THE **GAZE** /   E **LABYRINTH**

THE **GAZE** AND THE **LABYRINTH**

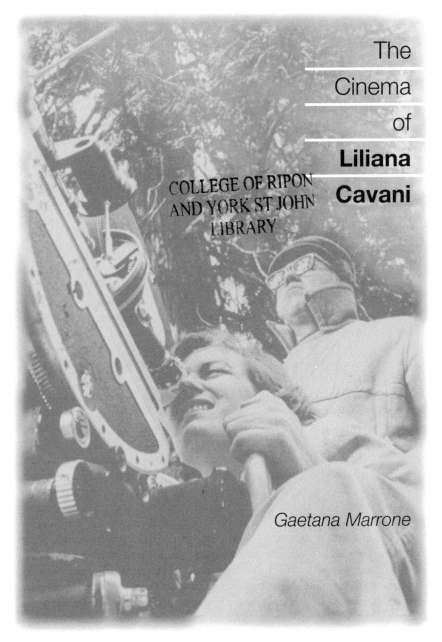

The
Cinema
of
Liliana
Cavani

COLLEGE OF RIPON
AND YORK ST JOHN
LIBRARY

Gaetana Marrone

PRINCETON UNIVERSITY PRESS · PRINCETON, NEW JERSEY

Library of Congress Cataloging-in-Publication Data

Marrone, Gaetana.
The gaze and the labyrinth : the cinema of Liliana Cavani /
Gaetana Marrone.
p.   cm.
Filmography: p.
Includes bibliographical references and index.
ISBN 0-691-03193-2 (alk. paper). — ISBN 0-691-00873-6
(pbk. : alk. paper)
1. Cavani, Liliana—Criticism and interpretation. I. Title.
PN1998.3.C4M37 2000
791.43′0233′092—dc21   99-27242 CIP

This book has been composed in Berkeley Book

The paper used in this publication meets the minimum
requirements of ANSI/NISO Z39.48-1992 (R1997)
(*Permanence of Paper*)

http://pup.princeton.edu

Printed in the United States of America

10   9   8   7   6   5   4   3   2   1

To Paola Tallarigo

Contents

List of Photographic Reproductions ix

Preface xiii

Acknowledgments xvii

Introduction 3

PART ONE. THE LABYRINTH: COGNITION AND
TRAGIC IMAGINATION 15

1. *Francesco di Assisi*: The Medieval Chronicle and the Establishing
of Physical Reality 17

2. Realism against Illusion: The Ceremonial Divestiture of Power
in *Galileo* 37

3. Metaphors of Revolt: The Dialogic Silence in *I cannibali* 57

PART TWO. THE TRANSGRESSIVE GAZE: STYLE AS TENSION 79

4. Toward a Negative Mythopoeia: Spectacle, Memory, and
Representation in *The Night Porter* 81

5. Staging the Gaze: *Beyond Good and Evil* 116

6. Theatricality and Reflexivity in *The Berlin Affair* 140

PART THREE. METAPHORS OF VISION 159

7. The Architectonics of Form: *Francesco* and *Milarepa* 161

8. The Essential Solitude: A Conclusion 188

Notes 195

Filmography 251

Bibliography 259

Index 305

List of Photographic Reproductions _____

ALL photographic illustrations in this book are taken from Liliana Cavani's personal collection. They comprise photographic tests, production stills, and frame reproductions. They will all be referred to as frames.

Frame 1. Liliana Cavani and director of photography Giuseppe Ruzzolini collaborating on *Francesco di Assisi* (Francis of Assisi, 1966) 20

Frame 2. The laboratory of Pietro Bernardone, the cloth merchant 25

Frame 3. The pope's emissary, the embodiment of religious authority 26

Frame 4. Francesco (Lou Castel), a conventionally idle youth 28

Frame 5. Francesco and the crucifix in San Damiano 30

Frame 6. Close-up of Francesco and the *Christus Triumphans* 31

Frame 7. Mickey Rourke and the Byzantine icon in *Francesco* (1989) 32

Frame 8. Cavani directs Lou Castel 33

Frame 9. The civil action of Pietro Bernardone against his son Francesco 34

Frame 10. Francesco's symbolic and physical divestiture 35

Frame 11. The anatomic amphitheater at the University of Padua in *Galileo* (1968) 41

Frame 12. Anatomy professor Acquapendente refutes the Galenic school of medicine 41

Frame 13. Galileo (Cyril Cusak) works on "l'occhiale" (the telescopic lens) 42

Frame 14. Galileo at the telescope 42

Frame 15. Galileo displays a map of the Copernican system 45

Frame 16. Set design for Bernini's tomb of Pope Urban VIII by Ezio Frigerio 48

Frame 17. Galileo's interrogation by the Roman Inquisition 49

Frame 18. Close-up of the trial 49

Frame 19. The strategic tactics of the Inquisition: torture as a judicial game 50

Frame 20. The procession through the streets of Rome: Galileo wearing the penitent's tunic and hat 51

Frame 21. The reading of the official sentence by the Dominican commissary 52

Frame 22. The abjuration of Galileo Galilei 52

Frame 23. Giordano Bruno and the Grand Inquisitor 55

Frame 24. Antigone (Britt Ekland) and Tiresias (Pierre Clementi) defy the orders of the city-state in *I cannibali* (The Cannibals, 1969) 61

Frame 25. The architectural setting of mental institutions as agents
for training docile bodies   66

Frame 26. Antigone's interrogation at the military police headquarters   69

Frame 27. Antigone and Tiresias being chased at the Officers Club   71

Frame 28. Tiresias holding Antigone in his arms at the sauna baths:
a modern pietà.   72

Frame 29. Antigone and Tiresias set a white dove free in an empty
church   74

Frame 30. Tiresias holds a photograph of Antigone as he searches
through a pile of bodies   76

Frame 31. The public execution of Antigone and Tiresias in the
city square   76

Frame 32. Documenting horror in *Storia del Terzo Reich* (History of
the Third Reich, 1961–1962)   85

Frame 33. Max (Dirk Bogarde), the night porter   88

Frame 34. Cavani looking through the camera viewfinder with director
of photography Alfio Contini on the set of *Il portiere di notte* (The
Night Porter, 1974)   93

Frame 35. Max's morbid taste for sadomasochistic games   96

Frame 36. Max terrorizes Lucia (Charlotte Rampling) in an empty
room, shooting at her with a pistol   96

Frame 37. Max's camera rolling: an authentic 1940s Leica   98

Frame 38. Lucia, as a fifteen-year-old girl, stands naked among other
prisoners   98

Frame 39. Lucia on the merry-go-round while being filmed by Max   99

Frame 40. The last shot of the film as Max and Lucia walk away from
the camera   102

Frame 41. Close-up of Lucia witnessing an act of sodomy inside the
concentration camp   106

Frame 42. Wide angle of the same scene   106

Frame 43. Production still of Liliana Cavani, with assistant director Paola
Tallarigo, and Dirk Bogarde   107

Frame 44. Bert Beherens (Amedeo Amodio) dances for Max   109

Frame 45. Bert's performance embodies the visual stage of Nazism   109

Frame 46. Costume designer Piero Tosi preparing Charlotte Rampling
for the cabaret scene   112

Frame 47. Lucia/Salomè performs in the Nazi cabaret scene   113

Frame 48. Dominique Sanda (Lou Salomé), Erland Josephson (Friedrich
Nietzsche), and Robert Powell (Paul Rée) in *Al di là del bene e del male*
(Beyond Good and Evil, 1977)   118

Frame 49. The sodomization of Paul Rée   123

Frame 50. Lou, Paul, and Fritz as voyeurs, wanderers, and artists
of life   126
Frame 51. Lou and Paul at the Palatine   128
Frame 52. The homosexual transgressive games among the Roman
ruins   128
Frame 53. A re-creation of the photograph by Jules Bonnet originally
taken in Lucerne on May 13, 1882   132
Frame 54. The hysterical Elizabeth Förster-Nietzsche (Virna Lisi) being
comforted by her brother   134
Frame 55. Fritz encounters Doctor Dulcamara (the Devil) in Venice   135
Frame 56. The mask of death   135
Frame 57. Nietzsche's hallucinatory reactions to the ballet of Good
and Evil   136
Frame 58. A scene from the ballet   137
Frame 59. The dancers (Amedeo Amodio and Robert José Pomper)   137
Frame 60. Gudrun Landgrebe (Louise) and Mio Takaki (Mitsuko) in
Interno berlinese (The Berlin Affair, 1985)   141
Frame 61. The Aryan model at the Berlin Institute of Fine Arts   145
Frame 62. The mystique of the forbidden love affair   148
Frame 63. Continuation of the same scene   148
Frame 64. The lovers' triangle with Heinz (Kevin McNally), Louise's
husband   150
Frame 65. Mitsuko as a geisha   154
Frame 66. Cavani with Mio Takaki and costume designer Josoburo
Tsujimura   156
Frame 67. Mickey Rourke in the title role of *Francesco* (1989)   162
Frame 68. Chiara (Helena Bonham Carter) kneeling next to Francesco's
body in San Damiano   164
Frame 69. Chiara entering the tent where the story unfolds   165
Frame 70. Identical scene of the tent in *Milarepa* (1973)   166
Frame 71. God's physical sign: the stigmata   169
Frame 72. Lajos Balàzsovitz as Milarepa building the tower of stones   172
Frame 73. Identical scene in *Francesco* with Mickey Rourke   172
Frame 74. Lumley and Albert Bennett (Paolo Bonacelli) in the
automobile accident   176
Frame 75. Milarepa learns black magic with the Man from Nyag   178
Frame 76. Milarepa meditates on how to destroy his uncle's house   179
Frame 77. The tree of death   181
Frame 78. The fisherman of eternal life   181
Frame 79. Marpa looks upon his new disciple   182
Frame 80. The physical ordeals of renewal in *Milarepa*   184
Frame 81. Similar scene repeated in *Francesco*   185

Frame 82. Milarepa performs the funerary rites for his teacher Marpa   186
Frame 83. Milarepa walking toward the horizon in the closing scene   187
Frame 84. Ko Morobushi as the Butoh dancer in *Dove siete? Io
sono qui* (Where Are You? I'm Here, 1993)   190
Frame 85. The dancer lying naked onstage   191

Preface

IN 1974 the film *The Night Porter* roused European and American audiences into awareness of the work of filmmaker Liliana Cavani. Since then she has achieved an artistic recognition among cineasts and critics that remains unparalleled in the European film industry. The director of twelve feature films, as well as several documentaries and operas, she has claimed for her films the status of classical tragedies and has denounced the ideological mystique venerated by the auteurs of her generation. Since the beginning of her career, she has privileged "a cinema of ideas" that brings into prominence "the pleasure of telling a story." Her work constitutes a corpus of cinematic exempla for critics and theorists interested in both the rhetoric of film and the problem of dramatizing, as spectacle, sociohistorical concepts. Cavani's imaginative use of narrative devices is expressly conveyed in compositions that are striking for their sophisticated lighting patterns and subtle framing. She portrays emotional tension through stylistic ambiguity, abstraction, and the reduction of spatial instability to geometrical shapes. Cavani's cinematic personae experience the conflict between historical and spiritual reality, the present and the past. They are "rebels," "visionaries," "madmen"; they are the Tiresiases of the future.

Because of her choice of controversial themes, her graphic use of sexuality, and her forceful (a)political stance, Cavani has rarely been understood. Cavani's films, many adapted from literary sources, clearly reflect the formal difficulties of filmic representation: the intricate relationship between cinematic and literary thematics; the ways in which conventional plots can be subverted and redefined in visual terms; the plasticity of filmic time; the architectural construction of space as an effective mode of screen dramaturgy; the manipulation of the cinematic point of view. Her understanding of central moments in man's historical *iter* has given us films that suggest how an artist integrates or reconciles emotion and idea, intuition and intellect. It also points up the futility of some critics' attempts to categorize her work by means of stereotypical impressions, most notably as a filmmaker obsessed with the corporeality of Eros. Scant critical attention has been devoted to the inherent difficulty—at times absurdity—of reducing Cavani's art to such a univocal dimension. A revealing classification would focus on the nature of the author's artistic concerns: her distinctive mode of expressing thought in rich and complex visual language and the cultural icons that comprise her style and images. These aspects of her work have been either overlooked or relegated to background material. I view Cavani's cinema within the realm of the history of ideas. Works about the director have traditionally indulged in a thematic stance, frequently obscured by polemical contours. My approach is interdisciplinary and intertextual; it draws on philosophical discourse, literary theory, and European historiography to elucidate Cavani's complex cinema of "ideas." I am interested in exploring how these disciplines interact with cinematic codes, and how the director reworks certain recurring themes and existential preoccupations. Cavani holds a doctorate in classical literatures and is known for her propensity to engage in linguistic and philosophical investigations. She also received an early training in the pictorial arts from her father, a renowned architect. An accomplished stylist who attributes her inspiration to a prime idea that informs her "invention" of representational linguistic designs, Cavani forges new cinematic paradigms in each of her films. She has emphasized the linguistic event that assaults the audience's subconscious expectations. Her cinematic syntax, still operating in the objective world, gradually dissolves into an examination of characters whose existence is regulated no longer by philosophical truth but by aesthetic authenticity.

Although in Europe Liliana Cavani has secured a reputation as a committed intellectual and an uncompromising artist whose dedication to the *cinéma d'essai* remains undisputed, she is primarily known in the United States as the *regista eretica* (heretical filmmaker) of *The Night Porter*, the film that launched her into international stardom. Her importance as a "great figure of cinema" (as the prestigious French critics have called her) has been underdiscussed and undervalued. The limited understanding of Cavani's work in the United States is related to a practical issue: her films are unavailable to the general film-going audience in America, and when they do reach the art theater circuit, as is the case with the work of many European filmmakers, they are often mutilated by severe cuts. I have made an effort to account for a given film's various stages of editing, censorship, and distribution. I shall discuss films primarily in chronological order to preserve the historical record of Cavani's stylistic experimentations as well as to demonstrate the polyphonic quality of her narrative modes. Biographical details are invoked only if they pertain to crucial aspects of filmic productions or otherwise illuminate the director's way of thinking. I draw extensively on Cavani's own writings and interviews; from production notes, working scripts, and other unpublished materials. These sources provide a unique insight into the director's working method and creative process. Because of the limited bibliographical resources on Cavani available to the Anglo-American reader, I have also chosen to list comprehensive additional sources of study. Continental criticism has provided, for example, a small but significant body of theoretical writing, specifically in Italian and French. I devote little discussion to the history of the reception of the films—which in itself would constitute a major cultural inquiry into the ideological dynamics of European cinema.

My analysis concentrates on the director's underlying aesthetic, which views cinema as simultaneously narrative and spectacle, or, in Cavani's own words, "the memory of the spectacle as an event." I study each film as an artistic monad, but also as belonging to a coherent body of work. Cavani is an auteur in the theoretical sense of the word. As a highly individual director, she initiates and oversees the entire production process, from script to final cut. In my discussion of Cavani's work I retain a distinction between an early "realist" period and a subsequent "psychological" one, since it relates to the artist's ambivalent representation of and interaction with the phenomenal world.

Finally, the title of this book, *The Gaze and the Labyrinth*, which describes the focus of its two main sections, is emblematic of typical situations in Cavani's cinema: the ambiguous, intricate interlacings of the events narrated, and of the language that represents those events; the importance assigned to the gaze and the eyes in the genesis of desire, and thought as an opening to speculative reflection and the acquisition of knowledge. Each film projects a fundamental reaction to particular, sensitive, and controversial situations in contemporary society. Cavani's cinema is conceived as a transgression and revolt against all binding ideological and commercial codes or strictures. Her characters are compelled to a kind of transgression, one that enables them to transcend the prisonlike limits of societal structures and to venture *beyond the door*, her most compelling and poetic metaphor for man's ongoing ontological journey.

Acknowledgments _____

EVERY film book requires a special support system and comes to life as a collaborative experience. I wish to thank all those who have supported and inspired me in this work. Most centrally I must acknowledge Maria DiBattista, who has helped me reach the comparisons and observations expressed in these chapters, and whom I was privileged to have as my *prima amica* at Princeton; and my husband Gerardo, for giving me a visual sense of cinema.

My gratitude also goes to the late Piergiuseppe Bozzetti, Director of Cultural Affairs at the Italian Embassy in Washington, who facilitated my first encounter with the director; Renato Pachetti, past President of RAI Corporation in New York, whose generous sponsorship allowed me to view Cavani's early films at the RAI (Italian television) film archive in Rome; Giovanni Grazzini, eminent film critic and former President of the Centro Sperimentale di Cinematografia in Rome, for his hospitality and willingness to assist me in locating the director's graduation short and an uncut version of *Al di là del bene e del male*; Francesco Milite, at the Centro Library, for his gracious assistance; Paola Giuli, for her kind collaboration in tracing rare periodicals at the Biblioteca Nazionale in Rome; Mary Ann Jensen, the curator of the William Seymour Theatre Collection at Princeton University; and Effie Chen and her staff at the Interlibrary Office of Princeton University's Firestone Library, whose patience and skills made possible my compilation of the first comprehensive bibliography on the filmmaker. My special thanks to Liviano Ruoli, the Councilman of the Istituti Culturali of the Comune di Carpi, for inviting me to participate in the Cavani Retrospective in winter 1990, and to Lotar Film for its collaboration during the early stages of my research.

I would like to express my appreciation to Princeton University and the State of New Jersey Office of the Governor for providing me with an exceptional year's leave, during which, as a John Mclean Jr. Presidential Preceptor and as a New Jersey Governor's Fellow in the Humanities, I had the time necessary to preview and organize most of the director's archival material in Italy. I am also indebted to the intellectual community of Princeton University, particularly my colleagues in the Department of Romance Languages and Literatures.

At Princeton University Press, to Joanna Hitchcock, who first believed in this book, and my editor Mary Murrell, who has consistently encouraged and supported me in every stage of the publication. I was extremely impressed by their dedication to Italian cinema. I am also grateful to my readers, who understood the very nature of what I wanted to accomplish, to my copy editor,

Lauren Lepow, for her perceptive reading of my manuscript, and to designer Frank Mahood.

Special thanks to Robert Hunsicker at Pharos Studios in Princeton for the photographic reproductions.

To Liliana Cavani, who has made the writing of this book a human as well as an intellectual encounter, I am obliged for her personal hospitality and for permission to consult and quote from her private collections, which are the foundation of my research. I also want to thank her for her willingness to sit through several long interviews; and for letting me make free choices, a risk few filmmakers would take. For that trust, I am most grateful.

THE **GAZE** AND THE **LABYRINTH**

Introduction ———————————————————

I make films because they are the work-play I have
chosen in order to know, that is, in order to glance
around the corner.
  (*Liliana Cavani*)

In a 1974 interview with Ciriaco Tiso, Liliana Cavani defined her idea of cinema as "an instrument of exploration," "a form of knowing," the way in which her "thoughts took shape": "If the Lumière brothers had not given us cinema, I would have been condemned not to express myself, and I would have been either very unhappy or in an asylum."[1] The emphasis on filmmaking as a unique (and for Cavani irreplaceable) mode of personal expression and artistic "thought" places the director at the very center of contemporary debates on the nature and expressive potential of film. Cavani's forceful cultural, (a)political stance and thematic "transgressiveness" derive not from programmatic ideological criteria but from an innate disposition toward freedom of individual expression:

> I am not provocative but free. I am not repressed, nor autocensorial: I am spontaneous. My surprise at the paroxysmal reactions to some of my films is sincere. . . . Nothing is intentionally brought to the extreme in my work: the true freedom, which I have always enjoyed at my own expense, may allow me to adopt, without fears or limitations and always with rigorous professionalism, certain forms of expression that the filmic text demands. There is a demythologizing pragmatism in this process: while they are operating, surgeons chat about soccer; while I am shooting, I search for the practical solutions that are adequate to the idea without asking myself if they will turn out to be provocative or extremist. But the gusto for transgression is probably in my nature.[2]

Liliana Cavani's formative years unfolded during the final stage of the Fascist regime. Born in Carpi, in the province of Modena, the director comes from a region, Emilia Romagna, that has provided Italian cinema with eclectic and innovative cinematic artists. Like Bernardo Bertolucci and Marco Bellocchio, also *emiliani*, Cavani's formal education was literary, linguistic, and classical. She graduated from the University of Bologna under the tutelage of philologist Raffaele Spongano, writing a dissertation on the fifteenth-century poet and nobleman Marsilio Pio. Cavani initially intended to become an archaeologist, a profession she soon abandoned in order to pursue her passion for "the moving image" at the Centro Sperimentale di Cinematografia in Rome.[3] Cavani's upbringing placed her between two distinctively separate worlds: on her mother's side, the sphere of working-class, militant anti-Fascism, and, on her father's, the world of conservative, high-bourgeois values of 1930s landowners. Fascinated by her maternal grandfather, an inspiring syndicalist who introduced her to the thought of Engels, Marx, and Bakunin, Cavani would maintain, throughout her career, secular, nonpolitical ideals. In the early and mid-sixties, a time when young filmmakers collectively professed left-wing views under the influence of the writings of Antonio Gramsci, Cavani asserted unequivocally independent positions. Cavani never accepted a party membership; she played, however, a prominent role in advocating change in the name of greater social reforms and freedom. In Cavani's view, Italian directors were instrumental in establishing post–World War II cultural trends. They were responsible for national defects, whims, and virtues:

> I would list among the defects that of having nourished an ordinary Italian typology with certain comedies, among the whims that of having tried to make political cinema, among the virtues that of having contributed to the transvaluation of values such as the concepts of our liberal-Catholic-socialist culture which have been emptied out by thirty years of cultural autocracy ("Fascism") and by nearly thirty years of fear, tactical precautions, and strategies ("opportunism") that bring us to a sixty-year cultural and social deferral in the concepts of family, sex, woman, class idea, etc. In this group of virtuous directors I include the auteurs who are censored, vilified, cursed, troublesome.[4]

What constitutes Cavani's own mystique is a public persona created by the artist herself through her films, personal appearances, and critical writings. In the Italian cinematic scene, she most resembles Pier Paolo Pasolini. Both Cavani and Pasolini could analyze cultural epistemes lucidly and engage in literary and societal discourse provocatively; they could conduct rigorous intellectual inquiries into the ideas that inform cinematic and political codes. The heterodoxy of their artistic experience was signaled by the epithet *scandaloso*, used to brand both their work and their personas. Their activity was scandalous precisely because it disturbed bourgeois comfort with the established order and exposed social regimentation in its latent nature and brutality. As Giovanni Grazzini has recently reminded us in a tribute to Cavani, she is indeed *un autore scomodissimo* (a very disturbing filmmaker) in a film industry traditionally committed to farcical comedy and unwilling to confront intellectual challenges.[5] Critical responses to her films have been polarized according to these perceptions of her "scandalous" art: from Indro Montanelli's "propagandistic toxicants" (referring to *La casa in Italia*) to Vincent Canby's Berlitz Era syndrome applied to *Francesco*, with its international cast speaking English with various degrees of naturalness;[6] from Michel Foucault's endorsement of "l'amour pour le pouvoir" as a veritable archaeology of Nazism in *Il portiere di notte* to Félix Guattari's defense of the artistic composite identity of *Al di là del bene e del male*; to Anna Banti's and Alberto Moravia's praise of the director's originality, scrupulous intelligence, and imagistic reinventiveness as signs of serious, rare cinematography.[7] Cavani has had a successful career without compromising her aesthetic identity and has been able to reconcile *cinéma d'essai* with the materialistic laws dictated by the commercialism of the medium.

Unlike many auteurs of her generation, who began by independently producing their low-budget feature films, Cavani started as a freelance director for RAI-TV, the Italian state television network, where she became one of those charged with the cultural programming at channel 2. Her first major assignment was a four-part series on the history of the Third Reich. In assembling the archival footage released by the Istituto Luce, Cavani, who adopts the documentarian's methodological attitude, discloses the philological curiosity of a true humanist:

> I was most challenged by the research for documents. We filled rooms with German newsreels that we had called in from all over the world (in those days RAI had nothing). I spent months at the Moviola. At the beginning I had no specific plan; the Italian bibliography on the subject was scant. I envisioned the structure of the film at the editing table. They had given me a wonderful toy to play with, a lot of film: I must admit that I thoroughly enjoyed organizing the material. In those years (1962–1965) I was full of enthusiasm. It was a time when I was completing my formation and I was filling in my lacunae. The television experience was to me almost a continuation of my studies.[8]

At RAI Cavani tested the possibility of working within the television format, while seeking production opportunities that were at the same time cultural and cinematic. She avoided the standard use of video cameras and shot her documentaries in 16 and 35mm film.[9] Such compelling series as the *Storia del Terzo Reich*, *Età di Stalin*, and *La casa in Italia* were to originate a docu-genre and also marked the beginning of the director's notorious battles with censors. Angelo Guglielmi recalls:

> They were three long stories in which the events narrated were only a pretext to evoke the social perspective, the ideological culture, the moral tensions in which the facts were rooted. Information was no longer an arid piece of news but assumed an epic aura almost as if she were imitating (and perhaps in the memory of the terrible events narrated in them) the works of her beloved classical playwrights.[10]

The documentary experience was decisive. Cavani's first feature film, *Francesco di Assisi*, is inconceivable without the meticulous reconstruction of everyday reality mastered during the years of apprenticeship. Similarly, *Il portiere di notte*'s ritualistic stylization of form could not have been realized without the technical and psychological investigation of Nazism in the *Storia del Terzo*

Reich. What some critics have seen as Cavani's "television" style, including the predominance of medium shots and close-ups, a less mobile camera, and the use of a normal lens (50mm), result from an aesthetic choice. In the documentaries we can see Cavani developing her cinematic "poetics." Reality is interpreted by means of authentic details, clarity of conceptual exposition, and an analytical editing syntax.[11] The documentaries provide early evidence of her mature style: the use of flashback and explanatory voice-over; the demythologizing of reality; a certain tendency to "overstate" and experiment with narrative structures.

Cavani's documentary films, produced at a time when RAI-2 was acquiring a cultural identity, set a precedent. They also anticipated the filmmaker's future critical recognition, with its paradigmatic insistence on an artist seduced by the *diverso* (that which is different).[12] Cavani's films deviate from political and social conformity; she is the heretic who dissents from the intolerance fostered by "the divinity of Western culture." Her cinema affirms as it reassesses freedom against Fascist and clerical rhetorics. She denounces the human debacle of hierarchical orders of power, whether in terms of the blatant atrocities of Nazi Germany in *Il portiere di notte* or the racial tension of the American 1960s in *Il caso Liuzzo*.[13] Cavani's career attests to the artist's commitment to voicing themes of social concern with a visionary clarity. *I cannibali* perceived the collapse of traditional systematic assumptions about the stability of the juridical-political authority at a time when the militant body of the 1968 generation was still getting organized; *L'ospite* addressed the correlation between incarcerating structures and individual autonomy before mental institutions became a politicized issue; *Galileo*'s final shot zooms into the skeleton head of the pope, exposing the emptiness and decay of the papacy's repressive mechanisms. Cavani's films are not, however, a response to the guilt-ridden crisis of the Italian Marxist intellectuals of the sixties. From the beginning of her career, she spoke of "the death of ideology" and rejected all dogmatism. Unlike most of the ideological filmmakers of the 1960s, she did not collapse into the defeatist political reexaminations of a later decade; nor was she lured into a minimalist cinematic aesthetic she polemically termed "nano-neorealismo" (dwarfish neorealism) because of its lack of individual and social ideas.[14] If Cavani's cinema remains indeed political, it is in the Aristotelian sense: politics defines the essential participation of the individual in the social and civil life of the polis:

> "Political" is the action one does for the good of the "polis"—that is to say, of the city. The city provides that there be citizens: the first prerogative of the citizens is to know the rights and the duties that devolve on themselves and others. Art is not a duty but a right: only in this sense is it political. Sade, Dostoievsky, Nietzsche acted for the good of the "polis" even if they were embarrassing authors, even if citizens were mostly against them.[15]

The origins of these convictions might be traced to a decisive moment in her early development. Her anti-ideological stance may derive from a shocking event she personally witnessed as a seven-year-old child, the execution of partisans by *repubblichini* in the center of Carpi:

> Early one morning, at dawn, I heard gunshots: it was still dark in the town. As soon as I could, I went out and started running behind a group of peasant girls who were riding their bicycles. I arrived in the piazza. There were sixteen partisans on the ground, covered in blood. The repubblichini surrounded them with rifles aimed at the women, wives, mothers, and daughters, who were crying and shouting, wanting their dead in order to mourn and bury them. But they were not allowed to come near them for twelve hours because the repubblichini had decided to use those dead bodies as a warning to anyone who came to witness. . . . The adults did not notice me; they could not prevent me from watching, from imprinting in my memory those dead bodies, the blood, the rifles, the desperate crying.

> The image of those executed bodies affected me for a long time, even though I feel I may have been unconscious of it. During the day, I never thought of them, but at night I dreamt of them. I dreamt of that image for a long time. . . . And since I had no religion to help me understand, for me death remained a mystery that I could never explain with any ideology.[16]

It is Pasolini who offers us the best definition of Cavani: he called her a young idealist, a cross between Joan of Arc and Pisacane, a heretic and a revolutionary who disclosed signs ahead of her time.[17] The question of power and knowledge, which is central to her "philosophical" discourse, is posited within the spectacular settings of sociopolitical revolutions: Francesco, Galileo, Antigone, Max and Lucia, Nietzsche and Lou von Salomé are heretics in the etymological sense of "those who chose."[18] They are not apocalyptic prophets in the religious tradition. Cavani places individuals against all that represents conservatism and conformity; their freedom of bodily gesture is set against the rhetoric and the morality of power: "My characters bear contradictory signs: they oppose the rhetoric and the rituals of power, to which everybody else conforms. They glance around the corner: they are the devious and seductive children of society, they are its demons."[19]

Cavani's cinematic roots issue from sources as diverse as the De Sica and Visconti of *Ladri di biciclette*, *Umberto D*, *Ossessione*, *La terra trema*, to Dryer's *Vampyr*, Murnau, Lang, and Pabst.[20] Unlike many contemporary Italian cineasts, she did not succumb to French "contaminations"; she admired Hitchcock and Buñuel, who share her interest in narrative plots, spatial transference, verbal communication, and subconscious juxtapositions. Her relationship with neorealism was not doctrinal. She never credited the director with objectivity, nor did she believe in inculcating political or moral messages. Her cinematic realism can be expressed by the axiom "how things truly are for me."[21] She has never questioned the primacy of cinema as art, as an expression of human meaning through imaginative devices that ultimately transcend their objective materials. Her ontological stance entails the inevitable "sense of the ambiguity of reality" that Bazin found essential to Italian neorealism:[22] "Realism is such a cruel game," she claims, "that it is not easy to play it: I have always tried to play it in each of my films. . . . Cruelty, analytical egotism, and play are the means to achieve realism."[23] The game is a paradigmatic situation in Cavani's films; it represents a mode of imaginative behavior that explores fantasy and the limits of cultural conventions. Cinema is play; thus is the creative state of mind open to subversive subjects. Play is also the Nietzschean self-renewing impulse that "calls new worlds to being";[24] it connotes a pluralistic space for the actual becoming of Existenz.

> What is the truth? Perhaps a beautiful woman "who has her good reasons not to reveal her reasons"? Or is it a "baubo," a meaningless word as for the Greeks? I do not search for this "baubo" in my films. In making a film I play: playing is the only way to face big problems. Only playing makes you really suffer.[25]

In Cavani's "playful" cinema, characters are divested of their heroic aura and displaced into an ordinary, marginal level of experience: the legendary saint (Francesco and Milarepa, with their imaginative alignment between man and nature), the visionary scientist (Galileo torn to pieces by the Inquisition), the classical myth (Antigone murdered by treachery). Lou von Salomé marks with her words to a deranged philosopher the meaning of their revolutionary sublimation: "Our century is coming, Fritz!" Narrative strategies focus on an ironic deconstruction of the real by visual ambiguity and poetic complexity:

> Those who believe that neorealist films were "poor" and technically based on improvisation, ingeniousness, rather than professionalism are wrong. Not only were they as rich as was necessary, but they were even luxurious because they never indulged in vulgarity; they were very refined.[26]

Cavani's art can thus be seen to follow two major trajectories: the one, which is best apprehended in the films from *Francesco di Assisi* to *Milarepa*, concerns the figure of the idealist who transgresses—through serious play—the boundaries of conventional society in search of self-realization and identity; the second, which includes her "scandalous" German trilogy, describes a transgression more malevolent and dangerous, where the undoing of the historical time is enacted through the couple's abysmal, ruinous sexual fantasies, a mechanism of perpetual entrapment. One has to do with an extending vision: the Christo-centric image-magic of the experiences of Francesco, Galileo, Antigone, who see beyond their historical *limina*. In the latter half of her career, the complicity of film with transgression and voyeuristic compulsion becomes an actual subject of the film itself. The intricate refractions of the gaze in *Il portiere di notte*, *Al di là del bene e del male*, and *Interno berlinese* create, through harsh lighting and the inclusion of the movie camera in the frame, a distorted vision of reality. A centrifugal delimitation of space (Cavani tends to set up her actors to one side of the frame) conveys the characters' marginality as well as their desire to transcend a descent *ad inferos*.

In Cavani's cinema, characters are messengers of the future in rebellion against the powers ruling the present. They have all seen *beyond* the *limina* or, to use Cavani's metaphor, peered *oltre la porta* (beyond the door). For example, in *Francesco di Assisi*, the *limina* are the historical limits—or margins—to which the lepers and outcasts with whom Francesco identified were banished. Yet by the time of her 1989 "remake," transgression is more resolutely linked to a tragic conception of selfhood. Hamlet, Cavani reveals, was the text that inspired her characterization of Francesco. The tragic view of life, rather than the legal or social obstacles to self-fulfillment or human happiness, is what comes to dominate her cinema. All of Cavani's characters are driven by a will to know, a process that comprises Foucault's notions of violence and transgression. Power is not a restricted institution or structure; nor is it a force wielded by certain individuals: it is a complex strategic situation that entails a differential relationship of forces confronting one another.[27] Characters like Francesco, Galileo, Antigone, Anna, and Max do not judge the values of systems of power; they do not technically rebel against these values. They attempt to speak from the circumference instead of from the center of reality. Their experience, bound to repetition and transmutation, is realized at the boundaries of the city walls, the furthest limits of social intercourse;[28] they take a voluntary leap beyond the door that opens to an obsessive, transgressive ritual of death.

Cavani's cinema attests to this preoccupation, and a fascination, with violence and desire. Particularly it investigates the metastructures of social relations and emphasizes the force of a synoptic will guiding man through an oneiric labyrinthine journey, a dark winding process of action and affirmation that leads down to the monster's throat, the locus of the fallen knowledge of life. The labyrinth is a poetic metaphor that designates the predominant Cavanian architecture of the interior. Its geometrical linearity delimits the tortuous paths of an inner space. The labyrinth is also the place of initiations; its entrance inaugurates as it completes the movement of separation from a patriarchal order: the chronicle of Francis of Assisi, the odyssey of Milarepa ritualize the death of the former self attached to that order, as well as figuring the wholeness one attains at the labyrinth's center. This apparent paradox becomes more understandable when one remembers that the serpentine body of mystery with the Minotaur at its center is an ancient symbol of life, death, the discovery, and the ability to return.[29] Where Daedalus's master invention connects with the prison-cave image, as in *Il portiere di notte*, *Al di là del bene e del male*, *La pelle*, *Oltre la porta*, and *Interno berlinese*, it alludes to a demonic underworld, to a tension between order and chaos, to a quest without solution, with its consciousness of the binding patterns of an experience of pleasure and terror.[30] An obsessive ambiguity characterizes Cavani's labyrinthine psychological structures: lucidity and madness, dreams and nightmares, real and surreal, delirious forms of absolute beauty and the hegemonic image of death, the privileged ritual at the heart of her artistic world. The architectural complexities of the legendary work of art also evoke a journey through the darkness of the unknown, a Pirandellian abyss that refracts upon itself, as in a mirror, glorified chaos.

The distinguishing stylistic characteristic of Cavani's cinema is narration by a kind of visual demythologization of reality, a constant search for a linguistic apparatus that can combine *mythos* (narrative) and *dianoia* (meaning).[31] I perceive an initial analogical rendering of reality, which translates an idea into "concrete" visual signs: the *paupertas* of the Franciscan message projected onto a barren chronicle style in *Francesco di Assisi*; the optical dynamics of the scientific language projected onto the symbolic divestiture of power in *Galileo*; the dialogic nature of Tiresias's and Antigone's silence generating a mythopoesis of polyphonic acoustics in *I cannibali*; Anna's schizophrenia projected onto the docudrama framing of *L'ospite*; the ritualistic display of human nature onto the oneiric quality of the imagery in *Milarepa*. From *Il portiere di notte* the director's approach to the phenomenal world emphasizes the perceptional, as she composes to wider shots that privilege the details in the mise-en-scène and displays greater freedom in her choices of means. The idea now has a direct association with the function of the eye. In *Il portiere di notte*, the cinematography overstates half of the photogram; Max's body movements suggest that he has shifted toward a mirror image of the inner self. There is a displacement of geometrical equilibrium which metaphorically translates that of the power structure, Nazism, to which the protagonist's older political identity belongs. The composition attains a constant tension between the character and the background. Such a stylistic device reflects Cavani's unique approach to reality:

> In *Il portiere di notte* I always wanted half of the photogram empty. The director of photography used to tell me that it was not right. When the characters were alone, I wanted them to be on one side of the frame in order to accentuate their concentration and self-analysis, and enhance their inner world, their inner hell . . . It was as if my deepest self had surfaced and I was transferring it onto my films. Consequently, the necessity of double readings. I could see the characters beyond the story, as in Sophocles, where they pertain to the action but they are also personae who portray us, the spectators.[32]

Confining framing and controlled blocking signify discontent and tension; they exemplify the interaction between the artist and society, the ideal order of the self opposed to the madness of Being. Cavani's films convey a tangible, intense view of the world; *sense* and *perception* are sources of knowledge, the means to glance beyond the surface of things: they command the relation of the spatial to the conceptual world, as in the multiple gaze of *Al di là del bene e del male*. The eye becomes the figure of transgression and being, a figure of play in an act that concludes by questioning its own limits. The eye draws from its capacity to observe "the power of becoming always more interior to itself."[33] As an instrument and measure of truth, it is the depository and *fons* of clarity that has the power of bringing knowledge to light for Francesco, Galileo, and Milarepa. It is also a figure of inner experience: the asymmetrical, dissociative eye of Anna in *L'ospite*. In the negative logic of the gaze in the German trilogy, a predominant aspect of vision is isolated: the spiritually dominating look of Power that acts, often with violence, to contain and control what is about to escape, particularly when it is fixed on a "woman" in the position of icon and spectacle.[34] Such extremities of vision are manifest in the staging of luminous ballet performances by Bert, Dulcamara, and Akira in *Il portiere di notte*, *Al di là del bene e del male*, and *Dove siete? Io sono qui*. The eye can also be a political machine that sees without being seen, the eye that dissects and punishes, as it is in *I cannibali*. In Cavani's later films, the aesthetic experience of the gaze is communicated by the presence of movie cameras, photographs, reflected lighting patterns that capture the very essence of the cinematic eye: the mirror refractions of the lens as the symbolic space of creativity and imagination.

Cavani's montage techniques contribute to this often violent abrogation of the boundaries between known and unknown, fantasy and reality. They construct a "jarring" effect, caused by the unexpected intrusion of intense images in a carefully controlled context, such as the skinned body of the heretic in *Francesco* or the disemboweled American soldier in *La pelle*. The functional role of these images lies in Cavani's concept of wanting to know. By de-emphasizing editing conventions, she punctuates her films with powerful images that suddenly shock the audience. In *Il portiere di notte*, when Max steps on the broken pieces of glass in the bathroom, his facial reaction enables us to feel his bodily pain. Cavani does not begin with violence; she isolates the close-up and the foreground to convey moments of horror. Such scenes break out from the compositional frame of the film, obtrude as something alien. These compelling images, externalizing the artist's concern with the violence inherent in the sociopolitical power structures, provoke an unbearable degree of discomfort in the audience, whose quiescent state is disturbed, and whose repressed unconscious tensions are freed. The experience is cathartic; it releases and purifies the viewer's "ignorance," achieving an Aristotelian purgation from *pathemata* (feelings) that implies a detachment from both the work of art and the artist. In Cavani's films, the aesthetic phenomenon requires emotional and intellectual distancing, the awakening of reflection and consciousness. From Jean Cocteau's point of view, cinema is a powerful weapon for the projection of thought, even onto an audience unwilling to accept it. Cavani's cinematic syntax does not entertain or move the spectator but elicits a mental rather than emotional reaction:

> I do nothing to move the spectators. I am not interested in making people cry, but in making them reflect. . . . Cinema can be political only if it leaves the spectator uneasy, *derangé* or enthusiastic, in the face of something that has not been solved for him. Greek tragedies do not encompass solutions.[35]

Philosophical ambiguity points to the tragic, dangerous *limen* where conscious individuals strive to assert themselves against existent boundaries. It introduces an objective situation of doubt as a problematic state of being confused.[36] Doubt stages the condition that transforms a situation into a search; it is not inevitably a precursor of the acquisition of truth. The Cavanian characters probe the equivocal status of a negative mythopoeia. They undertake a journey away from Power/Order. They enter the door that opens the portals of subconscious associations and spiral down into the dark side of life, into the world where evil, suffering, and death dwell. The body is the principal empirical instrument through which they actualize their investigation. The fullness of existence is expressed by their privileging a marginal status. Like Francesco, they share the life of the outcast, outside the walls of the city; this is the locus of their revolution. Cavani's films demand that we be aware of the forms of expression that emphasize the symbolic space in which the lines delimiting experience and imagination are abrogated.

Cavani expresses thought and aesthetics through the representation of liminal human experiences that redefine outer/inner realities. In the Bressonian tradition, she conceives the filmmaker as a creator rather than a *metteur-en-scène*. Like Bresson she strives for economy and precision. A study of the director's work involves diversified critical approaches in light of which a stylistic discourse can be developed. It requires understanding of the social, political, and philosophical traditions at work in European culture. Her cinema embraces the narrative tradition of Mann, Musil, Dostoievsky; the classical dramaturgy of Sophocles and Euripides; the speculative horizons of Nietzsche, Bataille, Foucault.

The depth and significance of Cavani's work is already evident in her first feature film, *Francesco di Assisi*, which serves as an ideal transition from the early documentaries, technically impressive, to *Galileo*, *I cannibali*, and *Milarepa*. Although her early films disclose the signs of a promising director, her mature style results from years of experimentations with traditional cinematic tools and narratives. In Part One I analyze three films as exemplary of Cavani's early cinematic techniques: the architectonics of the image and the medieval

chronicle in *Francesco di Assisi* (chapter 1); the optical metaphor and the spectatorial embodiments of the anatomic theater in *Galileo* (chapter 2); myth and
the unconventional use of sound in *I cannibali* (chapter 3). These films establish
the way Cavani composes her frame according to dialogue. With *Il portiere di
notte* (chapter 4), Cavani enters a new, international stage. The *passio* guiding
her earlier characters—who were driven to confront the social, political, and
religious hierarchic establishment of their times—now becomes an inward
journey of the couple. The German Trilogy (*Il portiere di notte, Al di là del bene
e del male, Interno berlinese*) constitutes my focus in Part Two. Here passion is
agonistic and sensorial. Now the director seems concerned with the aesthetic
development of thought through visual images. In particular, these films address historical phenomena such as Fascism and Nazism, as symptomatic states
in which the human subject is understood only outside traditional established
morality (*Al di là del bene e del male* and *Interno berlinese*, chapters 5–6). Finally,
in Part Three I shall discuss her latest *Francesco*, a search for personal identity
that ideally recalls the geometrical symbolism of *Milarepa* (chapter 7). The two
films have stylistic and thematic similarities, and they represent a transitional
phase that affects the director's later work. Cavani's most recent films, which
include *Dove siete? Io sono qui* (chapter 8), move toward an agonizing process
of human self-knowledge and tragic isolation.

PART ONE

THE LABYRINTH: COGNITION AND TRAGIC IMAGINATION

Dedalus is the hero of the way of thought—
singlehearted, courageous, and full of faith that
the truth as he finds it, shall make us free.
(*Joseph Campbell*)

Every creative process is labyrinthine. The resulting
truth is the enigma, which always calls for an answer
without a conclusion, but it opens itself to
all possibilities.
(*Aurelio Pes*)

Francesco di Assisi: The Medieval Chronicle and
the Establishing of Physical Reality

> I am a craftsman who loves the image imprinted
> on film.
>   (*Liliana Cavani*)

LILIANA CAVANI'S first feature film, *Francesco di Assisi* (Francis of Assisi, 1966),
discloses striking early evidence of the director's stylistic powers. The raw imagery and the barrenness of the film's compositional geometry introduce a
man with an unusually intense experience of the concreteness of reality. In
representing a classical subject that had inspired such different artists as Giulio
Antamoro and Roberto Rossellini, Cavani opts to make of Francesco's *paupertas*
the analogical principle of the biographical and visual narrative: she divests
the figure of Francesco of all oleographic and legendary inscriptions, and portrays him as a "normal," "natural" individual who is "not particularly cheerful
nor taken by a saintly madness as the legends based on an excess of piety have
presented."[1]

Commissioned by RAI, and aired in two parts (on 6 and 8 May 1966),
Francesco di Assisi was acclaimed as the most controversial and successful program of the year. It initiated cultural debates and parliamentary investigations.
Giobatta Cavallari selected it to be shown at the Venice Film Festival, paired
with Rossellini's *La Prise de pouvoir par Louis XIV*. The film became the emblem
of emerging Catholic dissent for a generation of progressivist ideologues on
the threshold of major revolutionary upheavals. It led its main actor, Lou
Castel—the schizophrenic protagonist of Bellocchio's *I pugni in tasca*—to an
actual conversion: Castel, who completely identified with the part of Francesco, donated his income to extraparliamentary leftist organizations and came
close to ruining a promising career.[2]

After a quarter of a century, *Francesco di Assisi* retains its messianic appeal
intact. It is a film about the present, as Cavani claimed, where the accent falls
on the apostolic *agere* (to act) of the new man;[3] but it is above all a film about
the future, a symbol of the interpenetration of the historical and the spiritual,
between the secular and the religious. Cavani transposes the exceptional life
of a saint into a factual historical milieu. Francesco's exemplary human experi-

ence is enhanced by his relationship to quotidian reality. The film's barren medieval settings, which are wet, stony, and earthbound, contribute to this unusual effect. The film also dramatizes a physical process of gradual divestiture: Francesco's nakedness during the trial scene; his progressive shedding of the suit of armor, the luxurious clothes, the sandals; the refusal of property. Kaja Silverman has remarked that these quite literal divestitures, which signal the stages of Francesco's cultural estrangement, make unusually explicit the director's "obsession with the self-mutilating male subject."[4] Francesco's revolutionary interpretation of *possidere*, to possess, reverses the power dynamics of his historical times. A compound of *potis* and *sedere*, the verb "to possess" means "to occupy a space as a master," and it was originally applied to real estate ownership.[5] Francesco transgresses the conventional social limits and reestablishes this meaning anew. He leads us to the path that approaches the center of the maze, where he himself stands. At the moment of death, in the urgent contact of his emaciated body with the earth, we witness a gesture, both simple and illuminating, that holds up to his life a mysterious mirror: "Place me on the earth . . . naked . . . help me . . . on the earth" are the protagonist's last words as the end credits begin to appear on the screen. Francesco thus calls us to witness the humbleness of the body as an instrument to experience reality, while reminding us of the originally pantheistic bent of his character.[6] The superb final image of naked deposition sums up the nucleus of the film, implying again the burden of man's identification with Christ.

Cavani's interpretation of Francis of Assisi divided viewers, particularly the press and Catholic groups. The film was labeled "heretical, blasphemous, and offensive for the faith of the Italian people."[7] Italo Moscati wrote that "it broke the boundaries of television conformism by presenting both the concern and the hope of the religious event; it induced a verification of the simplistic hagiographic tradition and stimulated individual meditations on the significance of the evangelical message."[8] More specifically, the film attests to the difficulty of describing a rebel figure who does not actually oppose the *auctoritates* of his time but accepts them in order to transcend their imposing structures. Francesco's transgression represents the epistemological *fractura* that marks the birth of the modern world; his action is scandalous, in the sense that Foucault intends when describing the spectacle of the crucifixion of Christ—whose life Francesco imitates as a creative example of a constant personal search. "His was an existential and poetic enterprise rather than a strictly religious one," says Cavani, "Francesco did not want to be the leader of a movement, nor did he wish to found a religious order. His was a creative act, which escapes any codification, and therefore it was revolutionary."[9] Cavani's emphasis on the imaginative behavior of the Friar Minor, at once heuristic and improvisatory, explores the limits of cultural conventions, embodying the interrelationship of play and heroic significance.

Guided by her imagination, and by solid bibliographical documentation, Cavani recounts the life of the wealthy clothier's son with austerity. The film's narrative centers on exempla dating from 1205, Francesco's youth and war games, up to his death on 4 October 1226. Cavani identifies the main transitional scenes by burn-in intertitles: the trial (1207), the re-*aedificatio* of old churches (1209), the sanctioning of the Order of Friars Minor by Innocent III (1210), the mission to the Orient and his new disciples (1221), his illness (1225). Francesco is introduced through his privileged social status and idle fantasies. He is "the king of youth and the lord of rumpus."[10] His accidental encounter with the Christ of San Damiano sets history in motion. In Cavani's cinema, such a radical encounter always inaugurates the existential adventure of the protagonist: Galileo and Giordano Bruno, Antigone and Tiresias, Milarepa and Marpa. Through this interaction, a process of transformation is initiated, which leads by a tortuous, labyrinthine path toward an eventual resolution: like all that functions on the archetypal level, what is constellated by this I-Thou encounter operates as a unitary reality field.[11] The encounter with the Christ of San Damiano, signifying the turn from the contemplative to the active life, constitutes the film's master scene, Cavani's authentic model of spiritual conversion. Francesco, the idle *cavaliere*, is slowly transformed into a zealous soldier of Christ: the kissing of the leper, the poor man's rags, the barefoot beggars all dramatize how Francesco becomes God's fool, facing the ways of the world. His transformation concludes with the spectacular formality of the civil action brought against Francesco by his father, Pietro Bernardone. The trial throws the human system of justice into confusion. Francesco's laughter in the face of the formal juridical ritual attests to the collapse of social hierarchy; it conforms in certain respects to Bakhtin's description of medieval carnival. As Kaja Silverman writes: "Like the merriment generated by carnival, that induced by Francesco's deliberate self-loss attests to a dispersed subjectivity, and to a 'social consciousness of all the people.' "[12] The rebel-saint forces upon the established structures a radical redefinition of power. The whole episode is shot in an exaggeratedly theatrical style. Francesco's spectacular gestures make him the center of the crowd's attention. His nakedness, which makes him into a public spectacle, also signifies his second birth. The trial sequence, which concludes the first part of the film, locates Francesco's symbolic and real divestiture within a complex historical tradition; it identifies his *paupertas* as a revolutionary act, and his nakedness as a primary, visual image of emancipation from structural and economic bondage. As the Franciscan biographer Julien Green notes:

> The scene of stripping, in an age when shame had not yet been confused with prudery . . . was one of the forms of public penance. To strip himself of the external signs of wealth, of the clothes in which he had tasted all the pleasures of the world— and the pleasure of a fine appearance meant a good deal to him—to abandon the

Frame 1. Liliana Cavani and director of photography Giuseppe Ruzzolini collaborating on *Francesco di Assisi* (Francis of Assisi, 1966)

pride of his youth, showed everyone that Francis violently repudiated his entire past. The renunciation in the presence of a crowd was in itself, according to the medieval mentality, a juridical act. From now on, Francis, with nothing to his name, was taking sides with the outcast and the disinherited.[13]

In a compelling synthesis of iconography and social history, the transfiguration of the Friar Minor leads to a new mode of teaching and practicing faith. Naked again, except for a crude smock, he undertakes an itinerary that leads him to the revival of abandoned churches, most prominently San Damiano and La Portiuncula—each destined to play a critical role in his life. He adopts the mode of the simpleton's preaching, rather than focusing on abstruse theological controversies; he acquires his first followers (Bernardo, Pietro, Rufino, Leone, and Chiara) and establishes, after an audience with the pope, the Rule of the Order. The rising dissent among his learned brethren eventually causes Francesco to isolate himself on Mount La Verna.

As this bald plot summary suggests, *Francesco di Assisi* moves within the limits of a specific genre: the medieval chronicle. The dependence on this genre has some formal repercussions. A chronicle requires a plot development clearly rooted in an eyewitness account of facts that follows a chronological order. Cavani's cinematic technique relies on handheld camera setups, portable lighting, punctuated by documentary film editing. Cavani chooses to shoot the film in black and white because that look suggests the tonality of news footage. She intended to tell the story from the perspective of a reporter who was going to record the great scandal of the time:

> Mine was a contemporary eye: my camera was going to record the scandal created by this character. Besides this decision, which concerns narrative, I also considered a technical one: I wanted to use the Arriflex for what it is, a 16mm camera, agile, flexible, built to shoot news, and avoid the pretense of having a Mitchell, as new directors often do. The camera determined the style of the film. There was no ambiguity between the instrument and the intention.[14]

In Cavani's chronicle, the event functions as a story element. In distinguishing various levels of conceptualization in the historical work, Hayden White has taken "chronicle" to refer to the primitive components in a historical account, mediating the unprocessed record to an audience of a particular kind.[15] Cavani's intention to reconstruct history from the perspective of a contemporary eye associates narrative with the unedited vision of the unreflective chronicler. Her rudimentary approach, however, does not exclude temporal or narrative complexity. In Cavani's hands, the chronicle does not depend on suspense and shock; these dramatic effects are alien to Cavani's treatment of Francesco's story. When a certain visual shock is attained, as in the scenes of the physical divestiture during Francesco's trial or Rufino's preaching in the cathedral, its impact is cleverly muted or reversed: instead of cutting to dramatic close-ups to emphasize the "scandalous" image, the director shoots from a bird's-eye point of view. In later films, what I have called the jarring effect of her editing technique replaces this type of shot. While Cavani's "chronicle style" shows signs of her previous documentary experience—she relies on some of the conventions of a genre she had already used as a vehicle for explicitly social and historical themes—the characters possess a depth that transcends the limitations of uninflected chronicle. This conflict between the documentary realism of the reporter and an existential picturing of reality as spare, barren, tangible is characteristic of Cavani's cinematic compositions. Tiso has perceptively described "the structural verticality that prevails on the horizontal narrative" of Cavani's symbolic cinema.[16] This tension does not support the objective view that the camera is trying to convey. There is an essential purity in the composition of the rustic imagery, which acts as a stylistic equivalent to Francesco's spiritual state and his search for an existentially concrete exemplum. Throughout her career, Cavani experimented with different genres and transcended their strictest conventions. Critics have not failed to notice that, despite its reliance on its chronicle features, *Francesco di Assisi* engages in "a genuinely new mode of storytelling."[17]

The film's narrative organization is structured in *quadri* (tableaux). The *quadro* is a scenic composition designed for the use of space as an interior. Cavani's interiors are formally established and defined by the dynamics of the close-ups (faces, hands, feet, etc.) and by the spatial relationship of the decor to the body. Photographed from a predominantly frontal angle in a medium shot, the tableau introduces the human figure against a rigorous and stable background, architecturally dominated by vertical lines.[18] Solid forms, such as doors, arches, walls, stairways, become privileged points of visual reference. A pictorial flatness qualifies the geometry of her shot-compositions, while the power of the image is displaced onto the emotive contours of the face, which Cavani regards as the diegetic locus of the film. The camera's incessant panning from one face to another becomes the structural narrative sign. Placed in direct relation to the object of representation, the spectator becomes the unifying center of the story, the one who composes in a simultaneous vision the series of images or the sequence of the events recorded. The internal dialectic of the tableau is articulated by the interplay of physiognomy, costume, and behavior. We can observe this dynamic at work most spectacularly in the scene depicting Francesco holding a torch in front of the Christ of San Damiano. This scene, constructed against the medium of flashbacks, emphasizes the initiatory meaning of the protagonist's journey. The torch symbolizes love as *caritas*. Francesco brings the light toward the painting as if to restore life to the crumbled church, providing a very poetic image of reillumination and renewal. Cavani's ideal of transcendence accounts for her use of the tableau as a theatrical metaphor, which transposes the temporal sequence of the story into a spatial continuum that, as in later films, highlights the figures' density and independence within a historical mise-en-scène. In creating the depth-experience of a dynamic space definable by sculpted backgrounds, Cavani stresses the idea of extension contained in Gothic architecture. She aims the light at a certain angle on the stone walls, which causes a shimmering effect. This lighting strategy persists in *Francesco*, where vertical and horizontal lines seem to merge into an extended sphere of light to enhance all tactile forms of the inner space. As Cavani explains: "Giotto registers the most beautiful chronicle of Franciscan acts. But they are static: I have tried to give them life through moving images."[19]

From a thematic point of view, the tableau illustrates a single concept: *paupertas* as evangelical virtue and ontological *principium*. It is the *paupertas* of Christ who takes on a human essence. This Christological *humanitas* of Francesco is central to Cavani's interpretation. She removes the saint from the hagiographic tradition and introduces him as a man in whom "we can recognize ourselves, whom we can meet and understand beyond the bigotry of sterile and too often banal devotion."[20] Francesco operates within a fundamentally concrete model of life. In him there is no fracture between *gestus* and *verbum*, deed and word. His is a character, says Cavani, posed midway between those of Gandhi and the young people who feel "an instinctive desire for love, trust, ideal values."[21] Yet Francesco is both alike and different; his simple and stripped humanity, while exemplary, is experienced at the limits of (human) nature and ordinary experience. Pietro Bernardone's son also reveals heroic attributes that traditional sources document: Madonna Pica's improbable delivery in a stable, a divine father, miraculous occurrences.[22] In the film, the first shot of Francesco is on a horse, while he is engaged in military exercises to prepare for his journey in Terrasanta. Max Weber, who has discussed feudalism and patrimonialism as the main variants of traditional domination, stresses that, in the feudal style of life, the *game* was an important means of training physical and mental character traits. It was not a pastime. The knightly orders of medieval Europe considered the game as a serious aspect of life that had "a special affinity with spontaneous artistic interests and helped bar the way to all forms of utilitarian rationality."[23] Francesco's heroic quest emerges from a *cavaliere* image to comprehend a Messiah myth. Christ-centered kingship was distinctively characterized by the mixture of monk and knight postulated in the orders of spiritual chivalry. Like the historical Jesus, Francesco symbolizes both the divine and the mortal aspects of humanity, whose integration is necessary if spiritual transcendence is to be achieved.[24]

The quest narrative unfolds as a polemical antithesis between institutional *auctoritas* (the ideology of temporal power in which the paternal figure and the *doctores* of the Church are invested) and the protagonist's individuality, which is expressed in the ethico-theological categories of *humilitas* and *sublimitas*. The Franciscan dicta form the basis of episodes within a chivalric dramatic structure whose main acts are the denial of power and subsequent banishment from the community, and the search for a new identity at the *limina* or extreme margins of conventional reality. Francesco's transgression restores us to a world defined by the experience of its limits; it exposes "that narrow zone of a line where it displays that flash of its passage, but perhaps also its entire trajectory, even its origin."[25] Transgression and the limit depend on each other. Arnold van Gennep has shown that all transitional rites entail a phase of expulsion, marked by the severance of the individual from a preexisting social structure. Francesco's action is set against a structure of order in which the father figure stands as his societal and cultural antithesis. Cavani concentrates on the symbolic and spatial area of cultural transitions, during which the liminal being is in an ambiguous and indeterminate state, frequently likened to death, to darkness, and, in later films, to bisexuality. The gnosis acquired at the liminal stage implies a change in being.[26] She emphasizes the ontological status of the *avventura attuale* of the protagonist:

I do not aim at social messages or anything else. I have always loved my work because in doing it I have learned something; something about myself and others. I explore my curiosity to the fullest; my work is like an open journey with which I try to answer, from experience, some ancient questions; but then I ask more questions and the search continues.[27]

Francesco is presented as alienated from the society of the rising mercantile class—to which he belongs by patrimonial rights. Later he is isolated by the Brothers in a dispute involving his refusal of *proprietas*. Property, according to the Franciscan ethos, precludes *caritas*, the theological virtue that rules the Franciscan *actio*: *caritas* is the *pietas* of the Christ. Christ's archetypal essence is translated into the symbol of the Cross: his thought is expressed by Francesco's *voce mentale* (voice-over); his word is realized in what Cavani sees as the creative behavior of the Friar Minor. For the son of the rich merchant of Assisi, action is quintessential to preaching; it enacts the doctrine enunciated in the prologue to the Gospel according to John, the simple faith of the first Christians: "In the beginning was the Word. . . ." The *Word* ("Logos" in Greek) is God in action, creating: "And the Word became flesh and dwelt among us. . . ." To realize this religious imperative, Francesco divests himself of all material goods and becomes a social outcast, before climbing to the sacred mountain where his apotheosis might occur.

The film opens with two parallel scenes that establish secular and religious authority: Pietro Bernardone, the cloth merchant, and the pope's emissary are both endowed with the symbolic and legal function of maintaining Order. The violence of the opening tableau, in the textile factory of Francesco's father, is transferred onto the visual projection of postural dominance by the *padrone*: the camera frontally "attacks" the workers as they are accused of having ruined a valuable piece of cloth. The film treatment describes the sequence thus:

In the steam that emanates from the boilers, the workers weave, wind, and keep the fire going. A foreman discovers that a piece of cloth has been damaged and cruelly strikes some dyers at random. Pietro appears, commands that silence and work be resumed; that is what they are paid for. His measured tone reveals a solid man, aware of his power.[28]

The initial shots establish a series of cultural antinomies that define liminality within the status system: padrone/worker (property/absence of property), father/son (state/transition), concrete/abstract (secular/sacred). The frontal shooting and the iconographic stasis of the entire scene call immediate attention to the existence of the camera and the eye behind it. They also draw the spectator into the sphere of the worker. Cavani operates on the conviction that the objectivity of the visual image should serve the story. The strategy is familiar to Cavani's viewers. The human situation is filmed so as to highlight its inherent tension. The master is introduced by a low-angle shot, framed within an

Frame 2. The laboratory of Pietro Bernardone, the cloth merchant

arch and backlit in silhouette. These are real persons in a real Assisi; human images sculpted as icons against a static background. Iconicity is Cavani's establishing technique in the early films. The opening sequence of *Francesco di Assisi* stands out in this respect, for it emphasizes a linear perspective and depth of field. We can sense the director's compositional ability, particularly in her

Frame 3. The pope's emissary, the embodiment of religious authority

placement of the figures against their backgrounds. Cavani indicates a prefer-
ence for medium shots and close-ups, as she concentrates on physiognomy.
Through the composition, she arranges the geometrical lines of architecture to
accentuate the tension in the frame. A confining, prisonlike mood, stressed by
the close-ups of the workers' sweat, conveys the dirty, stone feel of Pietro
Bernardone's factory. When Francesco's father appears in the doorway, his
body blocks the light, the only sustenance of life in the workplace.

At the very beginning of her career, Cavani manifests a preoccupation with the tension between the body and its background. Traditionally, the background corroborates both the narrative and the spectator's perception of the characters' moods and situations. In the opening scene of *Francesco di Assisi*, the dungeonlike setting behind the workers informs the otherwise materialist existence of the dyers with a sacral quality. It is apparent that Cavani aims at transcending the effect of verisimilitude captured by the prominent use of a handheld camera and normal lens. The initial shots transcend the visual and verbal distinctions of darkness/light, low/high, dirty/clean, the corporeality of human existence (sweating, coughing), and the physicality of the ambience (heat, dust, steam) to project a hieratic symbolism. A similar effect is created by the background behind Francesco, in our first glance at Lou Castel. It is an open space delimited by solid walls marking the boundary between order and chaos, structured space and *communitas*; the changing concept of medieval civic identity is revealed in the vision of the neophyte's upcoming new status: the blending of spiritual and secular powers united in one person.[29] Metonymy makes his figure bigger than life, an ideal knight against the imposing grandeur of the architectural lines. This commanding low-angle shot also anticipates the stark loneliness of the quest hero. The first shot of Francesco is a zoom into the pole guiding his war games. The ambience is that of an arena of action— the playful training against the "Saracino"—and it reflects the mood of a conventionally idle youth, at ease within traditional social limits. An analogous effect is re-created during the trial scene: cold buildings entrap the body of Francesco, the rebel, who is placed at the center of the piazza, as the scandalous monster of his time. Buildings affirm such oppositions in later films as well. The baroque theatrical settings of Galileo's trial by the Inquisition are a stylization of the labyrinthine paths of power; so is Antigone's torture machine: they create a readable context for the public gaze. In Cavani's later work, backgrounds become aggressively powerful in contributing to the film's dramatization of forces in conflict.

The principle which informs the protagonist's quest is a human desire that is displaced and heightened into a state of drunken madness: "matto," "malato di mente" (fool, madman) are the epithets shouted by the crowd to Francesco, as ceremonial spectacles of mockery are performed. What Foucault considers "le grand thème de la folie de la Croix" receives an ambivalent treatment in the film.[30] This ambivalence can be traced in two iconographic images of the martyred Christ. There is the crucifix in San Damiano, "a painted Christ crumbled under the rain and the sun," who has the fixed stare of the Italian illustrations of the late twelfth century: it emphasizes the divine qualities of the Christ who seems alive (open eyes, erect body posture) and, as *Christus Triumphans*, superior to the agony of the Cross. The other representation is the Byzantine cross, with "the dimensions of a man," in the cathedral of Assisi.[31] It portrays

Frame 4. Francesco (Lou Castel), a conventionally idle youth

the suffering of *Christus Patiens*, whose bent head, closed eyes, and wounded chest all work to stylize death and sacrifice. Both images incorporate the spirituality and physicality so crucial to the Franciscan impetus: with an imploring gaze fixed upon the hallowed countenance of Jesus, Francesco strives to articulate an *imitatio Christi*. In Cavani's recent *Francesco* only the Byzantine icon is retained, this time to suggest confusion and loss of identity.

Francesco's journey is expressed and guided by the exempla of the Cross. The filmic episodes, which are shot against authentic reconstructions of medieval settings, concern not a process of sanctification—miracles and legends are eliminated—but the search for the essence of Being. In his search, says Cavani, Francesco begins "to renounce many things which used to seem important, until he realizes that only the relationship with truth is the essential fact, the meaning of life."[32] The arduous quest for the truth is rendered by repeatedly delimiting lines in the visual composition, which realize the prison metaphor. The characters are often shot against a background that blocks their action; in the exterior shots, people are displayed in suffocating and aberrant postures. Only the Christocentric image gives the highest expression of man's wisdom, as Foucault has argued.[33] Cavani builds up to Francesco's final confrontation with his brethren, as he engages in a brief altercation about the futility of wearing a hair shirt ("cilicio"). Set against a foggy, constrained environment to evoke a sense of entrapment, and shot with a grainy film stock, this crucial scene incarnates the recurrent theme of *agere poenitentiam*. Francesco ventures on a labyrinthine exploration of his new followers: his spiritual consciousness and his concrete mode of thinking have no direct analogy in the hierocracy's medieval verbal conventions, abstract and rational. Telephoto shots accentuate the character's relationship to the crowd set in the background: he appears to be dominated, visually as well as orally, by the figures towering above him. Framed at the center of the maze, he comes to question his own directions. A centripetal, public gaze always encircles such Cavanian characters, whose body movement is choreographed to expose their defeat in the historical present. Here the path out of the dilemma ("he's a madman," "he's a fool," "he's an ignoramus") is voluntary isolation on Mount La Verna. As Joseph Campbell writes, the passage of the hero is fundamentally inward, "into depths where obscure resistances are overcome, and long lost, forgotten powers are revivified, to be made available for the transfiguration of the world."[34]

Following the oral-literary tradition, Cavani complicates such images by evoking the sphere of the ordinary; her linguistic models, also taken from colloquial speech, are intended to provide a mimetic translation of the *sermo humilis*, of the Franciscan *simplicitas*. Francesco executes an exemplary mnemonic replica of the biblical word: he is above all the *idiota*, in the archaic meaning of *simplex* and *illitteratus*. In order for the message to be accessible it must be simple and plain.

Frame 5. Francesco and the crucifix in San Damiano

The sequence of the trial objectifies the Franciscan message. The specular reciprocity between the example traced by the life of Christ and Francesco's practice is marked by sensorial realism: the eye and the ear are the dominant sensors in the apprehension of reality. The camera follows Francesco going through the crowd of leering spectators with a carefully framed succession of spectacular pans. The establishing shots of the bishop entering the city square are static, long takes that maximize the enduring and unchangeable nature of the hierarchical pyramid structure of the Middle Ages. During the reading of

Frame 6. Close-up of Francesco and the *Christus Triumphans*

the legal proceedings, conducted by Pietro Bernardone against his son's "rebellion and dissipation" (which lead to a suspension of kinship rights and subject Francesco to a de jure exile), the protagonist is shown cornered and surrounded by high stone walls. Cavani works with a juxtaposition of echoing voices (whispers, shouts, laughter) in order to sustain the effect created by the camera eye: the mad voyeurism of the crowd, cheering at the scandalous exposure of the rebel-saint. Cacophony reproduces the harshness of Francesco's symbolic and physical divestment. Cutaways of people's faces express individual responses to the spectacle. The scenes are brilliantly choreographed according to these reaction shots. Once again, Cavani represents figures of power (Pietro Bernardone, the bishop, the lawyers) through violent frontal compositions and low-angle shots, which convey the threat of authoritarian oppression. A similar result is constructed through her use of sound and montage during the scene of Francesco's encounter with the young leper ("frightened as a wounded deer"), who is legally expelled "outside the city walls" by means of a

Frame 7. Mickey Rourke and the Byzantine icon in *Francesco* (1989)

strange religious ceremony.[35] In her remarkable study of urban experience in the medieval world, Chiara Frugoni has described how every event that disturbed the peaceful unfolding of a life regulated by laws was in fact represented as occurring in the open.[36] The city walls enforced a violent division between the interior of the city whence the outcast is forcefully driven and the place, beyond them, of his punishment. In this episode of the expulsion of the leper, the words chanted by the priest resound like alien, distant voices in a nightmare. The handheld camera jolts relentlessly back and forth, side to side, as if to perform the dismay felt by Francesco's eye and ear when confronted with such a terrifying spectacle. The mobile camera highlights the act of seeing and its disturbing emotional impact. Francesco reveals his heightened power of sight and sound, which become more active as his new social status is defined.

Frame 8. Cavani directs Lou Castel

Frame 9. The civil action of Pietro Bernardone against his son Francesco

In June 1966, the newspaper *Orizzonti* organized a debate on *Francesco di Assisi* as a way of answering the numerous letters it had received about Cavani's film. It invited the director herself, Pier Paolo Pasolini, Ludovico Alessandrini, film critic of the *Osservatore romano*, and the theologian Adriana Zarri. Pasolini, while endorsing the film as an aesthetic triumph, expressed ideological reservations about Cavani's liberal, secular perspective. In his opinion, the film showed little awareness of the "delirious and sublime aristocracy of religion" and attempted to insert Catholicism into a petit bourgeois mentality by substituting moral and social stances for the sense of the sacred:

> Cavani has "Westernized" Francesco. She has divested his Middle Ages of the Oriental matrix that its socioeconomic conditions objectively had. She has eliminated the Oriental elements (hunger, death, dirt, hopelessness, barbarism), which were part of Francesco's world, and has substituted petit bourgeois elements for them. This is her historical violence . . . I dissent from the film's perspective and its absence of a sacred myth. The "bank clerks" who become the saint's followers, as well as his

Frame 10. Francesco's symbolic and physical divestiture

disciples, are miscast; their faces lack the sacral solemnity of the myth. The only poetic faces are those of the pope and the bishops. The great, the authorities, the powerful are ontological, mysterious, for a petit bourgeois; they are not problematic characters; they are dei ex machina and, in the film, sterling, ambiguous characters. The face of the pope is the only absolute face, and, in this respect, disconcerting, just as in myths. It does not take on problems but solves them for inscrutable reasons. This is religion.

Like his followers, St. Francis is a dilettante of religion. His nature remains that of his father and mother: he cannot help it; hence his irrationalism. It is the typical bourgeois strategy (I use this term psychologically) to confront the Other. Cavani's Francesco does not succeed in being different, in being a saint.[37]

Francesco di Assisi is not the product of bourgeois religion. In Cavani's interpretation, the classical archive of Franciscan texts reveals that the medieval meaning of the saint was not primarily ethical, metaphysical, but artistic: a powerful, pictorial raiment for fundamental Franciscan ideas. The character portrayed by Cavani presents a substantial deepening of the Christian message: it exults in the sacredness of quotidian reality. It stages a performance of absolute freedom in revolt, an existential and poetic example enacted in the image of the perilous adventure.[38] Few filmmakers would assert such a stand in a pre-1968 climate.

Francesco's marginality encompasses a notion of open morality against the bounds of hierarchical judgment. Maria Corti has called this type of paradigmatic, symbolic interaction in medieval culture "a transgressive *diverso*," that which values the alternative element of all its oppositions (*low*/high, *body*/spirit, *madness*/wisdom), and by so doing becomes the established antimodel.[39] Cavani asks us to pay attention to the interplay of social and artistic tensions. In her first feature film, the director experiments with narrative structures; each shot is calibrated to the rhythm of the life that it illustrates. Even in this early stage, the film evokes an unmistakable Cavanian mood. The camera is used with considerable control; the images work to displace the legendary in the direction of the ordinary; medium shots and close-ups enhance a narrative subjectivity that questions documentary realism. Cavani was training herself in a cinematic method that would prevail in her first noncommissioned film, *I cannibali*, in which the director's demythologizing pragmatism would return to the naked truth of a myth. Francesco becomes the pure archetypal conscience in a world of brutal rationality. This is emphasized in the film's final scene, when the body of the Friar Minor is laid down to die on the barren earth of La Portiuncula (as he had requested of Brother Elias). This ending transposes Francesco into the realm of anthropology: in becoming human, religion finds its cultural roots.

Francesco di Assisi expresses the tension of Cavani's later films: the images imply a criticism of the social system but do not advance a message of militant reform. Cavani's vision of the Franciscan world is detached; it does not sympathize in any direct way with established religion. The novelty of *Francesco di Assisi* is in the representation of a revolutionary, modern character who does not oppose his times, remains deeply medieval in his sensibility, and yet has the capacity to create an archetypal exemplum. Cavani was beginning to develop a kind of film that was different from what contemporary auteurs were showing audiences. Indeed, she entertains a very personal relation to social discourse and establishes a cinematic style through which her authorial voice will be identifiable in the films of the next decade.

2

Realism against Illusion: The Ceremonial Divestiture of Power in *Galileo*

> Realism in itself is not art, but there must be
> harmony between the genuineness of feeling and
> the genuineness of things. I try to force reality into
> a form of simplification and abbreviation in order
> to reach what I call psychological realism.
>   (*Carl-Theodor Dreyer*)

IN CONFRONTING the Galileo affair, writes Alberto Moravia, Liliana Cavani had two choices: "either to make a simple didactic film, almost an imaginary documentary (like Roberto Rossellini's film on Louis XIV), or to make a historical film and reconstruct, as much as possible, Galileo's drama in its psychological details. . . . She preferred to make the first film, but not without some flashes of the second; the originality of *Galileo* lies precisely in its simple and direct realistic approach, as well as in its pedagogical intent."[1] As Moravia realized, Cavani's *Galileo* (1968) is not strictly a historical film. History merges into a drama revolving around the defeated figure of the astronomer from Pisa: the director called it "un'opera a dibattito," a film for discussion.[2] The historical component in the tragic outcome (the abjuration) is represented by the Church, whose spiritual and corporeal dynamics present the terms of the conflict and debate: the dogmatic abstractions of the hierarchic body versus the empirical grammar of the new science. In its psychological component, *Galileo* comprises, along with *Francesco di Assisi*, *I cannibali*, and *Milarepa*, Cavani's quest theme, a tale of heroic action, which invariably depicts "heroism" in its ironic guise of defeat and develops the nondiscursive language of power through the progressive estrangement of the individual. Francesco, Galileo, Antigone, Milarepa are heroic characters displaced in the direction of the human: their catastrophe becomes a social event; their tragedy is almost a clinical investigation of a sick society.[3] The ironic displacement of these heroic figures contributes to a certain stasis in the action of the film: characters tend to withdraw into a subjective space, the prisonlike construction of the Cavanian interior. Catastrophe becomes meaningless, since neither the Pisan's abjuration nor Antigone's public execution will deter future revolutions.[4]

The most scandalous scientific case of the Counter-Reformation primarily involved questions about the search for truth. The polemics surrounding the

Galileo case mediated issues concerning physics, astronomy, and cosmology, but they also addressed broader epistemological inquiries. In its larger historical ramifications, the case helped to determine the separation of science and philosophy and the departure from authority as a criterion of scientific knowledge. Galileo's research—an eloquent exemplum of the pursuit of truth—is what interests Cavani. If Francesco's *caritas* attacked the core of medieval feudalism, Galileo's discoveries divested the Church of the illusory permanence of its authority in matters concerning scientific truth. At this stage of her career, Cavani's intention was not to convey a historical lesson, but to present a study of the forces of power and order within a defined sociohistorical context that would also serve as a metaphor for a universal situation. Francesco, Galileo, Antigone personify the unrest of their times; they are not men of the past. Cavani describes this intent to an anonymous reviewer:

> We live in an era of great moral confusion and absolute indifference toward any type of problems or principles. Ideals are dormant, if not dead; we have all abjured our ideals in order to continue living. Nobody would dare to climb on a pulpit and openly denounce the illness of our society. If he were to do so, he would be considered a fool. Why not, like Galileo, adhere to the "system," fight it as much as necessary, try to eliminate its defects, and somehow manage to make our ideas triumph? This would be the equivalent of reaching an ideal of freedom.[5]

In Cavani's cinema, the triumph of power always manifests itself in the ritual of the trial that is primarily social in nature. *Galileo* depicts the tragedy of a revolutionary intellect, an Illuminist *ante litteram*, as Cavani called him, who happens to find himself, without realizing or seeking it, at the center of the greatest scandal of his times.[6] In Cavani's ironic view, Galileo is a forerunner, but he is above all a man operating within, and answerable to, the dominant systems of his era. The first man who could glance beyond the established limits of the sky is ultimately blind to the consequences of his belief that his proofs could reverse the established modes of power. Galileo's naïveté informs the dynamics between science and authority. His search for truth and knowledge—the eye, the light, the circle, which symbolize his findings—is counteracted by the darkness of obscurantist structures. For the Pisan, writes Cavani, "culture is either free from power or it is dead":[7] death is the predominant image associated with the papal apparatus. For example, the Medici tombs were substituted for the Vatican, the original meeting place of Galileo with Paul V and Urban VIII. These funereal settings anticipate the outcome of the scientist's traumatic acceptance that error cannot be rectified: his abjuration.

Galileo is structured around each dramatic step or scene in which authority displays its power: the anatomical amphitheater, the proceedings of the Holy Office and the Inquisitor's gaze, the burning of the heretic's body, the carnival and judicial rites, the spectacular staging of the abjuration. The film follows

Galileo from the beginning of his teaching position at Padua (1592), under the aegis of the Venetian Republic (including a hypothetical encounter with Giordano Bruno), to his research on the matter of light and the telescopic lenses (1609–1611) after he goes to Pisa as the mathematician and philosopher of Cosimo II de' Medici, to the Inquisition's official admonition (1616), his summons to Rome by a special commission under the direct control of the pope (1632), the trial and abjuration in 1633.

Cavani's film elaborates this dramatic narrative as an allegory of the revolution in cognitive conditions:

> Galileo was inside a great movement of ideas. He was not a solitary man, looking through a telescope. First of all the telescope had come from abroad; someone else had invented it. Scientific Europe is all there. It is a scientific revolution born within a learned society; it is the scientific revolution of the processes of knowledge.[8]

Galileo's experience is representative of a central moment of modern history. Francesco expressed the popular revolution of the Middle Ages; the *Sidereus Nuncius*, as part of a learned, scientific movement, embodies the bourgeois values of that society as well as its revolutionary energies. The epoch into which Galileo was born was one in which the power of authority was supreme in every sphere of human activity—philosophical, religious, and political. For the Pisan, observation and reason replaced dogmatism in matters of scientific investigation. His methodological preoccupations led him to question and reject dogmatic truth, hence his anti-Aristotelianism. As he says in a famous passage of *Il saggiatore* (The Assayer, 1623), philosophy, as nature's great book, is written in mathematical language. Nature is comprehended by numbers, while history is the aggregate of that which has no relation to mathematics. Thus the actual number with which the mathematician works designates the precision of the scientist's findings, comprehensible to the inner and outer eye, and acceptable as a figure of cognitive demarcation.[9] Galileo was aware of the dangers of illusion based on sensory evidence; only mathematical rules could convey reliable evidence and verify the findings of experimentation. His dictum "without mathematics, one wanders about in a dark labyrinth" clarifies the relationship between the realistic essence of Galilean knowledge and the illusion of the philosophers' and theologians' dogmatism. To the human intellect, the universe appears as a labyrinth, decipherable only through a physiology of perception:

> Philosophy is written in this great book that is constantly open before our eyes (the Universe), but we cannot understand it unless we first learn how to interpret the language, and understand the characters, with which it is written. It is written in a mathematical language, and the characters are triangles, circles, and other geometrical shapes; without these instruments it is humanly impossible to decipher a word; without them one wanders aimlessly about in a dark labyrinth.[10]

The opening sequence makes this shockingly literal. Close-ups of the brain, photographed in high angle, effectively concretize the argument between dominant, classical epistemologists and the hypothetical prefigurations advanced by Galileo. The camera zooms into the complex system of the nervous fibers, as anatomy professor Acquapendente refutes the Galenic school of medicine. Lukács has referred to Galileo's new language and new alphabet as an unequivocal, transparent image of the new mode of reflecting reality.[11] This perception ratifies and extends the Copernican rupture with the geocentric, anthropomorphic vision of the Ptolemaic universe.

In Galileo's story, Cavani sees striking parallels to the cultural situation of the late 1960s. Her revolt against institutional stagnation is retold through the Galileo affair.[12] In Cavani's creative reconstruction of Galileo's drama, orthodoxy and order are increasingly challenged by the lucid realism of scientific language represented in the film's dialogue:

> GALILEO: Professor, is it not true that you feel hot and cold with your senses and that you don't ask Aristotle whether you should cover yourself or not?
> CREMONINI: My dear colleague, are you making fun of me?
> GALILEO: But tell me, when a suit is tight, don't you have another one made?
> CREMONINI: What are you trying to tell me?
> GALILEO: The same is for science: we use a theory until we realize it has become too tight![13]

This lucidity contrasts with the violence of the film's scenic forms, the forms in which power exhibits itself. "There is a remarkable realism, and modernity, in the dialogue," Cavani argues, and "a certain theatricality of the sets and costumes that allowed me to relate the 'vero' (truthful) with the 'finto' (fake)."[14] The director develops what I call an "optical" style to express the interlacing of the intellectual with the religious body. The optical perspective, accomplished by strategic frame composition and camera placement, duplicates the dynamics between the freedom of the inquisitive eye and the limits imposed by the blind obscurantism of the Church. Cavani extends this dynamic to every formal aspect of the film, in the contrast and interaction between ordinary and pompous sets, light and dark colors, austere and sumptuous costumes. The simple and clear reality of science makes its way into the high style of religious ceremonials. With this juxtaposition of images, Galileo emphasizes the complex and tangled relation of realism to illusion.

Cavani's film treatment makes explicit the revolutionary parameters of Galileo's science: "For Galileo the stars are not 1,027, as Aristotle says, the limits are given by the human eye. With an adequate instrument one can see thousands of stars." In establishing what is transgressive in Galileo's experience, Cavani also provides her audience with a key to interpretation in the realism of the visual imagery. Cavani's style validates the instrument of Galileo's cultural revisionism: Galileo at the telescope (with its small disks of various diameters)

Frame 11. The anatomic amphitheater at the University of Padua in *Galileo* (1968)

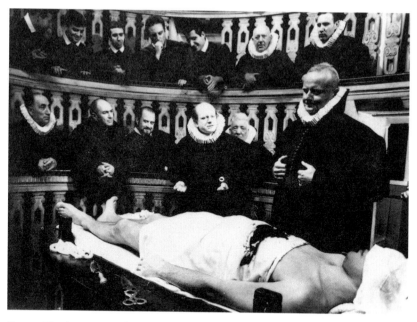

Frame 12. Anatomy professor Acquapendente refutes the Galenic school of medicine

Frame 13. Galileo (Cyril Cusak) works on "l'occhiale" (the telescopic lens)

Frame 14. Galileo at the telescope

is the key image for her. She manipulates the lens and the camera angle to magnify or reduce objects, and, in so doing, she visualizes the dialogic nature of the telescopic lenses, whose concave and convex surfaces alternately create the optical effects of inflation and *reductio*. This alternation defines Cavani's compositional strategy. Indeed *Galileo* reveals the director's imaginative skill in scenic organization. The spectator enters a realm of lavish display of baroque architecture and decor. The optical style translates the very nature of Galileo's revolutionary concepts as well as the lines of his historical boundaries.

Although *Galileo* follows a chronological sequence of events, it is not a biographical film. The film's narrative exalts the spectacle that encompasses what Cavani terms "la tragica avventura di questo personaggio" (the tragic adventure of this character). The importance of Galileo's experience, according to Cavani, rests on his "dispute with a (socio-moral) cultural system that is crystallized in the past and, by favoring scientific immobility, not only prevented science from being free, but was also the direct cause of social stagnation."[15] The director maintains a classical narrative structure and dramatizes the tragic event into acts or spectacular "numbers." The title role is played by Cyril Cusack, who interpreted the film as a story of the "tormented search for man's origins and destiny."[16] Cavani concentrates on the narrative construction of an *avventura di idee*, which generates tension between the discursive strategies of the protagonist and the a-dialogic nature of the social background. The labyrinthine theological enunciations of the *doctores* of the Church lead to insidious circumlocutions: a rhetorical (and visual) movement without escape, which anticipates the final abjuration. Cavani's compositions transgress established symmetrical lines; she plays with form and asks the spectator to master the ratio of cinematic spatial reality. For example, in the dialogue between Galileo and the newly elected Urban VIII (who as Cardinal Maffeo Barberini had been the scientist's patron), the pope and his entourage oscillate within a scenographic space that reinforces the sense of physical and learned limits of their debate: Galileo stands docile, unable to utter a complete sentence, while the clergymen move relentlessly along the sinuous forms drawn on the marble floor. This scene expresses a fundamental ontological rapport of the body with spatial reality; a rapport that Foucault has called, in *Surveiller et punir*, the mute solidity of the modern individual as object. *Galileo*'s cinematic style broadly points to André Bazin's "asymptote of reality" (life itself made spectacle), a term the French critic used to explain the way in which Vittorio De Sica and his screenwriter Cesare Zavattini interpreted cinema. More specifically, Bazin discusses *Umberto D*, a film Cavani has acknowledged as instrumental in her becoming a filmmaker.[17]

Galileo does not reject traditional cinematic spectacle. The film opens and closes with theatrical sequences: the anatomy amphitheater at Padua and the circuslike setting in which the abjuration is performed. The stage directions in the published screenplay read:

> A wooden stage for the spectators and an ample baldachin for the most reverend
> Grand Inquisitors. Overall it looks like a great circus where the principal "number" is
> performed by Galileo, no longer a man, but a tamed little monkey. From the towering
> baldachin a signal begins the ritual, or rather the spectacle.[18]

The script notes emphasize the use of ritual in order to reinforce the permanence of the Church. In representing the interplay of disciplinary technologies
and the empirical nature of Galilean science, the film tends to duplicate these
ritualistic models of power: not only are there two heretics (Bruno and Galileo)
but there are also two trials, sentences, and public executions. There is also a
double perspective in the visual presentation of the filmic reality—the illusionary versus the real—which is highlighted by Cavani's predominant use of low-
angle shots. The film is indeed anomalous in relying on limited camera mobil-
ity. There are almost no camera moves and only a few descriptive dollies. It
relies on close-ups and pacing to punctuate the emotion of the dialogue.

The opening sequence in the anatomy theater ("a castle of circular benches,
a small tower of Babel") establishes the cultural core of the tension between
the protagonist and powerful figures who are about to witness "an extraordinary and scandalous event, a desecration of the human body."[19] As the dis-
sected specimen is elevated from the floor and the anatomy lesson begins, a
high-angle shot clearly defines the desolation of the scene. This point of view
will create ironic distance throughout the film. Galileo's dispute with the Aristotelian *doctor* entails the risks and perils of transgressing the institutional *limina*, of asserting the ground of free inquiry and experience, unhindered by
Scholastic metaphysics and its theology—subservient to the cultural *cursus* of
Aristotle, Galen, and St. Thomas Aquinas. His revolutionary quest dramatically
culminates in the trial, which the authorities must conduct to restore order.
As Pope Urban VIII states, the scientist "had dared enter where he should not,
into the most grave and dangerous subjects that one could possibly raise at
this moment."[20] The trial enacts a ritual of divestment and banishment. *Galileo*'s
tragic action ends with the defeat of the hero: the objectification of the scientist,
the submission of the body through the control of ideas, "l'esprit' comme
surface d'inscription pour le pouvoir" (the mind as a surface of inscription for
power)[21] are expressed in the "assurda filastrocca" (absurd rambling rhyme)
read by one of the cardinals. When recited by Galileo himself, the *filastrocca*
becomes "un testo tragico che riguarda tutti" (a tragic text that concerns everyone): the penitent's eyes, no longer focused on the universe, turn toward the
reverend judges; photographed from a low angle, the Inquisitors appear "to be
projected into the sky as if they were God."[22]

The film's theatrical settings reinforce the oppressive power of these ceremonial rituals. In each setting, the body of the heretic is progressively displaced
onto the margins of the frame. *Galileo* begins with a juxtaposition of voices,
accompanied by shots of men speaking various languages of learning, each

Frame 15. Galileo displays a map of the Copernican system

placed in a different cultural background: the Aristotelians, the Ptolemaics, the Peripatetics, who claim traditional geostatic views; and the Copernicans, the Pythagoreans, who advance geokinetic theories. The opening shots identify the confusion that reigns at a time of extraordinary scientific revolutions. The great Pisan, who teaches mathematics with obvious discomfort and anguish (signaled by his repeated attempts to remove his academic collar), no longer believes in the Ptolemaic "panzane" (nonsense). The cultural climate of the opening scene appears to be favoring a dialogue; but Galileo needs to provide a theoretical account of, and a justification for, his new scientific discoveries. His initial instrument of empirical experimentation is the telescope, the rudimentary "Dutch toy" brought to him by Paolo Sarpi. For Spengler, the discovery of the telescope is Faustian: by "penetrating into spaces hidden from the naked eye and inaccessible to the will-to-power,[the telescope] *widens* the universe that we possess."[23] Galileo's transgressive eye puts into question the very nature of truth and man's freedom to acquire knowledge. His knowledge is neither speculative nor strictly materialist: it entails a mathematical procedure.

The film cuts from a very stylized opening—which reveals the artificiality of the academicians—to the realistic settings of Galileo's research laboratory and living quarters. Throughout the film, Galileo represents symmetry and logical clarity, as is emphasized by the straight geometrical barrenness of his environment. A rational, formalistic geometry (lines and angles, circles, triangles, rectangles) contributes to the illusion of moving toward something real, peering through a spiral or a tunnel, as in the amphitheater at the displayed body, or during Galileo's encounter with Giordano Bruno on the iron staircase. J. T. Frazer has seen in the geometric metaphor "an intellectually pleasing static image that conjures up the experience of watching moving bodies."[24] From Hipparchus to Copernicus, astronomers have used geometrical models to explain the kinetic energy of the sun, the moon, and the planetary orbits. The cognitive pathos of the Galilean geometrical configurations demonstrates various forms of scientific consciousness. The circle represents universal space itself, but it also refers to the limits of the established truth. Photographed from a low camera position in subterranean rooms, the stark contours of the celestial sphere often appear to entrap the scientist against a confining background, as in the windowless classroom at Padua where Galileo impudently argues that "the sphere is the symbol of perfection, but man's idea of it is imperfect."[25] The circle as a symbol of perfection and sight is also the geometrical body of the error of tradition. In this scene, Cavani works on reaction shots to emphasize the subject's paradoxical situation, as he fights to control his increasing anguish and fear. She dares to present a variety of visual and dramatic devices that succeed in structuring the most provocative illusion staged by an absolutist and blind power against Galileo's naïveté.

   Galileo is the story of the negativity of dialogue, in the sense that intellectual dialectics are absent, or applied externally as false rhetoric. In Galileo's encounter with Urban VIII, this is shown to be a fortiori true. The dialectical axis has as one pole the traditional acceptance of science within theological interpretations, and, as the other, the threatening discoveries of the new science. The simplicity of the Pisan's performance is counterbalanced by the highly controlled, argumentative responses that have been perfected by the Church hierarchy. Cavani's blocking emphasizes the spatial enforcement of control. The astronomer is exiled to the edge of the frame, his figure reduced to a Lilliputian size. Such compositions convey the constant surveillance of eyes of power: the pope climbs up to his magnificent throne, from which he stares down on Galileo. The scenography and the costumes create the illusion of a motionless organization of space, what Bazin has called the "tortured immobility of baroque art";[26] the utmost attention is devoted to the details of clothes, objects, and architectural design. The baroque corporeality of the seventeenth century triumphs together with its disciplinary techniques. Cavani's insistent use of close-ups guarantees that this triumph is blatant and visible.

   The visual rhetoric of *Galileo* exposes the eloquent rituals of the Church. The director collaborated with the cinematographer Alfio Contini (who would also photograph *Il portiere di notte*) and the set designer Ezio Frigerio in order to give the film a specific look. "The film does not draw from the paintings of the time," says Cavani, "I was not interested in a photographic reproduction of the period but in the ideas I wanted to express. . . . The colors were selected with extreme care, fabric after fabric, wall after wall."[27] The most telling example is the film's final sequence with its reaffirmation of traditional religious symbolism and technologies of power. Cavani announces the artifices of the Church in numerous ways: colors, sets, costumes, body postures, telephoto shots all convey a world of highly controlled rules. In the sequence of Galileo's last attempt at conversing with Urban VIII, before the Inquisition's proceedings begin, the labyrinthine design of the pope's circular and aimless movements, coupled with the geometrical inscriptions of the floor, projects the idea of a theologian's maze at the center of which the scientist is trapped, unable to escape (or utter a word).

Galileo's body becomes the scandalous monster at the very center of such an overpowering architecture. The splendor of the pope's golden attire set against the dark gray of the Medicis' funereal monuments in the background renders the illusion of light cast into a somber, incarcerating interior. Extreme camera placements, bird's-eye view and Dutch angles, add a sense of the "abnormal" a-dialogic nature of the encounter, a relationship of anguished distance, which visually underscores the drama of the heretic of the Counter-Reformation. The music of Ennio Morricone becomes an integral element of this static ensemble: it evokes the ominous atmosphere of Church rituals and the poignancy of the protagonist's apprehension in the face of the solemn apparatus.[28] At the end, the solemn notes of Haydn's *Te Deum* work as an ironic comment on the corrosive emblem of power (Bernini's funereal monument) to which Pope Urban VIII entrusted his ephemeral greatness. The Church of the Counter-Reformation cannot contain a science of unlimited hypothesis: the possible and the actual will never meet in history.

Galileo's central narrative event is the trial. Its cinematic representation, accomplished by frontal deep focus and fixed lenses, emphasizes the artifice of abstract disciplinary mechanisms. With the grandeur of its mise-en-scène, the trial epitomizes the profundity of Cavani's imagery. The spectacular, orchestrated dialogue of the Inquisition discloses the legal and political definition of power and its complex ways of exercising control over Galileo. The two overwhelming attributes of the trial are space and movement: the flat, two-dimensional, towering figures staging the Inquisition versus the docile, centered body of Galileo. The body that has to be disciplined and observed is made most visible at the center of the space of internment.[29] As in the closing scene, Galileo's figure transforms the spectacular into the psychological: his body invalidates every visual excess associated with the repressive mechanisms of his adversary. The magnificent sets and costumes fade before the universal questions posed by the scientific intellect as he confronts his inquisitive judges.

The emotional nuances that define the protagonist's attitude are humbleness, resignation, and anguish. Cavani's script specifies that "from high above, on their thrones, the cardinals watch Galileo with pity."[30] As Pietro Redondi reminds us, this was a time when both religion and politics were arts that centered on the gaze.[31] The sequence of shots during the interrogation evokes a

Frame 16. Set design for Bernini's tomb of Pope Urban VIII by Ezio Frigerio

dramaturgy of alienation, based on the tableaux. The trial is staged in "a circular marble room with many niches in which thrones are situated with about ten cardinals seated upon them. In the center, there is a table for the commissary general and the fiscal procurator, and a bench for the accused Galileo."[32] The Inquisitors are set against stark, white walls. The camera's low angle accentuates their postures in a Dreyer-like composition. Dreyer's tendency toward monumentality, the sculptural and the static, is re-created by Cavani as a means through which she achieves the penetrative force and accretion of consciousness that constitute the essential stylistic quality of this scene.[33] The rigorous judiciary procedures interlock in a succession of frames, whereby the political technology of power and of object relations dissects the scale and distance of the control.

The Galileo affair was a very serious affair of state. The pope's official scientist was suspected of new, dangerous doctrines: only through his official condemnation could the scandal be counteracted. Galileo is depicted standing erect, his hands clasped over the incriminating *Dialogo sopra i due massimi sistemi* (Dialogue Concerning the Two Chief World Systems, 1632). The scenographic space complements the unfolding dramatic action; the sequence is regulated by the deliberate pacing from facial shot to facial shot. The camera lens, set

Frame 17. Galileo's interrogation by the Roman Inquisition

Frame 18. Close-up of the trial

Frame 19. The strategic tactics of the Inquisition: torture as a judicial game

slightly below eye level, unbalances the framings, so as to decipher, in the signs of the face, the soul of the character. Galileo's figure is positioned prominently in the foreground: here the style of the tableau works to bring weight forward; it breaks with the more classical scenography of *Francesco di Assisi*.

In representing his struggle, Cavani focuses not only on the field of power but also on the soul of the man who must retain its unity against darker forces. She makes him human enough to understand that his opponent cannot be proven wrong. The drama relies on the effect of the rhetorical organization of the pictorial space. The religious ceremonials exhibit a psychological balance: Galileo's strength lies in his accepting, like Francesco, the legal jurisdiction of historical times. History will rehabilitate the scientist and the supremacy of the mathematical proof; the trial will remain a symbol of the Church's obscurantism.

Cavani displays her ideal of the truth through the depiction of implacable acts of punishment—and the confession that must follow and complement the strategic tactics of the institution. When the two Dominican fathers coerce Galileo into the sight of the instruments, which were efficiently designed to help the heretic confess the truth and repent (the commissary's warning), he is petrified. As a judicial game, torture is applied to the body of the heretic to challenge his definition of the truth; its persuasive mechanisms test the knowl-

Frame 20. The procession through the streets of Rome: Galileo wearing the penitent's tunic and hat

edge acquired at the *limina*. The visual impact of this scene anticipates the curiosity that drives the crowd to the spectacle of the scaffold. Doubtful "of being a madman, of speaking in an unknown language," Galileo submits to the ordeal of penalties:[34] the procession through the streets of Rome on a mule, wearing a penitent's tunic and hat; the *supplice* of the reading of the official sentence; the oath sworn as a public spectacle; the final banishment. During the conclusive act of the judicial drama, played out on 22 June 1633 in the church of Santa Maria sopra Minerva, Galileo's body language breaks down, exposing, in his nakedness and inertia, the visible signs that he who has tried to engage in dialogue with the system finds himself exausted by it.

Throughout the film, carnival rites (as well as judicial rites) mask the repressive forces of power. Popular festivities, with their licensed anarchy and teratological fantasies, are *signa* of the utopian character of nonhierarchical universality.[35] For example, the episode in which Galileo exhibits his telescope at Palazzo Barberini is set up by a grotesque, licentious scene revealing a procession of hooded men in black, carrying the effigy of a woman with a label on her chest that reads: "Heresy is dead." As the people's games begin, Cardinal Barberini

Frame 21. The reading of the official sentence by the Dominican commissary

Frame 22. The abjuration of Galileo Galilei

ventures to look through the subversive object displayed on an easel. The geometric simplicity of the telescopic lens contrasts with the deceptive appearance of the theatrical grandeur presented by the Collegio Romano to the public at carnival time. A cautious Robert Bellarmine (the great Inquisitor of Giordano Bruno's trial) marvels at such extraordinary effects, drawing a precise, threatening analogy to the Bruno affair. The burning of the catafalque supporting the effigy creates the visual illusion of a cross, transforming the scene into a suggestive stage set for Bruno's imminent execution at Campo dei Fiori: the man of reason, who sought to free religion from "imposture" (impostures), and the scientist, who claimed to be neither a visionary nor a heretic, embody the defeat of culture against a backdrop of the splendors of the baroque age.

In reconstructing the Galileo affair, Cavani exercises considerable poetic freedom. Her most notable departure is the role assigned in the film to the (historically undocumented) encounter between Giordano Bruno and Galileo. These men represent complementary curves of the same lens: they both see beyond the *limina* of their time, one as a philosopher, the other from the perspective of mechanics, geometry, and mathematics. Cavani shares her perspective with Aldo Tassone:

> Bruno is a man who looks at the past, while Galileo looks at the future. Bruno's rebellion occurs inside the Church and addresses theological issues: he claims that the Church must understand the new science and accept it. For Galileo (he is perhaps the first secular rebel) theology is one thing, science another. He does not ask the Church to understand the new science; he asks for scientific freedom. For Galileo, science is based on experience, religion on faith; they are two different things.[36]

This conceptual and methodological distinction between Bruno's and Galileo's philosophical investigations is visually projected onto the spiral staircase on which Cavani sets their dialogue. Like the cylinder-shaped *cannocchiale* (refractor), the spiral alludes to a transpersonal aspect of their confrontation. It is an optical illusion that draws the eye into infinity. Galileo, who is, in the director's words, "a man who before saying must see, and says according to how much he can prove," is framed at the very center of the spiral, facing the sky; while Bruno, "the philosopher who must create a system for a cosmology, before speaking of a cosmogony," is blocked, facing the depths of the tunnel created by the downward spiral curves.[37] The subtle conceptualization behind the composition of this encounter belies the ephemeral spectacle of the Church's Inquisitional rituals, which will determine the fate of both revolutionary minds. During the interrogation, Galileo does not delve into the binding argumentative questions advanced by the Jesuits, who have been trained in dialectics. While waiting for his sentence at night in a cell at the Holy Office, he is transfigured into an accused who is no longer afraid of anything or anyone. The author of the *Dialogo* cannot explain himself except through a dream, where he has no real interlocutors:

> I am going to say what I think. First of all I regret having come here to submit to you like a fool. I believe in what I wrote in my book . . . and I have no intention of recanting it . . . Furthermore, I am convinced that it is beneficial to the Church; not harmful . . . What damage could it cause? and what sin have I committed? . . . I have always believed that the Church loved the truth and fought ignorance. But I was wrong; otherwise your tribunal has nothing to do with the Church. . . .[38]

Throughout this chapter I have noted how the decor in Galileo's environment is habitually barren, allowing for a tableau effect. The pure white space of the cell, with a peculiar window designed not to permit a view of the exterior, evokes a limbo-like confinement: the figure of a crucifix on the wall seems to be suspended in a luminous emptiness. On the other hand, Bruno's cosmological dialogues with the Grand Inquisitor stage two strong minds who forcibly denounce independent, irreconcilable languages. Bruno's crusade against an oppressive and obscurantist orthodoxy and his anti-Aristotelianism are threatening and thus call for the full power of the most authoritative word in the vocabulary of seventeenth-century Roman Catholicism: heresy. Even the high clergy, Jesuits and Dominicans, compete "for a sort of primacy in the control of culture."[39] Cavani's original version of Bruno's death at the stake, a physical portrayal of the body's martyrdom, with its agonizing pain and cries, was censored because of its violence. Shot entirely in a long take, this powerful scene is hauntingly supported by Morricone's echoing sound track. Owing to the direct intervention of the Vatican, RAI television immediately withdrew the film from circulation and sold it to Cineriz.[40] We may wonder how this sequence relates to the film's major thesis that Galileo was not a weak man but one prepared to do what the ignorance of his times demanded in order to survive. Bruno's philosophical commitment makes it difficult for the institution to accept him. To Cavani, Galileo represents the progress of science extending to a systematic trial of apprehending reality. He neither judges nor preaches against the system that attempts to encompass his knowledge.

The scene in which the Venetian academicians refuse to look through the telescope best delineates Galileo's historical role: his adversaries did not want to be disturbed in their solemn faith in the Aristotelian system. Stanley Cavell, who has seen in Galileo the beginning of modern skeptical thought, has questioned whether such figures are comic or irrational.[41] This element of skepticism is part of the Cavanian definition of character: to admit ignorance ("I do not know") as a step to knowledge; to admit fear as a human quality. Galileo departs from theoretical deductions to prove that scientific facts can be circumscribed within general mathematical laws. Cavani has called *Galileo* her "most secular film," where nothing is transcendental.[42] This is clear during Galileo's

Frame 23. Giordano Bruno and the Grand Inquisitor

dialogue with Cardinal Bellarmine: for the scientist, truth is an instrument governed by logic, calculus, and mathematics; for the theologian, it entails ordering processes.

An appalling naïveté characterizes the protagonist's behavior, a trait most of Cavani's characters bear in common:

> These transgressors do not know they are transgressing. They do not make speeches. They are not preachers nor moralists. They are spontaneous *pueri*. Wisdom is made of the simplicity of the *puer* . . . Galileo finds it normal to see what he saw and to believe in what he believed. He did not think this could go against the rules of the game of the human consortium with religion. He became a transgressor against his will. He has the naïveté to go to Rome convinced that science belongs to the intelligence of everyone.[43]

Galileo's abjuration is the defeat of his naïveté. He understands, however, better than Bruno, that the historical situation of the Church could not allow for independent heretical solutions. Cavani's characters are always defeated at the level of the historical present. Francesco and Galileo move from within their acceptance of traditional power structures beyond the boundaries set by their religious and social institutions. Galileo sees an unequivocal, naked truth that cannot exist within the delimited space to which the body of the rebel-scientist is confined. In the prisonlike room where he awaits the sentence, Galileo, supervised by the conventional eye of Father Charles, is barred from light. The intolerance of the Church is not equated with religion, which, for Cavani, always objectifies a cultural mythology. Galileo's abjuration creates the *fractura* of the Counter-Reformation; it is "an act of faith in the future."[44]

The essential service of Galileo's new science to religious institutions is to divest them of their idolatrous apparatuses; hence the film's tendency to emphasize the body as a subject (the papal audiences, Urban VIII's lunch with Bernini, the accuracy of the body's posture for the funereal monument) or as an object of power (the burning of the heretic, the incarcerating effects of the interior designs). The intellectually vigorous arguments of Galileo's investigations, which guarantee the autonomy of logic, must be silenced, because autonomy of scientific culture would divest the Church of its ceremony and its power. As an intellectual director, Cavani defends the autonomy of scientific culture: this is the social task of cinema.

3

Metaphors of Revolt: The Dialogic Silence in *I cannibali*

Numberless wonders / terrible wonders walk the
world but none the match for man.
  (*Sophocles*, Antigone)

Not to speak does not mean that one has nothing
to say.
  (*Béla Balázs*)

I CANNIBALI (The Cannibals, 1969) is Cavani's first film to rely on an independent production company. The director presented the idea, which was inspired by Sophocles' *Antigone*, to Enzo Doria for Euro International Film. She outlined the story as "a dramatic adventure that takes place in the future."[1] The resulting free adaptation of a play that Aristotle cited repeatedly in his *Politics*, and that Hegel interpreted as a paramount example of the clash between the highest ethical forces (the political and the religious), is imbued with an urgent concern for the problems of the polis. It addresses central issues of language, culture, and politics. The film is a passionate advocacy of man, as defined in the first famous stasimon of *Antigone* on human creativity and inventiveness: the human being recaptured as a primal, prodigious body of nature, capable of structuring order into chaos.[2] "Today," says Cavani, "our cities are like many Corinths, where the tyrant gives orders against nature. That is an obscene authority, the real scandal nature resists, because she is free and innocent, and she loves man, her son. We have seen symptoms of rebellion. My film wants to bear witness to this type of natural rebellion."[3]

Despite its commitment to bearing witness to a natural rebellion conducted in the name and cause of Nature, *I cannibali* is itself a highly stylized film. It is somewhat less realistic than *Francesco di Assisi* and *Galileo*. It retains the narrative figurations of Cavani's authorial voice, which, once again, takes shape in a series of social transgressions and physical divestitures. The director translates the naked truth of a myth into primitive signs and symbols that function as *prodigia* expounding the dramatic events.[4] In Cavani's own terms, we enter "the world of absolute metaphor,"[5] visually constructed by the camera gazing upon the agon between a totalitarian state and the human being. Characters are emblems of a disquieting contemporary situation: they evoke the hallucinatory atmosphere of the mid-seventies in Italy, which led the nation to terrorism and despair, a catastrophe brought about by the collapse of the student movement and of the revolutionary ideals of May 1968.

Sophocles' tragedy recounts the ordeals of Antigone, the daughter of Oedipus and Jocasta, who defies the fateful edict of her uncle Creon, the new king of Thebes, forbidding the honorable burial of her exiled brother's body. Creon has ordered that the corpse of Polynices is to be left lying on the plain, a prey for the birds, as an example to those who are the enemies of the country. Anyone who disobeys the royal order will be sentenced to death. As Creon declares to the chorus of the Theban elders, his edict is a test of patriotism and a punishment for treason. He warns, "See that you never side with those who break my orders."[6] Cavani's film focuses on the transgressive context of the play as defined by Creon's threat to his citizens. I cannibali opens on a horrendous sight of decomposing corpses amassed upon the wet streets of a modern city. Careless citizens step by and around the bodies, which appear as flattened shapes against the outline of towering buildings. This opening has an important thematic relevance for the film: under Creon, man has defied ancient laws and has entered into a nightmare world. These haunting images will recur as television broadcasts throughout the film to remind viewers of the terrible events inscribed by the power that has besieged the city. Only the daring of Antigone will challenge its authority. For Cavani, her rebellion is not a thing of the past but threateningly foretells the future. Hence the director's choice of an archetypal structure of the filmic narrative:

> Antigone? More than a model I search for a stimulus in the past. I do not think the past can be reproduced, but I do believe in myth. . . . In I cannibali, and beginning with Antigone, I intended to use the language of myth and universal symbols to avoid the revolutionary speeches that had become a cliché by 1969–1970. As everyone knows, two months following the events of May '68, all slogans, posters, and catchphrases were sold out and overused by the establishment. . . . I cannibali is not the chronicle of a revolution (I would have needed an entirely different language) but the spectral analysis of reality beyond the various episodes that characterized the demonstrations. I believe it is a comprehensive analysis, and primarily a discourse of generations.[7]

Cavani made some important changes in the Sophoclean tragedy that result in a disturbing, bleak tone. In Sophocles, Antigone acts out of respect for the divine law and the blood bond of kindred, which she considers above the human order of justice. Creon's denial of burial disregards an ancient devotion in the Greek household, since the funeral rituals were a duty of the women. In the film, Antigone's action is also motivated by a disgust for civic life, and her love extends beyond the family. She is made a bourgeoise who has other collective identifications so that Cavani can dramatize the constraints imposed on the individual by corporate structures of power. Hence Antigone's revolt is not strictly political. Some other crucial Sophoclean events are omitted. Most notably, there is no remission of Creon's order for the execution of Antigone, an alteration that transforms her suicide into a tragic will to enact the revolution. Also, with the exception of Haemon and Ismene, all characters are given appellatives that translate hierarchic forms of control, surveillance, and discipline: Father (the Prime Minister), Guard, Sergeant, Officer, Policemen, and so on.

By emphasizing May '68 as a period of generational tensions, Cavani targets living history and the way in which the formula of revolution is applied to the young rebels. She investigates a return to origins carried out on an individual level rather than on a group scale. As she explains, her elementary unit of communication is the language of gesture:

> The idea of the film originated during the great babel of 1968, when language became meaningless. I wanted to make a film against these kinds of speeches and restore the value of silence and pure gesture, gesture as word. And I also wanted to reclaim an ethical order. Sophocles believed in an inherent, ethical nucleus of reality.[8]

In Cavani's cinema, gesture is the effective means that provides a communication-language. Tiresias's prophetic function is highly developed in this direction, since he is specifically required to communicate through a rhetoric of signs: drawing (the fish), sound (utterances of words from an African dialect), and exemplary gesture (the burial) mark his representational inscription of the cinematic discourse. In the immediate post-1968 period, Cavani's experimentation with a language of pure gesture can hardly be overestimated.[9] In *I cannibali*, gesture is knowledge conceived as being, and it is embedded in that marvelous form of communication which is silence.

Cavani sets up *I cannibali* in the industrial city-state of Milan, which, according to the director's intentions, establishes the social and political atmosphere of a modern European conglomerate. In this setting, under a totalitarian regime, the bodies of the rebels who conspired against the state are left on display in the streets and in public places to serve as a deterrant to further conspiracies. Multilingual announcements affixed to walls warn against any removal of the dead. Only a young woman, Antigone, played by Britt Ekland, will defy the order. She comes from a wealthy family and is engaged to Haemon, the son of the Prime Minister. She becomes an outcast as she searches for her dead brother's body. Only a mysterious stranger, a modern Tiresias, who speaks an unknown language and communicates by allusive signs, will assist her in performing the funeral rites for Polynices. They are both denounced by the citizens, and eventually arrested and interrogated. Tiresias is placed under psychiatric observation and paraded by the media like a carnival spectacle. Antigone is subjected to torture and public execution. Her death, as

well as the stranger's assassination, will ignite new rebels to reenact their exemplary gesture.

Cavani's "spectral analysis of reality" is formally established in the prologue. The film opens by the sea when four children (three boys and a girl) discover the body of a man (Tiresias) swept ashore and try to awaken him. As the young man gets up and begins to follow them, two hunters arrive at the scene and shoot all the children dead. "A completely unprovoked murder," writes Cavani in the film treatment, "seemingly unexplainable, violence that explodes against the innocent." The wide-screen format helps define the physical relashionship of the characters to each other and to the environment, as the anamorphic lens captures the figures set against the distant horizon line of the land and the sea. The handheld camera is gazing upon the action as if it is in danger of being caught. Tiresias will have to carry this cruel image with him while he roams through the city streets. He will also carry a symbolic inscription of his awakening: a seashell that he takes from the dead girl's hands, as she is lying on the beach.[10] Then begins an extensive crosscutting sequence of corpses and the Milan skyscrapers. The conflict now arises from the juxtaposition of these static, symmetrical shots of claustrophobic buildings. The cold, wet dawn casts upon the cityscape a metallic sheen of light. The images of bodies on the pavement scream their horror. The title song, "The Cannibals," composed by Nohra-Morricone, calls out to rouse humanity to wakeful consciousness.[11] Throughout the film, symbols are par excellence like the language of children, who can understand a picture better than a spoken word. What is more typical of *I cannibali* is the use of relatively brief shots to build up a scene, punctuated by the rhythmic assonance of sounds. The opening of the film establishes Cavani's subtle approach with the camera, at once mobile and invisible, present and hidden.

Though *I cannibali* reflects in many ways the violence and political upheavals of its time, and is indeed a powerful depiction of bourgeois rationality, it remains mythic, ethical, and ceremonial. It portrays human life in terms of unrelieved bondage: a nightmare of social tyranny, which translates the ironic ambiguities of unidealized existence.[12] The central images are images of dismemberment, mutilation, and torture. The city takes the form of the labyrinthine metropolis, where emotion and tension convey a lack of communication. It is "fantapolitica" (political fantasy) in the sense Cavani ascribes to Kubrick's *Dr. Strangelove* (1964) and Frankenheimer's *Seven Days in May* (1964) in her film reviews for *Studium*: political fiction deals with both prophetic events and social critique.[13]

Cavani wrote the film treatment at the end of 1968. She draws from images of war and famine, as familiarized by photojournalism:

> One day, in a waiting room, I sat opposite a man who was reading a magazine. When he came across a photographic reportage on the atrocities in Biafra (it was three or four weeks after the outbreak of the war), he quickly skipped through the

Frame 24. Antigone (Britt Ekland) and Tiresias (Pierre Clementi) defy the orders of the city-state in *I cannibali* (The Cannibals, 1969)

pages as if not to see. This man was obviously "tired" of an event that was no longer "new." At this point, I realized that any accounts of violence and revolution would retain their emotional impact on the individual for ten or twenty days. Thus information cannot engage us politically. It has the numbing effect of a horror film. . . . Therefore, in *I cannibali*, I wanted to place this man in a situation where he could no longer avoid the corpses in front of his home, in a city full of bodies. He could no longer turn the page without stepping on them.[14]

The director's incisive statement about the origins of her inspiration illustrates how a photograph, as an *análogon* of reality, may comprise unlimited cultural conventions and expressive possibilities. Photographs shock us only if they represent something novel. The spectacular title sequence of *I cannibali*, a photographic collage of ultimate horror, approaches what Susan Sontag, in her book on photography, deems a negative epiphany, or the prototypically modern revelation. We are reminded that, in an advanced industrial society, the camera defines reality essentially "as a spectacle (for masses) and as an object of surveillance (for rulers)."[15] Cavani maintains that she simply photographed whatever people could see every day, and that her film materialized "the monsters of the spirit."[16] Indeed she relies on the kind of pathos that we associate with the iconography of industrialized photography. In such images, it is dominant (capitalist) ideology that codifies what constitutes an event.

Other manifestations of the subconscious areas of the mind are housed in *I cannibali*. Namely, the director's blatant allusions to her own life: her spectatorial embodiment in the scene of the dead partisans in the piazza of Carpi.[17] While the shock of photographed atrocities may result in the horrible's appearing more ordinary, this childhood memory exercises a strong impact on the visual construction of the film. The opening shots provide an aesthetic mediation between the documentary and an essentially poetic imagination, a referent and a memory flashback. They trigger a hallucinatory effect that is also a document. Cavani most effectively balances the recording and creative powers of the medium. To this end, she entrusted cinematographer Giulio Albonico with the challenging job of shooting in an improvised "documentary" style, due to the actual difficulty of filming under time constraints in the streets of a metropolitan city, blocking nonprofessional extras, coping with traffic, and dodging police surveillance. The director's intention was to reveal everything as if it were "uno stato d'animo" (a mood):

> This is my only film where I utilize a long 750mm telephoto lens in order to create a certain density in the image, a type of graininess, that would recall war newsreels. Also this long lens creates an optical softness around the edge of the frame, which gives the illusion of a memory recaptured, Antigone and the ancient text.[18]

The prologue and title sequence sum up a terrifying vision of a death-haunted world. They establish the act of violence as a primary gesture. As Moravia writes, the director succeeds in presenting "a message of 'pious,' consuming, and almost morbid sorrow."[19] Unlike the early films, *I cannibali* manifests minimal dialogue, a progressive elimination of the spoken word. The photography evokes a shadowless flat range of gray. In Cavani's view, the image is as realistic as the mysterious, magical image of a dream.[20] *I cannibali* moves within the boundaries of an "apocalyptic" nightmare journey. In the sixties, Umberto Eco defined Apocalypse as the obsession of the dissenter, resisting the image of total integration promoted by the mass culture. The apocalyptic lets us foresee the existence of a few individuals capable of transcending banality.[21] Antigone's refusal to abide by the law of the city-state is a gesture of great significance, transcending the performance of a symbolic burial.

From the beginning of the shooting script, the character of Antigone is portrayed in terms of both her physical and mental state; her corporeal vibrancy and silence contrast with the stagnation and wordiness of the figures of power. Under a flat overcast sky,

> Antigone walks in a specific direction. The expression of her face suggests anxiety. She looks down at bodies upon bodies lying on the ground. Suddenly she has the impression that she is being followed. She turns her head and sees a man in white,

similar to a pope dressed in traveling attire (as one sees on TV and in newspapers), walking in her direction. With his arm raised, he is blessing everything and everyone; he is followed by a truck sprinkler. Antigone begins to run . . . And the man dressed as a pope quickens his pace.[22]

As Giuliana Bruno argues in her study of Elvira Notari's city films, "the terms of female tension are literally mapped out on the road."[23] From the outset, Antigone is presented "streetwalking" in a futuristic Milan. She is literally caught fleeting through a maze of "strade della città" (city streets), hollow corridors, stairways, and claustrophobic buildings. The film opposes the idea of hegemonic forces, lying beneath the surface of regimentation, to the idea of movement inherent in Antigone's corporeal presence. She is indeed the charismatic witness of the metropolitan scene, her movement consistently underlined by a series of close-ups of feet. These shots reiterate the perception of transition and body flow implied in Cavani's frames. Further, the use of a telephoto lens with a shallow depth of field achieves an optical effect that results in a diffused picture, evocative of a dream state: the streets appear ominous, enforcing the notion that the metropolis has supreme claim on the citizens. The sound track also functions as commentary; its eeriness results from the fact that environmental wild sounds have been replaced with moments of silence. Among the natural sounds, the most audible is the echoing footstep. As Mary Ann Doane has pointed out, the sound track covers the excess that escapes the eye, for "the ear is precisely that organ which opens onto the interior reality of the individual."[24] Again, the director's allegiance to social discourse reclaiming transgression is epitomized in Antigone's outrageous defiance of the bounds established by the laws of the tyrant. As a threat to law and order, this female wanderer kinetically embodies a threat to law and order: her nonviolence demythologizes the coercive strategies and disciplinary tactics of the polis.

Cavani's emphasis on corporeality as the language of representation and mediation of revolutionary identity is nowhere more self-explanatory than in the film's working title, *Il tamburo di carne* (Drum of Flesh). On the first page, the original shooting script quotes a passage from Henry Miller's *Nexus* on the explosive energy still contained in dead particles of matter; the passage also discusses the resurrection of the flesh (Lazarus and Jesus) as evidence of cosmic regeneration. For the completed film, Cavani selects as epigraph two lines from *Oedipus Rex*, the prophecy that the king would leave Thebes as a blind man: "You with your precious eyes, you're blind to the corruption of your life" (470–471). The tragedy of human blindness and the primeval fears inherent in Sophocles' Oedipus confront us with the threat of being caught in the terror of an unknown future. With Oedipus, Antigone remains a key figure of antiquity; her life demonstrates the furthest stages of the construction of the self through physical *sparagmos*.

Cavani stresses the tribal, magical, and ritualistic aspects of the Greek tradition, as the film's final title (referring to Antigone and Tiresias) attests: "The white race has always called 'cannibal' or 'savage' those who are different. Today these people are the young, who are rejected for irrational reasons, such as growing long hair. One asks if they are good and one also fears them as if they were cannibals, dressed in feathers and leaves."[25] Thus cannibalism is not a metaphor for disorder, confusion, and civil division. It polemically addresses man's primitive unity with the earth, an authentic metaphor for cultural independence.[26] In savage life, all human powers and all natural powers can be condensed in one individual. Here it is Tiresias, the androgynous seer who speaks the language of pure symbolism and whom Antigone joins in his subversive view of a transformed society. This legendary mana figure, interpreted by the actor Pierre Clementi, embodies the power of inner sight and the ability to master the antinomies of life. He represents the man of the future, the revolutionary of tomorrow.[27] Truth is on the side of Tiresias, and Antigone will surrender her leading role to him. The central image and symbol of their interaction is the fish, a paradigmatic sign of active regeneration and potential life (the pagan phallus).[28]

The film relies on the kind of mythology that we associate with anthropological religion. On the nature of the director's approach to the theme of I cannibali, her cowriter, Italo Moscati, comments:

> Some critics were quick to label the film "Catholic from the left." Cavani and I both reject this statement, because, like all labels, it is limiting, and also because "Catholic from the left" often defines a type of intellectual whose actions are in sympathy with the system he verbally opposes. With some exceptions, this type may be ironically included among Noam Chomsky's "new mandarins" . . . a class specialized in furnishing justifications for the regime in force.[29]

Cavani places Antigone at the crossroads of action, building the plot around a tragic collision, not a single character's story. Antigone disobeys the laws of the tyrant to follow the unwritten, eternal laws of the gods. She will not tolerate the desecration of Polynices' body. Her ethos is heroic (she knows the punishment for her gesture), and, as Walter Kaufmann states, she is "the worthy successor of Prometheus."[30] She aims at restoring the old mythical rapport between the mantic and the manic. As Ismene's Fiancé puts it to Haemon in the scene at the polo club, "she is a little crazy." The madness of Antigone becomes the silence of reason against the collective (in)human laws of the political body. While Galileo emphasized the body of the heretic and spectacular rituals of divestment, here images of torture and mutilation signify the judicial order exemplified by hierarchical observation and interrogation. Galileo's illusion of a dialogic discourse with the Church was based on his belief in the power of words; Antigone cannot engage in a verbal dialectic with violence, since language is synonymous with patriarchal dominant culture. Kaja Silverman virtually synthesizes Cavani's cinematic discourse as "linguistic paranoia."[31] In the Kierkegaardian sense of the term, this *virgo mater* is silence, and the retrospection implicit in silence gives her a preternatural bearing.[32] The sight of gallows, pillories, and birch rods could extort Galileo's confession, but the pain of whips and blows, enforcing Antigone's examination, will not produce a disciplined body. In Antigone, revolutionary action questions the function of punitive power and the hierarchy that sustains it.

Cavani denounces capitalist rituals of political execution and the lust of the ruling class for sadistic power by isolating the implacable eye of the photographic lens as a device underlying what Northrop Frye has called "the tragic theme of *derkou theama*," or the humiliation of being constantly watched by a hostile eye.[33] The exercise of discipline exhibited in the opening sequence of *I cannibali* is intended to induce a normalizing effect among the citizenry. Its success depends on a mechanism that coerces by means of observation: particularly the telephoto lens gives a sense of both distance from and closeness to the multitude of bodies. The camera becomes the eye that must see without being seen, an art of the visible which secretly constructs a new knowledge of man. The techniques of subjection exploited by the apparatus of the state are projected onto the film's settings, which feature military and police headquarters, prisons, madhouses, government buildings, and places of execution: the spatial nesting of hierarchized surveillance.[34] Cavani's narrative shapes the topography of a carceral city (cold, wet, concrete, and enclosing): a network of gazes that supervise one another. The architectural mapping of the city allows for an articulated control of the individual in both external and internal space. From Antigone's first appearance in the metro, she is constantly being pursued and watched by fellow observers. Once she runs into Tiresias at the snack bar, and decides to follow his footsteps, they both become the quarry in numerous chase scenes, which are literally being filmed in transitional spaces (streets, paths, alleys, corridors). If the hand of Francesco exemplified *caritas* and the eye of Galileo defied the limits of the Ptolemaic universe, Antigone's foot inscribes her relationship to earthly reality and its generative force:[35] it is the instrument enabling her to step out of the dark prison of endless bondage instituted by the city-state. Milan becomes a theater of shock and horror, in which every movement Antigone makes will be observed in detail, each gaze participating in the functioning of power.

Cavani imaginatively portrays the geopolitics of the carceral city and its cynical enclosure of citizens in the scenes at the neuropsychiatric hospital, particularly the segment in the courtyard, where the prisoners are brusquely called to order by the attendants after playing the innocent prank of removing clothes from a girl while she is singing a ballad.[36] These young inmates, among whom Tiresias has been secluded after his capture, are the same who will follow his example at the end of the film. This scene exemplifies the very principle embedded in the architectural orchestration of mental institutions as agents for

Frame 25. The architectural setting of mental institutions as agents for training docile bodies

training docile bodies. As Michel Foucault points out, "what is fascinating about prisons is that, for once, power does not hide or mask itself; it reveals itself as tyranny into the tiniest details; it is cynical and at the same time pure and entirely 'justified,' because its practice can be totally formulated within the framework of morality."[37] Cavani's scrupulous concern with surveillance is shown in the perpendicular high-angle shots that establish the courtyard from the point of view of a watchtower. In such a fixed place, the slightest movement is being supervised and recorded by the guards. The opening shots compose the detailed geometry of a panoptic fortress: several black apertures are arranged in an octagonal plane displaying a rigidly controlled interior (*le jeu du regard*). The building communicates a sense of unresolved tension between its inmates and the central point of control that allows for a single gaze to oversee everything. A juxtaposition of bird's-eye views of the octagonal dungeon brings this scene to a close: they reinforce the feeling of looking down a tunnel, as if humans have fallen into an abyss. There is also a carnivalesque quality in the orchestration of the mise-en-scène. For example, the force-feeding of a hunger-striker in the hospital refectory leads to a temporary suspension of hierarchical order and gives voice to a symbolic resistance: all the prisoners join the protest in crescendo by rhythmically beating their utensils on the tables, to the accompaniment of animalistic war cries. In this instance of temporary inversion of power, the socially marginalized body is empowered through sound, "l'assordante concerto," or the deafening concert, as Cavani calls it in her stage directions. Sound defies the constraints of individual training and coding. Nonverbal communication defies the disciplinary gaze of the guards in the courtyard scene as well, where the same hunger-striker initiates the prankish game with the female inmate, turning the locus of the supervised quotidian life into a center of playfulness.[38] In the working script, this inmate is called Ghandi.

Disciplinary mechanisms of progressive objectification and instrumentation of the body find another striking illustration in the cell in which Haemon is imprisoned after being caught by the police. Disgusted by his father's refusal to help Antigone, Haemon gradually regresses into an animal state. The cell becomes the site for a metamorphosis:

> The cell seems empty. The guard carrying a tray of food does not see the prisoner; however, he knows that he is hidden somewhere, as always. He rests the tray on the table . . . A strange moaning comes out of the shower niche. Then the guard puts the tray on the floor and gives the prisoner a pitying look as he leaves. Haemon creeps out of the niche like an animal without limbs. He creeps along the floor like a serpent or a worm. He reaches the tray, sniffs it, and then snaps at the steak. Holding the piece of meat in his teeth, he quickly creeps back to his den.[39]

In this scene the camera is placed on the floor, emphasizing the perspective of an animal looking up. The lens focuses on Haemon crawling out of his protective den in order to reach the food. His somatic transformation epitomizes the visualization of symptoms of deviance. During his last encounter with an unsympathetic father, Haemon pits himself against the catalog of the shameful arts of repression: he declares himself mad, anarchist, eccentric, rebel, antisocial, criminal, atheist, and homosexual. In this scene, the father's rejection of Haemon climaxes his rivalry with the son. The dynamic impetus of their antagonism includes law and *logos*. As the voice of collective authority, the Prime Minister is concerned with hierarchical social order; his words exhibit absolute arrogance, the sin of *hybris*. While in prison, Haemon's language of bodily excess signals his refusal of structure and order, and an instinctual movement toward the world of nature in its most elemental state (of which the animal motif is symbolic). Serpents, also associated with the cult of Dionysos, represent energy, force, and the death/rebirth ritual.[40] The character of Haemon encompasses the horror of the modern condition, the interplay of desire and power. The subject is both helpless and subversive in his relation to the alien world of the father, the monstrous head of the authoritarian body of society. Haemon's metamorphosis enacts a primeval rite of sacrificial slaughter.

Society needs to perform its spectacles. In *I cannibali*, it largely takes the form of surveillance and examination. The "scandal" of Antigone is no longer encoded, as was Galileo's punishment, into a public ceremonial. This prisoner is systematically questioned in an aseptic, white room at the military police headquarters. Thrown into the dynamic of the interrogation, Antigone's body is physically affected: she is forced to sit on an office chair propelled on wheels, and she is constantly rolled around from one interrogator to another in a spinning, disorienting motion. Swish pans and soft-focus shots establish the abrupt pattern of the examination process and its techniques of intersecting observations. The camera tracks back and forth, positioned at the same level as the key interrogator, thus enforcing his subjective point of view on the audience. These shots, set against white limbo backgrounds, highlight the figure movements of the prisoner. The police officers surround Antigone in a circle and, as they close in on her, they alternatively slap, strike, and insult her. The fluctuations of the torture scene (choreographed like a dance), its optical montage, ensure that the exaction of the truth by pain and judicial tactics is effective: its echoing sound and music score foreground a feeling of entrapment. Here we also witness a process of discursive divestment that assumes overtly political dimensions: at first, Antigone mumbles cryptic sentences, then she draws a fish on the wall, and eventually she utters Tiresias's magic cipher of communication, *senà*. This enigmatic word punctuates Antigone's last encounter with Haemon in the police infirmary. She will not speak again.

Antigone's case is also displayed to politicians and sociologists in a sort of secretive mock trial at the Government Palace. Limping and disfigured, she is forced into a private conference room, where she undergoes further interrogation, only this time she faces physical divestment, with erotic nuances. The one-way dialogue between the female prisoner and the gentlemen sipping champagne exemplifies the role of the ceremonial enforcement of violence and ideology:

> FOURTH GENTLEMAN: Miss, I hope that you have not been hit in more delicate parts. I don't approve these methods.
>
> THIRD GENTLEMAN: She was caught at the Officers' Club with an eccentric person. Naked!

Frame 26. Antigone's interrogation at the military police headquarters

FIFTH GENTLEMAN: Well, I find nothing wrong with it, if you have *le phisique du rôle* . . .

SECOND GENTLEMAN: You have made a gesture . . . For your brother, one could understand . . . But why continue?[41]

Throughout this penal liturgy, Antigone resists the gaze of control and becomes solely intent on removing a thorn from her wounded foot. She who has been inscribed to motion is finally constrained to stillness. The inflated rhetoric of the Fourth Gentleman rationalizes Antigone's transgressive gesture: "You know that every advanced capitalist society embodies among its young a revolutionary potential. We, the experts, try to foresee it through statistical inquiries. Out of one hundred young people like yourself, 30 percent have a good potential. But, of course, one must distinguish between social classes."[42] At first, this character seems endowed with the role of the coryphaeus, or leader of the chorus, in Greek theater. However, Cavani warns us against a simplistic identification of either government figures or the crowd of curious spectators in the piazza with the classical chorus. We are reminded that the chorus distinctly participates in the dramatic unfolding of events onstage.[43] Both the experts and the crowd witnessing Antigone's execution are exterior to the structure of the spectacle. The sociopoliticians peer through the Venetian blinds of the palace windows with one pair of binoculars, which they have to share. This gradually leads into a fight over the control of the optical instrument: they end up elbowing, grabbing, and pushing at each other. Cavani's use of travesty suggests the lust for voyeuristic power on behalf of the hierarchy. The role of the people who are summoned as witnesses in the piazza is also ambiguous. As the director specifies, they are "passive spectators."[44]

A similar use of the gaze is exhibited in the episode of Tiresias at the television station, where he is being telecast by the reporters who tracked him down before the police got to him. He is being announced as "the man of the day," and named Mowgli, after Rudyard Kipling's hero of the jungle. Tiresias is tied up and kept under surveillance, a figure of misery and ridicule. He looks around in bewilderment; his countenance is antithetical to the self-contained posture of the anchorman. The criminal is displayed through multiple television screens, which also bring images of Antigone into each and every household in the city. He is presented as an eccentric, strange, and intolerant individual. Psychologists have been invited in a panel discussion to evaluate his case. In total puzzlement, Tiresias breaks free, turning a news program into a comedic chase scene, being pursued by TV cameramen as they continue rolling amid cables and studio equipment. Obviously excited about this unexpected turn of events, the anchorman urges his narcoleptic viewers "to enjoy the show" and reassures them that the captive cannot run very far. He paternally enjoins, "Stay calm, dear Mowgli . . . millions of people are watching you live."[45] As the voice of bourgeois hegemony, the anchorman controls an instrument of observation and capitalist reification. This scene opens with rows of TV monitors in the control room, thus reproducing the artificiality of the studio as a simulacrum of self-reinforcing power. The visual recording of Tiresias's body is conceived as a seeing apparatus and as a seen sign: he becomes visible as the mass media's property, an object of collective appropriation.[46] Television is shown as a privileged space of marginality, enacting a racist saturnalia of punishment: it censors Tiresias's image through enforced stereotyping. Here the representational practices adopted by the media incorporate a technical mutation of the body's exposure; they demystify parody. The ritual of *sparagmos* is exercised by the tentacular hold of the camera in terms of optical effects that magnify, distort, and relay the savage being, making him more fearful than he is. Tiresias is recoded by the lawful gaze of a modern society: television has replaced the spectacle of the scaffold in the town square.

As already noted, *I cannibali* relies to an unprecedented degree on an oneiric dimension. Cavani experiments with what would come to characterize her directorial desire in her films of the 1970s: her critique of the existing symbolic

Frame 27. Antigone and Tiresias being chased at the Officers Club

order is conveyed in a visible dream quality; the resolution of the images is diffused; the compositions are continually evolving. The sequence in which Antigone and Tiresias run naked through the streets of Milan is typical of the film as a whole. The director describes its spatial trajectory as "a nightmare, a grotesque crossing through the places and the institutions that represent power."[47] The chase maps out a maze of winding streets, hidden depths, and downward paths. It opens with one of Cavani's characteristic dolly shots running behind the characters. The camera follows Antigone and Tiresias inside the Officers' Club, rushing down some stairs, against the background of white walls. A place fit for concealment, this building is riddled with tunnel-like corridors leading to hollow, narrow rooms. At first, the fugitives hide in the sauna baths, where they strip off their clothes and cover themselves in sheets, white for Antigone, red for Tiresias. In the film, color is a primal language; along with music it cocreates the descriptive vibrance of the mise-en-scène.[48] In this empty ambience Antigone and Tiresias witness an unusual game of debasement, demonstrating the devotional power of the army clique: a proces-

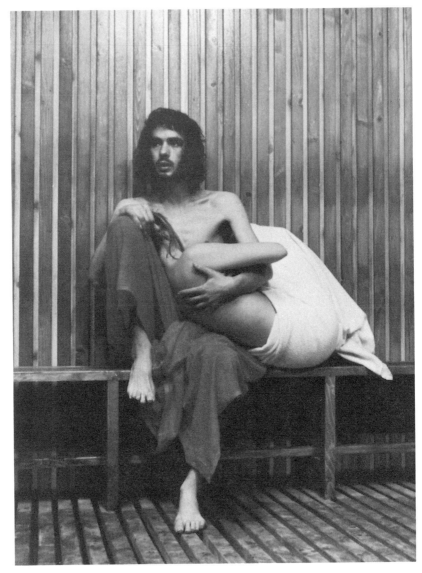

Frame 28. Tiresias holding Antigone in his arms at the sauna baths: a modern pietà.

sion of naked high-ranking officers, crouched on all fours, crawls between the legs of an adolescent boy who is wearing an oversize military uniform. This ritual evokes the vestiges of Mars, the god of war and sacrificial death.[49] The adepts offer no resistance to the cruelty of the little god. In the working script, the director's description of this scene is visually very detailed:

Crouched on the floor, naked, one stuck to the other, these men form a self-propelling serpent or caterpillar. In which direction is the caterpillar going? It is obeying the orders of a fourteen-year-old boy, dressed only in a heavy military jacket that makes him sweat. The caterpillar moves obediently, crawling on benches, coming down, and then going underneath the boy's legs, the way he wants it to be. The older members of the caterpillar breathe heavily and sweat profusely, but it does seem that they enjoy this act of subjugation.[50]

The boy's pleasure is in physically abusing the officers, and when he decides to leave, "the caterpillar made of ten heads looks up to him, with a disappointed and desperate expression, and so it tries to stop him from leaving. When the boy exits, the caterpillar follows him out the door."[51] Ennio Morricone's electronic beat accentuates the parodic quality of this ironic ritual of incorporation. This scene anticipates Pasolini's allegorical depiction of Fascist history in *Salò*, a film Cavani defended upon its controversial release in 1975.[52] Such a yearning for the past, as Millicent Marcus has pointed out, is a "recourse to the naked human body as an irreducible medium of communication, to a semiosis of corporeality unobstructed by the civilizing veils of clothing and the libidinal repression that culture has imposed upon it."[53]

When, at dawn, Antigone and Tiresias are forced to resume their flight in the streets, hunted down by police dogs, the luminous nudity of their bodies against the cityscape contrasts with the adornments of the soldiers' uniforms. These shots visually embody an important liberating effect: the silence of the naked figures running, as opposed to the pounding resonance of military boots. The camera dollying from behind the characters implicitly construes an interplay of different levels of reality and illusion: the blurring and shifting of gender identifications. Antigone and Tiresias assume a series of clothing disguises, each affirming their mutual identity against an ideology of exalted difference. As Kaja Silverman suggests, such reversibility in sexual roles alludes to dreams of androgyny in Cavani's cinema, orchestrating a male divestiture.[54] Other examples of transvestism include their dressing up in clergymen's robes in an empty church (where they also set a white dove free) and their wearing of uniforms inside a military recruiting barracks. *I cannibali* stages the ultimate parody of patriarchal dress: Antigone and Tiresias masquerade in the attire of powerful institutions, the Church and the army being the most prominent. The chase scene is very effective in conveying in a purely visual way the disruptive liturgy of Fascist demonization.

The final sequence sets in motion the mechanisms of identification with an ontological theatrical space. The closing shots come to question the civic function of the urban piazza in Italian architecture, which is traditionally that of a locus of encounters and social interaction; a space to satisfy the desires of the crowds. The piazza represents a distinctive form of public life and, as an architectural object, connotes a global ideology. Cavani's representational strat-

Frame 29. Antigone and Tiresias set a white dove free in an empty church

egies for the staging of Antigone and Tiresias's execution encircle their bodies
at the very center, watched over by the military police, as the citizens gaze
upon them. The lens's focal point remains fixed at the center; close-ups of the
machine guns firing accent the event. The coexistence of these two concentric
perspectives and shifts of gaze advance a vision: undifferentiated figures come
to the surface and begin to remove the rebels' bodies. Now the static, symmetrical shots of the opening sequence are counterbalanced by the in- and out-of-
focus shots of these silhouettes in motion, bringing the dead to a cave, drawing
a fish on its walls. Strategies of slowness and repetition help us absorb this
prolonging of perception. The techno-politics of punishment is based on the
idea of preventing future disorders. However, Antigone and Tiresias's death
transforms the ending into another beginning of the same ineluctable process:
Cavani's use of sound, mise-en-scène, and camera movement localizes the piazza as a microcosm of revolutionary action. As Roberto Calasso has reminded
us, Antigone's madness is *áte*, the divine infatuation without which "no towering form of greatness / enters into the lives of mortals."[55] For Cavani, the cave
represents a sacred ideal of life:

In the bowels of civilization, in the depths of our unconscious, there must be a reference point to help us open our eyes and see, to help us open our hearts and understand. Perhaps in pagan times? Or rather in animistic-prehistoric times? Wherever this point may be, we need to recapture our ancient human skin. These young people will be imitated by others. A seer and a prophet, young Tiresias has provoked something.[56]

The epilogue of I cannibali shapes the figures of the men of the future. The coming of Tiresias has exorcized the spell of present and future: the enclosing womb of nature will rescue humankind from the city of dreadful night, from the abyss of destruction. An isomorphic image of depth, the hollow cave (a kind of Etruscan catacomb) is the protective labyrinth of a sacred tomb, a profoundly archaic, form-giving and gestating receptacle connected with the symbolism of earth and water.[57] In the film, the presence of water is connected to the sea, and most of all to the humoral sheen of the streets, an effect Cavani created by using a truck sprinkler before each shoot. This specific look of the Cavanian exterior, at once stunning and oppressive, will identify all of her future films, beginning with Il portiere di notte. The metaphor of the labyrinth (of which the subterranean cave is a figuration) points to a mystical return to the mother, a mysterious vessel of communication. Cavani's cinematic style, which is oneiric, haunting, and mobilizing, gives an imaginative rendition of a classical myth as a fantasmatic ground for cultural debates. In the epilogue (a recognition scene) we apprehend the totality of contemporary life: history and actuality hypothesized in concreto in a sick society. I cannibali denounces the stasis of the human mind and the collective surrendering to the order of the Father. This is the tragedy of youth: "Today's young rebels," states Cavani, "have agitated something that for the first time has alarmed not only the bourgeoisie but also the repressive beaurocracy. Today's young rebels feel that their life as human beings is brought into play and they risk becoming a toy in the hands of politicians and the upper levels of the hierarchy."[58]

At a time when contemporary auteurs were turning to the cult of psychoanalysis and revolution, and Roland Barthes was announcing the death of the author, Cavani asserts her independent authorial voice against the confusion, the political ambiguities, and the lack of coherence of the post-1968 generation. In an epoch when power-knowledge was encoded in speech, I cannibali does not transmit thought but produces it. Beginning with L'ospite (The Guest, 1971) the director's use of a realistic scenario will function as backup to dream notes that are the stylistic trait of Milarepa. The former film, which originated from an actual visit Cavani made to female patients in a psychiatric hospital ward, is a case study of Anna's illness. The protagonist lives within a state of

Frame 30. Tiresias holds a photograph of Antigone as he searches through a pile of bodies

Frame 31. The public execution of Antigone and Tiresias in the city square

rupture, acted out to the music of Gioacchino Rossini and to the melodramatic staging of Maeterlinck's *Pelléas et Mélisande*. *L'ospite* is a film of heightened imagination in the context of docu-realism; the story of a woman in search of her individuality at a time when gendered power relations were nonexistent.[59] Both Antigone and Anna are cast into silence; they operate on the outer edge of our culture, at a point Foucault has called in *Les Mots et les choses* the frontier situation, the margin where communication, without words or discourse, renews the archaic power of gesture. As a first independent film, *I cannibali* anticipates the techniques of Cavani's films of the 1970s and 1980s. Some shots are emotionally poetic, as in Tiresias's searching for Antigone in the streets, among piles of bodies and ruins, holding up her photograph in a cry of despair and helplessness. The stunning framings of the later films have yet to surface, however; the photography evokes the tones and nuances of the German trilogy in the middle-range flat gray of the exteriors, a visual connotation that genuinely captures the architectural articulation of her future compositions. Most of all, the film's narrative structure introduces Cavani's inquiry into the realms of unconscious associations.

P A R T **T W O**

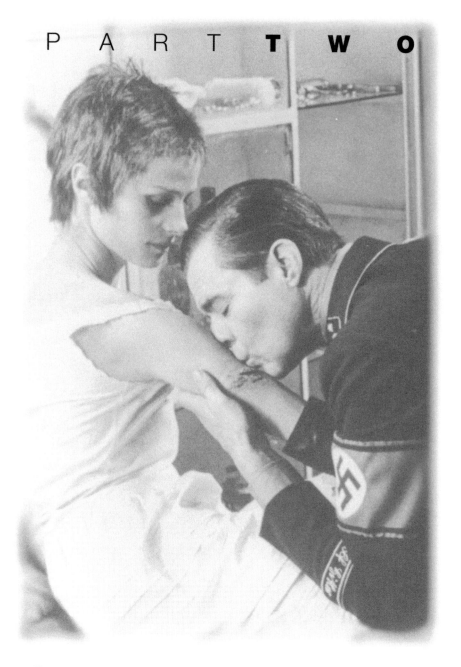

T H E   T R A N S G R E S S I V E
G A Z E :   S T Y L E   A S   T E N S I O N

I call experience a voyage to the end of the possible of man.
(*Georges Bataille*)

Every real effigy has a shadow which is its double.
(*Antonin Artaud*)

4

Toward a Negative Mythopoeia: Spectacle, Memory, and Representation in *The Night Porter*

The theme of carnal, civic, and religious passions
appears throughout my films.
Liliana Cavani

It is not a romantic story . . . it is rather a biblical
story.
(*Max*, The Night Porter)

IL PORTIERE DI NOTTE (The Night Porter, 1974) marks a turning point in Cavani's career. It is her first film to display mature stylistic and psychological preoccupations. The elaborate translation of a "scandalous" *passio* in a highly formalistic "interior" is accomplished by sophisticated cinematic effects. In dramatizing a spectacle (or scandal) Cavani relies on the gaze to explore the boundaries between interior and exterior, present and past. *Passio* is conceived on the Kierkegaardian model of erotic inclination; its greatest gesture, that of sacrifice.[1] From the Latin verb *pati*, *passio* signifies "suffering." *Passio* captures the experience of love in the purgatorial world inhabited by the Cavanian character in this second phase. For Cavani, *passio* is an instrument for the investigation of a slave society's brutality, but it also functions as a metaphor of violation and power. As for Bataille, being is violent *différence*. *Passio* favors a resurgence of archaic (repressed) desires and memories as play.

To render the violent *passio* that transfigures the present, Cavani departs from the "concrete" density achieved in earlier films and experiments with a perceptual kind of realism. Her directorial strategy refuses to separate the characters from their background. She evokes an oneiric dimension, a kind of a sinister limbo that encloses all existential interrogations; identified with an event of the past, the present is reenacted to the extreme possibility: the "humoral" solution of psychological (and physical) suicide. At a structural level, Cavani constructs images that convey the magic, subterranean qualities of a ritualistic descent *ad inferos*. The characters' despotic obsession with a love of darkness and a taste for lawless sexual rites does not project an absolute Manichaean duality. For example, Max murders Mario (the only witness who can identify Lucia), but he is not untouched: his pounding nightmare signals a revolt against the disintegration of experience. Psychologically, Cavani discloses an intellectual tendency to manipulate the visuality of sadomasochism, but she does it as if to exorcise the past and to extend that space, or threshold, from which her characters contemplate "the limit of credibility." As Cavani explains in an interview with Claire Clouzot:

> I felt the need to analyze the limits of human nature at the limit of credibility, to lead things to the extreme, because there is nothing more fantastic than reality. This is what I show in *Il portiere di notte*; it is only the beginning of reality. In the world, it is not virtue that prevails, but crime. That is why Sade is fundamental for me and he should be studied in school. *Il portiere di notte* is based on a pseudomasochistic story that is justified by the extreme situation in which both man and woman find themselves. It is the detonator that allows them to express themselves.[2]

The German trilogy—comprising, in addition to *Il portiere di notte*, *Al di là del bene e del male* (Beyond Good and Evil, 1977) and *Interno berlinese* (The Berlin Affair, 1985)—introduces a cinematic strategy entirely dependent upon the filmmaker's desire to follow her characters *beyond* the door and *into* the tortuous labyrinth of their unconscious expectations. In *Il portiere di notte*, Max enters the door that delimits a wet, foggy exterior ("A gray day, luminous asphalt, an aquarium-like atmosphere")[3] from the dark enclosure of the Hotel zur Oper, where his unexpected journey into memory and the past is about to begin. Wide-angle lenses are used to distort the outward appearance of buildings, particularly the hotel facade (by Otto Wagner), thus calling our attention to features of inner realities. In *Al di là del bene e del male*, Paul Rée's transgressive eye peers beyond the forbidden threshold of Fritz's hotel room; in *Interno berlinese*, Louise (the first-person narrator), once she passes the door into the Professor's studio, will recapture her scandalous experience at the Academy of Germanic Arts when her relationship with the Japanese Mitsuko transgressed the limits of race and sexual differences. These characters unveil their most hidden feelings and thoughts in an interior that becomes the theater of greater historical realities; they are themselves the spectacle that stimulates the viewers' unconventional responses. The plot, which develops through a series of flashbacks, projects the characters into drama that is larger than their present life: they are puppets of history. Cavani's emphasis is on content and representation itself:

> *Francesco di Assisi* and *Galileo* were made during a phase of professional unconsciousness. I filmed them with an enthusiastic impetus. Beginning with *Il portiere di notte*, the true facts, and the actors within the scenes, are not a reality. My point of view is beyond time, and beyond realism. The atmosphere of a place, a room, a road is transformed. My desire is to interpret them into a space of fantasy. They are mood

provoking (*stati d'animo*). In order to achieve this, I break the rules of cinematography; for example, I place lights to imply windows where none exist. This strategy evokes places beyond phenomenological reality, which make up my own reality, as in dreams.[4]

The metacinematic nature of the director's pronouncements illustrates the fundamental subjectivity of the filmic images. Cavani attempts to conceptualize some of the questions about artistic representation by looking beyond the classical forms of realistic diegesis as ascribed to a character or a place. She claims that reality does not exist independently of the filmmaker's perceptual act (a dreamlike state), that the objects depicted are constructions made by the perceiver.[5] It is clear that Cavani privileges images over dialogue to convey the characters' emotions. This visuality entails a certain ambiguity, which is reflected onto the formal complexity of her mise-en-scène. The films of the trilogy are marked by an intense elaboration of textures and authenticity of detail in set design and costumes. Cavani enlists art director Nedo Azzini (who worked on Bertolucci's *Il conformista*), costume designer Piero Tosi (Visconti's longtime collaborator), and Jusaburo Tsujimura, for Mio Takaki's kimonos in *Interno berlinese*, to visually execute the considerable audacity that removes her characters from a classical psychological narrative. Cavani cultivates "ambiguity" of her subjective vision in her choice of set design:

> It seems as if I accept reality, but indeed everything is manipulated and deformed by my point of view, by the choices I make. In *Galileo*, we designed the sets with a monumental, funereal character. It is the type of architecture that power chooses for itself. The backgrounds are built to tell a story by themselves. I use the word "ambiguous" to define my approach to reality, which is never objective but always subjective. Each individual set is carefully chosen as a participant in the story. Ambiguity lies somewhere between thought, fantasy, and the places we are used to seeing. They convey emotions that drive the story forward.[6]

Thus the specific nature of the German trilogy resides not in its being conditioned by the general economy of the Cavanian transgressive thematics (as critics have often argued), but rather in the "ambiguous" setting in which the director's subjective experience is imaginatively realized. Cavani is primarily concerned with the thematization of desire and pleasure in a repetition compulsion that exceeds the logic of history: play, spectacle, violent sexual and political power call into question their ideological origins as well as their stylistic bases. In *Il portiere di notte*, the characters literally self-destruct; they become exemplary of the barbarity of our times. Evil is frightfully human. The director remembers the making of *Storia del Terzo Reich* (History of the Third Reich, 1961–1962), a four-part documentary series in which Cavani utilizes films of the Nazis mostly found at the Istituto Nazionale Luce:

> I spent several months at the Moviola watching material that came from different parts of the world. I saw incredible things. The Germans loved to record every event on film, and they did it well. Hitler and his entourage loved cinema. My editor and I saw rolls upon rolls on the *Lager* and on the Russian campaign. One day we had to stop because we became sick. When the artists of the duecento attempted to paint the inferno, they were naive. Clearly there has been a progress in cruelty, in fact a true escalation. For whom did those cameramen think they were leaving those images? For monsters?[7]

Here it is not only a case of documented, sinister horror, of photographing the artifacts bearing the scars of irrefutable monstrosity (what Susan Sontag has termed "fascinating Fascism"), but of an unfathomable cruelty and consciously fabricated history. Saul Friedländer has stressed that "Nazism's attraction lay less in any explicit ideology than in the power of emotions, images, and phantasms," and that "a new discourse on Nazism will develop at the same level of phantasms, images, and emotions."[8] Film becomes a fetishized object that is preserved for the purpose of constituting a symbolic experience of the German past. Cavani focuses on the sites where the primal scenes of rampant National Socialism were played out, and the ways in which they were deployed in the name of cultural and national prestige: namely, how the spectacles were staged by the regime to disguise violence and repression. The iconography of *Storia del Terzo Reich* is designed to reveal the rhetoric and strategies with which Nazism appealed to its passive citizens. She avoids the dangers of ideological oversimplification and kitsch. The raw footage allows Cavani to evoke the pathos of an itinerant photojournalist, and to capture the essence of the despicable with highly charged dramatic images.

The adventurous journeys of Francesco, Galileo, Antigone, and Milarepa had taken them from the center to the margins of society, at which *limen* they experienced reality. Action and ritual occur at the center space, the locus of the hero's entrapment, trial, and tribulations. In *Milarepa*, the story of a Tibetan yogi's reincarnation, the male protagonist endures a series of ritualistic submissions to physical pain and lasting ordeals. As in *Francesco di Assisi* and *Galileo*, Cavani relies on her male characters to embody a dream of a moment beyond, since they alone inhabit a space from which divestiture is possible. In the films of the trilogy the main characters (a couple) theatricalize another transgressive relationship, again at odds with their times. They embark upon a journey of strangely narcissistic desire; they traverse intricate paths that eventually involve their expulsion from life itself. Desire finds its stage through the phantasmatic scene of male castration;[9] its complex dynamics figure complicity and ambiguity, pleasure and power. These characters reject the technical procedures of interrogation and trial, and decline the administration of punishment, or confession, as psychological therapy. Their transgressive discourse, which disrupts the symbolic order within which they operate, is fully sustained by retrospec-

Frame 32. Documenting horror in *Storia del Terzo Reich* (History of the Third Reich, 1961–1962)

tion and tension. The trajectory of representation traces a mobile *iter*, crossing the thresholds and boundaries of pleasure, unconventionally portrayed as fetishism, masochism, and sadism. The voyeuristic gaze is grounded in negation; it ultimately reveals the necessity of transgression itself. Thus transgression is not a vehicle for liberation but affirms the limitlessness into which it leaps, as it leads beyond a door that opens to an impersonal other (already within). In Georges Bataille's words, it is the inexorably splendid passion of a man brought to a higher level in the elevated mind, where he sees the light or, for Cavani, the beauty of the night: "I focus on a point before me and I imagine this point as the geometric locus of all existence and all unity, of all separation and all dread, of all unsatisfied desire and all possible death."[10]

The films of the trilogy are best apprehended if we analyze them as a coherent whole. These films were indeed conceived as a group: "I wanted to make a German trilogy," declares the director, "or I should say a Mitteleuropean trilogy, because we are all descendents from the same culture. I wanted to pay my debt to Thomas Mann."[11] Cavani relies on visual images to advance her narrative, while dialogue becomes scant and concise. The earlier films were constructed from a combination of individual scenes in linear fashion (each being a part in itself); now Cavani articulates her narrative on a scene-by-scene interconnection. The spectator is constantly made to *see*, to participate in a poetic gaze that encompasses the characters' transgression and ambiguity. The use of a mirror or other reflective surface in the mise-en-scène (in conjunction with the flashbacks) alters the temporal continuity of the story. Backgrounds are often out of focus: they provide implicit comment on the characters' emotional instability. The trilogy abounds in images and objects that symbolize the unlimited receptivity of the reflective eye: glass doors, mirrors, movie and still cameras, binoculars, glasses, spotlights convey a sense of the refraction of the spectacle of history. The couples who enact Cavani's spectacles endure multiplied and multifaceted relationships: Max and Lucia in *Il portiere di notte*; Lou and Paul and Fritz, Lou and Andreas, Fritz and Elizabeth in *Al di là del bene e del male*; Louise, Mitsuko, and Heinz, Mitsuko and Benno in *Interno berlinese*.

These films are also about cinema.[12] Cavani's image formation addresses camera placement—always stressing the act of seeing—body movement (from the puppetlike performance of Dirk Bogarde in *Il portiere di notte* to the slow, stylized gestures of Mitsuko in *Interno berlinese*), and composition, often highlighted by the inclusion of the photographic lens in the photogram. Max is first identified through the lens of his movie camera while filming a prisoner, Lucia. He focuses on the close-up of her face to let us imprint the immobility of her frightened stare, as she turns away from the bright light aimed at her. The camera eye also freezes the faces of the other deportees in the concentration camps as if to capture their last expression before they descend to destruction. Cavani also works with stylized backgrounds in order to convey tension through decor, lighting, blocking, and body posture. She experiments with a symmetrical displacement: the equilibrium of the composition is, in fact, shifted to the edge of the frame, emphasizing the marginality of the characters' identity and of their psychology. A vertical linearity dominates Cavani's settings; these lines frame the actor's body inside a space that projects the loneliness of the figure against an increasingly alienating background. The shots are tight, confining. The filmic architecture, which, as in Cavani's earlier films, conveys a sense of entrapment through bars, gates, walls, now becomes the dominant metaphor for the prisonlike environment of reality. For example, Cavani had Max's apartment entirely reconstructed inside the Cinecittà studios in order to represent faithfully the exact measurements of the workers' quarter in a Vienna suburb of the 1950s. These blocks of flats (called the Karl Marx Hof) were built mostly in the 1920s. In order to recapture the atmosphere of oppression and claustrophia inherent in such confined space, she used mobile walls with a careful selection of lenses. Figures are often entrapped within door frames; reflective surfaces duplicate and imprison the human image within its interior. The first shot of Max, after he recognizes Lucia, is a dolly move composing him to the right of the frame as he sits down in front of a reflected background. In these interiors, the distance between the camera and the figure seems determined by the eye that composes the shot. In the *speculum*, the unconscious becomes aware of its own reflection. Such an allusive and suggestive image encompasses, for Cavani, "the memory of ourselves."[13]

In his book on Kierkegaard's aesthetic, Theodor Adorno has pointed out how the concept of an idealist self is manifested in the recurring existential metaphor of the *intérieur*, signifying subjectivity and reflection.[14] Cavani's image of the interior defines inwardness, with the human subject occupying a personal space. For example, in *Interno berlinese*, the chamber inhabited by Mitsuko and Louise embodies the self-absorption of the characters outside history; stylistic strategies (such as the static camera) reinforce the idea that objects and sets become aestheticized, gaining meaning out of the primordial experience of a differential interior. The chamber is the primary site of spectacle, to which the central motif of the reflective gaze belongs, and also the real space that sets free the hallucinatory journey of playfulness. In *Il portiere di notte*, the interior is reduced to a quintessential and elementary experience. Cavani works predominantly with reaction shots, another effect of the refraction of the gaze. The Nietzschean slave views the world merely as a hostile exterior, to which he reacts: his action is therefore a fundamental reaction. Each film of the trilogy unfolds as one continuous interior sequence, showing the director's approach to interpreting action in deep-focus scenes.

These interiors are visual emblems of the inner reality of these transgressive characters: a concentration camp victim and an SS officer; the untimely intellectual ménage among Lou Andreas-Salomé, Fritz (Nietzsche), and Paul (Rée); a lesbian affair in Hitler's Berlin. Only by probing the unconscious can one understand the depths of such relations. The unconscious is not for Cavani simply the locus of uncensored, or consciously repressed, impulses. She also

Frame 33. Max (Dirk Bogarde), the night porter

probes the unconscious to understand its characteristic (Freudian) primary processes: the absence of time, interchangeability of master/slave dialectic, condensation. In Cavani's German trilogy, unconscious drives function within the logic of a space in which, as Ignacio Matte Blanco has described, every individual is an element of its class, and in which every relationship is symmetrical.[15] Here, the common denominator is a disorder of desire and a perversion of the will (sadism is directly associated not with pain but with a control of the will). The symmetrical logic of the individual relation to history determines for Cavani the frightening dynamics between the unlimited possibilities of the interior and the external limits and controls imposed by the reigning social power. Cavani dramatizes this symmetrical logic that underlies psychological and social disintegration. These characters do not need to know the past; they tragically reenact it in a real present in order to leap into the future. Max and Lucia resume their sadomasochistic games in the hotel room by regressing to infantile behavior ("My *bambina*," Max calls Lucia). In *Interno berlinese*, symmetry leads the lesbian lovers to a reality that transcends time and space, and conducts them to the realm of an ideal and deathless beauty—for which they are willing to dedicate (literally) their lives. Suicide is the sublimation of the erotic desire and paradoxically affirms the supreme purpose of life. In Dionysian terms,

dream and drunken madness are instruments of liberation; existence is ultimately an alchemy of the extremes. This is the Nietzsche of the *Krisis*, whose
convictions embrace an active, aesthetic nihilism. As Allan Megill imagistically
mediates: "Instead of drawing back from the void, we dance upon it. Instead
of lamenting the absence of a world suited to our being, we invent one. We
become the artists of our own existence, untrammelled by natural constraints
and limitations."[16] The predominant metaphor for the *Krisis* is the abyss.

Throughout the German trilogy the supremacy of desire is portrayed
through hallucinatory compositions. Cavani's "realistic" narrative structure is
enriched by poetic complexity; its pictorial expressionism recalls such aesthetic
rebels as Munch, Klee, and Kandinsky, in whose work the objectivity of form
is sacrificed to intensity and shock. Vienna is the city haunted by Kafka, Freud,
and the drawings of Egon Schiele. It is a city illuminated by a cold, aqueous,
humoral light (increasing haze and grayness); a tonality that signals psychic
disintegration. Max and Lucia, admits Cavani, are "a couple worthy of Klimt:
sophisticated, distorted, with a great taste for the underground."[17] They are
indeed tragic transgressive individuals. They seek a new meaning in life, self-
contained and provocative, defined against what Guattari called the "micropolitics of desire."[18] They do not engage in romantic pornography, as Vincent
Canby has claimed for *Il portiere di notte*, but represent the antithesis between
pouvoir and *amour*, where, in the end, "love reverses power, the superpower,
in total absence of power."[19]

For a general audience, Cavani's resonant sexual thematics are scandalous.
The scandal derives not from the images themselves but from the filmic context: desire is seen as a point of departure for freedom; but a free form of desire
is historically a scandal, as in the case of Lou Salomé, where her emancipation
challenges men in positions of power. Eros is the tragic essence of these films.
It is what Bataille has called the appropriation of life as far as death. The characters' *passio* is expressed by a creative élan; their obsession becomes a symptom
of the preoccupations of their times. "The erotic experience," asserts Cavani,
"does not happen to just anybody. It requires sophisticated culture and sensibility . . . Eros is a competitive form of love that spares nothing; it is a fight
toward courage, adventure, against everybody . . . This type of love is creative.
In order to exorcize it, we say that it destroys us. The lovers seem indeed to
destroy themselves. In reality, they regenerate themselves constantly, until
death, since death is not abstract to them; it is part of their experience."[20]

It was with *Il portiere di notte* that Cavani established her reputation as one of
the most provocative film auteurs of her generation.[21] The story concerns the
accidental encounter of a war criminal, an ex-*Sturmbahnführer*, Maximilian
Theo Aldorfer (Dirk Bogarde), and a concentration camp prisoner, Lucia Atherton (Charlotte Rampling), in a Viennese hotel in 1957, where Lucia, now mar-

ried to a prominent orchestra conductor, is staying while on tour. The couple replay the master/slave relationship that seems to have been the only thing they both genuinely cared about. After moving into Max's apartment (the new *Lager*), and while being haunted by a group of Nazi executioners, Lucia carries the fateful affair to mutual annihilation. "We are all victims or assassins," says Cavani, "and we accept these roles willingly. Only Sade and Dostoievsky understood it well."[22]

> I believe that in every place, in every relationship, there is a master-victim dynamic, more or less manifest and generally lived at an unconscious level. The maturity in each of us consistently restrains this energy, which remains repressed. War is a detonator: it widens the field of possibilities and expressions, breaks the repression, opens the dam. Because of the war, my protagonists have broken their repressions and live their roles with lucidity. They are interchangeable roles . . . When we are at war, the State monopolizes the sadomasochistic energy of its citizens, provokes it, and legalizes it. One may become a victim or an assassin within the law.[23]

Cavani combines the realism of the flashbacks with the hallucinatory vision of the present. From the title sequence, she establishes the ambivalence of reality by using both a wide-angle lens (for the facades of the buildings) and the zoom lens to venture through the door to Max's hotel. The night becomes a metaphor of the unconscious.[24] Once Max traverses this threshold, the first image the audience has of him is a glass reflection, which optically displaces him into something obscure; his actions are defined by controlled, mechanical gestures. The hotel lobby, Max's own territory, becomes the visible site of erotic and dark fantasies. Shot from below in a Dutch angle, it exaggerates the corpo-reality of Bogarde's role: the porter is the nerve center of the hotel, through which everyone communicates, and he also orchestrates the guests' desires. The opening sequence discloses Cavani's concern with the visual objectification of a human condition: her pictorial compositions generate intense, dramatic energy. She relies on depth of field consciousness achieved through wide-angle lenses and scant dialogue. The doorway motif, as narrative topos, is specifically developed in the form of elaborate lighting patterns (the light spills into the darkness) which enhance the reality that houses the night/unconscious. Cavani envisions the interiors with dark foregrounds, the key light emanating from another room (the light refracts off the walls and washes into the scene). This edge lighting brings out a certain texture in the reality envisioned. The sound track by Daniele Paris also comments on the scene: a lightmotif to Max's memory-dreams alternates with works of the great German musicians of the eighteenth and nineteenth centuries, almost to remind us by contrast, as Gian Luigi Rondi has suggested, what Mitteleuropean culture was like before the rise of Nazism.[25] Again, as in *I cannibali*, the most audible natural sound is the echoing footsteps, evoking the mystery of the (unconscious) journey about to take place. At the epiphanic moment of closure, when the couple chooses to end their seige, Max's theme inscribes their action in the threshold of interior/exterior, light/darkness. There is no musical comment to mark the moment when they are gunned down and their bodies fall like wireless marionettes on the cold, iron bridge.

Cavani's idea for *Il portiere di notte* goes back to her documentary years, her *Storia del Terzo Reich* and particularly *La donna nella Resistenza* (The Women of the Resistance, 1965), when she interviewed partisan women who had survived the concentration camps. Cavani was struck by the fact that only the victims wanted to remember and continued to revisit their sites of pain and (psychological) extermination. She recounts:

> Another woman from Milan, not Jewish, partisan, bourgeois, ended up at Auschwitz, and survived. When I met her, she was living in the suburbs in a rather modest house. I was surprised because her family was quite well-off. She explained to me that after the war she tried to fit back in with her family and to resume her contacts with those people who once knew her, but she could not take it and left. Why? Because she was shocked that after the war the world continued to function as before, as if nothing had happened, and in haste to forget the unpleasant and the sad . . . She began to feel guilty for having survived hell, for being the living witness, and therefore the bitter memory, of something embarrassing that everyone wanted to forget as soon as possible . . . I asked her which memories tormented her the most. She replied that she was still haunted not by the memories of a particular episode but by the fact that, in the *Lager*, she could fully test her own nature, what she was capable of doing in good and in evil: she stressed the word evil.[26]

Such an obsessive return to the site of death and horror may be ascribed to the symbolic processes of a funerary rite. The *Lager* becomes an object that haunts the survivor from the space of the unconscious, her journey enacting its own ritual of mourning: this particular victim endures the passage across the boundary of isolation and self-imposed exclusion.[27] *Il portiere di notte* raises the specter of an overriding guilt whose grounds are so real, and whose utterance is so terrifying, that it cannot be dismissed as an illusory, isolated (neurotic) reaction. It is a guilt of the unthinkable, heightened by the fact that few are willing to confess it (the impossibility of a direct relation to oneself). Thus the film calls for an anamnesis that refracts and symbolically enacts the ontological possibilities of guilt, the lonely alienation of Dostoievsky's underground man. In the first flashback, the montage of shots in the infernal Nazi camps, where the prisoners face, naked, the naked truth of fear, explicitly creates a profoundly ominous mood: the bodies are huddled together without dignity, stripped of their identity. The prisoners are displayed as if for a group portrait, showing their frailty frozen in time: each shot conveys a dramaturgy of suffering, which eludes, however, the pathos of period footage or still photographs. The viewer seems no longer to be watching a film but rather to be witnessing an event as it unfolds: the pulsing sound of Max's camera rolling (an authentic

1940s Leica) reinforces the audience's experience of participating in the raw-ness of a living moment. This scene of horror releases time from all bonds. No one speaks, but the terror is recorded by the camera lens: the grayness of the interior balances the humoral atmosphere of the Vienna streets, a gray zone that has visual association with spatial and temporal dispossession. The film's cowriter, Italo Moscati, explains:

> From the outside this city does not seem to be shaken by any visible, conflictual reality. But it is not so. The conflicts exist, and they are kept under a cold, conven-tional slab that covers everything. It is not the slab of hypocrisy that crushes and seizes life; it is the slab of power that has simply removed the physical presence of the Nazi symbols . . . The terrain on which these film characters operate is that of a society which has replaced the Nazi insignia with the insignia of wealth, or rather of an order founded on continuity and authority. What distinguishes them from every-one else, and also what gives them strength, is the common language that allows them to understand and communicate with each other. While the city seems silent or stammering, the ex-comrades attain their intended objectives. They appear to be a nostalgic sect of survivors; they are instead a power group acting with lucidity in order to support each other and increase their strength.[28]

This "common language" functions as a Fascist mechanism for coping with guilty memories. For example, Klaus, Hans, Kurt, Dobson, and Bert, the members of a fictitious psychoanalytical group, stage a mock trial to cleanse themselves of the guilt complex, which they diagnose as an illness of the psy-che, a neurosis. For all of them, language is reduced to the elementary use of ordering and describing. Only Max refuses to enter into its self-application and its madness; and he subsequently refuses to have his crimes erased. The monovision of the ex-Nazis is exemplified in Klaus's monocle (literally objecti-fying Fascist ideology).

In images of the Death Camp, what is imprinted is not a moment but its deferral: the past remains essentially memorial and "real." In order to achieve this effect, cinematographer Alfio Contini selected prime lenses without the use of any diffusion, which is commonly associated with flashbacks and dreams. He shot *Il portiere di notte* primarily utilizing fixed lenses with a normal focal length, and on occasion using a zoom lens in order to adjust for composition.[29]

Cavani discussed the victim's compulsion to enact the past, a kind of volun-tary repetition that compensates for a sentiment of loss and guilt, with a famous Holocaust survivor, who felt impelled by an obscure imperative to continually metamorphose his experience into storytelling itself:

> Years ago I spoke with Primo Levi for an entire afternoon. He remembered and remembered, even though he knew I had read his books, and that he could write many more books. I had the impression that Levi could speak, or, better, succeeded in speaking, only of that period of his life, as if he had never left. I also wondered if

Frame 34. Cavani looking through the camera viewfinder with director of photography Alfio Contini on the set of *Il portiere di notte* (The Night Porter, 1974)

the criminals were as traumatized as their victims. It does not seem so, at least not from their testimony at their trials. To admit remorse is to admit a sense of guilt, but their entire defense is based on the absence of guilt.[30]

In an interview years later, Levi himself confirms: "By now I am like a tape recorder; if you turn me on, I begin to remember for the others. For those who did not return but did everything to leave a trace. I am a witness of what exists at the bottom of the well of the night."[31] Levi, who called *Il portiere di notte* "a beautiful and false film," rejects Cavani's premise that the roles of victim and executioner are interchangeable: "Cavani knows a friend of mine, who was in the camps and who goes back every year to visit. She returns because she is a teacher. She takes her pupils with her to show the factory of death; but Cavani thinks that my friend does it for a kind of nostalgia, of the victim/accomplice. This is not honest. Her film is based on a wrong idea, more precisely on the idea Cavani has of sex. This has nothing to do with the camps. A case of aberration may have happened, but generally. . . "[32] Levi's criticism relies on the discomfort caused by Cavani's sexual portrayal, an approach that distracts him from understanding the film. Central to Cavani's interpretation is a metaphorics of reflection and enactment that transmutes the microcosm of the *Lager* into the macrocosm of a totalitarian society; also central is the consciousness of guilt that indeed shatters her characters at the bottom of "the well of the night." Guilt and self-betrayal are not marginal to the inherent ambiguity of the Cavanian erotic couple. In the German trilogy, it seems impossible to fully disengage creative action from the experiences of death and unbound sexuality, from metamorphosis and doubling. The brilliance and suffocation of Cavani's erotic images assure that their reality becomes naked: they point to the bottomless void and the vertiginous fall. At the limit of death, in a chaos of light and shadow, there is no catharsis. What is unveiled beyond the door is neither God nor nothingness: these characters experience death with the avidity of sadistic ecstasy.[33]

Lucia represents an ambivalent female archetype characteristic of the films of this second phase. At times virginlike and intensely ingenuous, at others endowed with tantalizing femme fatale gestures, Lucia controls the narrative movement. With Lou, Mitsuko, and Nina in *Oltre la porta* (a tale of incest), she configures the awareness of transgression and the shock of perversity, the ambiguous play of creativity and destruction of a (deviant) child. Max and Lucia embody the Dionysian monster, caught between remembering and forgetting, representing and repressing. They are not psychopaths but tragic characters who continue to play out the historical times that made their relationship lawful. Their subversion relates to power and domination originating in violence: it is a condition of social death. These are demons that can be exorcised but not defeated. Cavani visualizes their dark experience through a specular vortex. Her sophisticated formalism dictates, for the viewer, an uneasy awareness of the extended and multiform creative game of the trapped couple. During their long period of erotic seige (confinement, starvation, and death), only the locked door forms a frame to the enigmatic threshold that signifies both access and boundary. To remember, to relive the past, is the only step toward the future these characters are capable of taking. For Max and Lucia, Fritz and Paul, Louise, Mitsuko, and Heinz, death is the ultimate, voluntary act.

Cavani's preoccupation with power and resistance is unceasingly challenged by her seeking out the limit-experience of sadism that would enable her to efface the boundaries between pleasure and terror, life and death. Indeed, Cavani's attraction to the Marquis de Sade calls for the creative power of unusual forms of eroticism. Max and Lucia perform, in a mutually consensual theater of cruelty (Antonin Artaud's political stance against the existent order), a reenactment of excessive violation and enslavement under controlled situations, a kind of Foucaultian search for a potentially transformative truth. Cavani's stylistic tension and fragmentation are intensified by means of increasing silence. "A characteristic of their relationship," says the director, "is that they say little or nothing. Because their mutual experiences in the past have already spoken for them. They understand each other with gestures and looks. As now: they share a gesture of love (others would call it erotic) that is the reproduction of an ancient gesture ("riedizione di un gesto antico"). But with a difference: now she suggests it, not him."[34] Silence is the expression of the sensory binding between their intensely shared past and the present:

> Max had given free play to his "morbid" taste for sadomasochistic games. He chained Lucia to the bed so he could better caress her. He had her arm subjected to torture so that he could kiss her wounds gently. He chased her into an empty room, and while she was naked and terrorized, he shot at her with a pistol. He forced her to give him sexual pleasure through degrading acts. Their strange relationship was a combination of profound tenderness and cruelty. They had created for themselves an emotional, mute, and turbid complicity. Lucia never spoke; however, she seemed to respond to these experiences without aversion, sometimes even with satisfaction.[35]

In the original film treatment, Cavani introduces Max as the founder of a religious sect called "The Christian Church of the Apocalypse." He is a sort of visionary, who attends to his own passion for writing sermons. Within this context, Lucia's wound attests to the bleeding of relics. The director explicitly highlights the universal dimension of Lucia's story when she explains why she chose to make her the daughter of a socialist activist. Contrary to what many critics have argued, Lucia is not a Jewish prisoner:

> Almost no foreign newspaper understood that she was not Jewish. In the film, I gave my cue to Mario, the Italian cook who remains in Vienna. I wanted to bring in the issue of victim/assassin in order to include all human beings, and not only to address the Jewish question. *Lager* means prison and abuse for every victim. I was

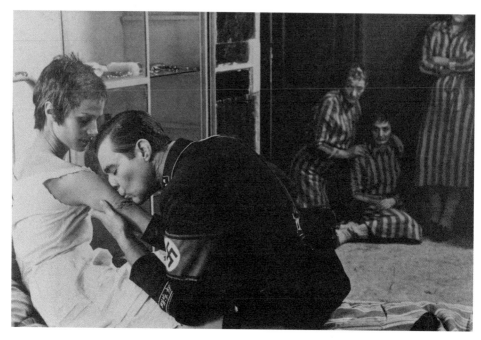

Frame 35. Max's morbid taste for sadomasochistic games

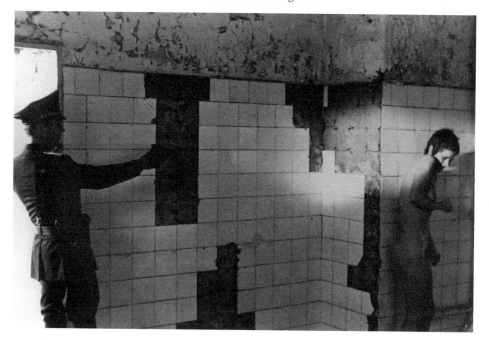

Frame 36. Max terrorizes Lucia (Charlotte Rampling) in an empty room, shooting at her with a pistol

concerned by this misunderstanding about my film. At times, critics pay little attention to cultural discourses and deform the reading of a film. I truly wanted to address
the dynamic between the ultimate victim and the ultimate assassin. My victim belongs
to any *Lager*. Indeed the most horrific were the Nazis, but there were also *Lager* in
the Soviet Union and in Brazil. I believe that it is essential to remember.[36]

During the initial sequence of the flashbacks, which is constructed out of
silence and unsynchronous sounds (Max's echoing footsteps as he approaches
Lucia, the cranking camera, offscreen shouts), Cavani strategically establishes
a dark form of communication between the victim and her torturer, a guilty
complicity that, in the present state, implies a withdrawal from the external
world and a heightened receptivity to fantasied (erotic) playfulness. The constantly shifting narrative point of view momentarily destabilizes the balance of
perception: inebriation and terror are sensations whose intensity and length
are paced very skillfully in the editing. It is Max who first recaptures the past
within a chronological and causal linearity (Lucia's arrival at the Death Camp,
the steps in her physical denudation) as he establishes the spatial articulations
of its staging. We see him masquerading as a doctor in the prisoners' showers,
recording sensational images: "Max was filming cruel scenes. And in the view-
finder, he came across a frightened fifteen-year-old girl, who stood naked,
among other prisoners."[37] It is Lucia's point of view that completes this flashback when she senses Max shining the movie light into her face. Alternatively,
the victim intervenes to disrupt the voyeuristic aggression of Max's gaze. In
two other scenes the captive ambiguity of Max's little girl is fully exhibited, her
glance always implying the presence of a sentient observer in whose viewpoint
the audience may partake: in the neutral spaces of the amusement park, when
Lucia is being photographed on the *giostra* (merry-go-round), and of the barren
stanzone da caserma (army barracks), in which she is being subjected to a mock
shooting against a white-tiled wall. In both cases, the sound of bullets emphasizes the hallucinated horror of humans being used as moving targets in a
hunting game of power and excess.

The *giostra* motif (vestigially carnivalesque) inscribes the couple's relationship in a language of silence and death. Lucia is dressed like a child (a light
dress, white socks, white shoes, and a ribbon holding her hair), the same attire
she wears at the end of the film, when she is actually executed. Max is in his
SS officer uniform. For Lucia, writes Cavani, he embodies "a lover, a master,
an unscrupulous father, and ultimately a god who amuses, torments, and loves
her."[38] This scene, played out against an Oedipal nostalgia, is designed to enhance Lucia's spatial suspension. She mechanically rotates up and down, and
spins around in midair, as if to expose a physiological fear of a fall: velocity,
downfall, and acceleration give the viewer the tactile impression of bodies without support, photographed in various angles of danger—even though thick
iron chains visibly secure the seats to a fixed center.

Frame 37. Max's camera rolling: an authentic 1940s Leica

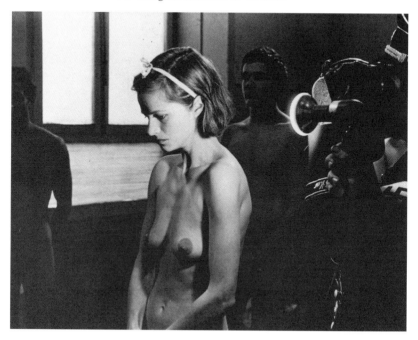

Frame 38. Lucia, as a fifteen-year-old girl, stands naked among other prisoners

Frame 39. Lucia on the merry-go-round while being filmed by Max

In the films of the trilogy, the game is no longer the Franciscan *ludus* but what Roger Caillois has ascribed to the excess of the *ilinx* (from the Greek word meaning "vortex") with the theatricalization of *mimicry*: a vertigo that swirls the players down into the abyss. The amusement park is a site of rapture because its "mechanisms of rotation, oscillation, suspension, and falling are specifically built to cause visceral panic."[39] The editing strategy adopted by Franco Arcalli reinforces the impression of impotence and debasement; at the same time, the shots convey the intoxication of Max's gaze. Arcalli builds tension by progressively lengthening the duration of the flashbacks. For example, when Lucia is first established in a close-up from the point of view of Max's camera (her face overexposed), she appears for only three beats, but, when she is reintroduced in a long shot with the other deportees, the scene unfolds for an extended period of time: its pacing simulates Max's subjectivity as obsession, while he is moving in on her. The sound of the camera and his echoing footsteps heighten the unconscious pulsations between real and ideal perception in the imaginary dispossession of Lucia. Max's memory sequences are enacted against an extreme close-up with an out-of-focus background in a shallow depth of field. Visually, this communicates a sense of hallucinatory memory trying to bring the past into focus. On the contrary, Lucia's flashbacks play with time, reflecting her emotional state (dizziness, nausea, instability, nakedness), a *mise-en-abîme* that evolves from the initial glaring of a bare light aimed at her face to the scene of the merry-go-round skillfully intercut with a close-up of Max's camera lens aimed at a fascinating object offscreen. Although the viewer is made aware of the spatial dislocation of these synchronous shots (Max is actually in the camps), it is always implied that he is filming her. Of her collaboration with her editor, a mythical name in Italian cinema, the director remembers:

> I met him one night at the house of some friends, and his presence reminded me of a fabulous, little-known Venetian poet called Baffo. Kim was not well known, but he was a true star among his friends, who admired him for his intelligence and his sense of adventure, which are very rare qualities, even in our business. I envied Bernardo [Bertolucci] for this collaborator and friend. And Bernardo out of his kindness and affection for me decided to share this friendship, and so he gave me this gift. I was preparing *Milarepa* and I needed very special collaborators, not just professionals, but people who were obsessed by the art of cinema. Kim was all that . . He loved images, even more than I did. I wanted to discard certain shots, but he recuperated them and studied them on the viewer by moving the film back and forth, while smoking his Gauloise. He knew how to select the best shot, and he also had a great sense of rhythm as very few others have . . . Then came *Il portiere di notte*, a delicate film, for its rhythm and its storytelling, which heavily relied on flashbacks and could have become boring. I did not want to use them all; however, Kim was successful in utilizing all of them. He made them indispensable for the plot structure and created suspense where I feared repetitiousness. It cost him thousands of Gauloises. And since I was also smoking, we were in a perennial fog guided only by the small light of the Moviola. Without him this film would not have been the same.[40]

The emblematic image of the merry-go-round evokes the fascination of a psychological suspense-thriller, with its effects of velocity and its rhythmic pacing of time. In a stunning visual prank of reversal, Max's phallic camera penetrates the last fortress in the (child's) fantastic playground. Visual pleasure is made of inebriation; it is savored at the edge of the paternal house: in the characters' role-playing, the mask takes on the vertigo. Significantly, Cavani's fair scene is dominated by the top of a merry-go-round that never ceases its circular motion. Here the circle engenders chaos. It might be said that this flashback alludes to the chaotic condition of Max and Lucia's erotic enactments.[41] Finally, in the scene which concludes the flashbacks, that of Lucia being forced by Max into an empty white room, while she is dodging the bullets, her juggling act implies a certain playful complicity. The low-angle camera pans from Max aiming a pistol at Lucia crouched in a corner, their points of view coming together to expose the duplicitous nature of the very body of the film. In Cavani's psychological drama, scenes such as this count more than the disclosure expected from the genre in the last few minutes of the film. Only the elegance and economy of Dirk Bogarde's performance (vaguely reminiscent of Losey's *The Servant*) can adequately translate the sadomasochistic brutality of this scene; and Charlotte Rampling's shy features can deflect the madness of desire into bourgeois respectability. Sadomasochism is a real (or potential) component of many relationships in Cavani's films of the seventies and eighties.[42]

Cruelty is lucid. It is depicted in visual details in one of the most controversial scenes of the film, that of Lucia throwing a perfume bottle on the bathroom floor. Max steps on the broken glass, playing a kind of mad game, which prompts the resurfacing of "another memory that they repeat with better wisdom."[43] Max's game manifests a radical tendency to enact painful strategies of autolaceration (he lingers on the sharp fragments of glass with bare feet). Contradictory signs of submission and revolt are revealed in this obstinate game of reversal. Pleasure and tension involve boundless excitation. Cavani risks making her audience squirm. The film demands that we reflect on the state of mind that motivates such an open defiance ("la sfida è aperta") between the two players. These are enigmatic figures placed at the entrance to the labyrinth before the challenge of either conquest or retreat. Contrary to Foucault and Artaud, Cavani's characters do not acquire consciousness in extremis but are driven to the *limen* and self-inflicted death out of extreme lucidity. As Bataille poetically insists, "the human being arrives at the threshold: there he must throw himself headlong into that which has no foundation and no head."[44] In Max's apartment, a site of tortured and powerful libidinal game, the couple finally drop their masks and appear without any play of light and darkness, preparing for the beautiful eruption of a luminous death on the bridge at dawn. Ciriaco Tiso perceptively writes:

> If the two protagonists had carried their cruel game to the very end, they should have died inside the walls of the apartment, under siege, physically as well as mentally exhausted; but they wanted to become "victims," and this makes them normal, the *normal* victims of a historical *abnormality*. Thus the end makes us wonder what these two characters are searching for on that Viennese bridge at night . . . they finally ask to become normal, and for this reason they reappear out of the apartment (back into History) in a pathetic image that ends in melodrama.[45]

Of all the images in the final part of the film, that of Max and Lucia walking away from the camera, enframed by the towering structure of the bridge, is the most haunting and beautiful. As in the title sequence, the only sound is the echo of footsteps: the camera dollies across the bridge and, once they are shot, zooms in. In this expressionistic cityscape (gray and wet), the solid limits of the bridge seem to disappear into a limitless expanse where sky and water dissolve. The last shot imprints a fluid space of transition, which evokes the unreal existence of death (the distant toll of a bell).

Some critics denounced all too quickly the erotic context of the film and labeled it "Next Tango in Vienna," a parodic analogy to Bertolucci's 1972 formalist fetishization of a Parisian encounter; some others hailed it as "The Classic You May Never See."[46] Cavani was blamed for representing heavy-handedly

Frame 40. The last shot of the film as Max and Lucia walk away from the camera

the boundless erotic playfulness that drives an ex-prisoner back into the arms of her ex-torturer. Vincent Canby even argued that the film should be considered romantic pornography, literally "a piece of junk."[47] Peter Bondanella vehemently addresses this issue:

> When *The Night Porter* first appeared, there was little in Cavani's former career to foreshadow the tremendous polemical but favorable reaction to the film in Europe or its utter condemnation by the New York critics. One delirious writer described the work as "a thinly-disguised Fascist propaganda film" or a "high point in social, cultural and political barbarism," proving once again that the term "Fascist" as employed by leftist reviewers in this country has been completely emptied of any meaningful historical or intellectual content.[48]

Bondanella's delirious critic is Henry Giroux, who reviewed the film for *Cinéaste*:

> Hailed in the American press as "a charming piece of romantic pornography," *The Night Porter* is a thinly-disguised Fascist propaganda film that glorifies sadism, brutality and exaggerated machismo. The film's uniqueness lies in its refusal to employ the standard subtle use of technique and content to mask its ideological message. Its barbarism rests not only in its audacity to extoll Fascist principles, but also in its attempt to legitimize the death of millions of innocent victims at the hands of the Nazi machine.[49]

To reduce this couple to repressed sexual yearnings is to misread the characters by subscribing to the very notion of genital aberration encoded in the B-movies of *la mode rétro*.[50] Given the context, Susan Sontag's colorful description of Fascist regalia is exemplary: "Sade had to make up his theater of punishment and delight from scratch, improvising the decor and costumes and blasphemous rites. Now there is a master scenario available to everyone. The color is black, the material is leather, the seduction is beauty, the justification is honesty, the aim is ecstasy, the fantasy is death."[51] Porn is passive and its goal is deflecting gratification, an on-screen theatrics of debauchery (mostly in close-ups), where the body performs ritualized exertions. As Robert Stam suggests in his discussion of the priapic nature of cinematic pornography, "on the actresses' faces we read, usually, the simulation of desire, and on the man's, grim duty, aerobic perseverance, the solitude of the long-distance comer."[52] In *Il portiere di notte*, what is important is not Max and Lucia's resuming their scandalous relationship but the way it has been visualized. Cavani's sustained effort to designate the interplay of the look as a simulacrum for an aestheticization of the body politic is blatant in the imagery relating to theatrical performances (particularly the dance sequences with Bert and Lucia/Salomè). She achieves this effect by virtue of refraction and repetition in an endless labyrinth of what I would call the dialogical angles of her subliminally haunting images. For example, the scene at the Volksoper, when Max first joins Lucia in the audience after they meet again, is crucial to an understanding of the essentially symmetrical relation between the past and its liberating deployment of performer/spectator dialogism in the present. Onstage, Lucia's husband is conducting the first act of Mozart's *Die Zauberflöte* (The Magic Flute), whose playbill we saw posted at Max's hotel in the opening sequence. The use of this specific opera evokes an incongruously ironic mood, because of its portrayal of brotherhood as considered in the context of the elite of the SS officers. The essential feature and appeal of the entire scene is the exaltation of the audience by the "Pamina and Papageno" duet, celebrating the blissfulness of married life, or, for Cavani, "the tragedy (in the Nietzschean numinous sense) of the Feminine and the Masculine as a duality that finds a *coniunctio*."[53] Mozart is known for his distinct interest in spectacular forms. Max's imposing presence at the Volksoper initiates the shocking awakening of pleasurable and haunting images in Lucia. Though profoundly moved by the music, she is not emotionally involved with the performance onstage. Memory structures the past as representation of representations: the camera shifts focus from the stage to Lucia's glance as she turns toward the intrusive spectator. Bogarde's countenance is described as follows:

Max wears his hotel uniform, inappropriate for the occasion: however, nobody notices him, no one knows who he is, nobody knows his story, with the exception of one person whom he gazes at with intensity. After all, that is the only reason he came to the opera, to look at Lucia Atherton. Lucia Atherton did not see Max enter; but now she "senses" him. She turns her head to meet his piercing stare. She is overtaken by a strong emotion; it is an emotion that is almost imperceptible from the outside.

Lucia Atherthon fights to ignore Max's presence, not to "feel" his troubling eyes fixed on her. She is tempted to turn her head or to do something to break the spell that Max has cast upon her. He knows that she cannot leave and also that Mozart's music provokes an atmosphere of exaltation especially for love themes. Max is fully aware that he is perpetrating emotional violence on the woman. That is exactly what he set out to achieve.[54]

Lucia's role is that of a silent but active player, as she was/is in the emerging images of the past. Cavani stresses the fact that "Lucia Atherton 'sees' Max who caresses a very young Lucia."[55] This statement literalizes the essence of cinema: it re-presents before Lucia a set of images, signifying the total absorption of the subject in the picture itself. Lucia becomes the spectator of her own self-projection, an imagistic translation of interiorized sense experience—this also explains the oneiric dimension of the film. Max and Lucia continue to pursue the projected spectacle of themselves in the pervasive and poetic imagery of the flashbacks. When Max and Lucia look at themselves in the mirror, each sees the reflection of his or her own life in the plane of consciousness of the other; they apprehend themselves through the eyes of the other. They are not the chained prisoners in Plato's cave: they light the fire that casts their own shadows. Lucia's flashback, with her hands chained to a bedpost, staring almost devotionally at Max, epitomizes the use of the gaze in Cavani's cinema. This scene (entirely shot in extreme close-ups) is set up by Lucia's nervously twisting her hands while Tamino's solo is sung onstage. Cavani cuts to the past, to a close-up of her hands chained; then the camera pans to Max in his glaring uniform, caressing her body. Oral pleasure and the allure of the mobilized gaze are exposed in the final close-up of his fingers playing in her mouth (a symbolic penetration).[56] She is a prisoner now, as she was back then. It is the darkness of the opera house that encloses these absorbed players; memory becomes a terrain for reproducing the couple's unconscious exhibitions. Lucia looks within herself through Max's eyes; and he needs her gaze to reconstitute his own self-identity. It is a double process of reversal of power relations that establishes the sublimation of sexuality through solemn composure and ritualistic game. If the theater is a classic image of the *intérieur*, so is the staging of the flashbacks: the Death Camp becomes the image of the *intérieur*'s vitality and fantasy.

In another scene the panoptic spectacle staged by Max's flashback is played against the "Pamina and Papageno" duet: Lucia and other inmates are caught staring at an act of sodomy between two men. The frontal flat lighting enables us to pick out the spectral faces of these human larvae watching the analytic spectacle of the male body through the bars of their bed frames. This scene, shot against a black limbo background, relies on the very physical threshold of spatial immobility and desire: the viewers' gaze effectively captures an unstable copulation that leads to perverse and morbid sexuality.[57] This destabilizing, horrific scene (it represents the victim's initiation to the Death Camp) ends with Max's interrupting Lucia's viewing of the act and recruiting her for a "medical" examination. He takes her away into the light, through a doorway, his action a reflection and an extension of the sovereign power of the SS uniform, but also of the ways in which spectatorial desire impinges on the filmic experience. Max's flashback conveys an intricate interplay of consciousness on the threshold of spatial/temporal manipulation. Cavani explores the spaces of the gaze through the editing, the framing (action and reflection occur at the extreme edge of the frame), and the dynamic shifting of focus from foreground to background (or vice versa)—a technique that sets up memory sequences and brings the past into a sharp focus of reality. To describe the actions of these characters as pornography is to disclaim an important contextual meaning, which is crystallized by the stylization of the actors' performance and the long takes.

In *Il portiere di notte*, the horrifying world of Nazism becomes abstract, a figural exploration of forms. Cinematically, it evokes Luchino Visconti, the filmmaker Bazin called the most aesthetic of the neorealists. For Cavani, Vi-

Frame 41. Close-up of Lucia witnessing an act of sodomy inside the concentration camp

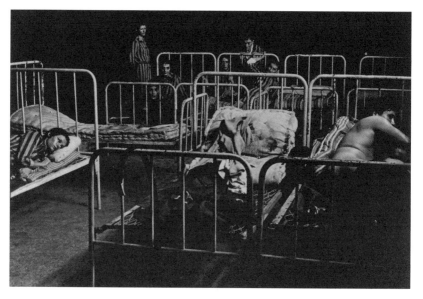

Frame 42. Wide angle of the same scene

Frame 43. Production still of Liliana Cavani, with assistant director Paola Tallarigo, and Dirk Bogarde

sconti was the least provincial of the neorealists: "He always dealt with themes quite different from mine; but we both made a film on Nazism. I loved *La caduta degli dei* (The Damned, 1969) and I may even quote from it. In the end, my characters are dramatic mannequins like his; but in my film their objective was quite the opposite: in *La caduta*, they were punished mannequins, defeated and guilty; in *Portiere*, they are two demons, the symbol of a two-faced reality; thus they are exorcized but not defeated."[58] During the release of the film and the battles with censorship, Visconti publicly endorsed *Il portiere di notte*, defining it as "an atrocious, cruel, and terrible film that leaves you breathless."[59] The issue of a Viscontian citation is particularly contained in the theatrical configuration of sets and props, and in the philologically "realistic" details of the costumes by Piero Tosi, who worked on most of Visconti's films from *Bellissima* (1951) to *L'innocente* (1976). Such aestheticism will find full application in *Interno berlinese*, where Mitsuko's stupendous kimonos embody the corporeal visuality of private/national identity.

Games of erotic enslavement and domination also reflect the paradoxical historical situation in which Max and Lucia perform their *passio*. "My protagonists," says Cavani, "acted their role according to the law until 1945; when they meet again in 1957, their roles are outlawed. They may appear to be psychopaths; they are always the same, not psychopaths, but tragic. It is a tragedy to live a role outside the historical time that produced and allowed it."[60] Fetishism, masochism, sadism—terms often used to define Cavani's erotic travesty of Nazism—portray the creative level of the imaginary. Nazism is not, in fact, "real" in the film. Cavani transforms the Nazi mythology in a specular, spectral multiplication of models and unfolds a profound analysis of the ambiguous nature of man as he operates in history. Max's apartment/*Lager* becomes the prison in which freedom can be attained only by repetitive, self-destructive actions. The puppetlike performance by Bogarde reveals the signs of historical premeditation; it contrasts with the perverse, luminous beauty of Charlotte Rampling, the existential cipher of fate. Lucia and Max show the fundamental face of Nazism, the cold exhibition of a rational violence perpetrated on the individual. By being *diverso*, Max emphasizes the exceptionality that may occur within controlled systems of power; he is dangerous to their very survival and must be eliminated along with his victim-partner. Max's answer to his ex-comrades during a group therapy session is even more pertinent:

> KLAUS: As always we must find out if all this is already known to our enemies. Or if I have managed to get into the archives before them . . . and Max can remain in the shadow, which is what he wants.
>
> MAX: I never thought it was quite enough just to burn all the papers. I want to be left alone, just to live in peace. To live like a church mouse.

With Max and Lucia a whole cinematic tradition that interprets Nazism only as perversion and homosexuality dies.[61]

In discussing the film on Italian television, Jean-Louis Bory defines the seduction of the horrible: "Horror has a link with beauty, innocence, and the victim. The ultimate horror is not that love is possible in an 'interior' (the concentration camp), amid humiliation and death. It is the birth of a strange bond between the SS and his victim. Cavani has shown this horror with disturbing violence. Nazism is the spectacular apparatus of a system that uses humiliation and suffering as instruments. It is a film on seduction, the seduction that was the spectacle."[62] In *Il portiere di notte*, as for *Interno berlinese*, Nazism is a spectacle that the eye perceives at a distance. A scene that exemplifies such an approach is Bert's dancing in front of the SS officers, and later for Max alone. The sequence (which begins in the present with Bert seated in front of a mirror putting on makeup) is shot with reflected lighting patterns: Max holds a theatrical spotlight aiming at the very center of the "stage." The mirror reflections of Bert's body create the illusion of doubling and projection, a visual effect that Cavani exploits to cut to the past. Here, a maximum of distance is introduced between the Dionysian vision of the naked classical dancer and the disturbing atmosphere of awe that surrounds him: the cold gaze of hierarchically empowered men in uniforms. An extreme wide-angle lens establishes a big, stark gray room where Bert dances below a large photograph of Himmler,

Frame 44. Bert Beherens (Amedeo Amodio) dances for Max

Frame 45. Bert's performance embodies the visual stage of Nazism

the omniscient eye of power. The key light for this scene comes from the exterior, through high windows, creating a soft directional light behind the dancer. Cavani choreographs the dance with bold, mechanical movements set to the sound of Strauss's *Der Rosenkavalier*. Elation and deliverance transfigure Bert, as his present world of differentiation and fragmentation disappears. As Angela Dalle Vacche has pointed out, Bert represents the spirit of the German *Volk*.[63] He embodies the visual stage of the regime, an introspective and ethereal projection of the national self: sculpted bodily postures and gestures are taken as figurative political icons.

The key element of Bert's performance is abstraction; its vehicle is seduction. A most emasculated presence in terms of power relations, Bert becomes threatening to the eyes of a male audience, because in dominant ideologies, as Laura Mulvey has shown, "the male figure cannot bear the burden of sexual objectification. Man is reluctant to gaze at his exhibitionist like."[64] In Bert's hotel suite, a stage of spatial illusion in which he directs the look and creates the action, Max is still wearing a uniform and still obliging the dancer's compulsion for a male audience. Bert's dancing for the SS officers incorporates a sacrificial ceremony, expressing the most numinous of feelings: his bodily rhythms translate the visceral world of Nazism. What makes this scene so important is that Bert's dance is intrinsically connected with threat, his gestures signifying enticement and deceit, his movements ambiguously ethereal. A play of light and shadows underlies the intercutting between past (high-key daylight) and present (low-key lighting). In the past, the male dancer expresses the unity of the national self when he energetically plunges into the light onstage, his homosexual dilemma drawing ironic attention to the very nature of the German popular consciousness. In the present, Bert dances only for an inattentive Max in a confined space, a site of darkness that keeps out all natural sources of light. Here his dance becomes a tired game of seduction and vanity. These contrasting lighting patterns reflect the hypnotic power of the dancer as well as the manipulation of the German soul that Nazism practiced on a large scale. Bert's performance ends with an injection of Luminal administered by the doctor-photographer: the dancer's body is transformed into a painfully distorted figure lying on a bed, as in a drawing by Egon Schiele. The split configuration of Bert's mirrored self anticipates the end of the film: Bert Beherens becomes the couple's executioner. In *Il portiere di notte*, evil is bound to "the supreme instant when everything that was form will be on the point of returning to chaos."[65]

Cavani translates primary eroticism into an erotic primitiveness of the images: the mythology of desire retraces a stage that is a pure "reduplication of an ancient gesture," what Max calls a biblical story. The heterosexual framing of Lucia/Salomè in the Nazi cabaret scene counteracts the homosexual world of the decadent dancer. Bert visualizes the homoerotic cult realized by the narcissistic corps of the SS, with its sculptural Olympian elegance and bold seductiveness; Lucia's cabaret performance (woman as icon) externalizes the psychological key to understanding the allure of the uniform: "They were like black angels," says Cavani, "the beautiful angels of the night. They were, in reality, imaginings created by a choreographer."[66] This extraordinary *scena atroce* is recounted by Max to Countess Erika Stein, a permanent guest at the Hotel zur Oper, like Bert. In the film treatment, Cavani describes the scene as follows:

> One night, in 1943, during a party, they all gathered "there": Hans, Klaus, Bert, Dobson. They had been drinking. Max requested that Lucia sing for him, and she, dressed in oversize trousers, with suspenders that could hardly hold them up, bare-chested, and an SS hat on her head, resting on her short hair, she sang hoping for a gift, as Max had promised her. She sang a popular song by Marlene Dietrich: "Wenn ich mir was wünschen dürfte." At the end, a big box was brought in containing the severed head of Johann, a prisoner who had once tormented Lucia. With this in mind, Max had thought of the story of Salomè and the Baptist. Lucia bit her hands till they bled without a cry.[67]

This flashback is set up by Max while he is serving dinner to the Countess, who advises him "to file Lucia away," in other words, to eliminate her. The opening shot is that of an officer wearing a doll-like mask. Lucia performs amid a decor composed of Nazi regalia and sex symbols to an audience of leering officers, prostitutes, and masked musicians; their waxen appearance evokes the fright they once aroused. Her voice is guttural, her movements teasingly inviting: she "imitates with seductive gestures a primadonna of a cabaret."[68] The room is smoky, dark, and bathed in blue, sepulchral hues. The effect of this color (set against the dark, unlit background) creates a sense of tension and disembodiment: it emphatically evokes the atmosphere of the cabaret-spectacle. As an object of the combined gaze of the spectators and the male protagonist, Lucia is displayed as a body/image for their fascination and fantasy. The Dietrichesque dancer (a recurrent topos in postwar cinematic representations of Fascism) is a culturally identifiable fetish, which embodies the legacy of the Third Reich. The cabaret offers a particularly stereotypic type of representation; it implies that the viewer has an immediate, enjoyable identification with the glamorous female performer. Lucia as a body to be looked at is exhibited in highly stylized poses, but one should remember that Marlene Dietrich was often a controller of the look, not just an object of the gaze. Max succumbs to the lure of Lucia's unconventional sexuality and thus empowers her to control the stage. As Lucia/Salomè is dancing, the camera, never level, creates tension. In one shot, when she leans against the column, the camera actually tilts from left to right, a subtle move that conveys the distorted reality of the spectacle. Also, the wall behind the dancer is black and white, emphasizing the horizontal line that cuts through the frame as the camera moves.

112

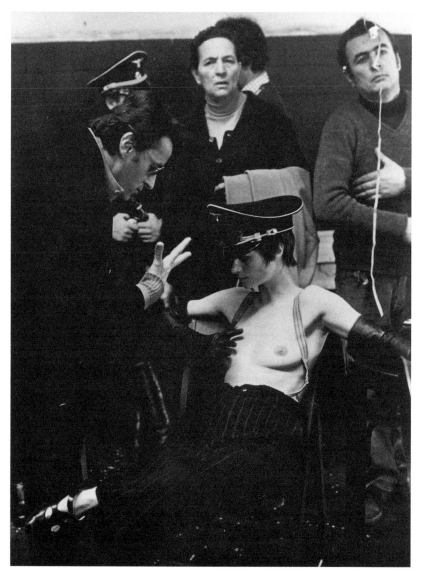

Frame 46. Costume designer Piero Tosi preparing Charlotte Rampling for the cabaret scene

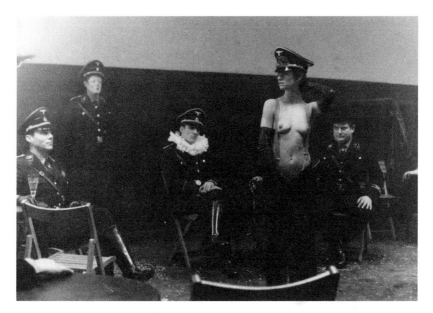

Frame 47. Lucia/Salomè performs in the Nazi cabaret scene

In contrast, the reaction shots (close-ups) of Max are level, as is the delivery of the gift box when the dance is over. Insofar as it is identified with Max, the power of the gaze retains its control over the pleasurable facade of the spectacle: an atmosphere reminiscent of the German expressionist theater that preceded the rise of Hitler. Sets and lighting evoke an eerie phantasmagoria that visualizes the interaction between chaos and power. In this scene, Max's voyeurism (associated throughout the film with sadism, debasement, and the unconscious) takes on the form of fetishistic scopophilia focused on the look alone.[69] The executioner places the gift in front of his victim, so that he may enjoy the precise moment of the unveiling. When the box is brought to Max's table, extreme close-ups allow the viewer to witness Lucia's childlike anticipation (Salomè embodies the child; the Greek word that describes her is the diminutive *korasion*, little girl) reflected in Max's elusive smile. A close-up of his hand wearing a black leather glove as he reaches to uncover the exorbitant offering functions as an eerie artifact. Cavani concentrates on the process by which Lucia's curiosity turns into natural revulsion, a transformation also mirrored in Max's disappointed look. We are not in the inferno of the *Lager* but in that of the cabaret, of "a special cabaret that does not draw from the reality of the concentration camp, but from the iconography that cinema and literature have given us of the *Lager*."[70] Lucia/Salomè offers a parodic and excessive depiction of the Dietrichesque singer, resembling a drag version of the mythical star. The practice of transvestism, which blurs gender distinctions, operates as a symbolic disavowal of the gazer/master. The dance is disturbing because we are horrified at the horror of Lucia's symbolic execution: she stares at her gift in silence as she is bound to share the fate of Herodias's daughter. During this scene, the couple's (childish) body language expresses the regressive nature of their love bond:[71] Johann's severed head seals their complicity in time and space.

Cavani portrays Salomè's dark passion through an astonishing vision of ambivalent sexuality and mimetic desire at work: Lucia/Salomè embodies the double threat of female attractiveness and destructiveness, but it also participates in a decadent attack on patriarchal culture. Cavani's treatment of the Maccabean princess does not draw from the pictorial tradition, which inscribes Salomè's subversive power in narcissism and sensual appetite (as in Beardsley's drawings for Oscar Wilde's play or Moreau's "Salomè Dancing before Herod," which combine a sense of strange beauty with sadomasochistic eroticism).[72] Indeed, Cavani's filmic images enhance the iconography of the cabaret spectacle, with the opening tableau of Pierrots, carnival masks, and macabre setting. Lucia is not the self-reflexive femme fatale embodying a terrible, natural force (like Salomè) but rather a figural representation of the androgyne, or the exaltation of incest (her bondage to the Father), a theme the director would later address in the character of Nina in *Oltre la porta* (Beyond Obsession, 1982).[73] Lucia's dance ruptures the limits of the hierarchical language of power, specifically mocked in the mimetic figurative style of the Dietrichesque number. A ritualistic demystification of Nazism is also embodied in Max's gift (a male gift), which sanctions the brutal reality of dominance. This ritual involves the act of stripping, a clothing metaphor (a constant feature in Cavani's films): Lucia dances as a bare victim of the Death Camp in Fascist regalia (long black gloves and SS cap), a far cry from the elusive veil symbolism associated with the biblical princess. While Salomè's dance draws from this symbol its connotations of deceit and disclosure, Lucia's travesty of a cabaret icon asserts a desire for a naked, unmediated experience. Max's ex-comrades (the lawful defenders of patriarchal culture) must reject the couple's affair and eliminate the dangerous female threat. Thus Cavani's visualization of the cabaret interior, a self-created world of projection and imagination, defines the Lucia/Salomè story as a performance about power: Lucia becomes the unveiled and the unveiler, a threat whether she looks or is gazed upon.

In the framing story of a cabaret siren, an icon of pleasure has been tranfigured into a spectral, haunting site, revealing the interplay of control and subversion, Eros and Thanatos. Lucia empowers herself in the dance scene, but through dance, she also accepts death. The biblical figure faces death as soon as she kisses the severed head of John the Baptist (a gift from Herod). Max and

Lucia represent a predetermined role assigned to them by power; their strength is to accept it. Cavani's originality in treating such a controversial theme is not in their sadomasochistic exchange but in her transformation of Nazi mythology into an ambiguous and creative encounter in history; it is the spectacle that translates Max and Lucia's relationship into repetitive gestures, a sign of sociopolitical fate.

5 _____

Staging the Gaze: *Beyond Good and Evil*

The dream of erotic love takes us to such heights
only so that we can make that leap, from the sky
down to earth, down below.
(*Lou Andreas-Salomé*)

He passed from the depth of night into deepest
night.
(*Thomas Mann*)

CAVANI'S most ambitious film, *Al di là del bene e del male* is also among her most
commercially successful.[1] It recounts the affairs of Louise (Lou) von Salomé
(Dominique Sanda) with Friedrich (Fritz) Nietzsche (Erland Josephson) and
Paul Rée (Robert Powell). Félix Guattari has perceptively called this film an
apologue about the relationship between desire and power: "I felt I was being
watched by a woman. A woman with a composite identity, who is at once
Liliana Cavani, Dominique Sanda, Lou Salomé, but also certain women with
whom I have lived in similar situations."[2] This sensation of "being watched" is
the key to Cavani's mature style. It suggests a departure from the classical
depiction of the gaze and the phallic identification upon which masculinity
relies. Cavani's authorial subjectivity, as Guattari suggests, is opposed in nature
to traditional classifications of authorship. Indeed Cavani's images challenge
the coherence of the male ego. They are disturbing because they call into question the very notion of representation as embodied in the optics of a traditional
(male) spectatorship: they map a topology of seeing otherwise.

In response to such issues, Kaja Silverman has argued in her study of male
subjectivity that the look is situated on the side of desire (and the disposition
of lack), while the gaze is ascribed to "otherness and iridescence."[3] Cavani
strips the male look of its masculine ostentatiousness and strives to dispossess
it of its patriarchal legacy. This translocation is engineered by a form of phallic
divestiture that systematically projects the male subject from a leadership role
to one of subordination via masochism.

Al di là del bene e del male enacts interpersonal conflicts through the characters' attempt to entertain new experiences; to invent life against the decadent
morality of the nineteenth century; to adopt a position of social and sexual
marginality. As Lou declares upon meeting Paul Rée, she simply "wants to

live."[4] In Nietzschean terms, Lou Salomé's experience of life is posited as the most vital law of being: experience is total, hallucinatory, and isolating.

These conflicts are staged through fantasmatic, or erotic, tableaux: the homosexual couplings among the Roman ruins at night, Paul Rée's encounter with a prostitute at the Berlin train station, the ballet scene in Venice, Paul's sodomization. "The fantasmatic generates erotic tableaux or *combinatoires*," points out Silverman, "in which the subject is arrestingly positioned—whose function is, in fact, precisely to display the subject in a given place."[5] Particularly, the tableaux dramatize the shocking encounter of the marginal male subject with (symbolic) castration and specularity, in overt defiance of the classical image of male desire. Fritz's and Paul's hallucinations, dreams, and nightmares are fantastic fragments projected out of the psyche's deepest longings and inhibitions. Cavani's characters share the ideal of subverting traditional models of seeing and knowing. For example, in the opening sequence, Paul's transgressive eye opens the door to Nietzsche's hidden encounter with a prostitute and opium. This scene sets up a succession of witnessing rituals that Cavani renders with fluid camera moves and reflected images: from Lou's and Paul's spying on homosexuals engaged in a sexual encounter to the numerous disruptive, explosive glances that define the interplay between desire and power as a ritual of submission and control. Lou, Fritz, and Paul all seek to liberate themselves from the constraints of fin de siècle European society. But only Lou crosses the boundaries of accepted behavior and remains free. The transgressive process will lead Fritz into madness and Paul into a ritualized initiation into death.

The title *Al di là del bene e del male*, a direct allusion to Nietzschean ethics, refers to the way these enigmatic characters are affected by their life together, beyond the dangerous life-destroying concepts of Good and Evil, which constitute the basis of all morality. They reject structures of domination (marriage, family, the relationship of the couple). Nietzsche perceived the very concepts of good and evil as masks, concealing the self-interest of dominant power groups. Cavani explains: "Nietzsche opposes the type of morality that is gradually instilled into us; he calls for a breach of ideas and for the need to see reality in its true complexity and not merely as black and white. He tries to tip the scale of values in order to see if 'Good' in reality may be evil, and vice versa. From a psychoanalytical point of view, 'Good' and 'Evil' bear a different meaning. There are people who live their sad and painful routine and are frustrated because they lack the courage to invent a way of being. It is a malady."[6]

According to Nietzsche, individuals must first change themselves so that they may change society. They must become undisciplined, unstable, and different. This notion of *différence* constitutes the philosophical perspective that foreshadows the characters' revolutionary experimentation—in relation to which the fantasmatic scenes are also organized. "One day there will begin a new day," proclaims Fritz to Paul at the beginning of the film, "Do you know

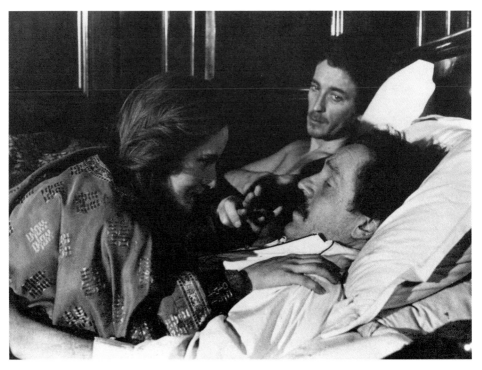

Frame 48. Dominique Sanda (Lou Salomé), Erland Josephson (Friedrich Nietzsche), and Robert Powell (Paul Rée) in *Al di là del bene e del male* (Beyond Good and Evil, 1977)

when? When we will say yes to everything that was once forbidden, scorned, and cursed! Only at that time will we become immoral at last."[7] And he introduces himself to Lou with nihilistic frivolity:

> FRITZ: I am the messenger you were waiting for.
> LOU: What are you announcing?
> FRITZ: Egoism: a wrongly despised virtue.
> LOU: You are speaking to a scrupulous woman.
> FRITZ: And you to the most virtuous man you could ever meet.
> LOU: Why should I believe that?
> FRITZ: The fact that I am immoral.[8]

Cavani's viewpoint reflects the conviction that Nietzsche has radically transformed the whole concept of thinking within the cultural horizons of fin de siècle Europe. At the end of the film, Lou unexpectedly visits her old friend at his mother's house in Naumburg. She finds him playing the same lied by Mahler ("The Song of the Pilgrim") that Peter Gast (alias Heinrich Köselitz) played on the piano during the opening sequence. She gazes into Fritz's blank expression and announces the coming of the new century. His sister Elizabeth interjects: "I don't want any Jews in my house!" Unaffected by her prejudice and hostility, Lou answers: "Can't you hear Fritz? He's playing the music of a Jew." She slowly walks away and approaches her carriage with her face glaringly lit. Her luminous smile greets the future.[9] As the carriage rattles through the autumn light, there are flashbacks of Lou and Fritz mischievously rolling around in the dark pine woods, alone with the sunshine. In the closing shot, we are drawn to the light that emerges and disappears through the time tunnel of trees, a metonym for material progress, the boundless horizon that links the historic future to the present. The carriage travels away from the camera toward the light: these images point back to Lou as the embodiment of Nietzschean subversiveness. In this scene, the fusion of sound and light is physiologically externalized in the perception of the chromatic quality of warm colors accompanied by Gounod's waltz from *Faust*. As Gilles Deleuze states, for Nietzsche, "man imprisoned life, but the superman is what frees life *within man himself*, to the benefit of another form."[10] Lou is instrumental in liberating the "other" speaking voice against the rigid limits of social rationalities (ethnic, sexual, cultural), the various orthodoxies of organizing life that Foucault, in *Les Mots et les choses*, calls an ontology of the annihilation of beings. This ambiguous and precarious being is an iconoclast, like Fritz, who ignites her power to show and reveal the truth. As the ideal figure of the *Übermensch*, Lou embodies a change, the advent of a new form of existence without neurosis.

Lou Andreas-Salomé was a writer, a militant socialist, and a pioneer in the new science of psychoanalysis, who traveled and worked with the cultural elite of Europe (Nietzsche, Rilke, Freud, Wedekind). In *Al di là del bene e del male*, Cavani identifies Lou with "the desire that becomes the point of departure for freedom."[11] However, free desire is a form of scandal. Lou embodies the Nietzschean obsession with transgressive sociointellectual experimentations. She recognizes and accepts herself more than Fritz and Paul will ever accept themselves. In her case, acceptance entails the idea of playing a sexual role that does not have an end in itself but is a creative, deconstructive game countering turn-of-the-century societal values.

What disturbed the critics most about this film was not the erotic content but the games Lou played—and apparently mastered. In our society, it is intolerable that a certain type of female gaze can be directed toward what Guattari calls the "micropolitics of domestic life":

> In fact it is necessary to distinguish between a temporary relationship and a lifetime project that puts into question the very structures of marriage. Nietzsche's sister and family would gladly tolerate a life of concubinage, but not the disruption of a sacred

institution. Therefore, we are confronted with a conspiracy, "a war machine of love," which questions all values established on the exterior and the interior of each character, values introjected, thus assumed. The film shows how this war machine is transformed into an "infernal machine," which tends to destroy the characters.[12]

Lou is not in love with a seductive, transitory experiment; she is of a truly revolutionary mind, which debates the structures of an institution (marriage) of her society. Her eroticism progresses through multiple stages. The male characters' self-destruction suggests the presence of the repressive, external structure that encloses them. In *Al di là del bene e del male*, desire is the starting point for a search for freedom, but its actualization is not permitted by the established powers. These "demonic" revolutionaries are as defeated by their time as Francesco, Galileo, and Antigone were.

───────────

The story takes place in Rome in 1882. Paul Rée, a young Jewish writer from Leipzig, brings a doctor to the Hotel Minerva, where his friend and intellectual mentor Friedrich Nietzsche lies in an opium stupor. Fritz refuses to admit the doctor; on the other hand, he does welcome Madame Thérèse, a prostitute with whom is well acquainted. A distraught Paul is about to leave, but not before peeking through the door at the tawdry encounter. Later on, in the socialist salon of Malwida von Meysenburg, he meets Lou Salomé, a twenty-one-year-old Russian emigrant from St. Petersburg. Both bored, they desert the party and begin to wander among the ruins of the Palatine, where they come upon a homosexual erotic game. Lou's fascination with and avid curiosity about the unforeseen spectacle is counteracted by Paul's traumatized disavowal of this libidinal infraction and by his impulsive desire to marry her, an offer she refuses (as she will later refuse Nietzsche). Yet Lou agrees to an experimental ménage à trois, an erotic and intellectual alliance. But Fritz must reckon with a hysterical Elizabeth, who takes an instant dislike to Lou and will attempt to have her expelled as a Jewess and a political threat.

In an interview with Lietta Tornabuoni, Cavani comments about these characters' creative endeavor:

> The trio inspired me as one character with three heads, with whom one could progressively identify. Today's intellectual is a bourgeois who sits at a desk. These three were not intellectuals; they were artists of existence, experimentalists of life. It was their masculine-feminine psychological ambivalence that stimulated me; it was emblematic of some personal anxieties of mine, which, I believe, are everybody's: we all have different faces and yet we feel we have only one.[13]

And she further explains her view of the complexity of erotic feelings:

Traditionally, a man thinks that he must live with a woman and a woman with a man. In truth, life may be invented, and Lou Salomé tries to invent her life in a ménage à trois. This relationship is not particularly sexual; it consists of a unique relationship among three friends who decide to live together . . . and they might as well have been four or five. Sex does not necessarily play a role in their situation. . . . So you may ask, why would the story of these characters intrigue me? Because they have been very influential for culture, and for the communication of experiences. For better or for worse, their private project became exemplary and symbolic, since these characters recorded their experiences in writing, which was their form of communication. Thus their private life became public. Even though we may emphatically reject it, we do assimilate it on a cultural level.[14]

Nietzsche's friendship with Lou Salomé spans from April through November 1882. In a letter to Paul Rée from Tautenbourg, Lou writes about her long walks with Fritz and praises the blissful state of solitude in which their shared philosophical soul unites with the spirit of nature: "In our dialogues, we unwillingly reach the bottom of the abyss, a dizzying place where one has the sensation of grasping onto solitude and testing the lower depths beneath the surface. We always followed the paths of the chamois, and, should anyone have listened to us, one might have thought that it was an encounter between two demons."[15] Inevitably, jealousies arise between Paul and Fritz over Lou's affections, turning their association into a game of dominance, erotic couplings, in which Salomé often takes on the position of observer of her male interlocutors.

The failure of the experiment brings Lou and Paul to Berlin—where Lou is eventually trapped into marrying the Orientalist Karl Andreas and Paul will end up serving as a doctor in poor neighborhoods. In pursuit of better health, Fritz becomes a wanderer, like Zarathustra. This utterly lonely man goes to Italy: first Venice, a site of intoxicating hallucinations, and then Turin, where in January 1889, after a severe seizure, he is confined to a private asylum. The sudden outbreak of his madness signals his imperiled male identity and its crisis. At the end, the film exposes the social problems of these itinerant "artists of existence": Paul drowns in the river Inn after a brutal sexual assault (an accidental murder or suicide), his violent death played out as a Saint Sebastian masquerade; Fritz is reduced to a shadow of a man, repossessed by his mother and sister; Lou, after a last visit to Fritz, leaves with a younger lover, her ultimate disobedience to the oppressive authority of the male voice. Her action vindicates the Nietzschean questioning faculty that resounds in the world *Ausblick* ("outlook") of the Madman in *The Gay Science* (1882):

"I come too early," he said then; "My time has not come yet. This tremendous event is still on its way, still wandering—it has not yet reached the ears of man. Lightning and thunder require time, the light of the stars requires time, deeds require time, even after they are done, before they can be seen and heard."[16]

For Prometheus, hanging between a world of freedom and a world of bondage, it is the dawn of a new divine power in man.

Summarizing the story of *Al di là del bene e del male* is easy, and interpreting it is even easier if we remain within the parameters of a biographical sketch. But this is not a historical film, although Cavani's dialogues reflect Nietzschean thought—particularly *Ecce Homo* and the philospher's correspondence with his sister.[17] Once again, we are reminded that the types of characters who preoccupy the director in the German trilogy are those who initiate a symbolic inversion of social hierarchies: a female committed to a transgressive encounter (Lucia, Lou, Louise); a man in a historical role of power (Max, Nietzsche, Benno); and a husband who mediates in the background (Anthony Atherton, Karl Andreas, Heinz von Hollendorf). It is not sex at the center of Cavani's thematics, but the familiar topos of death, the will to chaos, or the triumph of Dionysos. In *Al di là del bene e del male*, death is no longer the ineffable rite of expulsion of the earlier films; it has embraced all the possibilities of being, and, at the same time, it has exhausted them. As histrionically formulated in *Also Sprach Zarathustra* ("My death I praise to you, the free death which comes to me because I want it"),[18] Paul Rée's "suicide" and Nietzsche's syphilis (the disease affecting the protagonist of Mann's *Doktor Faustus*, a work Cavani seems to have had in mind)[19] are conscious acts of strong will (*voluntas superior intellectu*). They can be seen as examples of human affirmation in the face of mortality. Death is evoked with laughter, a recurrent and impious desacralization in Nietzsche's writings.

In one of the most critical scenes in the film, Paul pays a prostitute for permission to watch her sexual act with a porter (whom he also pays to perform). The visual articulation of this eerie night scene pivots upon lack and the projection of insufficiency onto the figure of the porter. Paul is the character confronting a black chaos ("l'ignoto"). His drama is visibly shown as the extreme of passivity, a condition of profound excitement and directional energy.[20] Cavani also stresses, in terms that prepare the ground for Paul's death, the primal function of this ritualistic *copula*, which finally releases the voyeur from his inhibitory fascination with Lou: "It is the first step toward an acceptance of his feminine nature."[21] According to the script description of this encounter, the director introduces Paul in a state of hallucination, calling the symbolism of the body into play, as in the later scene of his sodomization. The rhythm of the seminaked human bodies, intensified by the flames of a nearby bonfire, evokes the beast dances of the spring festivals of Dionysos: ritual affirmations of life with all its terror. Representation centers on the cultic symbol of the phallus, whether in the inflated form of the erect member of the porter (an erotic play of universal attraction that Cavani emphasizes by tilting down to a close-up), or in the rigid shape of a bottle, which the drunken revelers forcibly use on Paul for their orgiastic ritual of dismemberment and sacrifice.

Frame 49. The sodomization of Paul Rée

   Both scenes appeal to the primordial resonances of an archetypal rite, in which Paul becomes possessed and metamorphoses into glorious intersubjective alterity, at once part of and irreducible to the world of the same and the other. At the beginning of the sequence depicting Paul's death, Rée is fraternizing with young workers in a local tavern. Later that night, they all walk out in a state of jocose, drunken frenzy. At dawn, the young men lead Paul down a secluded path near the foggy bank of the river Inn and begin to beat him. Throughout this scene, the emphasis lies in the scandalous. The imagery resembles that of Saint Sebastian, a fantastic tableau with which Paul identifies. Within this montage, he is completely naked with his back to the camera. His hands are tied to an abandoned iron crane, and he is held down by a group of men while one uses a bottle as an instrument of sodomy. The final shot frames Paul's contorted body in a violently extreme composition against the abyss below. As a privileged site of inversion, this Dionysian tableau allows the marginalized subject momentarily to take center stage. The spectator inhabits Paul's terrified suffering, in astonishment and complete anguish. These disconcerting images attack fin de siècle decorum and ideology; they function to dissolve the conventions of bourgeois realism. In this sense, the staging of Paul's death embodies heterogeneous forms of masking.[22] Cavani radicalizes the pictorial topos of Saint Sebastian by linking it to the obsessive images of Paul's frightened and yet allured gaze during his nocturnal wanderings with Lou at the Palatine. As Freud has shown, feelings of unpleasure and pleasure trigger unbound excitation. Cavani's epistemological focus on the body as the site of vision suggests that the perceptual field maps the characters' techniques of observation. These flashbacks set in motion the course of mental events, thus sustaining a form of inferential thinking that evokes the sexual tableaux. From the outset, Paul is led to the orgiastic rituals by following Via San Sebastiano.

During the shocking sequence of his sodomization, in a Bacchic delirium of the tearing apart of the body, the fantasmatic transformation of Paul into Saint Sebastian triggers a heteropathic identification. He undergoes a symbolic deliverance from the mysterious numen of the mother (the water of the river is associated with the female) and of other daimones: a frightening moment when the individual stands at the boundary between annihilation and a renewed life. Intoxication is a forerunner of truth. In the scene of Paul's death (portrayed in an extreme long shot), the violence is accentuated by a subtle pacing of the editing that focuses on the convulsions of the soul. Violence hits Paul's flesh as it does the body of the martyred Saint Sebastian.[23] His erotic death is visualized in the iconography that depicts the saint. The sodomization of Paul Rée with a bottle is edited by Franco Arcalli without any lingering on the violent act. Arcalli does not enhance the sadistic impulses of the act of seeing. Ultimately, this scene is inspired by the cry of the Magician in *Zarathustra* for the eternal tortures caused by the cruel huntsman: "Thou mocking eye that stares at me from the dark."[24] In the glowing flesh of the young saint, we perceive the man of the Christian era, weakened by his erotic impulses and crucified in Christ.

Here we find most of the essential characteristics of a libido myth in reversal: original homosexuality, vulnerability, and subjugation. Therefore, the piercing of the arrows of pain comes to signify a state of morbid introversion. Paul's death is an act of union with oneself, and also a self-violation, a self-murder.[25] At the threshold of death, Paul's extended, echoing laughter culminates a mental masquerade of Nietzschean aphorisms: man is his own sacrificer, his own huntsman. Paul Rée has indulged in a personal, tragic fantasy: he dares to cross the *limen* of sexual difference and challenge the phallocentric apparatus of ambient morality. His libido drowns in its own depths (also a predominant image in Nietzsche). The infliction of pain is indeed incidental to the masochist's pleasure. Within this scene, life exhausts itself in the completeness of the moment: an illumination of intoxication and ecstasy, bliss and blasphemy.

The fantasy of the arrow-bottle visualizes Paul's struggle for personal independence: he projects himself of his own free will as a target inviting death. This act of self-exposure is figured in an iconic male image, thus attesting to a final gesture of self-assertion, beyond the stage of unconscious fantasy: Paul looks upon the martyred body of Saint Sebastian both as the subject and the object of a sacrifice. In this scene, Cavani displays a total freedom of thematic invention unbounded by biographical realities.

Paul Rée reappears during the séance set in Professor Staudenmayer's house, in which Lou participates. The exteriorization of Paul's psyche as a "presence" entails the exaltation of the *coincidentia oppositorum*. Paul appears in a pool of light and confesses to his audience, "Since I discovered that I am a woman and had myself violated, I am very happy." The scene concludes with the sound of his paradoxical, insistent, mocking laughter. His laughter recalls Bataille's dazzling spell of laughter that opens up a world of scandalous joy.[26] We are told that the medium had to reach the bottom of the abyss ("dal 'basso' ") to find Paul in the embrace of demons. Only Lou understands Paul's triumphant attitude of anticipatory self-depreciation and bursts into convulsive laughter. Paul's laughter is grounded in excess (from the Latin *excedere*, "to go beyond") and separation. It indicates the moment when the character challenges himself. As Robert Stam puts it, what Nietzsche values in the Dionysian experience is "the transcendence of the individuating ego, led to feel a euphoric loss of self as it is subsumed into a larger philosophical whole."[27] For Cavani, the séance is the most Nietzschean scene in the film: "This man returns from the other world to say that he has become what he is and he is happy. He laughs. Laughter and pleasantry are the first signs of reality, and of seeing the truth. His apparition is Nietzschean. He has become Nietzschean; at last he laughs about himself consciously."[28]

In *Al di là del bene e del male*, dramatization lies in the act of seeing and its multiplicity of passionate questionings and probings. As voyeurs, wanderers, and experimentalists of life, these characters are able to convey their feelings to each other at an emotional and intellectual level. Seeing reveals an interdiscursive network of looks, gazes, and visibilities that constitute the narrative topoi of Cavani's investigation into an erotics of knowledge. Seeing sketches an epistemological terrain that doubles as a topography of desire, mapping the diverse nuances of characters' relations, exchanges, and reflections as discrete zones of visibility. As Gilles Deleuze has clarified, the notion of visibility refers not to the way in which a subject sees (since the subject who sees is himself a locus within visibility) nor to the data of a visual meaning, but to "complexes of actions and passions, actions and reactions, multisensorial complexes, which emerge into the light of day."[29]

Take, for example, Cavani's logic of the gaze in the title sequence, the tangible way in which the director defines the camera as *techne*, or an instrument in the service of representation. In a subtle choreography of moves/gazes, Cavani calls our attention to the cinematic language, its ties to illusion, and our faculty to see. Like an eye wandering around, searching, and wanting to see more closely, the camera pans from the assemblages of monumental facades and, as if attracted by the music of a piano, moves through the window of the Hotel Minerva, where Nietzsche lives. When we are first introduced to

Frame 50. Lou, Paul, and Fritz as voyeurs, wanderers, and artists of life

the philosopher, Paul's look fulfills the role of the observer in any classical representation. But in the opening scene, Fritz's hotel room becomes a place of visibility for male malady, establishing the perceptual themes of light and dark, seen and not-seen. Contrast lighting emphasizes the interplay of bodily visibility/invisibility and creates a sense of visual separation between exterior and interior. Nietzsche is lying on a couch, in casual attire, smoking opium. In the dark reality of his fragmented body (its anatomical figuration reconstructed by close-ups), the familiar visitor is bound to perceive the mental condition that now imprisons his friend's opaque glance. A combination of camera moves (tilts and pans) and sound sets the scene to evoke the fundamental corporeal basis of Nietzschean philosophy. This proved controversial. Fritz's radical postures throughout the film were criticized as inappropriate for a man of thought.[30]

The open doorway, the space behind and in tension with visible actions, is a visual representation of the locus at which the subject either opens to transgression (and achieves knowledge) or remains a voyeur. One must remember that Nietzsche promises insight for the transgressor, and that the acquisition of knowledge is an essential form of transgression. In the films of the German trilogy, the doorway motif is a symbol of approach to the unconscious. The act of seeing represents the breakdown of the *limina* of the existing (social) order and the disclosure of being. The most telling elucidation of this trope occurs at the beginning of *Al di là del bene e del male*, when Paul looks across the threshold of a doorway as Nietzsche engages in sexual relations. Paul Rée's voyeuristic impulses are established as ambiguous. His point of view could be that of looking through a keyhole, similar to looking through a camera view-finder (thus his vision is restricted to a narrow aspect ratio). Only when he crosses the boundary of life and death is he freed from the restraint of voyeur-ism and conventional morality (the message he delivers at the séance). In the scene of Paul spying on Fritz and Madame Thérèse, the centripetal direction of his look focuses on the spectacle that is staged in the foreground.

This radical visibility marks the relation between seeing and being seen throughout the film, a series of witnessings of powerful performances—such as Paul's encounter with a prostitute in Berlin, or that of his (self-)execution. Scenes of violence, nightmares, and hallucinations inscribe the trio's unattain-able dream; they are sculpted into the erotic settings of the tableaux. In *Al di là del bene e del male*, to see is transgression and resistance; to see becomes the experience of being. The characters' search for the place of meaning or truth, in order to master the masks of reality, is dangerous. Ultimately, the bearer of the look must confront his hallucinations, risking madness (Nietzsche's last mask) or even death.

Al di là del bene e del male also mobilizes light. Watching identifies with the camera eye and with the light that brings the images to life. It is the homosexual lovemaking, staged out in the archaeological park of the Palatine, that most brilliantly advances the theme of visual (and sexual) ambiguity. Epitomized in a dialectic of bodily visibilities, the erotic games signify the discovery of a more nocturnal world, a dimension of indefinite unreality where, as Foucault reminds us, Sade had placed sexuality from the beginning.[31] From a distance, we see Paul and Lou framed at the threshold of the Roman ruins, witnessing a group of youngsters' unconventional sexual encounter: the boys, most likely prostitutes, are caressing and kissing an ecstatic, half-naked young man. Paul and Lou were led to this enchanted site going down Via San Sebastiano, guided by a man with his oxen carrying a torch. A dolly shot uncovers the empty paths, conveying a bizarre feeling of mystery and excitation. They make their way through a maze of ancient ruins consisting of arches, pillars, stone walls, and comprising interlocking paths, or "walks." Many shots at the Palatine evoke labyrinthine topographies. Paul and Lou first stop behind a pillar and gaze upon the elusive movements of bodies, lit by a fire casting animated shad-ows.[32] In this sexual vision, the motion of the flames mirrors the sensual cou-pling and rubbing of the bodies, a kind of liberating deployment of sexuality, a transgressive writing with light. Their insistent eyes move in the direction of the hypnotic light that exposes the spectacle to the gaze. The camera pans from the observers to a wide shot of the scene incorporating both players and spectators. The game played by the boys unfolds in an asymmetrical center,

Frame 51. Lou and Paul at the Palatine

Frame 52. The homosexual transgressive games among the Roman ruins

against the ruined boundary of walls. What was initially a casual walk ends up stimulating Lou's visual curiosity. Associated with her desire to see (to know) more, it expresses her distinct form of receptivity and spontaneity. In her discussion of spectatorial embodiments and architectures at the turn of the century, Giuliana Bruno points out, "The lust to find out leads to a fascination with seeing, a perceptual attraction for sites, and consequently the formation of spectacle."[33] Thus Paul and Lou's attraction for the transgressive sides of the visible is embedded in spectacle. "The scene is not demeaning," specify the script directions; "it is very much in harmony with the strangeness of the place and with the mystery that surrounds it: it has rather something magical and ancient: at least all this comes across through Lou's eyes, because Paul seems upset and tries to drag Lou away."[34] Subsequently, the two friends happen to separate and go in different directions. They are oddly driven to a series of erotic tableaux and spy upon the kinetic mapping of the archaeological maze. Paul has been completely possessed by this moment. Forgetful of self, he plunges into chaos, his interior secret masked in his spontaneous offer of marriage to Lou (which concludes the scene). It is sex that both speaks and reveals, provokes and produces: what is presented to "the lust" of the eyes is the zone where one perceives one's being in the crossing of the limits.

In order to heighten the drama at the Palatine, Cavani, rather than focusing on the event itself, concentrates on the characters' faces and their reaction to the scene. She also conveys the ambiguous play between light and dark, as the images flicker on the screen. The scene is lit by flames that project silhouettes of color onto the faces of the observers. The alluring visuality of homosexual erotics is mainly articulated by reaction shots that express the true meaning of the scene: an active gaze transforms the shapes of stone and the undefined bodies in motion into a representational landscape. The effect achieved by Cavani is atmospheric and sculptural. The bodies are lit from below, casting tall shadows to convey a drama of perspectives, a staging that breaks off sensuous limits and draws the eye into itself. The same source of light (the fire) discloses who sees and what is seen in a game of reflections, abrogating the classical distinction between players and spectators. Cavani's compositional strategy is inscribed within a blend of naturalism and fantasmatic transfiguration. The flickering light, supported by the sound of whispering, forces Paul and Lou to intensify their senses, so that they can truly capture this occurrence. The configuration of the scene shows that the archaeological sites are not merely backgrounds: they embody the structure of (unconscious) desire. Throughout the film, fantasmatic scenes interrupt the characters' labyrinthine trajectories. They entail excessive acts that portray being at the limit as a corporeal spectacle of visibility. Erotic excess is a mode of questioning and disturbing value systems; excess, or that which produces "scandal," becomes a "provocation" to overcome current social principles.[35]

In *Al di là del bene e del male* the body is perceived as a social and erotic landscape. This choreography of the gaze mediates all future spectacles. A similar effect is created when Lou and Fritz visit the crypto-portico of the Palatine and scrutinize the ancient Roman frescoes on its walls, barely lit from small windows high above. In the subdued and musky darkness of the subterranean gallery, the erotic scenes (particularly the coupling of two men and a woman) become beautifully transparent. As sexual tableaux, these images transmit the characters' play of desire as well as the (sexual) excitement always emanating from Lou.

Cavani subverts the dynamics of power and pleasure by projecting heterogeneous desire onto the male bodyscape, and by displacing the alignment of masculinity with the spectatorial gaze. The audience must confront a spectacle of (male) pleasures that exist primarily in darkness. What we see at the Palatine is mediated by the effect that the tableaux have on the voyeurs. Our sense of what is happening depends on how much we can reconstruct from Paul and Lou's dynamics of looking. Cavani sets an imaginary stage for a pagan ritual of beauty and unbound sexuality, a game of inferential transgression visually encoded in the bodies of the young participants, who appear as ethereal phantoms. She interprets the scene in a warm, earthy tone, which evokes the sphere of the unconscious. Its explicit sexual imagery speaks of fantasy and representation played around the bodyscape:

> In the nineteenth century, and still today, what are so many Northern scholars or elegant bourgeois foreigners searching for in Italy? The beauty of nature, the remains of classical antiquity, the culture of the past, but also a fantastic, free, pagan happiness, embodied in beautifully gracious boys and girls, similar to the ones portrayed in the ancient vases and sculptures. For many, the descent to the South has been a vitalizing experience, an initiatic journey of self-discovery, surrendering themselves to sensations and desires that were once repressed.[36]

For Paul, the erotic tableaux are a lookout point. He is highly attracted and repulsed by the act of seeing. His excitement and marriage proposal to Lou counteract his feelings of impotence and entrapment. This is significantly expressed in the shadowy figure of one of the boys, who breaks away from the group and is "overtaken by a true and strong *fou rire*."[37] The boy's laughter echoes in the night for an instant; it widens the range of the audience's perception of the visual images: it is the sound that attracts Paul into the labyrinth of the Roman ruins. To interpret the reaction on Paul's face (enhanced through close-ups), we foresee the beginning to a journey of self-discovery, of mastering repressed feelings. In *Al di là del bene e del male*, as we have seen, laughter has cognitive meaning; it signals a process of unveiling. The irrevocable moments at the Palatine consume Paul throughout his life. In the form of flashback images they build up to the erotic fantasy of his tragic annihilation.

Within this configuration, the unconscious establishes the virtual source of light in the film.

At the deepest level, Paul's spiritual adventure lies in integrating and normalizing his psychological complexity. His reaction to these night encounters disguises an atavistic memory of fear. He is seduced by the shocking body movement of the players, but he also experiences a childlike inebriation at finding in Lou a possible redeemer. Voyeuristic impulses bring us back to childhood. A similar case of obsessive compulsion for looking is shown in another controversial scene: the ineffable game of watching Lou urinate into a Chinese vase at the time the trio lives in Leipzig. Lou's playful act of enslavement introjects a kind of regression to childhood for both Fritz and Paul. As Eros turns creative, it inhabits infantile plenitude and unity. In Guattari's words:

> The micropolitics of the superman is conducive to "becoming a child." The micropolitics of desire forces Paul to question his own sexuality, and to become a woman. Lou's micropolitcs achieves the goal of her becoming a poetic and literary being. In reality, we have nothing to do with the subjective polarities of man-woman, but with something that relates to childish love or poetic love (which are nonetheless also true loves) more than a traditional oedipal situation.[38]

Throughout the film, Lou is the irradiating center of playfulness. For Lou, sexuality without sex is a way to resist the agency of sex, which ties desire to matrimonial rites. Her view relates to the agonistic relations between free beings. She strives for a different type of relationship that is unique in our social field. In *Al di là del bene e del male*, the objective world of virility is construed by the gaze; knowledge of this world comes through the senses; the characters' subjective mode of experiencing life is framed at the threshold of perception and cognition. They travel. It is the travel of Faust: to immerse the spirit in temptation, not to save it.

This is recorded in the visual documentation of their life together in a photograph taken in Lucerne on 13 May 1882 by Jules Bonnet. The photographer's studio is a Nietzschean pantheon of the future, a site dedicated to the creative medium of the new art of photography. In the picture, Salomé is standing in a cart holding a horsewhip, being drawn by Fritz and Paul. The whip signifies actions that traditionally violate moral norms. The composition, which in Cavani's film duplicates the original historical document, is faithful to a certain extent: the detail of Lou standing higher than the two men. The photographer has been instructed by Fritz to catch them in such a playful, odd posture. Cavani visualizes the ambiguity of Lou's appearance in a pose of sexual dominance, an erotic embodiment of male deviant desire (in her other hand, she holds a bouquet of flowers).

But Lou's female desire consists of living to the limits of the experiential and of transgressing those limits with enthusiasm. She is engaged in reality, not fantasy, and she gets into trouble when the two are integrated. In fact, this

Frame 53. A re-creation of the photograph by Jules Bonnet originally taken in Lucerne on May 13, 1882

scene is a flashback that surfaces to sanction the end of the trio's experiment, when Lou is coerced into marrying Karl Andreas. During the emotional scene in which she informs Paul of Karl's attempted suicide, she glances up at a framed photograph on her desk. Then the film cuts to the flashback of the actual scene of the photograph's being taken. The photograph memorializes a moment within the erratic trail of these itinerants at the height of their ménage à trois. It crystallizes an image of erotic playfulness in the visual texture of the film. After the flashback, Lou grabs the photograph and smashes it to pieces. The still image is the fetishist object of an erotic experimentation that has been interrupted by Karl. It becomes a locus of the articulation of filmic meaning. From this scene onward the film builds upon a hallucinatory atmosphere of dramatic confrontation (the ballet sequence), which significantly reinforces Nietzsche's slipping into madness. As Cavani puts it, it is as if "the characters were in a horse race one behind the other."[39]

In the relationship interconnecting Lou Salomé, Paul Rée, and Friedrich Nietzsche, conventional gender roles seem to dissolve. In the project of the "sacred trinity," Cavani sees a transgression of what one commonly calls masculine and feminine: sometimes the man seems to be Lou, Fritz and Paul the woman. Indeed the most important thing, even if it is at an unconscius level for Lou, is to break the roles, to confront knowledge with a criterion that could be either masculine or feminine. I think that Lou saw herself primarily as a "being," not as a man or a woman. This was clear for her, and partly for Paul. Fritz may seem the most violent in his desire to destroy the myths, certain behavioral modes; in reality, under certain aspects, he is the most traditional of the three except in certain particular moments that I thought I could detect in his work. . . . In my opinion, what fascinates these two men (about Lou) is a certain ambiguity. The great charm of Lou is in her having somehow something of a boy. Not an ambiguous femininity, as one would say today, but more mentally "ephebic" than physically.[40]

It is the female character who undertakes to assert a desire of her own. Lou's trajectory is mobile, carrying her within the boundaries of new forms of desire. In her, female pleasure rests on the dynamics between ambiguity and complicity with male desire. But Lou never submits to erotic dominance, as is clear from her refusal to adapt to Karl Andreas's phallic monopolizing desire. She remains unscarred even by what may seem a compromise. In the moment of her breaking (Karl's suicide attempt), she retains power over her body. Cavani's Salomé is positioned at the *limina* of the patriarchal order. She denounces its logic; she embodies its deviance. If "the episteme of the Feminine is anarchy," as Cavani says, then Lou *is* the world of the Feminine.[41]

In Cavani's cinema there are no ordinary modalities of life, such as the ones codified by the bourgeois family. Lou's distaste for all that defines the perfect model of a Russian housewife (from which she has escaped) makes her sensitive to experimenting in an environment hostile to such experimentations, particularly when women are in control of the action. The power of the tradition that Lou defies vividly informs the character of Elizabeth Förster-Nietzsche. Elizabeth's mad rage makes a spectacle of female hysteria. In one scene in the script, enraged by her brother's tardiness for lunch, Elizabeth violently dissects "with her nails and hands a roasted leg of pork as if she were dissecting the body of a mortal enemy."[42] In the actual film, the pork roast is replaced by a chicken (a more visual figuration of *sparagmos*). The entire scene is shot in one continous take. Elizabeth is filmed in a cavernous, dark environment sitting alone at the head of a formal dining table. As the clock strikes, the camera dollies toward her as she peremptorily instructs Trud, the maid, to serve her. The ticking of a clock paces her movements. She stares at the dish, slowly puts down her knife and fork, and begins to dismember the meat. The camera zooms in on her hands and then tilts up to the reaction of the shocked maid. This civilized individual, who eats on the hour, forgets herself and becomes a savage as an antidote to Lou's imposing presence. Here we are given a corporeal spectacle of visibility, a strategy of degradation and puerile irreverence that

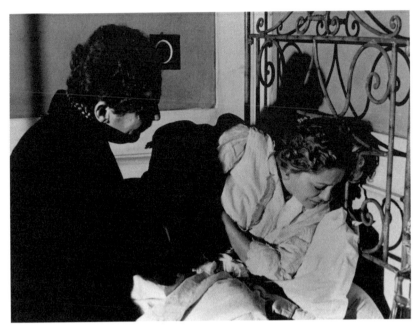

Frame 54. The hysterical Elizabeth Förster-Nietzsche (Virna Lisi) being comforted by her brother

employs a kind of surgical mutilation to translate the pathological stigmata of cultural rigidity. The following morning, Elizabeth is caught voraciously devouring a Bavarian pie for breakfast; after an altercation with Lou, she is overcome by fury and regurgitates. Elizabeth's lust for food exposes the vulnerability of her individual identity: her neurotic reaction can be defined as an impulse to appropriate authority from Lou—who is perceived as a rival and whose power must be incorporated. Her histrionic acts stage an infantile scenario that unveils and reenacts the discovery of prurient family secrets (unresolved incest fantasies and fears). These scenes are intercut with a flashback of Elizabeth and Fritz as children gazing upon their aunt Augusta's sensuous cleansing rituals. Erotic impulses and hysterical behavior converge in this visual representation of female malady. Elizabeth is intense in physicality. In the film, the strictures of official culture, which define Elizabeth Föster-Nietzsche's sexuality, are realized in Virna Lisi's powerful performance: loss of control, dismay, and defeat unmask the social proprieties Nietzsche's sister valued and exploited.[43] For this role, Lisi won Best Supporting Actress at the Venice Film Festival.

In the second half of the film, we find the characters at the limits of the will. Now they wander from dark to dark, through hallucinations and deliriums, in a maze haunted by the hegemonic image of death. The climactic point is the

Frame 55. Fritz encounters Doctor Dulcamara (the Devil) in Venice

Frame 56. The mask of death

Frame 57. Nietzsche's hallucinatory reactions to the ballet of Good and Evil

moment at which Fritz encounters Doctor Dulcamara (the Devil) in Venice
and is led into a game of perpetual entrapment: the ballet of Good and Evil.
"The ballet changes the tone and the rhythm of the film," Cavani admits, "in
the beginning, the rhythm was rational, and later it is emotional. By becoming
mad, Nietzsche allows Paul Rée to be a homosexual and allows himself to turn
into a child. . . . I was not interested in 'sex' but in their complicity, a feeling
stronger than friendship and love."[44] In a scene shot in an obsessive Kafkaesque
mood, the enchantment of the dance stems out of its inherent ambiguity between resemblance and illusion, as in a play of mirrors reflecting dreams and
visions. To the senses, the ballet appears deceivingly real/surreal, rational/
magic: it embodies the ultimate challenge of the opposites. Framed at the margins, and leaning against a wall, Fritz watches the material embodiment of his
nightmares. Good and Evil perform at center stage in an empty, dark room.
The warm light projected onto the bodies of the dancers enhances a game of
instincts, impulses, and seduction. Animated shadows are cast on the walls,
visualizing this final confrontation. In the last years of his life, Nietzsche increasingly used the image of the dance as a metaphor for his thought.

The poetic dimension of this scene rests on the purely visual nature of these
antinomies, reinforced by the film's use of chiaroscuro lighting. The two naked
male dancers perform an outrageous erotic drama: a red-haired man (the Devil)
takes off his mask and begins to dance with a young man (Christ). Fritz is

Frame 58. A scene from the ballet

Frame 59. The dancers (Amedeo Amodio and Robert José Pomper)

attracted to the spectacle by the sound of whispers. The ballet enacts a sacrificial rite. The duality of good and evil is subliminally unified in death: in the end, Evil strangles the Good. Dance, lightness, and laughter are the attributes of Dionysos. For Nietzsche, the creator is a dancer. Thus the ballet surpasses the domain of narrative by visually dramatizing (Nietzschean) ideas. At different levels of tension, it entails a perceptible metaphor of knowledge.

Fritz's hallucinations in Venice freeze narrative time. The descriptive function of the dance universalizes the motif of going in and out of light. This scene is atemporal since it occurs in Nietzsche's mind. His isolation has forced him into an abyss wherein reality has vanished. Another compelling scene is his encounter with Doctor Dulcamara in Piazza San Marco. All around him there is coldness. This scene opens from the back of Fritz's coat as he walks away from the camera. At a distance, Dulcamara enters the frame from the left and walks past him. As this mesmerizing figure exits the frame, there is a cut to Nietzsche's reaction: when he turns his head, we see a close-up of a man wearing a white mask (the typical mask of a Venetian doctor of the nineteenth century). Dread overcomes him as he approaches the exulting Dulcamara, now transformed into a naked man staring at him with demonic contempt, casting a sinister shadow upon Nietzsche, almost the phantasm of a horrible Faustian pact. This is followed by a series of shots of Nietzsche intensely staring at this apparition as it walks away toward the canal. The black cape of the mysterious apparition is a phallic symbol of copulation. The opacity of the man's stare sets up a spectacle in which the gazing subject is being dispossessed to its limits: the dancer stands still, naked, his cape blowing in the wind. The final shot is of Dulcamara standing on a gondola departing in silhouette (identified with water, Dionysos stands for uninhibited libido).

Fritz's hallucinatory state is interrupted by the sounds of waves, which bring him back to reality. Dulcamara's elusive features become a haunting omen:

> He has a long black cape that reaches down to his feet and an old-fashioned black, broad-brimmed hat. His appearance is impudent and full of charm. He gradually gets closer and closer, and just when he is about to come across Fritz, a gust of wind blows the cape open for an instant: the man is revealed naked. Fritz is the only one to have noticed that a white body wriggles within the dark material of the cape. Fritz becomes disturbed. He turns his head and tries to follow the figure with his eyes, but loses him from sight.[45]

It is a young gondolier (Christ) who eventually leads Fritz to approach Doctor Dulcamara for a cure for his syphilis. He is given seven more years to live. In *Al di là del bene e del male*, Cavani's approach to storytelling has been altered in an ostensive way: she seems to show more than tell; she demands that we master the nuances of the experience of seeing. As Giovanni Grazzini writes, this film is "a page of transgressive history in which the Nietzschean conflict between Dionysos and Christ is colored in poetry."[46]

As in the stellar firmament there are sometimes two suns which determine the path of one planet, and in certain cases suns of different colours shine upon a single planet, now with red light, now with green, and then simultaneously illumine and flood it with motley colours: so we modern men, owing to the complicated mechanism of our "firmament," are determined by *different* moralities; our actions shine alternatively in different colours, and are seldom unequivocal—and there are often cases, also, in which our actions are *motley-coloured*.[47]

Cavani's characters engage in a fight that can never be won; hence the Dionysian melancholy in her films of the trilogy.

6

Theatricality and Reflexivity in *The Berlin Affair*

> As the philosophy of professors exclaims, there is de-
> sign and unity in universal history, but in the life of
> every individual. . . .
> (*Arthur Schopenhauer*)

A PROVOCATIVE story of forbidden love in prewar Germany, *Interno berlinese* continues Liliana Cavani's examination of transgressive relationships. Her view about the very possibility of such relationships grows more scandalous as she adapts Junichirō Tanizaki's novel, *Manji* (The Buddhist Cross, 1928–1930), to a Westernized setting. The director admits that she was utterly captivated by Tanizaki because of his passionate idealism and his "uncanny ability to guide us inside the most minute action."[1] In translating the Japanese story for the screen, Cavani brings the action forward in time, placing it in the Berlin of 1938 amid the upper echelons of the diplomatic corps.[2] Adolf Hitler is poised to march into Austria. On the home front, the Führer pursues his "purifying" campaign against every aspect of the national life opposed or indifferent to the politico-ideological features of Nazism. The very daring of Cavani's approach has perhaps contributed to the film's historical neglect, but in the context of today's newly awakened multicultural awareness, Cavani's film reasserts its revolutionary conception of gender, ideology, and cinema itself—particularly in her radical exploration of interiors as a concrete metaphor for subjective interiority.

The film begins with the obsessive attraction of the wife of a German diplomat, Louise von Hollendorf (Gudrun Landgrebe), for the daughter of the Japanese ambassador to Germany. Louise sees Mitsuko Matsugae (Mio Takaki) at the Institute of Fine Arts, where they both take drawing lessons with the art instructor Joseph Benno (Andrea Prodan), an earlier conquest of Mitsuko's compelling charm. Captivated by the Oriental girl's beauty, Louise uses her as a model for her sketching exercises. Gradually she is entrapped in an unconventional affair. Louise will carry her obsession to a suicidal end that also involves her husband Heinz (Kevin McNally), an ambitious career officer at the Ministry of Foreign Affairs. Mitsuko eventually plays the married couple off against each other until their affair with her is publicly censured by the regime's high command (Heinz is asked to resign, and he is threatened with deportation). In a typical Japanese ceremonial ritual, all three drink poison. But hours

Frame 60. Gudrun Landgrebe (Louise) and Mio Takaki (Mitsuko) in *Interno berlinese* (The Berlin Affair, 1985)

later, to Louise's bewilderment, she awakens and understands that Mitsuko intended to take Heinz instead of her. Cavani confesses: "I really do not know how to interpret Louise's survival. Even after reading the book I kept asking myself this very question: whether you love the person you leave behind or the one who remains with you."[3]

Cavani treats the relationship between Mitsuko and her three erotic "adepts" as that of a mystical body of worshipers and their mysterious, enigmatic goddess. In the film, says the director, we detect the "symbols of a private, interior cult that dominates the exterior; it is a cult rooted in myth, the fantastic, and religion. . . . Ultimately, it is the story of an idol and her adepts: in many ways, it is a 'religious' story."[4] Its enactment within this particular historical moment is obviously intentional.[5] This is the period of Germany's Nazification, in a climate of heavy moralistic enforcement, a necessary condition for the manic defense mechanisms that served to mold effective national obedience. The elegant formalism of the diplomatic corps in Hitler's Berlin creates a climate of rigorous conformity and moral control of the life of the individual. It also conveys the elaborate narcissistic foundation of the Germans' relation to the Führer and to the ideology of National Socialism. The Japanese girl alters this conformist and hygienic life.[6] Her deployed narcissism comprises difference (as boundless diversity) and otherness as a threat that intrudes from the outside: she represents the breakdown of powerful collective identifications. At first, it is only Louise who is attracted to Mitsuko, but later on she will have to share her lover with both her own husband and an ambiguous foreigner, the art instructor Joseph Benno. It is he who constitutes the fourth point of the "Buddhist Cross" (an archaic swastika) that inevitably yokes them together and seals their tragic destiny.[7] For Louise, Mitsuko embodies a fantasy of recapturing the purity of the self unmediated by group (psychological) conventions. "Perhaps," Cavani argues, "personal emotions intensify only when there is an evil regime on the 'outside.' "[8] In a country that has put all its faith in the Führer, this private scandal can only end in a spectacular ritualization of Eros and Thanatos.

In *Interno berlinese*, Nazism is the ideological pyramid that functions as a point of departure for the narrator's memory. It serves as an ideal foil to the acting out of the intensely personal "religion" embodied by Mitsuko and her three adepts. The director's objective is clearly stated:

> For me, a dictatorship is the most irreligious moment in history, because its leader and the hierarchies in power take the place of a divinity, while instead they are a caricature. As a consequence, they cause imagination to become scandalous and impossible, and also religion that feeds on fantasy. . . . With their religious passion that has nothing in common with dictatorship, my characters are not anti-Nazi; however, they become "other" than Nazism, which they oppose, even if it is not overtly expressed in the film.[9]

In the opening scene, Louise represents the world of individual thought by re-creating her past experience on the stage of history.[10] She recounts her story in flashback to an old university professor, who is blacklisted by the regime owing to his controversial erotic books. *Interno berlinese* unfolds as a kind of *Kammerspielfilm*, even though it avoids the temporal strictures of the classical German model. All major drama occurs within the same interiors: from the Professor's study (the central representational nucleus of Louise's process of invention), to the Art Institute, to the chambers of the erotic encounters (the brilliance and suffocation of Louise and Mitsuko's couplings). The very premise of the film, as a reviewer points out, implies that the characters are linked by a common cultural complicity so that their playful, scandalous game is plausible and the spectator/voyeur may participate: this game originates "from within" and always interprets the logic of the outer world.[11]

Louise is the focal character whose voice for the viewer is authoritative. She tells the Professor how she was driven by an obscure imperative to surrender to Mitsuko's spell of seduction and enslavement. As the scene opens, we see the Professor in a long shot seated in silhouette, typing an inscription from Schopenhauer. The bell rings, and he opens the door to an elegant lady who seats herself at his desk and begins to tell her story. Her voice and manner attempt to conceal her profound nervousness, betrayed by her lighting a cigarette with trembling hands.

Throughout the film, Louise is the narrative reflective presence; Mitsuko is the specular, visual icon. They represent two facets of Cavani's vision. In order to enhance the illicit lesbian relationship, Cavani places Mitsuko in front of paintings (which are in soft focus) and limbo backgrounds to create the effect of looking into deep space. When she cuts to reversal shots of Louise, she composes her within the rectangular frames of windows or doorways—the regularity of plane geometry, which tends to enforce a sense of psychological entrapment. She portrays this unbridgeable alienation by visually framing Louise against gates, fences, and walls, her gaze often interrupted by figures or objects placed in her line of sight. Louise looking through the iron gate at the Japanese Embassy, trying to catch a glimpse of Mitsuko, exemplifies the inaccessibility of the young woman. Louise's passion for Mitsuko is literally barred. As Louise is increasingly subjected to the cruel disclosure of Mitsuko's sexual audacity (her encounters with Benno at the Hotel Leipzig, her deviant lovemaking to Heinz while Louise is lying next to them in a state of semiconsciousness), she becomes a captive of desire, tormented by the entangled interrelationship orchestrated by the Japanese idol. This desire is clarified by the initial allusion to Schopenhauer. Ultimately, as Hayden White writes, Schopenhauer professed to unveil life as it really was: "a terrible, senseless striving after immortality, an awful isolation of man from man, a horrible subjection to desire, without end, purpose, or any real chance of success."[12]

Behind Louise's imaginative authority as a narrator, there is the Kierkegaard-ian dialectical reduplication of the truth, a process that comprises finding what has been lost and awakening it to life anew. This is an indispensable premise of the emotional logic of *Interno berlinese*: it constitutes the narrative frame of the film, which is not a confession. For Kierkegaard, repetition connects to the essence of creation; thus the aesthetic reveals the religious. It bears comparison to the Platonic *anámnesis*, or recollection, the truth as a summons to the pri-mordial image: we can know only what we re-cognize. Louise's quest is for the re-creating of an experience that is between memory and oblivion, grieving and nostalgia. Recollection becomes a process of self-projection within an inte-rior space, a kind of teleological suspension. Just before the first flashback, Cavani begins with a medium shot of Louise, who remarks to her silent inter-locutor, "It all began when I stopped coming to your literature classes, as a matter of fact when the party forced you to resign owing to political motiva-tions." The camera proceeds to show Louise arriving in front of the Art Insti-tute. The Steadicam first picks up Mitsuko stepping out of her car, assisted by a chauffeur. Throughout the film, Cavani cuts to Louise's face witnessing the unfolding of events. The self of the story is already a differential repetition grounded in the economy of telling as consciousness. During this entire open-ing scene, the music is set to a rhythmic heartbeat, underscoring Louise's un-easiness. The sound track, composed by Pino Donaggio, supports not only the dramatic theme of the film but also its religious aura: it evokes a visual interplay between light and dark, corporeal fullness and lyrical abstraction.[13]

Louise's dialectical interpretation of memory has insistent correspondences with visual metaphors: the eye is the ideographical sign of the film. Memory becomes the real name of one's relationship to oneself, or, as Deleuze puts it, "the affect on self by self."[14] Cavani underscores the individuality of the re-peating voice; she has realized the superiority of representing the first person, as it surfaces in the eye of memory. Louise's initial recollection is shot from a subjective point of view. Cavani exercises "the modality of the physical eye," which establishes a temporary identification between the character and the spectator.[15] Louise's storytelling seeks a conclusion that can lead to a new be-ginning (repetition is oriented to the future). The end of the film emphasizes the tension of culture on the margins: before the Professor is arrested by the Gestapo, he hides a manuscript inside a box of chocolates, which he hands over to Louise. She is entrusted with the publication of his last novel, a gesture of acknowledgment from the former mentor to his disciple.

In this view, the speaking subject has entered into the order of signification and has crossed the boundaries that separate her from the coercive imaginary relations of Nazism. Cavani associates the couple's erotic performances with history and with the political body in prewar Germany by universalizing the terms of representation—most prominently the narrative architecture of catas-trophe and pathos. As the only survivor of the Buddhist Cross, Louise refuses

Frame 61. The Aryan model at the Berlin Institute of Fine Arts

to assume the traditional role of mourner: she consciously and creatively inhabits the frame of storytelling to move beyond the condition of loss. She becomes aware that she shall never know why the idol chose to leave her behind. Her physical endurance attests to the remarkable self-control of this lover/heroine. Her discourse enacts a ritual of ecstatic mourning for meaning, for beauty, for transcendence. Louise insists on the testamentary dimension of every word she utters during her last encounter with the Professor. She emphasizes two essential features of the German society of her day: the public character of existence (the participation mystique) and its pronounced verticality of differences.

Such differences are carefully staged in the visible signs of deviant love affairs. They address the morality of everyday conduct, private life, and pleasure. At the Art Institute, Joseph Benno reprimands Louise for repudiating the German model in favor of Mitsuko ("The Institute provides a splendid Aryan model and you continue to ignore it"). The low-angle shot of the art instructor reminds us of power and authority; the echoing sound of his footsteps accentuates Louise's act of transgression.

Another ostentatious example occurs when Louise and Heinz participate in the plot to uncover General Werner von Heiden's homosexuality and practically ruin his career. The sequence begins with the couple in an elegant dance hall, where Louise entices the young piano player to her home. The tension between the pianist (the general's lover) and the von Hollendorfs is created by the editing and the low-angle geometrical shots (a certain insistence upon a frontal mise-en-scène). The decor in Heinz and Louise's house is cold, with its jagged edges of shadows and walls, its sparse furniture. The sets are designed to construct strong linear patterns, framing the human figures.[16] These images of the individuals listening and gazing into space create the effect of a static dance of despair. When the music stops, Heinz's cousin Wolf reveals himself as a high-ranking officer in the Gestapo. Upon leaving, von Heiden calls attention to the illusion of (heterosexual) conformity: "It is impossible to defend oneself against vulgarity." In reviewing the film, Alberto Moravia singles out Louise's comments upon her role in the moralizing campaign of the regime.[17] She describes her involvement in the homosexual trap: "It was a lynching . . . in my own house . . . the moralizing campaign was in reality a defamatory, purging campaign against those generals and officers who were an obstacle . . . during those days I intensely thought of Mitsuko as of a refuge." These so-called perversions, intimately associated with sentiments of inferiority and isolation, are means to escape from the psychological stagnation that prevails in public life. They exalt the characters' independence of social exigencies.

There is no deception practiced on the audience as the flashbacks occur. The chronological organization of the narrative evokes the nostalgic reemergence of scenes wherein transgression of the historical time itself originates.[18] Cavani establishes a sense of nostalgia during Louise and Mitsuko's first encounter at the art studio, where Mitsuko's beauty is seen to embody both a perfect form and an archaic conception of corporeality. Throughout the film, Louise perceives Mitsuko as an ethereal vision (the art lessons), a physicality (the sexual encounters), and a spirituality (music and light). In the end, Mitsuko evokes the ambiguity of "the sweet angel of death" (as Lino Miccichè calls it)[19] that Visconti envisioned in Tadzio, the young aesthetic idol of Aschenbach in *Morte a Venezia*. In contrast to Arcalli's editing strategy in *Il portiere di notte*, which conveys the compulsive quality of the protagonists' regression, in this film, the editor, Ruggero Mastroianni, selects a more linear and controlled style—as does the actress Gudrun Landgrebe in her approach to her role.

On the other hand, Mitsuko appropriates for her own use the one type of feminine authority the culture admits as legitimate for an idol. The enticing performance of Mio Takaki is gestural; it evokes the ritualistic nature of religious ceremonies and their rhetoric of allusion and silence. Her impenetrable face (self-contained like that of a Japanese theater mask) is heavily made up, while her measured and subdued tone of voice reveals an aggressive sexuality. Her elusive *figura* disturbs the spectators' expectations. She embodies a heterosexual female fantasy. When Louise draws Mitsuko's portrait in her home, the model is seated in front of a dark background. Such spiritualization of the human face is despatialized in the close-ups, the exchange of glances heightened by eyeline-match editing. Mitsuko's face fills the frame, her strong-willed eyes fastened upon Louise. These shots disclose Mitsuko as a temptress, who lures Louise into the tumultuous depths of a life that knows no limits. Mitsuko proceeds to dress Louise in a kimono; she wraps the obiage around her waist: the silk sash becomes an object of play and tension as she pulls Louise toward her. Amid the subdued sounds of the rustling clothes, the women kiss and make love on the floor. It is a play of pure performance, which visualizes a divestiture leading to the abrogation of racial difference. At the end of the film, Mitsuko uses the obiage to tie herself to Heinz and Louise in the suicide ritual.

As the source of Louise's initiation into the sacred mysteries of Eros, the Japanese woman retains an instinctive alliance with the erotic through the sublimated form of the transgressive sexual act. Copulation recaptures its ancient pathos. Death takes on a special dimension, which is urgent, essential, religious, and mythical.[20] As for Tanizaki, sexual transgression, formalism, and classicism are the dominant traits of Cavani's filmic structure. Her approach to Eros and sexuality might be viewed as a kind of palimpsest in which classical culture is overwritten by modern formulations: Sade (particularly La Philosophie dans le boudoir, 1795), Bataille, and Artaud. Cavani discards sex per se (as a genital act); she envisions sexuality as the multicentered creative stage of theatricality. Eroticism combines sophisticated gestural freedom and stylized pathos. The slow, stylized erotic "dance" performed by the transgressive couple in the interiors virtually opposes the strict movements of the military displays (the realities of official power) on the outside. The Cavanian interior poetically suggests the possible transcendence of social (and historical) tensions.

Once again Cavani defines the meaning of life, self-contained and provocative, against the micropolitics of desire, a trait of Cavanian characters that often brings them to express their sexuality beyond any conventional male/female definition.[21] In Interno berlinese, women disclaim man's virtual monopoly over power. For Cavani, eroticism is a strategy that deploys a transgressive cinematic language: the violation of sexual taboos is reflected as a violation of discursive norms.[22] In common with Luis Buñuel, a filmmaker she admires, Cavani links formal to sexual and social transgression. This is especially manifested in the sexually scandalous scenes in Mitsuko's Japanese setting, where we are shown the ritualistic theatricality of erotic performances. The claustral intimacy afforded by this relationship embodies fantasies of centrality, unity, and mastery, in sharp contrast with the familiar notions of rupture and fragmentation empowered by the Nazi imagination. The interiority of these characters is objectified in interior settings and transgressive rituals: the traditional cinematic space assigned to the female subject (the domestic space) is transformed into a locus of ecstatic orgasm and violent ideological critique.

Mitsuko is the true master of the action. Her cruel game of enchantment is executed through the narrative figuration of ceremonial rituals of divestment: from the initial gift of the kimono, a ceremonial object of initiation that attracts

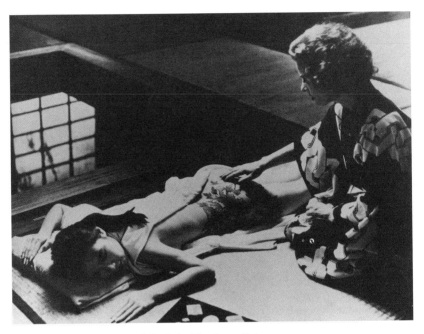

Frame 62. The mystique of the forbidden love affair

Frame 63. Continuation of the same scene

Louise into a new erotic alignment (the symbolic stripping away of her Western sartorial exuberance); to the gradual undressing in which Mitsuko reveals a tattoo as her exclusive ornament; to her dressing up as a geisha, a blinding sensuous epiphany. Throughout the film, men's attire symbolizes male devotion to Hitler's mad fantasy of self-abnegation and duty. These erotic scenes rely on controlled, mechanical postures, supported by a display of intricate clothing. The act of drinking is also a recurrent motif, ranging from tea ceremonies to the consumption of intoxicants, to the final collective suicide by poisoning.[23] In Japanese culture, ritual hara-kiri represents victory over the material world. For Cavani, suicide represents the "true use of one's body."[24] Ultimately, the orgasmic spasms of love connect to the spasms of death. Photographed from a predominantly low-angle camera position, with the characters at the center of a scenographic space, the erotic encounters of the interior celebrate a scandalous repudiation of the exterior (bleak, shadowless, gray, wet). Two worlds thus face each other on the proscenium, the inner space of individual fantasy and the broader external space of historical discourse, each playing out its real drama. During Mitsuko and Louise's last encounter inside the Japanese Embassy, the lovers are interrupted by the sounds of guards and their dogs as they project their ominous silhouettes on the paper screens, foreshadowing the manipulation of the soul masterfully practiced by Hitler's regime. As noted earlier, the von Hollendorfs are threatened with deportation when the liaison between the two women is disclosed.

The libido displayed by the logic of the stylized copulations is reduced to well-defined looks, exchanges of gazes, movements, and postures. In the films of the German trilogy, Cavani exalts the shifting of gender roles, freed from social inhibitions. Pleasure and dread are experienced in such a way as to evoke a kind of Bataillian excess.[25] Death becomes the excess of life itself over rupture. Cavani's images capture the contradictory nature of violation. She exploits historical interdictions in order to heighten the very actions they were intended to negate. "What interests me most in people's lives," says the director, "is when they choose to live for something other than themselves, something they judge to be bigger than their ordinary, flat existence. Critics call this obsessive; I prefer to think of it as a passionate interest in the transcendental, and as such connected with spirituality and religion."[26]

Interno berlinese exposes the filmmaker's fascination with the aesthetic coordinates echoed in Oriental art, more distinctively with the low, straight-on camera angle identified with the films of Yasujiro Ozu. As Noël Burch suggests, such an angle endows the film with a ceremonial quality: "This peculiarly Japanese reaction is perhaps difficult for us to appreciate fully, except insofar as religious and other ceremonies in Japan do take place close to the floor and involve low bows and prostration."[27] Cavani places the camera slightly below the eye-line, violating the axis of action in the interiors. Her compositions evoke at times the two-dimensional surface of Ozu's framing; however, she

Frame 64. The lovers' triangle with Heinz (Kevin McNally), Louise's husband

does not renounce Western strategies of depth representation. She deploys a mobile camera, utilizing dollies and the Steadicam, to enhance the erotic impulses of the act of "excessive" (repetitive) lovemaking. The dynamics of representation involving Mitsuko include sexual ambiguity in its visual configuration, the fantasy of going beyond gender. Eros is a (Platonic) force that searches for the timeless; it is also the Bataillian mystery of lacerating truths, a delirious need for sacrifice. In the opening sequence at the Art Institute, the images are fetishistic, disclosing the desire for the idol itself, not in order to possess it (because Mitsuko remains unknown and unknowable), but as a source of an illumination, the effects of which cannot be defined by words. For Louise, Mitsuko represents the lure of a transcendental order, of unadulterated immaterial truths, against the simulacrum of false appearances produced by Nazism. She is first seen in a low-angle shot as she steps out of a diplomatic automobile, followed by Ume, her personal attendant. As she walks up the steps of the imposing building, the camera tilts up slowly, keeping her in the center of the frame. This shot establishes a connection between visual representation and fantasy as Louise gazes in awe at the spectacle before her. Inside the institute, the daughter of the Japanese ambassador displaces the German model exhibited by the school by calling attention to herself. The chamber aesthetic of Cavani's trilogy is here brought to a new level. The camera captures an intense choreography of gazes, as it dollies around the circular configuration of the art studio. Louise decides to turn away from the nude model at the center of the studio and begins to sketch a portrait of Mitsuko instead, under the close scrutiny of the art instructor and of the group of gazing students. In the next scene, Mitsuko enters the room and walks through the middle of the circular chamber space positioning herself at the outer edge of the circle, in front of a pool of light emanating from a window. In order to make Mitsuko's face resemble porcelain, Cavani uses extremely diffused lighting (usually filtering it through tracing paper and silk). When she crosses the circle, her theme music is introduced, then fades, as if a ray of light enters the room. When it stops, the spell has been cast on Louise; the divine essence has asserted her presence. The incorporeal world of the music prepares for the feeling of transcendence. Mitsuko's theme is formally orchestrated with the camera's movements, intensifying our anticipation of her eventual appearance.

Mitsuko does not represent ideas; she is the idea. She evokes Schopenhauer's aesthetic encounter with a (Platonic) world of unbroken beauty.[28] Beauty becomes the point of departure for an anamnesis, the exposure to the light of the ideal essence. This private idol, who operates through a pictorial quality, exists so forcefully that in her presence the allure of the national icon is dissipated until it disappears. She asserts her existence by her placement within the composition: Mitsuko becomes the dominant figure, and her body is usually situated in the center of the frame and shot frontally from a low angle. Throughout the film, the lighting is brighter on her face than on any other character's. The place from which Mitsuko speaks is the realm of beauty. The dread (and ecstasy) Louise feels in her presence is mystical, not merely aesthetic.[29] When Mitsuko enters the art class, everyone notices her presence. The camera follows her as she moves toward the most brightly lit part of the room. The lighting on her face alludes to an event that is being announced and expected. Contemplation is not a mechanism by which desire is negated, but a self-reflexive process by which desire doubles its representation. Mitsuko is dressed in a delicate violet kimono, the visual equivalent of a perfect apparition. Violet is the mystic color; it reflects the numinousness and allure of the archetypal image.[30] Louise offers Mitsuko the rapt devotion that National Socialism would claim of her: the light cast upon the idol depicts the intensity of worship. This produces a state of (aesthetic) devotion, whose character implies a total surrender to the object of contemplation. In Nazism, the state of religious devotion is a phenomenon of mass self-demonization. In a way, Cavani equates Mitsuko's beauty with the most violent forms of transgression: her cruel beauty implies its underlying historical transcendence. Hitler himself was a kind of mirror of violence and ambiguous sexuality. Ultimately, as Moravia points out, it was characteristic of the frustrated conformists in totalitarian states to take

refuge in decadent and funereal passions that counteracted the healthy appearance of their ideology.[31] In *Interno berlinese*, Cavani is concerned with transcendence, with a transcendence of the historical milieu and the language of her
previous styles.

This film is purposely designed to be hieratic in its cinematic strategies: the
blocking is stylized, the camera movement slow, and the editing seamless.
Cavani stages the erotic encounters as ritual performances. The actors are confined to the foreground, forced within a narrow space, even though there is a
great sense of openness behind them. The individuals remain still, while the
camera dollies and pans around them, slowly revealing the domestic chambers.
The film's framings implant Mitsuko within a privileged zone. For example,
when Louise visits Mitsuko inside her studio at the Japanese Embassy, she is
seated and centered in a low-angle medium shot, with a caged bird next to
her. This shot is constructed against a darkened background that progressively
leads the eye toward a spatial continuum. When Cavani cuts to a reverse angle
of Louise, there is a predominance of rectangular lines, which converge into a
corner, thus intensifying Louise's growing sense of enslavement. A transitional
dissolve reveals Mitsuko sleeping on the floor partly covered with a white sheet.
Slowly, with her hand, Louise lifts the sheet, exposing a flower tattoo imprinted
on the young woman's lower back and thigh. The tattoo symbolizes the transformation of Mitsuko into a pictorial tableau. This quiet, sensual encounter is
followed by the scene of Mitsuko's jealous outburst and dramatic threat of
suicide, which frightens Louise. The Dutch angle on Mitsuko, as she tears the
sheets off Louise's bed, emphasizes her anger and dominance, but also exhibits
the exaggerated facial expressions seen in Kabuki theater. When they meet
again, Mitsuko is dressed up as a geisha. Blue light bathes the room in an
unearthly illumination, marking it as the scene of devotion. The camera dollies
back from a profile of Louise entering the frame in medium shot to establish
Mitsuko center frame. She sits in an almost frozen pose, with a mesmerizing
look on her face (made up in white). Japanese theater masks, particularly those
of female personae, are blank and static, their impact relying on lighting and
the actor's movements.

There is another interesting aspect of the same scene: the camera starts off
behind Mitsuko and then pans over to reveal the silhouettes of the embassy
guards with their dogs projected onto the screens. The frightening visuality of
these ethereal phantoms, heightened by the pounding sound of their footsteps,
disrupts Mitsuko's musical theme. The geisha is propped up on pillows against
a golden background, the corners of the tatami effaced by the placement of the
flat cushions. Louise's body is composed in a worshiping posture, consistently
filmed from a high angle. They are both lit by paper lanterns placed on the
floor, the warm light flickering on their faces. Louise's body gravitates toward
this hypnotic icon as if it were discovering a new religion: she has entered the
world of mysticism. On one hand, the camera's close scrutiny invites the view-

er's participation; however, the theatricality of sets and lighting elicits detached observation. In this scene, the formalistic elements and traditional thematic components of Japan are synthesized. The blue color (suggestive of death) makes its ceremonial appearance. This novel effect foreshadows the solemn suicide ritual that ends the film, once again strictly choreographed by Mitsuko. Moreover, this entire sequence is typical of Cavani's directorial approach: she cuts straight into her scenes with no particular transitions, framing the characters in the middle of their movement.

Interno berlinese introduces sexuality as an ambivalent mechanism of spiritual ecstasy. For Cavani, the word "interior" defines both a dwelling space and an internal state of the characters:

> *Interno berlinese* is a discourse about "un interno" (an interior); it is an inner discourse. The lighting is subservient to an interior dialogue of a private religion. For example, in a temple, you may find torches as instruments of illumination. In my film, however, there is present an overall luminosity that originates from open spaces and windows as if the people inside avoid the exterior and consider it a place they cannot identify with. My itineraries are all interiors.[32]

As the director acknowledges, the architectural design of the interior becomes a site where the imagination not only is the object of investigation but also constructs the scene of the cinematic *écriture*. These interiors are set as art studios, diplomatic offices, hotel rooms, and particularly the most important chamber: the drama is actually taking place within the walls of a home. The articulation of this inner space gives the film its peculiar dramatic rhythm. The characters' movements are deliberately slow and calibrated, their gestures ritualized. They represent the dynamism of desire in contrast with an exterior that denies the mythology of a private affair. Cavani utilizes the illusion of false perspective by carefully placing objects and figures within the frame and scaling down their size. The optics of a camera lens is different from seeing something with the naked eye (each lens gives you a different perspective). In *Interno berlinese*, the director primarily uses her favorite 50mm lens for the wide shots and the 75mm lens for the close-ups. This choice of focal lengths approximates that of a painting, and it is the closest to the human eye; it creates a field of reflection oriented toward an interior space. Mitsuko is "porcelain," a work of art, an inner image. She moves so gracefully, as if her feet did not touch the earth.

Against this elaborate ritualization of the interior, the theme of Nazism is drawn across a field of subtle visual allusions. Cavani argues that the game of erotic pleasures intensifies the repressed morality of the larger national body: "Since nothing could contrast more with the rigorous repressed morality of the official side of Nazi Germany than the passionate abandon that seizes my characters, there was no need to show a single swastika, or brown shirt, or have Hitler shrieking into microphones. If we succeed in achieving what we

Frame 65. Mitsuko as a geisha

are striving for in the making of *The Berlin Affair*, that overdone atmosphere will be grafted upon every single shot."[33] For Cavani, swastikas and uniforms are the symbols of a caricature of religion. Her mise-en-scène employs devices similar to those utilized by the regime. As Kracauer observes, the Nazis knew that "allusions may reach deeper than assertions and that the contrapuntal relation of image to verbal statement is likely to increase the weight of the image, making it a more potent emotional stimulus."[34] Indeed, she abstracts interior spaces to such a degree that setting becomes a spectacle in itself, and this abstraction evokes a mystical geometry. As in Japanese ceremonial rituals, gestures, words, and objects are used to express a precise meaning; they must be rigidly executed.

The most beautiful of all the ceremonial sequences occurs during Louise's encounter with Mitsuko made up as a geisha. Mitsuko's postures and facial expressions are studied. She communicates with Louise in slow, rapturous utterances. There is a poetic echo in her words. The geisha acts as if she were being observed by others. Her body is transformed into the site of theatricality. A certain pictorial flatness evokes the Kabuki interior, which has little perceptual depth. This scene is at all times presentational, the closest to Ozu's surface organization of the shot. Mio Takaki had to learn the subtlety and complexity of ancient movements, which also include the art of wearing the kimono. In the film, the kimonos are ceremonial objects designed to serve in a cult (like the Nazi uniforms). Their specific use signals changes in the character's psychology; their chromatic harmony of colors and the exaltation of certain privileged hues tell the story. They establish an emotional boundary between the character and a situation.[35] In *Interno berlinese*, our perspective shifts to the frame, to the pervasiveness of lights and lines, to the positioning of the body. The Cavanian *interno* becomes a locus of a visible invisibility.

The director of photography, Dante Spinotti, admits that Cavani's strength lies in framing, and defines the style of *Interno berlinese* as "realismo splendente" (heightened realism). He describes how this effect was accomplished:

> We shot in studios, so that we had better control over the interior sets. We relied on the best color timer in the world, Academy Award–winner Ernesto Novelli, in order to achieve the purest colors, precise tonality, without having to rely on gels during the production. This was essential to define the characters as representative of two different, antithetical worlds. I designed a special hard light that could also be bounced and used as a soft source in order to get a more realistic look. . . . In a conventional cinematic technique, I used a small iris on the lens, which allowed me more depth of field. To do this, I had to raise the lighting to a certain level, which I do not think compromised realism. On the contrary, we achieved "un realismo splendente."[36]

The belief that film as an art form relies on realism is Spinotti's trademark as a cinematographer. No matter how abstract or fantastic the story may be, his approach is to be faithful to reality. For *Interno berlinese*, he creates a visual dichotomy (interior/exterior); his photography is suggestive, real and poetic. He dutches the angles slightly in order to visualize the intensity and the mystery of the characters. Cavani presents cultural traditions, the German and the Japanese, that celebrate the erotic experience as a ritual of light and color. Particularly, the predominant color, a dark plum, adds visual sensitivity to film's complexity by ensuring the sharp contrast between the intensely lit zones (emitting pure luminosity) and the darker areas. This use of color represents the characters' state of mind and captures the atmosphere of the interior. As the film progresses, it gradually evolves into darker tonalities. The visual playground ranges from the diffused lighting of the art studios (reflecting the Platonic ecstasy) to the language of dark interiority, the somber colors of the von Hollendorfs' claustrophobic decor.[37] Spinotti uses edge lighting to separate the figures from the backgrounds. Lighting becomes an abstracting element, accenting the symmetry of the frame space.

Interno berlinese remaps a discourse of gender and representation that escapes conventional codifications. Cavani's emerging understanding of what she has called "the memory of the spectacle as event"[38] places the ritual of desire at

Frame 66. Cavani with Mio Takaki and costume designer Josoburo Tsujimura

the center of a complex sociohistorical performance, of which women are the protagonists. Women understand better than men that the creative model of survival is the articulation of such desire. They hazard a suicidal leap into the beyond that opens to a future of incredible, enriched knowledge. In the visual topography of the Cavanian interior, a microhistory is mapped out. As Giuliana

Bruno notes, the spatial paradigm in relation to female discourse bears on a psychoanalytic referent, for what is experientially female is the inscription of desire in a spatial practice.[39] Cavani's emphasis is on corporeality.

The films of the German trilogy place the audience in a provocative position. Cavani's images question dominant iconic modes. Her themes, as critics have often emphasized, are an important part of the film. They should not, however, obscure her visual achievement. From the very start of her career, Cavani experiments with cinematic grammar to enhance her narrative structures. In the German trilogy, camera placement and composition become the most important expressive instruments of the story. Cavani explores the spaces of the gaze, focusing on the interior as the locus of female fantasy. Although at times the camera may be identified with the characters' point of view, it usually maintains an objective distance. Still, in *Interno berlinese*, as in *Il portiere di notte*, the presence of the movie camera within the frame often reinforces the voyeuristic aspect of the collective/private spectacle. It is from the perspective of the audience's perception that we speak of theatricality in the film. In Cavani's cinema, the stage is a place for viewing, but it is also a temporary site of the liberation of the imagination from the social code.

The German trilogy captures the Cavanian film at its best. Cavani's cinema supposes a certain type of audience, capable of transcending traditional modes of narration. For many, the jarring effect of her images and editing strategy can be too disturbing. In *Il portiere di notte*, the notion of knowledge as the violation of the *intérieur* is eroticized and enacted as spectacle. The camera remains static in order to allow the eye the time to explore the frame and become involved in the story. In *Al di là del bene e del male*, the audience is required to use their senses in order to fully participate in the characters' mobile gazes. In *Interno berlinese*, the play of mirror, the refractions, the masks give way to silence and gesture, which mediate a world of inner reality. Cavani asserts her presence as the producer of the look and works to pit her films against the strategies of dominant culture.

PART THREE

METAPHORS OF VISION

Francesco is not a man of the past; he may not even be of the present. He is a man of the future.

Francesco: a story from a "slice of life" that, at times, after a long day's work, reminds me of only one other literary character that I love, *The Idiot* by Dostoievsky.

(*Liliana Cavani*)

To become zero . . . the necessary point of departure . . . the absolute freedom.

(*Lumley/Milarepa*)

7

The Architectonics of Form: *Francesco* and *Milarepa*

IN ANNOUNCING her second film about Francis of Assisi in 1988, Liliana Cavani emphasized that without Mickey Rourke she could not have made such a complex film about a saint whose life is "a classical metaphor, like Hamlet's."[1] Upon the request of producer Giulio Scanni, she began developing a script together with Roberta Mazzoni in November 1986. She recounts:

> For my next project, I had in mind another film, involving a woman astrophysicist in the main role. But the producer Giulio Scanni asked me: "Why don't you remake *Francesco*? A year or so ago even Antonioni was considering this idea, but it was never realized." I told him that he must be joking. "But it's a beautiful story," he insisted. Well, I thought about it, and in rereading the books on the saint . . . I saw that I could produce something very different, not a remake.[2]

The selection of an actor whose charisma relies on the physicality and instinctuality of his performance signals Cavani's intention to give prominence to the body in her reconception of Francesco. The protagonist's search for identity is now epitomized in the word "contatto," as it signifies the relationship between man and God:

> The word "change" is central to my film; the word "contact" is the fulcrum of the story. In a certain sense, San Francesco is *for me like the thirteenth apostle*. Francesco carries the burden of the Sermon on the Mount upon himself. "Deus mihi dixit" is the Latin phrase, "the credo," that for Francesco establishes precisely "the contact," and this contamination has inspired the young, the secular, and the Catholics to follow him.[3]

In its etymological sense of "to touch" and to be "infected," contact exemplifies the necessity to experiment throughout one's life and body. The first gesture that Francesco/Rourke makes, in order to approach his new, transgressive world outside the walls of Assisi, is sharing the elemental life of those who do not possess anything. He experiences the deprivation of *proprietas* by using "fratello corpo," "fratello asino" as he calls them. *Francesco* (1989) re-creates the poetry and the personal cost of entertaining such an idea about experience; it uses an expressionist photographic style that is charaterized by harsh, realistically corporeal light. Cinematographer Beppe Lanci (who replaced Ennio Guarnieri after three weeks) selects soft-focus for the face and the surface of

Frame 67. Mickey Rourke in the title role of *Francesco* (1989)

the body, and direct, contrast lighting for the backgrounds. The resulting effect places an emphasis on the movement of the human body, shot against the sharp intensity of the settings. The body thus becomes the geometrical locus of all existential questions, the point of intersection between substance and spirit. Through the use of the body, one knows, and one actualizes the great contact of the conscience with mystery. Francesco has a perceptive rather than a contemplative frame of mind. He breaks with the Manichaean tradition that views the body as negativity (sin). Many of Francesco's followers do not understand that in order to imitate Francesco they have to follow "fratello corpo"; that theology implies the knowledge of the factual, thus of the body, and the contact (*tactus* and *gustus*) of the experiencing subject with spiritual reality.

Francesco is structured as a series of encounters, from the protagonist's first glance at Chiara of Assisi in his father's shop to the body's last journey to San Damiano before the official burial in order to take leave of the "cristiana" whom he had accepted as his "father, mother, brother, and sister."[4] The encounter is both a spiritual and a perceptual contact. Pictorially, it is realized by a scenic composition organized around the use of space as an interior that the body fills. Cavani describes it in terms familiar to anthropological religion: "*Francesco* is a film of encounters. Francesco takes a path, follows the Gospel; it is initially a ritual. The ritual becomes creative in the precise moment when his gesture embodies the purpose of his life and expresses his existence."[5]

In the opening scene, Chiara (Helena Bonham Carter) is kneeling on the ground as Francesco's body, wrapped in a shroud, is being carried in to San Damiano and placed in front of the crucifix. As the camera booms down, Chiara moves over, kisses his hand, and lies next to him, with her head facing down. Through this *analogia visionis*, the Francescan *imitatio* has only one original source: the iconic image of the Byzantine Christ, of which the Friar Minor is a *speculum*. In this film, the portrayal of Francesco's death differs from the end of *Francesco di Assisi*. The emphasis subtly changes from an allusion to Christ's Deposition to a more reflective, specular, and imagistic representation.

Narrated in flashback, a few years later, by Chiara and five of Francesco's first followers in a white tent set on a mountain (an ascensional image), the film establishes a temporal sacrality that is reminiscent of *Milarepa* and departs from the strict chronicle format of the earlier version. The editing cleverly interweaves images of Francesco's life with those of the narrators recounting the story—this part constitutes the *cornice*, or frame, of the film. Gabriella Cristiani, the film editor, has adopted the elliptical style of cutting from Franco Arcalli, whom she once assisted. As she mentions in an interview with Stefano Masi, Arcalli was known for his cutting on movement, a technique she also applies to her work.[6] Cristiani subscribes to a sense of perceptual fragmentation and charismatic fascination with the *corpus* of Francesco. Thus the flashbacks become a site of the articulation of the filmic experience.

Chiara's arrival is announced by the wind, a sound that paves the way for a new consciousness to take form: the wind is a cosmic chord; it evokes a sense of awe. Chiara's arrival to the tent is shot from the inside through a triangular opening (an image also recurrent in *Milarepa*). This shot establishes the geometrical configuration of the film as a whole; it also conveys the feeling of a mystical apparition. The door is suggestive of an entrance to a shrine, a threshold leading to the innermost inwardness. It signifies the boundary between the profane and sacred worlds.[7] Cavani has expanded the character of Chiara of Assisi to fuse social reality with the essence of the Franciscan message, the viewing of Christ's life as a pattern of action. The tent becomes the creative center, an accessible site of the soul states. In *Francesco*, we must acknowledge the essential contribution made by the camera's geometrical framing to the profound intensity of the film. Cavani argues for a "visual writing"; her mise-en-scène foregrounds concrete configurations of the conflict between the private and the social, charisma and structure.[8]

In the film, the transgressive, dialectical process—secondary now is the social critique—is ruled by the personal itinerary of each narrator, who relates his or her own unique encounter with Francesco. Under the tent, Chiara and the Brothers model a human hierarchy that becomes a metaphor for the vertical structure of the social ideals of the Middle Ages. Chiara's body remains the

Frame 68. Chiara (Helena Bonham Carter) kneeling next to Francesco's body in San Damiano

Frame 69. Chiara entering the tent where the story unfolds

originating agency of storytelling (she takes position at the center). In her compelling presence, the oral tradition (her words) is being recorded. It is Chiara's face that signals the *incipit* of the story, a flashback to the first time she saw Francesco: "His image has filled my existence since childhood."[9] The voices of the individual narrators weave a discursive heterogenity, but again, the images conjured up by memory are closely linked to those of the hierarchical dissolution of Francesco's historical times. Most prominent among the images are the skinned heretic that marks Francesco's first encounter with the Gospel, and the high-angle shot of the naked bodies amassed in a ditch (a photographic reminder of Nazi concentration camps) during the war between Assisi and Perugia, when Francesco was taken prisoner (1202–1203). The materiality of writing is visually represented by the Brothers' constantly working—for example, weaving a basket and mending the tent. It is Leone's hand that transcribes the spoken word—as he did once for Francesco.

Francesco is also a film about silence. It is best approached as a metaphor of melancholy and angst. Francesco's *passio* has turned into tragic isolation. The camera high-angle point of view diminishes the *cavaliere* image that supported the narrative action of Lou Castel's Francesco. The drama unfolds within visible structures of containment, such as walls. Open doors, archways, pillars compose the film's visual architectonics. In reviewing the film, Gian Luigi Rondi spoke of "the terror of the 'dark night.' "[10] In other words, watching *Francesco* is like looking into the depths of a tunnel. For example, the scene of Bishop

Frame 70. Identical scene of the tent in *Milarepa* (1973)

Guido and Francesco walking together under the cloister (at this time Francesco is told to form an order) is mazelike and confining. It is shot in contrast lighting with long shadows, as if the source of illumination were candles and oil lamps. This circular perspective, with arches and pillars, conveys also the feeling of a transitional journey. Francesco's whole body participates in the dynamic of the close-up, which fills the screen surface: from the feet, which first enter the frame in the opening scene and symbolize the physical endeavor of Francesco's journey; to the hand, which Chiara kisses, an emblem of *caritas*; to the nose, which follows the hot bread or accepts the scent of the lepers, a sign of the *humilitas* of the Friar Minor; to the torso, which emerges from Lake Trasimeno, an apparent inconsistency with the saint's iconographic tradition, which, after Thomas of Celano, images Francesco as a small, feeble man.[11] In the scene at the lake—which is followed by Francesco's gift of his armor, the vision in Spoleto, and the return to Assisi—the body signifies both the renunciation of the "materialistic" adventure in the Orient (to become rich and noble) and the birth of a new knight, the spiritual complement of the *corporeus*. On this subject, Alberto Moravia writes that "Cavani has seen Saint Francis in a 'historical' style," referring to the fact that he is an earthly man, made of flesh and bones.[12] In the blocking of the body (frontal medium shots), one can detect Cavani's Apollonian veneration of the human figure, which is seen as both a sensual and an ideal form. Cavani emphasizes the saint's spiritual and corporeal reality and formalizes Rourke's psychological performance, which transforms such an extraordinary experience into a complete mode of being. One of the most remarkable and controversial scenes is Rourke's unabashed ballet on the snow. He dances around naked, as if he becomes one with the earth and the air. He makes snow figures that represent his human desire for a wife and children in order to tame his libidinal urges.[13]

The paths of Francesco's journey can be reduced to a system of mental and physical states: from the initial splendor of the images highlighting Francesco's devotion to *la gaya scienza* of legendary Provence (sumptuous clothing and food, heightened by warm colors) to his progressive physical decay, reflected in the smock, untidy beard, fasting, gray tonality, cold lighting, and a landscape that is wet, dark, spectrally medieval. The transformation of the body releases a visual energy that confines as it attracts the spectator's eye. Francesco's body is physically confined within a rigorous background, whether it is the boundary/wall of the city or the mountainous rocks of his solitary wanderings; the shed at Rivo Torto or the caves on Monte Subiaco, which Francesco called his "carceri" (prisons). This is a claustrophobic film of interiors: it is a film without a sky. Assisi is cinematically reconstructed in the Rocca Paolina, the subterranean city of Perugia. Cavani viewed this ancient place (instead of the historical Assisi) as the ideal site in which "the first hidden anxieties of this handsome, rich, and much loved Francesco take shape."[14] By eliminating the pictorial quality of the sky, the director creates a psychological space-time continuum that relates to the inner loneliness of Francesco's experience at the *baraccopoli*, the ghetto of the poor. The sky becomes a projection of the character's interior; it configures the space of the soul. The tonality of the *baraccopoli* is livid, and so are the people, with their rags and their huts. In this dark, steamy, cavernous setting, human beings are imprisoned in a dehumanized state. Tragic chaos was a driving force in Cavani's modern interpretation of *Francesco*, and she used the film *Blade Runner* (1982), directed by Ridley Scott and scored by Vangelis, as a reference.[15]

Cavani employs a centrifugal compositional technique in which the film's visual lines are directed toward the *limina* of the frame, thus displacing the symmetrical relation of body to the background. Thematically, these boundaries refer to a character who, like Dostoievsky's idiot, ironically becomes "a kind of *pharmakos* in reverse."[16] When Francesco is alone, he is placed to one side of the frame, a technique that emphasizes his concentration and spirituality. Only in the epiphanic moments is his body centered, as in the opening sequence in San Damiano when Francesco's body is left on the barren stone, aligned with the wooden crucifix above the altar. This composition reappears in the scene of the stigmata, where an emaciated Francesco is lying on the rough-textured stone. The physical reality of the wounds (the imprinted signs of Christ) is visualized in the details of the rocky landscape, the spring water, and the color of blood. This emotional scene is memorable largely because of Rourke's performance: the viewer senses the commanding force of this charismatic character, who suffers agonies of fear and doubt. The Stigmatization concludes the narrative sequence of the flashbacks. Chiara unveils its iconography: "He said nothing . . . I medicated him, I bandaged him without asking anything. I thought . . . I thought that love had made his body identical to the one he loved. I asked myself if I could ever love so much. . . ." The film ends with a close-up of Chiara's radiant face as it fades to black supported by the music of Vangelis. We are in the realm of anagogic mystery, the journey of man from the subterranean cavern (the archetypal image of the womb, a place of mystery) to an apotheosis on a mountaintop. In *Francesco*, as in *Milarepa*, we witness the transformation of the labyrinth from confusion and tragic chaos to order, from blindness to vision.

Francesco d'Assisi was a film of the sixties with specific thematic and stylistic influences (Paul Sabatier's biographical work, Giotto's frescoes, Cimabue's painting). The use of the body formalized the dialectical relationship between the capitalistic underpinning of paternal power and the new meaning given to the social order by Francesco's experience. In *Francesco*, the polemical thrust of the images persists when the father figure is introduced: in the allusiveness of the bathtub scene, when the naked bodies of Pietro and Francesco face each other, anticipating future contrasts; or in the sequence of the social divestment during the trial, when the verbal culture of the patrimonial power is counteracted by the silent, gestural culture of the rebel-son. Pietro Bernardone is no

Frame 71. God's physical sign: the stigmata

longer a despotic father but an earthly *pater*, imperfect and materialistic, who denounces his son but also spies on him and dreams, until the end, that his son may return home.[17]

Following the oral-literary tradition, particularly the *Legenda Trium Sociorum* (The Legend of the Three Companions), Cavani emphasizes the figurative aspects of bodily gestures, while the romantic aura of Cavani's earlier *Francesco* is diffused. Rather than being portrayed as ignorant, Francesco is now confused: he is a man who descends into a labyrinthine underground that has oneiric dimensions between the apocalyptic and the demonic. The darkening of consciousness has in the film a precise visual codification: smoke, fog, dust, wind, rain are all images reinforced by diffused photography. The archetype of the center, which Cavani retraces in the mandala symmetry of *Milarepa*, is enriched by images of stairs, circle, house, fortress, cross. The inorganic world is represented by the stone, a great emblem of the timeless.[18] *Francesco di Assisi* was a film about the present; its message was conveyed by the transgressive experience of the rebel figure. *Francesco* is a film about the future, as the electronic sound of Vangelis establishes from the title sequence. For Cavani, it is a film of mature experience. Notwithstanding, the two versions share similar directorial traits (Rufino in the cathedral of Assisi, the trial) and register identical camera movement and choreography. *Francesco* is photographically more corporeal and imaginative, while the first film was more experimental and abstract. To translate this perceptual and yet timeless nature of the Franciscan imagery, set and costume designer Danilo Donati creates an ambience charged with intense realism: "We began with the cloth, the wood, and the nails to reconstruct our Middle Ages; an epoch that alludes to the metaphysical. We can only reproduce its essence, its scent, without being too particular."[19] *Francesco* departs from Cavani's preceding productions (with the exception of *Milarepa*) because it is introduced as a film of hope. The photography deepens the background with intense pools of light that form a luminous spiral. The film values the "night" and "confusion" as steps toward light; it portrays the drama of a lonely man. When Francesco begins his ascent to the sacred mountain and receives the stigmata, the film celebrates his transcendence in the mystical delirium.

Francesco is the summa of corporeality in the cinema of Liliana Cavani. The body is the locus of the violence of history: the shock image of the skinned heretic, the pile of dead bodies, the prisoners' bodies in Perugia, the hallucinatory figures of the lepers in the *baraccopoli*. The body is the locus of expressivity. It is also the locus of cosmic wisdom, the focus of a sensorial realism of the nose (one smells the new reality), of the eye (one sees and is seen), of touch (the kiss given to the leper), of sound (indistict, guttural voices). The experience of the body restores human contact with mystery. Rourke's Francesco is not the Nietzschean neurotic, epileptic visionary of 1966. He is Nietzsche's man of the future identified with the splendor, the physicality and deification, of *passio*, adventure, and knowledge. Cavani's corporeality reflects conflictual, contemporary situations. In an interview with Pierre Riches, Cavani speaks about the making of *Francesco*:

> To make a film is an experience that often costs me a lot. I ask myself questions. In this case, I asked many. Francesco made me confront various contemporary issues, which we talk about and which cannot be ignored. For example, today there is this idea, this habit of delegating our own power to the State, even our need for love, for advice, and our assistance when we are lonely, sick, or near death. We delegate everything. . . . In life, we all walk on thin ice; if for someone the ice cracks under his feet, it is too bad for him. Francesco is still valid today for his immense sense of consciousness. His concrete way of living brotherhood is extraordinary and very modern. It is our last frontier. It is an idea that moves beyond the contemporary into the future. Utopia? Perhaps, but it is a marvelous idea.[20]

Francesco's distinctive trait is his capacity to change, to lead a life of constant search and actualization. The ability to change and the epistemological emphasis on the body as the site of vision are also central to *Milarepa* (1973), a film that the director has defined as concerned with "the process of knowledge," and has often compared to her historical characterization of Francis of Assisi.[21] In light of this representational interest, to make her second film on Francesco, Cavani chose to return to the mountains of Abruzzo, in the exact location where she shot *Milarepa*. She managed to trace the very same pegs that she once utilized to support the tent of Marpa, Milarepa's teacher. The set of *Francesco* was built in the same spot.[22] Francesco is the Western man who searches for being, peace, and inwardness of body and soul; his empirical form of life translates into the factual situation of poverty. His transformation from wealth to a beggar's life parallels the steps of Buddha (from prince to mendicant); his life is reminiscent of a sannyasi existence. Milarepa is a poet, a sorcerer, and a hermit who lived in Tibet during the eleventh century. The mystical immediacy of his experience is the medium through which religion is conceived (for the early Franciscans, theology was practical knowledge). In an interview with cowriter Italo Moscati, Cavani explains that *Milarepa* becomes the story of a young man of today who identifies himself with the character of the medieval Tibetan poet:

> He travels in his own mind; he enters an adventure from which he seems to be excluded; instead it involves him intimately. Once again, considering the fact that this film is regarded as a kind of fable, it was not a journalistic piece that interested me but the search for an experience which is hidden behind contemporary life. The young man, who studies in a university and has a professor who guides him to work on the sorcerer Milarepa, is related to Francesco and to the characters of *I cannibali*.

Frame 72. Lajos Balàzsovitz as Milarepa building the tower of stones

Frame 73. Identical scene in *Francesco* with Mickey Rourke

However, he is a unique figure. He is a student who comes "after" the revolution . . .
He looks toward the East, to the Eastern tradition, not to Mao: to an ancient language
that he does not understand; to a religion that is a way of life, a philosophy.[23]

Thus *Milarepa* is an analysis of various forms of consciousness. It is both a
spiritual and a scientific investigation of reality. Consciousness is a boundary
situation, its formal visualization embodied in a kind of liturgy of the camera
lens, an archaic geometrical style. Cavani labors with the movie camera to
interrogate the external worlds of the protagonist's metamorphosing experiences, to make them reveal their innermost truths. In reviewing the film, Pier
Paolo Pasolini speaks of "the mad rationality of religious geometry":

> What an extraordinary experience (almost forgotten) to see a *truly* beautiful film.
> Cinema pertains to the same order of life: for this reason, one senses the artificiality
> of a film that is *truly* beautiful when watching it, but after a while, it resurfaces in
> one's memory and becomes real, even though it may be only a dream. Liliana Cavani's
> *Milarepa* is one of these absolutely rare films. One does not remember it as a film,
> but as perfect Geometry, in which a real, visual experience has been inscribed and
> crystallized. It is a curious experience. In reality, we are bound to live in a perennial
> "subjective" perspective: the camera is always closed to our eye, the angle is always
> determined from where we see, and the visual field is always the space with our body
> standing in the center. . . .
>
> I would never have conceived of using such a premise, in any other film except
> *Milarepa*. It has been a long time since such a beautiful film appeared on the screen,
> a film that so openly exalted the expressiveness of cinema. Furthermore, the Geome-
> try that synthesizes all possible points of view in Milarepa's life (once *lived* and *seen
> as lived*) has so to speak technically the character of the religious vision of reality. This
> is always so polyhedric and omnicomprehending (the gaze of "rational" sainthood is
> that of a sublime, true, cubist painter, who sees *all* the surfaces of objective reality
> simultaneously).
>
> In Cavani's film, the itineraries of Milarepa, who is searching for knowledge or for
> an initiatory form of knowledge through which to interpret life, are crystallized in a
> series of lines rhythmically arranged: a sequence of static shots and rather irregular
> compositions (with pans and zooms) on a "profilmic" world that is also strangely
> geometrical: an Abruzzo, barren and blue, oftentimes with clouds and moving fog
> over the rocky planes, lost in a profound solitude.[24]

Indeed, cinematic expression prevails as Cavani's primary point of interest.
The film has been visually set up with the contemporary sequences emphasizing a dull, latent image. The flat surfaces of walls vanish into a play of light
and shadow projecting the protagonist's sense of disintegration and his dissatis-
faction with the conformist society that surrounds him. This modern part functions as a *cornice* for the religious experience of Milarepa. It also establishes the
oneiric dimension of the film that contributes to a sense of longing. Cavani

ignores the prescriptions of biography and chooses to pursue her thematic and visual purpose beyond the limits of genre. After visiting Nepal and witnessing the crude reality of destitute villages, as well as the beauty of the people, the director chose to reject a semidocumentary approach and discarded the idea of filming in the East: "As soon as I returned, I decided that I could not do the story of Milarepa, but I could tell 'a' story related to the book of Milarepa."[25] Once again, the body of the actor serves an essential function in the psychological regression of a contemporary character into another culture. Lajos Balàzso-vitz, whom Cavani cast in the title role, is, in her own words, the ultimate character: "Lajos does not invent; he plays himself in doing Milarepa."[26] The film epitomizes the dynamics of consciousness, what Moscati has called the questioning of humanity's "obscure boundaries": the biological, the irrational, and the unconscious.[27]

It was Elsa Morante, whom the director visited regularly, who inspired Cavani to read *Vita di Milarepa*, translated by Anna Devoto for the Adelphi publishers. In his introduction to the autobiography (originally transcribed by Rechung, one of Milarepa's disciples), the Orientalist Jacques Bacot depicts the figure of the sorcerer-poet according to the physiognomy handed down by the Tibetan iconography: "A bizarre young man, with a disconcerting temperament, whose pale complexion is matched by a physical vigor that does not experience exhaustion, whose elastic features clash with an extraordinary tenacity, whose naïveté (one of his teachers considers him an idiot) hides an abstract intelligence, solely directed toward the absolute. A voluntary helot, Milarepa was considered 'abnormal,' like every great saint and mystic."[28] Balàzsovitz is thoroughly congenial in the part. Cavani, who has centered most of her films on the experience of male characters who retreat from power, stresses how Milarepa invariably anticipates her social concerns of the mid-1970s. She makes him the son of a working-class mother—no longer the heir to a small landowner, as in the original text—because she believed that this was the only class in Europe capable of regenerating itself, of avoiding the conditioning power of bourgeois culture.[29]

In 1991 she recounted to Silvia Costa: "I was marching in a protest rally, which at that time was a common occurrence. As I looked around, I noticed young boys wearing gold Rolexes and very expensive leather jackets. I asked myself: but with whom am I marching? So I decided to leave the rally."[30] For Cavani, *Milarepa* is "un'avventura moderna, fuori dell'ordinario" (a modern adventure, out of the ordinary): "It is as if one trips all of a sudden, or one finds oneself in an accident that forces one to stop and think, pushed out of the old, familiar paths."[31] It is a spectacle of unrelieved absorption. It is as if the camera is executing the director's inner mood during the shooting. First and foremost, Cavani resists the temptation to invoke the Orient as the quintessence of esoteric culture and as a simplistic antithesis of all that is "Western"— what Edward W. Said has called "a Western style for dominating, restructuring, and having authority over the Orient."[32] The life of Milarepa becomes an account of a spiritual journey into the unconscious depths of the human being.

Set in a contemporary industrial city, the film begins with the story of a university student, Lumley, and his professor, Albert Bennett, who has guided him to translate an ancient Tibetan book. On their way to the airport to catch an airplane for Nepal, they get into a car accident. With them is Bennett's wife, Karin, who runs for help. While the professor lies in a dangerous, transitional state between life and death, Lumley is confronted with the task of assisting his teacher and of performing a liminal rite. Guided by his imagination, he recalls the translation of Milarepa's journey and his struggles for self-awareness. The film visualizes the three stages of Milarepa's experience in search of a teacher. His experiences range from the depth of black magic with the Man from Nyag, where he is forcibly influenced by his mother's desire for revenge against his father's family, to the wisdom of Marpa, the white lama who teaches him obedience, discipline, and knowledge. The same actors play the main roles in both present and past: Lumley becomes Milarepa, Bennett is Marpa, and Karin is Damema, Marpa's companion.[33]

Cavani's film concentrates on Milarepa's apprenticeship, a transitional stage that requires his enduring a series of physical ordeals, the utmost self-abnegation, and an oneiric journey. The director shows little interest in the unfolding of the plot, with its chain of biographical events, but rather focuses on Milarepa's spiritual world. She visually portrays a progression from darkness (the subterranean cave of the Man from Nyag) to light (the ethereal tent of Marpa) by stripping the backgrounds of density and working with diffusion. Static shots are at the center of our visual field, her imagination investing them with emotion and meaning. She avoids exotic landscapes and highly stylized interiors. Milarepa's religious way of life is extravagant enough, as was Francesco's experimentation.

The film opens in a noisy, alien urban setting with the main character in a telephone booth trying to make a phone call. His relationship to the exterior is essentially one of separation. The desolate gray of the empty streets conveys his state of mind. Cavani's main objective is to portray a young man's eerie detachment from the world and from himself. Lumley leads a solitary life; his mental absorption in scholarship irritates his mother, who works in a factory to keep him in school. She wants a better life for him and his little sister. Lumley's yearning for the wholeness of existence is established in his quest for knowledge, rather than in any more metaphysical endeavor. As he finds himself involved in the car accident with the Bennetts, and he begins to revisit the sites of Milarepa's itineraries (so often imagined and dreamt about), the central image becomes that of an oneiric descent: the cracked glass/mirror of the windshield suggests the exchange of the original identity for its reflection. Milarepa's story is suspended between existence and essence, reality and ideality. It comes into Bennett's consciousness at the instant of his tragic break with reality and

Frame 74. Lumley and Albert Bennett (Paolo Bonacelli) in the automobile accident

extends beyond him in magnificent fragments that seem to surface out of fantasy and recollection.

Through the looking glass of Lumley's creative imagination, the adventures of Milarepa are largely suggested by a world of dream and poetic language. It is clear that, for him, meaning is a matter of an alteration within consciousness, where identification and represention coexist. The scene of the automobile accident—the driver loses control of the vehicle, which plunges off the highway, rolling down an embankment—establishes the style of Cavani's approach. The camera becomes an embodied eye looking through obstacles, as if there were a screen between the eye and reality. Visually fractured images are rendered by shooting through the broken glass of the car, the cloth fibers hanging at Milarepa's mother's house, the straw hat of the old fisherman, or the sheets of Marpa's tent, which create geometrical shapes (triangles and quadrangles). Most prominently, the fog acts as a filter and diffuses the itinerant body of Milarepa against the horizon line.

The psychological preoccupations of *Milarepa* reveal an impulse to reenact a liminal state straddling life, death, and reincarnation. Or, in Cavani's own words, the obsession for the resurrection of the flesh: "Milarepa ends up offering his body (indeed his own body) to the salvation of all creatures, insects included."[34] The protagonist's ability to confront death is part of a living process of transformation that begins at birth. In this context, the Western notion of death becomes inappropriate. The theme of death, which in one form or another has fascinated Cavani since childhood, is inextricably tied to the theme of the journey. The character of Albert Bennett, at first somewhat puzzling, has a particular bearing on Lumley's state of mind. The accident is, for the cultural tradition of Tibet, parallel to a mortuary rite. The time lapse from a person's demise to reincarnation is conceived as a journey through the *bardo*, a transitional stage that is situated neither here nor there.[35] Bennett attains this status when he assumes Marpa's identity. He becomes very much a man in transit. The death of the great master provides the requisite motive force to form what in Buddhism is the only aspect of time, that of coming into being and passing away. Man is connected by countless threads with the past and the future. Their specific energy is projected onto basic elements (water, earth, fire, air, and space). As Lumley says, "Marpa and young Milarepa were once spiritually united in their past lives."[36] Thus each individual forges a bond with the whole history of humankind.

The topography of Milarepa's journey is labyrinthine, a series of paths filled with dangers, demons, trials, and unexpected encounters. The sets are designed to represent interior landscapes. The labyrinth is a classical metaphor for learning. Take, for example, the fantasmatic geometrical shapes defining the dark subterranean dungeon where the sorcerer from Nyag operates, or the corporeal visuality of the designs imprinted in Marpa's tent, a locus mapping out the intersection of knowledge, power, and desire. Within the cultural boundaries of Zen meditation, the paths traveled by the main character toward self-awareness are negatively figured through a teaching that destroys any illusionary conception of reality. Milarepa's labyrinthine experiences represent a search for an ideal form of life in which reality can be annihilated and the self mastered.

Cavani is clearly more interested in conveying the experience of identity than in accounting for aspects of Milarepa's background that provoked his need for such an experience. His first itinerary follows the desire for power/ knowledge involved with black magic, toward which he is directed by his mother, an ambiguous female archetype, who demands revenge against her husband's brother (he refuses to relinquish the property that lawfully belongs to them after the death of Milarepa's father). The mother's murderous thirst installs the son as an agent of her obsession with power, from which she feels excluded by her social and economic position. She sends him off to master a discourse capable of destroying their village. This affirmation of knowledge creates a progressive enslavement to violence. The journey to the Man from Nyag is synthesized in the ominous structure of a labyrinth used *in malo*, an imposing construction without any space of passage; its inextricability (angling corridors, tunnels) connotes death. As Cavani specifies in her script directions, the monastery of the black lama "has no doors to enter."[37] Here the iconography of the labyrinth suggests the "image of the lost direction," as Frye has called it, with the demonic counterparts of geometrical images: the sinister circle and

Frame 75. Milarepa learns black magic with the Man from Nyag

the sinister cross.[38] The image that configures Milarepa's state of mind, when he learns black magic and becomes capable of annihilation on a staggering scale, is the circle executed in red chalk on the ground of the infernal cavern.[39]

This scene sets up the devastation of the uncle's house and the killing of everybody inside during a wedding celebration. It begins with a static, high-angle shot of Milarepa sitting in an underground cell with his legs crossed, sculpted like a statue in front of a charged interpsychic space: the red circle. He meditates on his spell. A ray of light is cast upon him, thus drawing our attention to the composite character of the new disciple. The light is centered on his face, aimed between the eyes, and forms a circle around his body. This image visualizes the creative energy at work. From his intense stare the film cuts to his mother weaving in the enclosed space of her home. She suddenly gets up and goes to the door. Her frightened reaction suggests the horror she has just witnessed. Cavani's shot formation relates the intersubjective experience that forges the psychic bond existing between the two characters. It is the combined concentration of their forces that causes the leveling of the entire village. The mother shares her place with the son through identification and makes him the signifier of her own desire. The intercutting of corroborating shots makes this blatant.

Frame 76. Milarepa meditates on how to destroy his uncle's house

Upon his return home, when he is presented with the shocking conse-quences of his violent act (this tragic scene is shot with a handheld camera that emphasizes the rawness of destruction), Milarepa is taken aback by his moth-er's vindictiveness. She is simply portrayed as a grotesque lunatic. In the scene of her exulting recognition of her son's destructive powers, as she shouts and shakes her walking stick above the ruins of the uncle's house, her jubilation suggests a gratification long deferred. The mother acts "as the diegetic point of origin for the desire which finds fulfillment in the collapse of the village—in the collapse, that is, of a cultural order in which woman figures as lack, and from whose privileges she is entirely barred."[40] Milarepa decides to leave in the agonizing hope that his final, monstrous gesture can be cancelled or expiated by a commitment to total integrity. The Tibetan universe in which Milarepa lives is an elaborate construction where magic as a brutal agency encompasses the ritual of a descent to a demonic world of suffering. Milarepa's first compre-hension of depth experience is an act of destruction that is born out of his intense psychic communion with his mother.

Milarepa will not see his mother alive again. After he has mastered a higher level of spiritual discourse with Marpa, he returns to the village and visits her abandoned, decomposing remains. He removes fragments of her skeleton, takes them to a mountain stream, and pulverizes them with a stone. He mixes the fragments with water, which he drinks. This cannibalistic ingestion ritually unifies him with his mother. As I have shown in chapter 3, within Western culture, cannibalism as a metaphor stands for the ultimate signature of difference in a coded opposition of light/dark, rational/irrational. It is an oral ritual of resistance. Milarepa's act of incorporation evokes a kind of dissolving of the limits of the self through the physical commingling of self and other.[41] As Kaja Silverman remarks, the psychic constraints that result from the mother-son relationship are overcome in this scene: "Mila's cannibalistic incorporation of his mother permits her to participate in his liberating divestiture, and with him to transcend sexual difference. Together they make the journey to 'the snows of Laphis,' a journey that leads definitely away from both narrative and ideological closure."[42]

The theme of weaving, which is also associated with the mother, reflects Milarepa's dual itinerary of dissolution (the Man from Nyag) and of reconstruction with the white lama. The cloth that the mother weaves suggests Ariadne's thread; but her string serves no orienting purpose during the hero's transit to the center of the maze. In the fortress of the Man from Nyag, the intricate architectural design creates a sense of discontinuity, a rupturing of awareness. Milarepa must radically transform the image of the (mother's) thread into the idea of spatial continuity in order to reach the mountain of Marpa's monastery, with its inherent possibility of a return and a rebirth. This involves a process of territorial passages from one magico-religious site to another. Milarepa's labyrinthine wanderings of ascent comprise crossings of neutral zones (deserts of stone, marshes, glaciers) as well as of natural boundaries (mountains, valleys, torrential streams), which mark progressive rituals of consecration.[43] During this transitional stage, he encounters the tree of death, guarded by a deceitful hermit. This terrible sight, a bunch of severed heads hanging from the contorted branches of a leafless tree, catalyzes the epiphany of Milarepa's initiatic journey. He finds himself witnessing the most brutal form of violence against the human body. Milarepa, who is at first possessed by deeply human taboos, which rendered him organically incapable of disobeying his mother's rancorous will, looks at the tree with unprotected eyes. This haunting spectacle (a terrestrial horrific replica of the tree of knowledge) counteracts the images of an anxious Marpa waiting for the disciple announced to him by a dream. The scene of the tree of death is shot with a wide-angle lens that conveys a sense of its static exemplarity. For Milarepa, the vision of death is a profound reflection on his own: it is an appropriate symbol on his way to the demonic Man from Nyag. The pure image of the weaving evokes the filmmaker's freedom to inscribe her story in a mythical structure: the name Milarepa means the man in cloth.

Milarepa's encounter with the tree of death counterpoints an incident in which the main character comes across a fisherman performing the rites of

Frame 77. The tree of death

Frame 78. The fisherman of eternal life

Frame 79. Marpa looks upon his new disciple

eternal life. Milarepa's approach to the scene is shot through some bushes in the foreground. The camera is positioned from a high angle, as he walks along a riverbank and sees an old man grilling and devouring fish. There is a cut to the skeleton of a fish in the man's hands as it metamorphoses into a live fish (which he throws back into the river). This transformative ritual repeats three times. The image of the fire portends change and renewal; it underscores the opposition existing between escatological time and cyclical time, mortal and mythical dimensions. Fish are numinous; they represent potential life. They are also identified with knowledge. The man utters, "How could I destroy something without bringing it back to life?"[44] Eventually the fisherman offers Milarepa a map of the rugged terrain that will lead him to Marpa. In the next scene, he is shown taking the young man on a raft across the river. This experience visually defines the film's central theme of spiritual regeneration. The old fisherman is an intermediary figure, for Milarepa and the atemporal forces.

Milarepa's second itinerary is visualized in the mapping of the tents that constitute the monastery of the white lama. "For me," explains Cavani, "the tent has many meanings. It may mean the veil . . . the soul . . . freedom. . . . It is also a sacred place but mobile; it becomes a sort of 'mobile church.' It is a place where one can change because the tent seems to be suspended in mid-air."[45] The monastery is a sacred zone exemplifying an archaic enduring border of the spiritual domain. Within its boundaries, Milarepa is asked to undertake the trial of constructing and destroying a tower of stones: the weaving of the thread of regeneration is alchemically transmuted into the stone, a symbol of the immortal self. During this grueling endeavor he is forced to occupy a subaltern position (he is also denied access to Marpa's tent). As Mircea Eliade has pointed out, "any real act, i.e. any repetition of an archetypal gesture, suspends duration, abolishes profane time, and participates in mythical time."[46] The building of the tower enforces the notion of a male subject who is associated with the interiority of a private, bound space.[47] Milarepa accepts his own sacrifice, ready to serve a higher ideal. The meaning of existence lies in the fight against the evil within himself. He rises to the test, without attempting to shed his responsibility even when his body has been physically debilitated (bleeding and bruised). He undertakes the last crucial step: he breaks the rules of normal behavior and retreats to the wilderness. Like Francesco, he exposes himself to the charge of folly. He is eventually rescued by one of Marpa's disciples, so that he may perform the funerary rites of the great master. Milarepa's journey is rewritten in the myth of the eternal return: knowledge, poetry, and magic constitute the marvelous irrationality of the dream.

Spatial representation designates the loci of Milarepa's spiritual itinerary. In Buddhist ascesis, the discipline of the body is a condition for the discipline of the mind. Cavani's compositions evoke a sense of continuity, as if there were a trajectory aiming at a moving point in space. For example, the closing shot emphasizes a vanishing-point perspective and, therefore, deep space. In the topos of the journey, life and death have a rapport of continuity. Death is only one in a series of steps. The film's last few scenes are superbly conceived in the tradition of Cavani's powerful finales. The protagonist moves away from the camera. We see him walk up the mountain facing the clouds, attempting to reach the horizon. As in fairy tales, the magnitude and height of the mountain allude to his fulfillment. The film is intercut with scenes of Lumley walking along the wide asphalt road where the accident occurred. The conclusion is a figurative expression of what is happening to the main character. The last stage of his journey leads to the totality of being and to the abrogation of the Western self. As Eliade writes, the labyrinth is "the defense, sometimes magical, of a center, of a richness, of a meaning. To enter it may be a ritual of initiation, as in the myth of Theseus. This symbolism models existence that, through numerous trials, advances toward the center, toward oneself, the *Atman*, to use the Indian term. . . . Life is not made of one labyrinth: the trial renews itself."[48] At the end of the film, the spirit of Marpa is left behind, his bodily substance transmuted into mythical form. As Milarepa slowly walks toward the horizon, the teacher whispers with an enigmatic smile: "Do not turn around, young

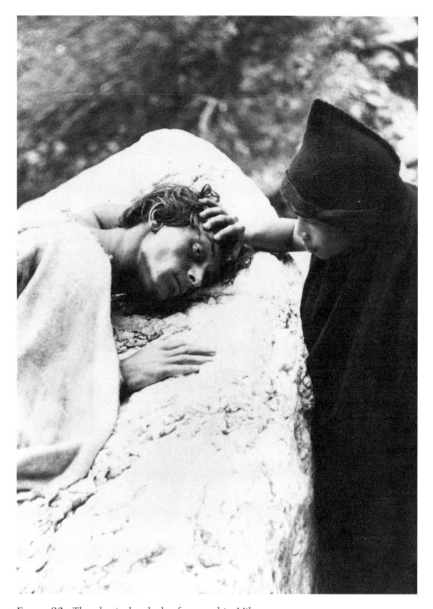

Frame 80. The physical ordeals of renewal in *Milarepa*

Frame 81. Similar scene repeated in *Francesco*

Frame 82. Milarepa performs the funerary rites for his teacher Marpa

man . . . Do not ever turn back." The last image of Marpa is the spirit empiri-
cally seen. The camera's slow inquiry and the studied compositions undermine
a diffused, melancholy sense of the passing of time, of the old master vanishing
and yielding to a new one.

Milarepa is a poem of vision, an homage to the processes of knowledge,
enriched by the cosmogonical myths of the initiation of the hero. Wind, rain,
water, fire, snow, fog all are elements of the material setting in which the action
of the film unfolds. They evoke the very essence of Milarepa's real world. They
create that emotional aesthetic impression which Pasolini singled out in his
review. Also Lino Miccichè emphasizes the film's setting: "boundless horizons,
scattered huts surrounded by clear mountain light, solitary figures with sparing
movements, minimal dialogue and gestures convey great suggestion and vi-
brant intensity."[49] These spatial elements constitute the zero degree of experience. Faced with the emaciated figure of the Tibetan lama, we perceive a modern fable of a generation in defeat, the elusive meaning of our existence.

Francesco and Milarepa are young men in search of identity, who enjoy
a privileged status in Cavani's cinematic discourse. The director's emotional
investment in their stories betrays a remarkable desire for change in the power

Frame 83. Milarepa walking toward the horizon in the closing scene

structures of their time. These figures depart from a kind of gospel of experience to become intense spokesmen for the clarity of being. Mankind must be
rescued not individually but all together from the madness of modern civilization. This is the sacred duty of humanity toward its future. Francesco and
Milarepa are very lonely figures who exist at the *limina* of their culture. They
are not heroes but individuals whose charisma lies in their spiritual conviction
and in their experimenting upon themselves to arrive at a new form of existence
for others. They are like children: creative and selfless. Both choose not to
renounce dream and poetry.

8

The Essential Solitude: A Conclusion

WHILE completing *Interno berlinese*, Cavani was once again faced with a question about her obsessively sexual historical themes:

> Critics have written that in *La pelle* I was a victim of the American myth, and that in *Il portiere di notte* and *Al di là del bene e del male* I tried to express the ambivalence of masculine/feminine, transforming cinema into a kind of sadomasochistic psychoanalytic session. My generation, which grew up after the war, cannot ever forget history, and so, in any case, I still want to continue telling stories about our Europe.[1]

One of the projects that Cavani considered undertaking in the eighties was a film on the Italian premier Aldo Moro, who was kidnapped in March 1978 by the Red Brigades and was executed on 9 May of that year. She gives a chilling assessment of what was the most serious terrorist threat to the democratic state:

> A personality like Moro is of great interest to me because he is someone who died in the same way as he who did not refuse the hemlock . . . I am intrigued by the profound *pietas* he has shown everyone to the very end. In death, he returned dignity to life . . . I am also intrigued by the fact that, as a practicing Catholic, he had the complex of Antigone, or a sacred idea of life. Therefore, if I ever make a film on him, I intend to avoid the contingency of casual politics and focus my discourse on his life and politics in the absolute sense of the administration of the polis, of civil commitment. . . .[2]

Cavani's reference to Socrates assigns Moro's personality an institutional, civic identity that transcends local or ephemeral politics. Such an enlarged, even idealized form of civic consciousness also inspires Cavani's own "historical" cinema, beginning with her documentary films at RAI and culminating in her cinematic portraits of Francis of Assisi, Galileo, and Nietzsche. Cavani's cinema is essentially a way of seeing, as Foucault suggested, "the conditions in which human beings 'problematize' what they are, what they do, and the world in which they live."[3]

Cavani's latest film, *Dove siete? Io sono qui* (Where Are You? I'm Here, 1993), signals a return to the Italian contemporary scene. The film recounts the love story of Fausto (Gaetano Carotenuto) and Elena (Chiara Caselli), an adventure in the world of the deaf, an homage to silence.[4] Fausto belongs to a wealthy family who has raised him to be "normal," while Elena comes from a working-class background and struggles to complete her high school studies. As the director explains, the title signifies "the need for an encounter: between people of different cultures, minorities, and races."[5] Clearly, this film does not advance an inquiry into the social problems of the deaf. It is rather "an experience that enables us to understand diversity and tries to enrich the lives of 'normal' people . . . to reflect on the Babel, the confusion, the noise of the 'normal,' and to focus on the hidden means of communication that rely on silence, thought, and fantasy."[6]

Dove siete? Io sono qui returns to some of the filmmaker's concerns of the late sixties, particularly the themes of isolation and silence explored in *I cannibali* and *L'ospite*. Most familiar is Cavani's dramatizing the deterioration of Italian sociopolitical life through the institutional body of family and school. Fausto and Elena's daily existence is made vulnerable by simple practical jokes, humiliation, and even overt threat. Yet Fausto and Elena do not blame society for these vexations. They do not show mistrust or suspicion of others. Their encounters are characterized by joy and pleasure. The most effective moment of the film is when Fausto rescues the Butoh dancer Akira from a bar fight and, as a result of this friendship, discovers a new art form.[7]

The one common denominator throughout Cavani's films is the use of dance, with its powerfully emblematic gestural codes. In *Dove siete? Io sono qui*, the four dance sequences celebrate the vitality of a form of communication that is not spoken. Particularly memorable is the first image of Akira (Ko Morobushi) lying naked on a bare stage against a black background. The performance begins with the slender figure of the dancer arising from the floor and reaching up toward the light. His body is crouched (painted with white lead), his knees bent, his head shaved, his eyes closed. Akira's body suggests a stylized birth from pain and darkness. Prior to his performance onstage, the dancer is seriously beaten up during a fight. His injured body has had to be carried to the theater. Akira's dance manifests the stigmata of pain and also expresses the desire to transcend physicality and (perpetual) disintegration in a return to a luminous origin. In the end, the dancer has overcome his pain and stands upright facing the audience. For Cavani, "this brief scene stresses the theme of rebirth, or at the very least it creates a setting for the epiphany of a god."[8] Throughout the performance, in order to sense the vibrations of the music, Fausto touches the speakers. A vision emerges from silence, allowing voiceless words to be born: the body of desire (*nikutai*) is subliminally inscribed in Akira's movements.[9]

That same night, Fausto stands outside in a pouring rain with his arms outstretched in the air. He is lit by a blue light, framed half-naked, finally freeing himself. The encounter between the Butoh dancer and Fausto becomes an engagement in which they efface each other. Beneath appearances, there exists a profound need to avoid the babel of words, the squalid artificiality of the sounds that the "normal" compulsively utter. Ko Morobushi writes on the meaning of Butoh:

Frame 84. Ko Morobushi as the Butoh dancer in *Dove siete? Io sono qui* (Where Are You? I'm Here, 1993)

Frame 85. The dancer lying naked onstage

To dance is to attempt to give a name to something that is still unnamed, like a cloudy vapor moving in front of us, which sometimes we believe we can reach, but it hides relentlessly.

To dance is the excitement without end in front of this horizon, which constantly backs away. It is the pleasure of a neutral zone, where life and death become profoundly entwined.

To dance is to restore the body to its nomadic happiness.

Dance, and thus *Butoh*, is an unstable, endless process between apparition and dispersion.[10]

In the second dance performance, the scene fades up (from a slightly high camera angle) on the stem of a rose being held by a figure as he enters the frame from the left, in a medium shot. The dancer, dressed in a long white coat, slowly moves to the center of the stage, predominantly lit in blue. In a close-up, his face is white, bearing the marks of aging; his eyes are closed. This figure resembles a mummy who is attempting to retrace the steps of an ancient itinerary. The rose in his hand appears as a heavy burden. The floor is covered with sand, which evokes the surface of a mysterious planet, or the moon. At the end, Akira rotates his body facing the light, then walks backward, disappearing into the darkness, raising the rose above his head. Simultaneously, the light beam closes like a curtain. This dance sequence is intercut with close-ups of Elena watching the performance specially arranged for her by Fausto. The sensational images created by Ko Morobushi are violently primitive and disquieting. Morobushi's style, like that of his teacher Tatsumi Hijikata, is bold, provocative, and transgressive, quite remote from the lyrical performances of Kazuo Ōno, the legendary founder of Butoh.

These performances are reminiscent of the dance scenes in *Il portiere di notte* and *Al di là del bene e del male*, where the dancers project their controlled movements through the proscenium to the audience beyond. Bert and Lucia/ Salomè choose to present the body as the techne of pleasure, while Fritz's hallucinations in Venice are a prelude to his final dissolution into madness. However, the Butoh dancer is in a speculative (rather than theatrical) relationship with his own nascent identity as other: he suggests radical newness. Akira expresses a unique subjectivity that opens to a kind of immanent, original universe. The empty stage, where he performs, is significantly evocative of the primeval surface of the earth. In another scene, with Elena at school attempting, with great difficulty, to read, an apparition of Akira materializes. Her anxious voice is intercut with an image of the Butoh dancer, his coat blowing, standing motionless in a pool of blue light. The imagined stage becomes a symbolic space that embraces a poetics of estrangement, and yet it opens to the possibility of self-acceptance. This sequence is oddly instantaneous and low-key. It has nothing like the extraordinary psychological density of Fausto's vision of Elena's funeral.

Akira's last performance occurs during Fausto's long vigil in a hospital as he awaits news of Elena's condition after she has been violently attacked by a group of youngsters. In a dream sequence, Fausto is leaning over Elena's coffin in a church. A blue light on his face cues to the dance scene. Akira appears with a red rose, moving very slowly from left to right. Imperceptibly, the camera dollies and zooms toward his face as he carefully places the rose on her coffin. Throughout the performance the dancer gradually steps out of blue light and enters into a warmer light. When Fausto wakes up, he is relieved to find out that Elena has survived the ordeal. He begins to recite Catullus, her beloved Latin verses: "Da mi basia mille, deinde centum . . ." (give me a thousand kisses, then give me one hundred more). In the last shot of the film, the camera dollies with Fausto as he moves through a long corridor toward a glimmering blue light. In the Japanese tradition, white and blue, which are the domain of Akira's performances, are the colors of death. Blue suggests transcendence. It always stands in relation to the darkness from which the dancer emerges. Within this context, the Butoh dance mediates the experience of death. This final sequence fails to give the film the thematic tension of an earlier version, where Cavani clearly intended to end the film with Elena's death.[11]

Dove siete? Io sono qui shows what is quintessential in Cavani's cinema: her obsessive need to make differences visible, to rediscover the limit. The rhetoric of isolation that dominates the dance sequences is a denunciation of human hypocrisy, the emptiness of language. The Butoh performances in particular exploit cinema's ultimate visual capacities. *Dove siete? Io sono qui*, a sensitive film, was not a commercial success. It represents a pause in Cavani's career, in which she sets up a very small stage, after the spectacular *Francesco*. Her next film, now in preproduction with the working title of *The Seventh Circle*, is based on a book by Leonard Simon. It is a psychological thriller, to be shot in English between London and Rome.

As of this writing, Cavani has completed her twelfth feature film. Her fascination with cinema as a means of exploring the most vital problems of European culture has made her one of Italy's most influential filmmakers of the generation after Visconti, De Sica, and Fellini. She views European sociohistorical life as a struggle between the marginal, the transgressive, the diverse, and the accessible, the normal, the generally social.

Cavani's cinema commands our attention and imagination in the way classical theater did. It establishes a debate on the anthropological nature of man as an entity who is part of a specific culture. Her cinema is the cinema of tragic act, as a vehicle for transcending reality. It is essentially a creative act, a constant individual search for a truth that is not doctrinal but created:

> I believe that people want to see adventures of ideas, especially stories that capture their attention, disturb their dreams and decisions, and affect their lives. These adventures ought to provoke in the spectators' mind the power of doubt and anxiety with which they cannot easily come to terms.[12]

Cavani's cinema of ideas dramatizes the essential solitude of a subject. Her latest films pay homage to silence, gesture, and vision. Perhaps beauty remains Cavani's most important political category. Her characters are allured *oltre la porta* by the mysterious seduction of a (transgressive) beauty that leads them to yearn for transcendence. Cavani's characters bear the playfulness of the Nietzschean *puer aeternus* (eternal child), whose function lies in trespassing the boundaries and exciting new creative play. In Cavani's cinema, the ancient topos of the *puer* symbolizes the idea of a "play that is divine because there is no promise / nor hope to gain."[13] It is the leading idea of Cavani's vision of the world. In this world, only play, as the Dionysian *puer* and artists engage in it, discloses the creative forces of constructing and destroying, without any moral judgment, in eternal ingenuity.

Notes

Introduction

1. *Liliana Cavani*, Il Castoro cinema, no. 21 (Florence: La Nuova Italia, 1975), p. 2. All translations are mine, unless otherwise cited. Ciriaco Tiso's monographic study is the most comprehensive analytical work on Cavani to date. For a critical introduction, see Francesco Buscemi, *Invito al cinema di Liliana Cavani* (Milan: Mursia, 1996). Also: *Liliana Cavani*, Schede Registi SPF no. 8 (Rome: Centro Studi Sampaolofilm, 1975; Daniela Schettino, "La cinematografia di Liliana Cavani" (Diss., Università degli Studi di Lecce: Facoltà di Lettere e Filosofia, 1976–1977); Paolo Bosisio, "Liliana Cavani," *Belfagor* 33, no. 2 (1978): 173–190, 158; Arnoldo Garcia del Vall, *Liliana Cavani* (Madrid: Editorial Fundamentos, 1980); Paola Tallarigo and Luca Gasparini, eds., *Il cinema di Liliana Cavani: Lo sguardo libero* (Florence: La Casa Usher, 1990); Primo Goldoni, ed., *Il cinema di Liliana Cavani*, Atti del Convegno: Carpi, 25 February–3 March 1990 (Casalecchio di Reno, Bologna: Grafis Edizioni, 1993). I shall list relevant reviews in the discussion of individual films. Quotations and bibliographical references without a page number are taken from the director's Archival Collection.

In 1990, Cavani's hometown, Carpi, established the "Associazione Fondo Liliana Cavani," where the director's films are preserved and are made available for consultation.

2. Lietta Tornabuoni, "Intervista con Liliana Cavani," in Tallarigo and Gasparini, *Lo sguardo libero*, p. 14.

3. In an interview granted on 10 May 1990, Cavani confessed that she decided to give up archaeology because of her poor knowledge of German, a language she considered necessary to any serious research in that field. When Cavani enrolled at the Centro Sperimentale, the Italian film school founded by Mussolini in 1935, she was the only woman to be admitted to study directing in 1960. Biographical information on Liliana Cavani is scarce, often inaccurate. She insists on privacy because she believes in the autonomy of art from autobiographical explicability. By effacing her authorial persona, the director has enforced the absolute centrality of interpretation. For further details, see Dacia Maraini, "Liliana Cavani," in *Ma tu chi eri? Interviste sull'infanzia* (Milan: Bompiani, 1973), pp. 75–87; Tiso, *Liliana Cavani*, pp. 29–31; Aldo Tassone, "Liliana Cavani," in *Parla il cinema italiano* (Milan: Il Formichiere, 1980), 2:109–121; Tallarigo and Gasparini, *Lo sguardo libero*, pp. 12, 13–18, 153–154.

4. Tiso, *Liliana Cavani*, pp. 20–21.

5. "Lo scandalo della verità," in Tallarigo and Gasparini, *Lo sguardo libero*, p. 141.

6. In his article, Montanelli attacks attempts by ambivalent TV industry decision-makers to resist freedom and anticlericalism. He lists Cavani's documentary as one of the TV programs that perpetuate confusion and resentment. "Il teleschermo avvelenato," *Corriere della sera*, 6 May 1964, p. 3. Canby laments the fact that "Europe is entering its Berlitz era of movie making," and that the standard use of English has neutralized national characteristics. "Ici Se Habla Euro-English," *New York Times*, 4 June 1989, sec. 2, p. 1 (translated as "Le lingue tagliate dei registi," *La stampa*, 10 June 1989, p. 3). His position is debated in *La stampa* by Fellini, Bertolucci, Paolo and Vittorio

Taviani, and Cavani herself—who claims that her film provoked not "a crisis of culture but a widening of communication." Lietta Tornabuoni, "I guai della 'Berlitz Era,' " 11 June 1989, p. 3, and "Chi vive nella Berlitz Era?" 13 June 1989, p. 3.

7. P. B. and S. T., "Anti-rétro: Entretien avec Michel Foucault," *Cahiers du Cinéma*, nos. 251–252 (July–August 1974): 10–12; "Liliana Cavani and Félix Guattari: Una conversazione," in L. Cavani, Franco Arcalli, and Italo Moscati, *Al di là del bene e del male* (Turin: Einaudi, 1977), p. 174; A. Banti, "Un maestro e un'esordiente," *Approdo letterario*, October–December 1968, pp. 153–154; A. Moravia, "Antigone si arrende ai tecnocrati," *L'espresso*, 10 May 1970, p. 23. For a discussion of Cavani's critical reviews, see Buscemi, *Invito al cinema di Liliana Cavani*, pp. 139–148.

8. Tassone, *Parla il cinema italiano*, 2:109–110.

9. Bianca Sermonti, who devoted a study to Italian women television directors in the late 1960s, noted the incongruity of including Cavani in this group. "My type of filmmaking," Cavani insisted, "does not agree with television methods. I could never rehearse and organize a program just one week after the assignment. I need to plan, investigate, and research around the filmic text; my assimilative slowness makes me unfit for television directing." "Quando il regista è donna," *Rivista del cinematografo*, nos. 4–5 (1967): 260. The following is a guide to the director's television years; there is no critical study of her documentary films: G., "Alla TV: Pirandello," *Corriere della sera*, 25 November 1961, p. 6; Ialli, "Hitler al potere," *L'unità*, 25 Novemebr 1961, p. 8; Montior, "Il tamburo dei tedeschi," *Il paese*, 25 November 1961, p. 3; S. Su., "La tecnica della dittatura," *Il popolo*, 25 November 1961, p. 5; Scap., "La notte dei lunghi coltelli di Hitler," *L'avanti*, 25 November 1961, p. 5; Vice, "Televisione: Gli anni tragici dell'Europa," *L'avanti*, 2 December 1961, p. 5; G. C., "Litanie storiche," *L'unità*, 20 October 1962, p. 7; G. T., "Sui teleschermi: Secondo canale," *Il messaggero*, 20 October 1962, p. 8; M. Dol., "Hitler überall," *Il tempo*, 20 October 1962, p. 10; U. Bz., "Il flagello della svastica," *La stampa*, 20 October 1962, p. 4; V. B. "TV: 'Anni d'Europa' e il paroliere di turno," *Corriere della sera*, 20 October 1962, p. 8; Vice, "Una trasmissione sul nazismo," *L'avanti*, 20 October 1962, p. 5; G. C., "Germania demoniaca," *L'unità*, 27 October 1962, p. 7; G., "TV: 'Sesto piano,' " *Corriere della sera*, 27 October 1962, p. 8; G. T., "Sui teleschermi: Secondo canale," *Il messaggero*, 27 October 1962, p. 8; U. Bz., "Berlino in fiamme," *La stampa*, 27 October 1962, p. 4; G. C., "Controcanale: Stalin dal '34 al '40," *L'unità*, 22 December 1962, p. 7; G. T., "Sui teleschermi: Secondo canale," *Il messaggero*, 22 December 1962, p. 8; M. Dol., "L'età di Stalin," *Il tempo*, 22 December 1962, p. 12; V. B., "Le donne sapienti," *Corriere della sera*, 22 December 1962, p. 8; U. Bz., "Donne intellettuali di trecento anni fa," *La stampa*, 22 December 1962, p. 4; Vice, "L'età di Stalin," *L'avanti*, 22 December 1962, p. 5; G. C., "Controcanale: Conclusione infantile," *L'unità*, 29 December 1962, p. 7; Ivano Cipriani, "Stalin alla TV," *Rinascita*, 29 December 1962, p. 26; U. Bz., "Una serata politica," *La stampa*, 29 December 1962, p. 4; G. T., "Sui teleschermi: Secondo canale," *Il messaggero*, 23 May 1963, p. 8; U. Bz., "Burocrazia sotto accusa," *La stampa*, 24 May 1963, p. 4; S. Su., "Videosera: Congedo di 'Osservatorio,' " *Il popolo*, 29 June 1963, p. 7; I. C., "La casa in Italia," *Televisione*, no. 2 (1964): 99–101; Gabriella Guidi, "Liliana Cavani prepara un'inchiesta sulla casa," *Rivista del cinematografo*, nos. 3–4 (March–April 1964): 164–166; Alberto Pacifici, "Nove signore in cabina di regia," *Settimana Incom*, 5 April 1964, pp. 24–28; Mario Benedetti, "Baracche e ville con piscina: Queste le case degli italiani," *Incom*, 3 May 1964, pp. 10–14; G. C., "Controcanale: 'Ribalta' senza luci," *L'unità*, 3 May 1964, p. 4;

N. S., "Il respiro calmo della verità," *L'avanti*, 3 May 1964, p. 6; S. Su., "Videosera: I 'bassi' e le baracche," *Il popolo*, 3 May 1964, p. 5; U. Bz., "Mina recita 'Otello' accanto a Renzo Ricci," *La stampa*, 3 May 1964, p. 5; Montanelli, "Il teleschermo avvelenato," p. 3; I. Cipriani, "La casa in Italia, oggi," *Rinascita*, 9 May 1964, p. 27; "Saltata l'inchiesta sulla casa," *L'avanti*, 10 May 1964, p. 6; Indro Montanelli, "TV: Monopolio di complicità," *Corriere della sera*, 10 May 1964, p. 3; Ludovico Alessandrini, "Momenti delle telecamere," *Osservatore romano*, 10 May 1964, p. 5; L. Cavani, "Il teleschermo avvelenato" (Lettere al Corriere), *Corriere della sera*, 10 May 1964, p. 5; S.G.B., "Il guitto di Waterloo e l'inchiesta nascosta," *Giornale d'Italia*, 12 May 1964, p. 13; N. S., "Un ordine e un metodo," *L'avanti*, 17 May 1964, p. 6; U. Bz., "Deludente il 'Cantatutto' con Milva, Villa e Arigliano: Vigorosa e coraggiosa puntata dell'inchiesta 'La casa in Italia,' " *La stampa*, 17 May 1964, p. 5; Vice, "Da Cantatutto ai pirati," *L'unità*, 17 May 1964, p. 11; Ber., "Senza smalto," *Il piccolo*, 24 May 1964, p. 6; U. Bz., "I dispiaceri del sabato sera," *La stampa*, 24 May 1964, p. 5; A. G., "Sui teleschermi: Primo canale," *Il messaggero*, 24 May 1964, p. 10; Vice, "Controcanale: Un'assurda riforma," *L'unità*, 24 May 1964, p. 9; N. S., "L'inchiesta sul tetto che scotta," *L'avanti*, 31 May 1964, p. 6; Vice, "Controcanale: C'è casa e casa," *L'unità*, 31 May 1964, p. 9; R. G., "La casa in Italia," *Educazione e TV*, July 1964, 58–61; U. Bz., "La donna e la Resistenza in un'inchiesta televisiva," *La stampa*, 6 August 1964, p. 4; Ludovico Alessandrini, "Momenti delle telecamere," *Osservatore romano*, 1 January 1965, p. 3; Francesco Bolzoni, "Una regista televisiva tra i 'piccoli fratelli di Gesù,' " *Osservatore romano*, 2–3 January 1965, p. 3; G. C., "Indagine sulla pace," *L'unità* (Milan), 8 May 1965, p. 9; G. T., "Sui teleschermi: Secondo canale," *Il messaggero*, 8 May 1965, p. 10; U. Bz., "Intervista ai professori che hanno operato le gemelle," *La stampa*, 10 May 1965, p. 4; G. C., "La donna nella Resistenza," *L'unità* (Milan), 10 May 1965, p. 6.; M. Dol., "Le donne nella Resistenza," *Il tempo*, 10 May 1965, p. 11; G. C., "L''eroe' traditore," *L'unità* (Milan), 5 June 1965, p. 9; G. T., "Sui teleschermi: Secondo canale," *Il messaggero*, 5 June 1965, p. 10; M. Dol., "Primo piano: Pétain," *Il tempo*, 5 June 1965, p. 8; U. Bz., "L'imputato Pétain," *La stampa*, 5 June 1965, p. 4; Francesco Mei, "I connotati dello sterminio," *Il popolo*, 9 October 1977, p. 7; Giovanni Grazzini, " 'La camorra' vince ad Este," *Corriere della sera*, 10 October 1965, p. 13; G. Grazzini, "Settimo 'Premio dei Colli': Il cinema fruga la realtà," *Corriere della sera*, 4 October 1966, p. 13. See also Tiso, *Liliana Cavani*, pp. 29–38; Tallarigo and Gasparini, *Lo sguardo libero*, pp. 22–40; Alessandro Amaducci et al., eds., "Liliana Cavani," in *Memoria, mito, storia* (Turin: Archivio Nazionale Cinematografico della Resistenza, 1994), pp. 45–54; Lietta Tornabuoni, "Cavani: Solo la Storia ci salverà," *La stampa*, 2 July 1994, p. 13, and "Riscopriamo la Storia," *Rivista del cinematografo* 64 (August–September 1994): 36–37; and the following writings by Cavani: "Una regista alla ricerca dei piccoli fratelli di Gesù," *Rivista del cinematografo*, no. 1 (January 1965): 46–47; "I fratelli di Gesù nella bidonville," *Orizzonti*, 17 January 1965, pp. 24–26; "Le donne della resistenza," *Orizzonti*, 4 April 1965, pp. 6–7.

10. "Dalla TV al cinema," in Tallarigo and Gasparini, *Lo sguardo libero*, p. 127. Guglielmi was director of special programming at RAI-2. Cavani's problematic relationship with censors began with *La casa in Italia*, which documented the exploitation of low-income families by development entrepreneurs. RAI, under pressure, did not air Part Two. Cavani's denunciation of the developers' tactics prompted, however, the direct intervention of Pope Paul VI.

11. Natalia Ginzburg focused on these features in her review of *Storia del Terzo Reich*, reaired in 1977: "Outstanding, exemplary, for its clarity of words and images, and for its intense pacing." "La Cavani racconta l'orrore di Hitler," *Corriere della sera*, 21 September 1977, p. 15.

12. Etymologically, *diverso* signifies "deviation," *divertere* from *versus*. Giacomo Devoto, *Avviamento alla etimologia italiana: Dizionario etimologico*, 2d rev. ed. (Florence: Le Monnier, 1968), p. 136. This terminology is still retained; see Fernaldo di Giammatteo, "Cavani: La nausea del diverso, il rifiuto del dubbio," in Tallarigo and Gasparini, *Lo sguardo libero*, p. 135. For an understanding of the political and ideological language that has controlled criticism of Cavani since the first reviews of her documentaries, the following comments on *Storia del Terzo Reich* are exemplary: on one hand, she is accused of lacking courage for neglecting Spartacus in her depiction of Nazism (Monitor, "Il tamburo dei tedeschi," p. 3); on the other, she is praised for her impressive and objective reconstruction of the historical events (G., "Alla TV: Pirandello," p. 6; S. Su., "La tecnica della dittatura," p. 5). *L'avanti* calls her work "breathtaking" (Scap., "La notte dei lunghi coltelli di Hitler," p. 5), while *L'unità* laments Cavani's omission of the Catholic and capitalist forces contributing to Hitler's rise to power (Ialli, "Hitler al potere," p. 8; G. C., "Litanie storiche," p. 7, and "Germania demoniaca," p. 7).

13. The script for *Il caso Liuzzo* (1969), originally entitled *Intolerance*, was based on the true story of the American woman shot in Alabama after attending, with a black companion, a peace march organized by Martin Luther King, Jr. It was directed by Luigi Fina for the television series *Teatro-Inchiesta*. Cavani wrote two other treatments on American racism: *Black Jesus* (1965–1966), a musical depicting an American black as a Christ figure, and *Malcolm X* (1968). They were never financed. See Ludovico Alessandrini and L. Cavani, "Uno 'Spiritual cinematografico': Black Jesus," *Fiera letteraria*, 12 December 1965, pp. 6–7. On the relationship between cinema and racism, Cavani wrote, "A truly nonracist cinema is almost impossible because the man of Western culture has cultivated for two thousand years, within himself and society, intolerance as his only God." "Un cinema antirazzista non è ancora nato," *Rivista del cinematografo*, nos. 6–7 (June–July 1968): 374.

During this period, Cavani completed three unpublished teleplays: *Il caso Oppenheimer* (1963–1964), *Provocazione* (1965), inspired by Dostoievsky, and *Coriolano* (1967), adapted from Shakespeare's play.

14. Personal interview, 27 June 1989. Cavani rejected the ideologies of the 1960s because they were "heavy and intolerant."

15. Tiso, *Liliana Cavani*, p. 13.

16. Anna Maria Leone, "Contesto ma credo," *Il messaggero*, 16 December 1973, p. 3; Maraini, *Ma tu chi eri?*, pp. 82–83.

17. Cavani recounts Pasolini's assessment in her "Pasolini," *"La Biennale" Annuario* (1976), p. 1039. Carlo Pisacane (1818–1857) was a Neapolitan patriot and writer who died fighting against the Bourbons.

18. From the Greek *hairetikós*, originally connoting "election," "inclination," "proposal." *Dizionario enciclopedico italiano* (Rome: Istituto della Enciclopedia Italiana, 1956), 4:441.

19. Tiso, *Liliana Cavani*, p. 14.

20. For a list of the filmmaker's cinematic preferences, see Tiso, *Liliana Cavani*, p. 9; Tassone, *Parla il cinema italiano*, 2:122.

21. Tiso, *Liliana Cavani*, p. 10. "I do not believe in the objectivity of the director. It is always a person who makes a film, whether he has the soul of a bureaucrat or the instinct of a madman. Even the most engagé film requires the individual; just think of the great Russian cinema of the Pudovkins and the Ejzensteins. . . . Before reality I have first of all an attitude as a 'person' rather than as a director. Reality is a planet to be explored without preconceived ideas." Ibid., pp. 2–3.

22. André Bazin, *What Is cinema?*, ed. and trans. Hugh Gray (Berkeley and Los Angeles: University of California Press, 1967), 1:37. For a penetrating discussion of Bazin's notion of cinematic representation, realism, and ambiguity, see Noël Carroll, *Philosophical Problems of Classical Film Theory* (Princeton, NJ: Princeton University Press, 1988), pp. 104–120.

23. Tiso, *Liliana Cavani*, pp. 10–11.

24. Friedrich Nietzsche, *Philosophy in the Tragic Age of the Greeks*, trans. and introd. Marianne Cowan (Chicago: Gateway, 1962), p. 62.

25. Tiso, *Liliana Cavani*, p. 8. Baubo was the mythical wife of Disaule of Eleusis, reputed to have sheltered the grieving Demeter. She appears to be a hypostasis with phallic connotations. See Erich Neumann, *The Origins and History of Consciousness*, foreword by C. G. Jung, trans. R.F.C. Hull, Bollingen Series XLII (Princeton, NJ: Princeton University Press, 1973), p. 84, and *The Great Mother: An Analysis of the Archetype*, trans. Ralph Manheim, Bollingen Series XLVII (Princeton, NJ: Princeton University Press, 1974), p. 139.

26. Tassone, *Parla il cinema italiano*, 2:123.

27. See Michel Foucault, *Histoire de la sexualité*, vol. 1, *La Volonté de savoir* (Paris: Gallimard, 1976), p. 123; Gilles Deleuze, *Nietzsche and Philosophy*, trans. Hugh Tomlinson (New York: Columbia University Press, 1983), pp. x–xi. Cavani has acknowledged the congenial influence of Nietzsche's writings in an interview on 11 May 1990. She befriended Foucault at the time of the polemics surrounding *Il portiere di notte*, when the French philosopher openly defended the film.

28. The idea of limit is associated with the sociological concept of taboo. Truth is the product of a constant transgression of the limits of knowledge. See Charles C. Lemert and Garth Gillian, *Michel Foucault: Social Theory as Transgression* (New York: Columbia University Press, 1982), pp. 133–134, 137.

29. Edward C. Whitmont, *The Symbolic Quest: Basic Concepts of Analytical Psychology* (Princeton, NJ: Princeton University Press, 1978), p. 306. Mircea Eliade lists the wanderings in labyrinths among the patterns of a difficult road that lead to the center, a zone of absolute reality. Attaining the center is equivalent to an initiation. See *Cosmos and History: The Myth of the Eternal Return* (New York: Harper, 1959), p. 18.

30. See Penelope Reed Doob, *The Idea of the Labyrinth from Classical Antiquity through the Middles Ages* (Ithaca, NY, and London: Cornell University Press, 1990), pp. 24–25.

31. Tiso has addressed the issue in terms of *récit* and *structure*. See *Liliana Cavani*, pp. 25–26.

32. Interview, 27 June 1989.

33. Michel Foucault, *Language, Counter-Memory, Practice: Selected Essays and Interviews*, ed. and introd. Donald F. Bouchard, trans. D. F. Bouchard and Sherry Simon (Ithaca, NY: Cornell University Press, 1977), p. 45.

34. For the visual figuration of the feminine position in narrative cinema, see Teresa De Lauretis, *Technologies of Gender: Essays on Theory, Film and Fiction* (Bloomington: Indiana University Press, 1987), p. 44.

35. Claire Clouzot, "Liliana Cavani: Le Mythe, le sexe et la révolte," *Ecran 74*, no. 26 (June 1974): 38.

36. Ambiguous derives from *ambigere*: "to doubt," "to be undecided." *Dizionario enciclopedico italiano*, 1:344. In formal logic, *ambiguus* is opposed to univocal, as a word alluding to polysemy.

Chapter 1
Francesco di Assisi: The Medieval Chronicle and the Establishing of Physical Reality

1. Lucio S. Caruso, "Francesco, uomo normale," *Rivista del cinematografo* 40 (February 1966): 111. The idea of a film on the life of Francis of Assisi was proposed to Cavani by Angelo Guglielmi. After initial reservations, because of her secular background, Cavani accepted the challenge to present a saint who has performed a revolution *ante litteram*. She requested permission to shoot on location (Assisi, Gubbio, Bevagna, Spello) and in 16mm film. She was assigned a budget of thirty million lire and the assistance of an independent producer, Leo Pescarolo. *Francesco di Assisi* was shot in forty-nine days and became the first feature film ever to be produced by RAI-TV. It was released in June 1972 (blown up to 35mm). The film's original title, often printed in the curtailed form *Francesco d'Assisi*, is not elided.

Previous cinematic treatments of the subject include: Mario Corsi, *Frate sole* (1918); Giulio Antamoro, *Frate Francesco* (1926–1927); Roberto Rossellini, *Francesco, giullare di Dio* (1950); Raffaello Pacini, *La tragica notte di Assisi* (1960); Michael Curtiz, *Francesco d'Assisi* (1960). Cavani does not endorse Rossellini's didactic intentions and bases her film on historical and theological sources. She acknowledges particularly the influence of the writings of Teilhard de Chardin, who restored a cosmic perspective to the Christian message. Rossellini's film is a poetic prototype that never questions the conventional sainthood of the Friar Minor. In his analysis of Rossellini's films, Peter Brunette sees in *Francesco, giullare di Dio* the beginning of the director's interest in history but still allows the strong didactic vein. See *Roberto Rossellini* (New York: Oxford University Press, 1987), p. 128. Also, Gian Piero Brunetta sees Cavani's adaptation as marked by a "revolutionary élan" in response to the Rossellinian matrix. *Storia del cinema italiano dal 1945 agli anni ottanta* (Rome: Editori Riuniti, 1982), p. 705. In an interview for the TV program *Zoom*, both directors discussed their role as television filmmakers with Pietro Pintus at the 1966 Venice Film Festival. Rossellini flamboyantly claimed that "the auteur cinema could survive only in television," while Cavani praised the artistic freedom that RAI allowed to its authors: "*Francesco di Assisi* would never have been financed outside, especially in the version I chose to make, that is, the version of the truth, of bare reality, of not being spectacular in the common sense of the word." (Typescript, 8 September 1966, Cavani's Archival Collection.) For Cavani's comments on Rossellini's film as well as her approach to the subject, see Tassone, *Parla il cinema italiano*, 2:124; Sergio Trasatti, "L'inquietante Francesco," *Cinecircoli* 4 (March 1966): pp. 28–29; Mario Foglietti, "San Francesco come noi," *Il popolo*, 26 April 1966, p. 3; Mario Lucchini and Alessandro Zaina, "Intervista a Liliana Cavani," *Il cammino* (Annali francescani), November 1966, pp. 281–282.

2. Personal interview, 10 May 1990.

3. In her press release, the director speaks of *un'avventura ancora attuale* as well as of an archetypal story that expresses conflicts of class, family, and generation. Cavani was also inspired by a contemporary model, Charles De Foucauld and his *Petits Frères*, the subject of her documentary film *Gesù mio fratello* (My Brother Jesus, 1964). On this point, see her 1965 articles "Una regista alla ricerca dei piccoli fratelli di Gesù," pp. 46–47, and "I fratelli di Gesù nella bidonville," pp. 24–25.

4. *The Acoustic Mirror: The Female Voice in Psychoanalysis and Cinema* (Bloomington and Indianapolis: Indiana University Press, 1988), p. 221. On the theme of Francesco's nakedness, see also Tiso, *Liliana Cavani*, pp. 42–43.

5. See Devoto, *Avviamento alla etimologia italiana* p. 325. This is the revolutionary social role Francesco takes upon himself. He displaces himself into a new definition of space.

6. In this regard, I refer to the etymology of the Latin adjective *humilis*, that which is "adherent to the ground." It derives from *humus*, "earth." See Devoto, *Avviamento alla etimologia italiana*, p. 445.

7. I am quoting from the press release issued by Liliana Cavani in 1966 to address the parliamentary proceedings initiated against her film by a member of the right-wing party Movimento Sociale Italiano, the *missino* Cruciani. See also her letter to the Turin newspaper *Il nostro tempo*, now in L. Cavani, *Francesco e Galileo: Due film*, introd. Leo Pestelli (Turin: Gribaudi, 1970), pp. 110–113.

8. "La TV come mezzo di espressione: Si apre un dibattito sulle sabbie mobili," *Civiltà dell'immagine*, October 1966, p. 98. On the controversial reception of *Francesco di Assisi*, see "La polemica," in Cavani, *Francesco e Galileo*, pp. 107–113; Ivano Cipriani, "Francesco sul video," *Rinascita*, 14 May 1966, p. 22; I. Moscati, "Il fuoco fatuo dei critici TV," *Civiltà dell'immagine*, July 1966, pp. 9–12. Upon the film's theatrical release, Callisto Cosulich commented on the 1966 confrontational atmosphere as reflecting national identities: "The serious Italy and the hypocritical one of the holy pictures pinned on the walls; the secular or authentically religious Italy and the pharisaic; the democratic Italy and the clerical-Fascist." "Credere, disobbedire e combattere," *A.B.C.*, 7 July 1972, p. 62.

9. Daniela Pasti, "Bello, asciutto, estatico: E' il santo che fa scena," *La repubblica*, 26 September 1981, p. 4.

10. Julien Green, *God's Fool: The Life and Times of Francis of Assisi*, trans. Peter Heinegg (New York: Harper and Row, 1985), p. 144. The historical readings on which Cavani based her first version of the life of St. Francis include the *Vita Prima* by Thomas of Celano, Paul Sabatier's *Vie de S. François d'Assise*, and Johannes Jorgensen's *Francesco di Assisi*. Francesco's personality was directly reconstructed from his writing, including a selection from the *Fioretti*. On the typological motifs that command early Franciscan biography, see John V. Fleming, *From Bonaventure to Bellini: An Essay in Franciscan Exegesis* (Princeton, NJ: Princeton University Press, 1982), pp. 3–31.

11. See Whitmont, *The Symbolic Quest*, p. 304. One might point out that Cavani's shorts at the Centro Sperimentale di Cinematografia were entitled *Incontro di notte* (Night Encounter, 1961) and *La battaglia* (The Battle, 1962; working title, *L'evento*). The first film uncovers the subtle forms of unconscious racism in the story of a one-

night friendship between a drunken Italian and a black man. *La battaglia* is a particularly effective prototype of Cavani's critical epistemology and narrative devices. It stages the story of Theseus and Ariadne in a scenic theater by a group of young people. In the awakening of dream and imagination, the accidental killing of a black companion by a jealous Scotsman (Theseus) collides with the ideal world of innocence represented by Lucia (Ariadne). Cavani's treatment of the mythical quest shows control in visualizing the world of desire in contrast with the bondage of the world of experience.

12. *The Acoustic Mirror*, p. 221. It attests to the relevance of folk laughter as an element of Christian spirituality. The medieval imagination posits an essential congruence between hierarchy in the body (the highest element is the head) and the established allegorical framework of meaning. Francesco's individual experience of a new high falls within Bataille's kind of headless allegory. See Allan Stoekl's introduction to Georges Bataille, *Visions of Excess: Selected Writings 1927–1939* (Minneapolis: University of Minnesota Press, 1985), pp. xiii–xiv.

13. *God's Fool*, p. 84. On Franciscan poverty and permanent liminality, see Victor W. Turner, *The Ritual Process: Structure and Anti-Structure* (London: Routledge & Kegan Paul, 1969), pp. 140–147. Some of the attributes of the liminal personae are passivity, humility, silence, and nakedness: "to demonstrate that as liminal beings they have no status, property, insignia, secular clothing indicating rank or role, position in a kinship system. . . . It is as though they are being reduced or ground down to a uniform condition to enable them to cope with their new station in life." Ibid., p. 95.

14. Tassone, *Parla il cinema italiano*, 2:124–125. The Mitchell is a bulky and confining camera. Giuliano Gramigna and Giovanni Cesareo, among others, reviewed the creative potentiality of the *cronaca ideologica* in G., "TV: Debutto felice del 'San Francesco,'" *Corriere della sera*, 7 May 1966, p. 13; "Francesco non si piega alla regole," *L'unità* (Milan ed.), 9 May 1966, p. 7.

15. See *Metahistory: The Historical Imagination in Nineteenth-Century Europe* (Baltimore and London: Johns Hopkins University Press, 1973), p. 5.

16. *Liliana Cavani*, p. 45.

17. Sergio Saviane, "Il fratello della luna," *L'espresso*, 15 May 1966, p. 31. For its treatment of the Christ-Anthropos theme, this film is considered superior to Pasolini's *La ricotta* and *Il Vangelo secondo Matteo*: "Pasolini's story is not believable, because it is too polemical; Cavani does the opposite. Hence the strength of her work." Ibid. See also Filippo Celani, "Lo spettacolo della settimana: 'Francesco d'Assisi,'" *Osservatore romano*, 9–10 May 1966, p. 3.

18. For an excellent study of the cinematic tableau, see David Bordwell, *The Films of Carl-Theodor Dreyer* (Berkeley and Los Angeles: University of California Press, 1981), pp. 41–42.

19. "Il ribelle in perfetta letizia," *Cinecircoli* 5 (January–February 1967): 3. My observations on the Gothic form and its use of light are indebted to Otto von Simson, *The Gothic Cathedral: Origins of Gothic Architecture and the Medieval Concept of Order*, Bollingen Series XLVIII (Princeton, NJ: Princeton University Press, 1956), pp. 3–20. On the definition of the stone as the emblem of the Timeless-Become, see Oswald Spengler, *The Decline of the West* (New York: Knopf, 1932), 1:188. For Spengler, Giotto's art is only apparently a revival of the classical Apollonian way of feeling: it is Gothic. Arnold Hauser has observed that Giotto's treatment of space is unified and continuous, but its depth never extends beyond that of stage scenery. Like those who commissioned his

works (prosperous men who personified the first great period of middle-class culture), his art exercises austerity and objectivity. See *The Social History of Art*, 2 vols. (New York: Knopf, 1952), 1:287–288. Cf. Geörgy Lukács's discussion of medieval art and its specific social mode: "Giotto creates the pictorial form of a world that is a theater for human spectacles, boldly against the religious-allegorical form of decorative representation. His predominant function of spatiality, of a peculiar space for every single image, makes autonomous, artistic entities of all of his works. . . . Within these concrete, individualized spaces, men engage in action with solid, physical consistency and dramatic vehemence." *Estetica*, trans. Fausto Codino (Turin: Einaudi, 1970), 2:1451.

20. "Il ribelle in perfetta letizia," p. 3.

21. Ibid. Cavani also comments on her casting of a Protestant actor in the leading role: "Lou Castel is a born beatnik, a potential Franciscan. I just needed to look at his shyness, to feel his restlessness when he was talking, and knew that he was searching for genuine relationships between himself and the world. The character of Francesco cannot be improvised; there must be an inner resemblance." Ibid.

22. On Francesco's heroic aspects, see Corrado Bologna, "L'Ordine francescano e la letteratura nell'Italia pretridentina," in *Letteratura italiana*, ed. Alberto Asor Rosa (Turin: Einaudi, 1982), 1:729–797. It was, for example, the lack of this quintessential spirit of the Middle Ages, so conspicuously absent from *Francesco, giullare di Dio*, that prompted Pierre Leprohon to view Rossellini's film with reservations. See *The Italian Cinema*, trans. R. Greaves and O. Stallybrass (New York: Praeger, 1972), p. 136. Franciscan biographer Luigi Salvatorelli also lamented Cavani's characterization of a "failed hero." "San Francesco alla TV," *La stampa*, 19 May 1966, p. 3.

23. Reinhard Bendix, *Max Weber: An Intellectual Portrait* (Garden City, NY: Anchor Books, 1960), p. 364. On patrimonial government and paternal authority, in which sphere the conflict between discipline and individual charisma played a decisive role, see Max Weber, *Economy and Society: An Outline of Interpretative Sociology*, ed. Guenther Roth and Claus Wittich (Berkeley and Los Angeles: University of California Press, 1978), pp. 1153–1155. In reviewing Cavani's film, Antonio Petrucci remarks that the polemic against the proto-bourgeoisie is reflected "in the scene where a joyous Francesco and his first followers distribute their belongings playfully. And in so playing they manifest the Franciscan spirit that contrasts with the bourgeois seriousness of those who collect material goods." "Dietro i capelli lunghi dei 'provos' l'homo ludens reagisce all'homo faber," *Fiera letteraria*, 1 September 1966, p. 24. The revolutionary and the heretic have in common the tendency to form a group with strong ludic connotations. But once they have established themselves, the game is over, and the ludic dynamics is transformed into a power structure. Hence Francesco's resistance against forming an order.

24. On the *persona mixta* in the religious and political sphere, see Ernst H. Kantorowicz, *The King's Two Bodies: A Study in Mediaeval Political Theology* (Princeton, NJ: Princeton University Press, 1957), pp. 42–61.

25. M. Foucault, "A Preface to Transgression," in *Language, Counter-Memory, Practice*, pp. 33–34, originally published as "Hommage à George Bataille," *Critique*, nos. 195–196 (1963): 751–770.

26. See Victor W. Turner, *The Forest of Symbols: Aspects of Ndembu Ritual* (Ithaca, NY: Cornell University Press, 1967), p. 102; Arnold van Gennep, *The Rites of Passage*, introd. S. T. Kimball, trans. M. B. Vizedon and G. L. Caffee (1960; Chicago: University

of Chicago Press, 1964), 3d rpt., pp. 18–21. It must be remembered that the term "quest" derives from the Old French *queste* (mod. *quête*), with its Latin root in *quaerere* (to seek). See C. T. Onions, ed., *The Oxford Dictionary of English Etymology* (Oxford: Clarendon Press, 1966), p. 731. As the object of the medieval knight's pursuit, *quête* may be associated with a process leading to individuation.

27. "Quattro domande a Liliana Cavani regista," *Se Vuoi*, no. 5 (1967): 13.

28. Cavani's Archival Collection. In reviewing the film with Miklós Jancsó's *La tecnica e il rito* (Italy, 1972), Alberto Moravia defined the dialectical motif of violence as "impegnato" (engaging). "Faccia feroce fa carriera," *L'espresso*, 25 June 1972, p. 23.

29. On the changing concept of the city in medieval Europe, see particularly Chiara Frugoni, *A Distant City: Images of Urban Experience in the Medieval World*, trans. William McCuaig (Princeton, NJ: Princeton University Press, 1991), pp. 106–117; Arnaldo Fortini, *Francesco d'Assisi e l'Italia del suo tempo* (Rome: Biblioteca di Storia Patria, 1968), pp. 21–94; L. Salvatorelli, *Vita di san Francesco d'Assisi* (1926) (Turin: Einaudi, 1982), pp. 8–22.

30. Foucault interprets Christ as the one "who wanted to appear as a madman, in order to experience fully, in his incarnation, the miseries of the human fall." *Histoire de la folie à l'âge classique* (Paris: Gallimard, 1972), pp. 170–173. For the French philosopher, it is only with Dostoievsky and Nietzsche that the scandal of the Cross finds new power of manifestation. Cf. Joseph Lortz's discussion of Franciscan madness and drunkenness as a matter of exegetical argument: "Francesco was, and wanted to be, a fool in this world." *Un santo unico* (Rome: Edizioni Paoline, 1958), p. 33.

31. These attributes refer to stage directions in Cavani, *Francesco e Galileo*, pp. 35, 77. The text was originally published in *Rivista del cinematografo* 41 (August 1968): 503–512 (part 1) and 41 (September–October 1968): 577–587 (part 2). On the classification of the wooden crucifixes of the period, see, among others, Alfred Nicholson, *Cimabue: A Critical Study* (Princeton, NJ: Princeton University Press, 1932), pp. 29–31; Evelyn Sandberg Vavalà, *La croce dipinta italiana e l'iconografia della passione* (Verona: Casa Editrice Apollo, 1929), pp. 79–93. On the iconographic and exegetic depiction of Christ in Franciscan thought, see C. Frugoni, *Francesco e l'invenzione delle stimmate: Una storia per parole e immagini fino a Bonaventura e Giotto* (Turin: Einaudi, 1992), pp. 113–117.

32. "Il ribelle in perfetta letizia," p. 3.

33. *Histoire de la folie à l'âge classique*, p. 170.

34. *The Hero with a Thousand Faces*, Bollingen Series XVII, 2d ed. (Princeton, NJ: Princeton University Press, 1968), p. 29. Cf. "This means nothing less than that the conflict with all its excruciating implications must be endured consciously; we cannot seek to terminate it forcibly by taking sides, by enforcing a premature decision. Symbolically this amounts to a crucifixion; by our consent, our acceptance of this suffering we are nailed to the cross of the opposing drives." Whitmont, *The Symbolic Quest*, p. 228. Francesco's *stultitia* reflects the natural faith and *caritas* that Erasmus opposes to mechanical religious rituals: it is Christ's act of becoming a fool to save man notwithstanding his being the wisdom of the Father.

35. Cavani, *Francesco e Galileo*, p. 26.

36. See *A Distant City*, pp. 11–12.

37. Francesco Bolzoni, "Lo scandalo di Francesco," *Orizzonti*, 5 June 1966, p. 30. The director's friendship with Pasolini dates back to their first encounter in 1966, pro-

moted by Laura Betti, on the occasion of a private screening of *Francesco di Assisi*. She remembers him as a "sensitive and good-natured artist, who was extremely interested in the work of young filmmakers." Interview, 10 May 1990. On the symbolic transformation of the Franciscan episode in Pasolini's *Uccellacci, uccellini* (Hawks and Sparrows, 1966), see P. Adams Sitney, *Vital Crises in Italian Cinema: Iconography, Stylistics, Politics* (Austin: University of Texas Press, 1995), pp. 18–21. Gian Piero Brunetta views the Pasolinian concept of linguistic mimesis as an homage to the origins of cinema: dissolves, gestures, and sounds evoke primitive forms of communication. See *Forma e parola nel cinema*, introd. Gianfranco Folena (Padua: Liviana, 1970), pp. 59–60.

38. Cf. "Francesco, the beatnik number two after Christ, was someone who even today would annoy the conventional middle class and certain clergymen. As he did during his times. Because he said 'no' without compromise to the rising bourgeois system and to the traditional Church." From Cavani's film treatment of *Galileo* (Archival Collection).

39. See *Il viaggio testuale: Le ideologie e le strutture semiotiche* (Turin: Einaudi, 1978), p. 242. Emphasis is mine.

Chapter 2
Realism against Illusion: The Ceremonial Divestiture of Power in *Galileo*

1. " 'Galileo' di Liliana Cavani: In ginocchio davanti ai censori," *L'espresso*, 22 September 1968, p. 23. Anna Banti also singles out the film's originality in its didactic structure: "In our times of crisis, *Galileo*, which is equally distant from the rhetoric of the moneymaking historical film and from experimental demands, is a good acquisition for the seriousness of our popular cinema industry." "Un maestro e un'esordiente," p. 154. Peter Bondanella, among others, interprets the film within a more didactic context than Rossellini's study of Louis XIV. See *Italian Cinema from Neorealism to the Present*, new expanded ed. (New York: Continuum, 1993), p. 348. On this point, Cavani comments: "I am fascinated by a story; I work to develop it in-depth; I make a film as someone else makes a book, an essay, a photographic reportage, a painting. I never have a didactic intention in what I do. *Galileo* is the most didactic film I ever made. This was due to the fact that it was originally produced for a television audience. . . . The first part of the script was schematic. But in the second part—representing the conflict between Galileo and the Curia—I had more freedom to express my point of view." Tassone, *Parla il cinema italiano*, 2:126. See also Franca Faldini and Goffredo Fofi, eds., *L'avventurosa storia del cinema italiano raccontata dai suoi protagonisti 1960–1969* (Milan: Feltrinelli, 1981), p. 409. On the relationship between cinema authors and the television medium, see particularly Brunetta, *Storia del cinema italiano dal 1945 agli anni ottanta*, pp. 530–532.

Galileo was presented at the Venice Film Festival, under the auspices of its president Luigi Chiarini. It was caught up in the 1968 auteurs' boycott and received more polemical than critical attention. Though a member of the ANAC (Associazione Nazionale Autori Cinematografici), Cavani did not support the boycott on the ground that it was orchestrated by politicized factions: "My disagreement with the protesters in Venice derives from the fact that their revolution is merely an escape from the real problem facing cinema . . . which, as every author knows, is distribution. . . . The *pagliacci* in

Venice have gathered students from all directions, like a call for extras in a B movie. One would hope that these cinema authors—who paternally convince students to play the role of prophets—will soon and unequivocally reveal what they truly are: typical Italian bourgeois with a revolutionary ambition, which they express in bursts of useless words and gestures that aim at keeping things as they are." Typescript, September 1968 (Archival Collection). On this issue, see especially Sandro Meccoli, "Ecco il 'cartellone' delle ultime giornate," *Corriere della sera*, 3 September 1968, p. 13; Aggeo Savioli, "Il 'Galileo' ha trovato l'ambiente meno adatto," *L'unità*, 3 September 1968, p. 7; Claudio Sorgi, "Accolto il 'Galileo' con buona dose di consensi e polemiche," *Osservatore romano*, 4 September 1968, p. 5; I. C., "Cavani risponde ai suoi critici," *Paese sera*, 5 September 1968, p. 14; Claudio Quarantotto, "Cronache di una Mostra salvata dai borghesi," *Il borghese*, 12 September 1968, pp. 92–93; Mino Argentieri, "A Venezia è morta la vecchia mostra," *Rinascita*, 13 September 1968, p. 26; Faldini and Fofi, *L'avventurosa storia del cinema italiano raccontata dai suoi protagonisti*, pp. 431–432; Francesco Dorigo, "Chiarini alla mostra di Venezia," in *Barbaro e Chiarini: I teorici del cinema dietro la macchina da presa*, ed. Nino Genovese (Messina: Edizioni De Spectaculis, 1988), pp. 70–74.

2. Luigi Costantini, "Un Galileo precursore del Concilio," *Panorama*, 15 February 1968, p. 51. Ascribed to a historical matrix, Galileo's identity appears ambiguous to Pietro Pintus, in *Storia e film: Trent'anni di cinema italiano (1945–1975)* (Rome: Bulzoni, 1980), p. 90. For further discussion, see my "The Staging of Cavani's *Galileo*: The Historiographer's Art," in *Etica cristiana e scrittori del novecento*, ed. Florinda M. Iannace, *Forum Italicum*, Filibrary no. 5 (1993), pp. 139–146. *Galileo*'s production marks a historical moment in Italian cinema: it was the first collaborative effort with Bulgaria. The film was shot in 35mm (color) for six weeks in Sophia's studios and for the remaining three in Italy. The result set the standard for both film industries. Initially intended as a three-part series for the "small screen," it was never released by its main producer, RAI-TV. Sold to Cineriz, it was cut from 105 minutes to 92 for theatrical distribution in 1969. The reediting primarily excised the long scene of Giordano Bruno's execution at the stake. The film was originally R-rated. For production details, see Guglielmi, "Dalla TV al cinema," in Tallarigo and Gasparini, *Lo sguardo libero*, pp. 128–129.

3. See Northrop Frye, *Anatomy of Criticism: Four Essays* (Princeton, NJ: Princeton University Press, 1957), p. 284.

4. At the time Cavani produced *Galileo*, she also announced the making of *Coriolano*, a film depicting "the first major plebeian revolution in history." See Luciano Michetti Ricci, "Il vero pericolo è l'autocensura," *Settegiorni*, 2 July 1967, pp. 36–37. Also reported by Antonio Nediani, "La Cavani alle prese con la vita di Galileo," *L'avanti*, 18 October 1967, p. 5. *Coriolano* was never made because of problems with financing.

5. "Le idee di 'Galileo' e l'oscurantismo," *Cinema d'oggi*, 30 October 1967. "The film aims at telling the significance of the Galileo 'case.' The author's answer (debatable, of course) is that of a man of today who sees the terms of such a 'case' always represented in time." From Cavani's film treatment.

6. I. C., "Galileo nelle mani di una donna," *Paese sera*, 19 October 1966, p. 1 (Radio-TV).

7. From the film treatment (second draft). It is omitted in the final version.

8. Interview, 10 May 1990. Cavani's historical background on Galileo was primarily based on his letters. Further readings included Pio Paschini, Vincenzo Spampanato, Fulgenzio Micanzio, Giorgio de Santillana, Eugenio Garin, and Bruno Nardi.

9. "In number, then, as the *sign of completed demarcation*, lies the *essence* of everything actual, which is cognized, is delimited, and has become all at once." Spengler, *The Decline of the West*, 1:57. For a detailed analysis of the foundations of Galileo's new science of dynamics, see Ernst Cassirer, *Substance and Function and Einstein's Theory of Relativity*, trans. William Curtis Swabey and Marie Collins Swabey (New York: Dover, 1953), pp. 361 ff.

10. Galileo Galilei, *Il saggiatore*, in *Opere*, 13 vols. (Milan: Società Tipografica De' Classici Italiani, 1808–1811), 6:229–230. The explicit description of perception as a labyrinth is rare. Doob invokes the wondrous net described by Galen "as a complex interlace in which the animal spirits essential to accurate perception are manufactured." *The Idea of the Labyrinth*, p. 84.

11. See *Estetica*, 1:149–150, 157–158. For Lukács, the Galilean vision of the relations between science and biblical revelation achieves the dis-anthropomorphism of the reflection of reality. For a complex account of the spectatorial embodiment in the anatomy lesson, cf. Giuliana Bruno and her inscription of this popular spectacle in the cinematic apparatus: "The spectacle of the anatomy lesson exhibits an analytic drive, an obsession with the body, upon which acts of dismemberment are performed. Such 'analytic' desire is present in the very language of film, and its spectatorial codes." *Streetwalking on a Ruined Map: Cultural Theory and the City Films of Elvira Notari* (Princeton, NJ: Princeton University Press, 1993), p. 61.

12. Italo Moscati has described the film as a must-see and "a rare occasion to ponder on contemporary issues"; however, he objects to the analogy, drawn by several critics, between Galileo and the Czech leader Alexander Dubček. "Il Galileo di Liliana Cavani," *Cineforum* 8 (October 1968): 594. The invasion of Czechoslovakia by the Kremlin occurred on the night of 21–22 August 1968, a week before Cavani's film was presented in Venice. On this particular point, see Paolo Pillitteri, "I rapporti fra l'uomo e il potere nell'ottimo 'Galileo' della Cavani," *L'avanti*, 3 September 1968, p. 5; C. Quarantotto, "Una lezione di storia che non convince," *Giornale d'Italia*, 3–4 September 1968, p. 3; Gian Luigi Rondi, "Un suggestivo 'Galileo' sullo schermo della Mostra," *Il tempo*, 3 September 1968, p. 7; Paolo Valmarana, "Esempio di chiarezza il film della Cavani," *Il popolo*, 3 September 1968, p. 5.

13. Cavani, *Francesco e Galileo*, p. 118.

14. Interview, 10 May 1990.

15. From the film treatment. Galileo's subversive intellect makes him the forerunner of a new society potentially freer and therefore projected toward the future.

16. Cipriani, "Un irlandese ribelle nei panni di Galileo," *Paese sera*, 23 September 1967, p. 3. For his performance, Cusack was nominated for the Coppa Volpi at the 1968 Venice Film Festival.

17. See *What Is Cinema?*, 2:82. "I believe," states Cavani, "that I make films because of *Umberto D.* That film transgresses filmmaking itself." Interview, 27 June 1989. In 1997 Cavani received the "Premio Vittorio De Sica," awarded previously to Bergman, Tarkovsky, Kurosawa, Visconti, Fellini, and Blasetti.

18. Cavani, *Francesco e Galileo*, p. 182. Cavani visualizes such domestication of Galileo by actually having a monkey play with the spectators during the reading of the abjuration. The script (without stage directions) was originally published as "I dialoghi del film Galileo," in *Cineforum* 8 (October 1968): 598–624.

19. Cavani, *Francesco e Galileo*, p. 117.

20. Cited in Pietro Redondi, *Galileo Heretic*, trans. Raymond Rosenthal (Princeton, NJ: Princeton University Press, 1987), p. 256. Originally published as *Galileo eretico* (Turin: Einaudi, 1983). In view of documents newly released by the Holy Office, Redondi argues that, contrary to the official sentence, Galileo's indictment as a heretic originated not in astronomy but in physics: his atomistic intuitions challenged the dogma of the Eucharist.

21. M. Foucault, *Surveiller et punir: Naissance de la prison* (Paris: Gallimard, 1975), p. 105.

22. From the stage directions in Cavani, *Francesco e Galileo*, pp. 182–184.

23. *The Decline of the West*, 1:330.

24. *Of Time, Passion, and Knowledge: Reflections on the Strategy of Existence*, 2d ed. (Princeton, NJ: Princeton University Press, 1990), p. 32.

25. Cavani, *Francesco e Galileo*, p. 130.

26. *What Is Cinema?*, 1:11. Cf. Christine Buci-Glucksmann on the emblematic axiom of the baroque, *être, c'est voir*: "Thus from the beginning the baroque eye establishes itself as a new mode of seeing, which assigns the gaze an ontological 'optikon,' an epistemological and esthetic importance." *La Folie du voir: De l'esthétique baroque* (Paris: Editions Galilée, 1986), p. 29.

27. From the film treatment. In order to perfect such visual effects, Contini had to set up a laboratory in Bulgaria to develop dailies, and Ezio Frigerio moved to Sophia for five months to train the local crew to build sets and costumes (interview, 10 May 1990). In the films he shot for Cavani, Contini selected one normal prime lens and used the zoom for minor compositional adjustments. See "Alfio Contini: Il cannocchiale rovesciato," in *La bottega della luce: I direttori della fotografia*, ed. Stefano Consiglio and Fabio Ferzetti, pref. Emilio Tadini (Milan: Ubulibri, 1983), p. 18. On Cavani's approach to scenes and costumes, see Tiso, *Liliana Cavani*, p. 4; Faldini and Fofi, *L'avventurosa storia del cinema italiano raccontata dai suoi protagonisti*, p. 409. In reviewing the film, Tullio Kezich underscores Cavani's "remarkable capability to transform ideas into spectacle." "Galileo," *Bianco e nero*, nos. 5–6 (1969): 147.

28. Critics were divided on Morricone's score. Gian Luigi Rondi labels it "manneristic and presumptuous" ("Un suggestivo 'Galileo' sullo schermo della Mostra," p. 7); Giovanni Grazzini dismisses it as "insidiously distracting" ("Galileo: Ieri come oggi," *Corriere della sera*, 3 September 1968, p. 13); Claudio Quarantotto sees it as "out of place" ("Una lezione di storia che non convince," p. 3).

29. A body is docile that may be analyzed, manipulated, transformed, and improved. Thus "discipline constructs subjected and practiced bodies, 'docile' bodies. Discipline increases the forces of the body (in economic terms of utility) and diminishes these same forces (in political terms of obedience)." Foucault, *Surveiller et punir*, p. 140. In short, the *mécanique du pouvoir* dissociates power from the body. For a discussion of the connections that link a discourse to bodies, see the chapter "Les corps dociles" (pp. 137–171). The terminology applied by the Inquisition to the heretics retained four conventional formulas: *tractare, docere, tenere*, and *defendere*. On this point, see Guido Morpurgo-Tagliabue, *I processi di Galileo e l'epistemologia* (Rome: Armando, 1981), pp. 152–154.

30. *Francesco e Galileo*, p. 174.

31. See *Galileo Heretic*, p. 5.

32. Cavani, *Francesco e Galileo*, p. 169. Cavani's visual style does not follow the Brechtian alienation effect, which relies on the interaction between performance and spectators. Bertolt Brecht's aesthetic position brought him to underscore the social effects of Galileo's physical weakness (the abjuration). On Brecht's poetic practice and Galileo, see Walter Benjamin, "What Is Epic Theater?" in *Illuminations* (New York: Harcourt, Brace and World, 1968), pp. 149–150. When Cavani announced the making of *Galileo* in November 1967, she clarified her approach to Mario Foglietti: "In confronting the life of Galileo, I did not concern myself with the issue of being Brechtian or anti-Brechtian. This would have limited my scope . . . I studied the character of Galileo in search of the truth and to ascertain facts that might be exemplary, and a stimulus to reflect even today. As for Brecht, my Galileo will be more corporeal, pompous, solemn; these were typical characteristics of that period." "Tra un Brecht e un antibrecht c'è posto per un altro Galileo," *Il popolo*, 25 November 1967, p. 11. Also: "For me it was important to contrast the man of culture and power. Therefore, I tried to present a Galileo on trial, while in Brecht this aspect was only marginal . . . I was interested in the confrontation and the defeat of the 'man.' " From the press release dated 3 September 1968 (Archival Collection). On Brecht's more materialist Galileo, see C. Costantini, "Antibrechtiano il primo film su Galileo Galilei," *Il messaggero*, 21 June 1967, p. 10; G. G., "Il tormento di Galileo Galilei," *Bollettino italiano*, September 1967, p. 10; I. Moscati, "Un Galileo 'anti-Brecht,' " *Osservatore romano*, 18–19 September 1967, p. 5; Enzo Natta, "Galileo a braccetto con Marcuse," *Dimensioni* 6 (November 1968): 52. In Italy, Giorgio Strehler, who had been trying to stage Brecht's *Life of Galileo* since the early fifties, successfully premiered it at the Piccolo Teatro in Milan during the 1962–1963 season.

33. See Donald Skoller, ed., *Dreyer in Double Reflection* (New York: Dutton, 1973), p. 126. On Dreyer's organization of space and *La Passion de Jeanne d'Arc*, see Bordwell, *The Films of Carl-Theodor Dreyer*, pp. 66–81. Galileo's commission of inquiry was composed of three theologians: Monsignor Agostino Oregio, a specialist on the subject of the Eucharist, the Augustinian Father Zaccaria Pasqualigo, and a Jesuit, Father Melchior Inchofer. For a detailed discussion of the extrajudicial measures of the commission, see Redondi, *Galileo Heretic*, pp. 249–261.

34. Cavani, *Francesco e Galileo*, p. 177. In the first volume of the *Histoire de la sexualité*, Michel Foucault makes the following polemical claim: "One confesses—or one is forced to confess. When it is not spontaneous, or dictated by some internal imperative, the confession is extorted; it is driven from its hiding place in the soul or extracted from the body. Since the Middle Ages, torture has accompanied it like a shadow and supported it when it could escape no longer: the dark twins. Both the most defenseless tenderness and the bloodiest of powers need the confession. Western man has become a confessing animal." *La Volonté de savoir*, pp. 79–80.

35. See Corti, *Il viaggio testuale*, p. 241. Cf. Robert Stam: "The carnivalesque principle abolishes hierarchies, levels social classes, and creates another life free from conventional rules and restrictions. In carnival, all that is marginalized and excluded—the mad, the scandalous, the aleatory—takes over the center in a liberating explosion of otherness." *Subversive Pleasures: Bakhtin, Cultural Criticism, and Film* (Baltimore and London: Johns Hopkins University Press, 1989), p. 86.

36. *Parla il cinema italiano*, 2:131. Cavani has called Galileo a "modern hero," as opposed to Bruno, who, by suffering martyrdom, is "the hero of the past." Costantini, "Un Galileo precursore del Concilio," p. 52.

37. Interview, 10 May 1990. Cf. Whitmont: "The individuation path is also like a labyrinthine spiral in which we fear to lose ourselves." *The Symbolic Quest*, p. 93. Also: "Transgression, then, is not related to the limit as black to white, the prohibited to the lawful, the outside to the inside, or as the open area of a building to its enclosed spaces. Rather, their relationship takes the form of a spiral which no simple infraction can exhaust." Foucault, "A Preface to Transgression," in *Language, Counter-Memory, Practice*, p. 35.

38. Cavani, *Francesco e Galileo*, p. 179.

39. Ibid., p. 134. "Heretical" is applied here in the religious sense established by the patristic fathers in order to fight deviations. Bruno and Galileo are judged by theological standards, since their findings contradict the dogmatic truth of the Church. The intellectual component of their heresy is also voluntary, which makes their transgression a matter of moral guilt. Theirs are "voluntary errors." *Dizionario enciclopedico italiano*, 4:441. The Roman documents on Bruno's sentencing and execution insist on the "wretched obstination," and "pertinacious heretical intellect" of the accused. See Vincenzo Spampanato, *Documenti della vita di Giordano Bruno* (Florence: Olschki, 1933), pp. 197, 207.

40. For further details, see n. 2 above. On the polemics concerning censorship, Cavani declared, "I find it scandalous that we have in Italy a type of censorship that is blind to the vulgar violence of westerns, and the like, and then finds it hard for minors to see Giordano Bruno at the stake, and wants to cut it." From the press release issued on 5 September 1968 (Archival Collection). Two other films presented at the Venice Film Festival were sequestered by the Office of the District Attorney: Bertolucci's *Partner* and Pasolini's *Teorema* (which was indicted). Official support was underwritten by the directors of the ANAC, the French critics of *Cahiers du Cinéma* and *Positif*, and, among others, Robert Bresson, François Truffaut, Jean-Luc Godard, Louis Malle, and Alexander Kluge, the winner of the Golden Lion with *Die Artisten in der Zirkuskuppel: Ratlos*. See I. C., "Cavani risponde ai suoi critici," p. 14; Alichino, "La pericolosa Cavani," *Settegiorni*, 15 September 1968, p. 32; M. Argentieri, "Il tarlo del censore," *Rinascita*, 20 September 1968, pp. 23–24; Filippo Sacchi, "Misteri della censura: 'Galileo' vietato ai minori di 18 anni," *Epoca*, 22 September 1968, p. 130; Lino Miccichè, "Un salto nella verità," *L'avanti*, 29 September 1968, p. 8. Ciriaco Tiso defines the scenes with Bruno as "physical poiesis." *Liliana Cavani*, p. 55.

41. See *The Claiming of Reason: Wittgenstein, Skepticism, Morality and Tragedy* (New York: Oxford University Press, 1979), p. 261.

42. Interview, 10 May 1990.

43. Interview, 27 June 1989. "He had underestimated the ability of the hierarchy to conspire; he had also underestimated the fear of the few clergymen who had once defended him. He had not considered that the Church, as an absolute power, had always protected itself against controversies, not with open debates and questioning itself, but only with the force of its authority, power, and connivance." From the film treatment.

44. Interview, 10 May 1990. For a detailed discussion of the Inquisitorial abjuration, I refer to Italo Mereu, *Storia dell'intolleranza in Europa: Sospettare e punire. Il sospetto e l'Inquisizione romana nell'epoca di Galilei* (Milan: Mondadori, 1979), pp. 299–319.

Chapter 3
Metaphors of Revolt: The Dialogic Silence in *I cannibali*

1. "Film 'I cannibali' per Britt Ekland," *Corriere della sera*, 25 March 1969, p. 13. The film was shot in Milan and Rome during spring 1969 for a budget of 160 million lire. Enzo Doria was a young producer who had made his successful debut with Marco Bellocchio's *I pugni in tasca* in 1965. *I cannibali* premiered at the Spoleto Festival in April 1970, and, thanks to François Truffaut's backing, it was exhibited at Cannes in May. The film received wide critical attention. American distributors offered international release provided that Cavani would change the last fifteen minutes to create a happy ending. She declined. For production details, see Tiso, *Liliana Cavani*, p. 61; Tassone, *Parla il cinema italiano*, 2:132; L. A., "Britt Ekland a Milano," *Corriere della sera*, 3 April 1969, p. 15; Lia Quilici, "Madame direttore," *L'espresso*, 20 April 1969, pp. 13–17; Enzo Natta, "Due cannibali tra i ribelli insepolti," *Dimensioni* 7 (June 1969): 70–74; Giorgio Calcagno, "La regista del 'Galileo' spiega perché fa dei film anticlericali," *La stampa*, 21 August 1969, p. 7.

2. I have cited this choral ode (vv. 376–377) at the head of this chapter. In ancient Greek theater, stasima were sung by the chorus between two episodes. For a discussion of the importance of this stasimon to the theme of the play, see particularly C. W. Oudemans and A.P.M.H. Lardinois, *Tragic Ambiguity: Anthropology, Philosophy and Sophocles' Antigone* (Leiden and New York: E. J. Brill, 1987), pp. 118–131. All quotations in the text are from Sophocles, *The Three Theban Plays: Antigone, Oedipus the King, Oedipus at Colonus*, trans. Robert Fagles, introd. and notes by Bernard Knox (Harmondsworth: Penguin, 1984).

3. "*I cannibali* secondo l'autore" (Archival Collection). These handwritten notes were edited for the French press kit in 1972 as "I cannibali: Un Cri d'alarme." Ettore De Giorgis has pointed out that Cavani's *umanesimo* is her real religion, a commitment to human interests that avoids the abstract intellectualism of the 1960s. "L'impegno umano e artistico di Liliana Cavani," *Vita sociale* 29 (July–October 1972): 373.

4. The etymological roots of *prodigium* include both "prophecy" and "to lead." See Devoto, *Avviamento alla etimologia italiana*, p. 333. In her unpublished script notes, Cavani writes, "There is no spectacle without prophecy."

5. Personal interview, 11 May 1990.

6. Sophocles, *Antigone*, in *The Three Theban Plays*, p. 69.

7. Clouzot, "Liliana Cavani: Le Mythe, le sexe et la révolte," p. 37. On Cavani and the Italian political climate of the 1960s and of the 1970s, see C. Cosulich, "Cadaveri a Milano," *A.B.C.* (Milan), 27 March 1970, pp. 25–28; Marco Sorteni, "Una cinepresa sull'anima dei giovani," *Domenica del corriere*, 26 May 1970, p. 36; G. Fofi, *Il cinema italiano: Servi e padroni* (Milan: Feltrinelli, 1971), pp. 81–95; Pintus, *Storia e film*, pp. 93–100. The adaptation closest to Cavani's film (for its references to contemporary situations) is perhaps Jean Anouilh's *Antigone* (1944), where the protagonist is identified with the French Resistance movement during the German occupation. In Anouilh's

play, the omission of the character of Tiresias signals a desacralization of the mythical story. For a comprehensive introduction to the theatrical, operatic, and cinematic versions of Antigone, see George Steiner, *Antigones* (New York and Oxford: Oxford University Press, 1984), chap. 2. Steiner views Cavani's film as a platform for the women's movement.

8. Interview, 11 May 1990. Cf. Cavani on the function of Antigone and Tiresias's revolt: "It was very important that they have no slogans, that they are working alone, not as a group. . . . I was startled to see that books were being sold with revolutionary slogans and so were buttons and paving stones. In Italy there is even a Boutique of Contestation. They have everything there, including a doll you throw a brick at. When it's hit it holds its head and screams Ouch." Mary Blume, "Liliana Cavani and the Young," *International Herald Tribune*, 15–16 April 1972, p. 14.

9. Cavani's position on language, in its representational function, as a system of symbols, which articulates meanings through gestures, ought to be seen in its relation to the contemporary debates on semiotics. Umberto Eco, Gianfranco Bettetini, Christian Metz, and Roland Barthes have presented arguments that invaded popular culture and the performing arts. Among the Italian filmmakers, Pier Paolo Pasolini attempted a synthesis of semantic spheres and the creative act in his distinctive thesis of "cinema di poesia." For an outline of the central features of semiotics' contributions to the question of film language, see Eco, *La struttura assente: Introduzione alla ricerca semiologica* (Milan: Bompiani, 1968), pp. 152–158. Cavani's predominantly aesthetic position can be reconstructed through a wide-ranging selection of critical reviews, primarily her writings on Bergman, Antonioni, Malle, Resnais, Godard, Pasolini, Petri, and Visconti, published in *Studium* and in *Il nostro tempo* between 1960 and 1964.

10. "Only the children want to know, and they instantly pay the price. As soon as Tiresias awakens, he begins to utter a terrible prophecy already in progress." From the director's notes in the working script (Archival Collection). In Greece, people believed that a seer made his prediction come true by uttering the words themselves. For Cavani, the seashell is an instrument for transmitting knowledge, and whoever uses it is destined to die. In the beginning, the girl holds the seashell, and later Tiresias also listens to its sounds of prophecy. He will leave the object behind in the snack bar as a sign for Antigone to follow him. Gaston Bachelard associates the seashell with a poetic space of transcendental geometry and dialectic growth (the hidden and the manifest) in *La Poétique de l'espace* (Paris: Presses Universitaires de France, 1967), pp. 105–129. For Mircea Eliade, as the assimilation of the source of cosmic life, the seashell implies a second birth. See *Images and Symbols: Studies in Religious Symbolism*, trans. Philip Mairet (New York: Sheed and Ward, 1961), pp. 125–150.

11. The lyrics of "The Cannibals" (originally in English) are as follows: "Call me cannibal, / I won't die, / savage cannibal, / I won't die, / crazy cannibal, / I won't die, / pagan cannibal, / I won't die, / I'm happy and wild and free, / kill me if you can, / I will never lie down dead. / I'll just fly away / on my sky-blue horse, / I'll just fly away / happy that my mind is free." For a discussion of the opening sequence, see, among others, G. L. Rondi, "Lunga notte delle stelle per gli 'Oscar italiani,' " *Il tempo*, 26 April 1970, p. 10; F. Sacchi, "Ritorna con Antigone il dramma del potere assoluto," *Epoca*, 3 May 1970, p. 135. Rondi points to a Kafkaesque type of tension, particularly clear in the shots establishing the citizens' indifference to the corpses; Sacchi speaks of astounding and surreal images.

12. See Frye, *Anatomy of Criticism*, p. 238.

13. "Fantapolitica e verità," *Studium* 60 (July–August 1964): 523–526. On this point, see also her review of Otto Preminger's *Advise and Consent*,"Un coraggioso film americano sui retroscena dell'alta politica," in *Il nostro tempo*, 1 November 1962. Tullio Kezich speaks instead of "fantasociologia" and emphasizes Cavani's ability to transform docurealism into a spiritual journey. "I cannibali," *Panorama*, 7 May 1970, p. 15. Tiso also acknowledges that the premise of *I cannibali*, which he calls allegorical, is "occasionally political and essentially mythic." *Liliana Cavani*, p. 64.

14. Clouzot, "Liliana Cavani: Le Mythe, le sexe et la révolte," p. 38. Cavani confessed to Ornella Ripa: "I made this film as if it were poetry. . . . This film is irrational and completely different from *Galileo*. My feelings originated from real events—reading the newspapers, looking around, and being shocked. As a result, a tragic prophecy was born, *I cannibali*." "Solo i cannibali salveranno la città," *Gente*, 11 May 1970, p. 107. Here, "irrational" signifies nature and precultural being. See also the director's interview with Italo Moscati, "Per seminare inquietitudine" in L. Cavani, *Milarepa*, ed. I. Moscati (Bologna: Cappelli, 1974), pp. 37–38.

15. S. Sontag, *On Photography* (New York: Delta Book, 1977), p. 178. "Photographs were enrolled in the service of important institutions of control, notably the family and the police, as symbolic objects and as pieces of information" (p. 21). Like Cavani, Sontag specifically refers to photographs of emaciated Biafrans and of Tuareg families dying of starvation as having the effect of a replay of now familiar atrocity exhibition. Cavani recognizes that the success of *I cannibali* was determined at Cannes, and by the invitation of the New York Film Festival promoted by Susan Sontag, who had also attended "La Quinzaine des réalisateurs" during the selection of the European film entries. Personal interview, 11 May 1990. For the reaction of the foreign press to the film, see especially Penelope Houston: "*The Cannibals* is carried by a calm but rather freakish visual sense, a dislocation as disquieting as the corpses among the traffic. An intelligent, unexpected film, it seems well worth someone's trouble to import." "Cannes 70," *Sight and Sound* 39 (Summer 1970): 122–123. Also, Amos Vogel speaks of "an extremely effective and frightening central idea," in "One Festival Plus One," *Village Voice*, 9 July 1970, p. 57; and Larry Cohen highlights Cavani's visuality in "Italy's 'Cannibals' Needs, Deserves U.S. Distributor," *Hollywood Reporter*, 22 September 1970, p. 4. Roger Greenspun offers an opposite point of view in " 'Cannibals,' Modern Version of 'Antigone,' " *New York Times*, 21 September 1970, p. 55. Molly Haskell reports on the screening of *I cannibali* at the New York Film Festival and summarizes its debate with great clarity: "It is a one-track film which either sweeps you up in the simple audacity and exquisite elaboration of its conceit or it doesn't; if it doesn't, you are likely to ignore (or rather, not perceive as an issue) its obvious symbols and political oversimplification, and if it doesn't no amount of argument will persuade you." "After the Revolution (2)," *Village Voice*, 1 October 1970, p. 57.

16. Ripa, "Solo i cannibali salveranno la città," p. 108. Once again Cavani declares: "I am against ideology. I was born after World War I with a great desire to be outside any ideological contestation. *I cannibali* was my way to react to this." Interview, 11 May 1990. Two notorious events signaled the self-destructive potentials of the students' and workers' counterculture: the tragic and obscure death of Milanese publisher Giangiacomo Feltrinelli in March 1972, killed while attempting to attach explosives to an electric pylon at Segrate, and the Valpreda case. A friend of Fidel Castro, Feltrinelli operated

an armed clandestine left-wing group called GAP (Gruppo di Azione Partigiana), supposedly to fight a possible right-wing coup in Italy. A ballet dancer from Rome and an anarchist, Pietro Valpreda was the scapegoat arrested for the infamous bombing of a bank in Milan's Piazza Fontana on 12 December 1969. He was kept in prison for years and eventually cleared of the crime in 1985.

17. Cf. Cavani: "The first scene of I cannibali is an execution. While I was shooting, I realized that it was a shocking memory of my childhood." Leone, "Contesto ma credo," p. 3. In the introduction, I have quoted in detail Cavani's powerful description of this experience.

18. Interview, 11 May 1990. One should be reminded that the focus of a 750mm lens is very critical, particularly under low light conditions. Therefore, it takes a special cinematographer to keep everything in focus. The choice of the telephoto lens is very important because it covers a dual function: on one hand, it relays a dream state; on the other, it produces the effect of distancing the viewer from the action. This filmic style visualizes the nightmare mood of the post-1968 period.

19. "Antigone si arrende ai tecnocrati," p. 23. Moravia ranks the film among the best of the year. The film's opening sequence is unanimously praised by critics, even by such polemical reviewers as Goffredo Fofi, who attacks the director's stylistic and cultural intentions: "The nonconciliatory perspective of a world (our world) ruled by monsters is never sufficiently explained. Cavani casually combines mystical solutions (Christian, pagan, Third World) with the somnambulistic, unconvincing performance of mannequinlike actors." Fofi, Il cinema italiano, p. 124.

20. See Cavani, "Pensare e ascoltare," Annuario AIC (1989), p. 15.

21. See Apocalittici e integrati (1964) (Milan: Bompiani, 1977), pp. 4–5. For Eco, "Mass culture is anticulture. However, since it was born at a time when the masses had a highly contextual historical relevance in society, 'mass culture' is not a transient nor a localized aberration: it is the sign of an irretrievable decline, and the man of culture (as the last survivor of prehistoric times, and doomed to extinction) can only bear witness in terms of Apocalypse" (p. 4).

22. L. Cavani and I. Moscati, Il tamburo di carne, pp. 6–7 (Archival Collection). This working script was revised and published as "I cannibali," Sipario 25 (February 1970): 40–49. In the final version, the opening scene with Antigone was cut down to her simply noticing a curious procession preceded by a hieratic and aloof pope.

23. Streetwalking on a Ruined Map, p. 287. Bruno applies the street paradigm to the unruly woman, a nomadic character who lives outside society's basic rules.

24. "Ideology and the Practice of Sound Editing and Mixing," in The Cinematic Apparatus, ed. T. De Lauretis and Stephen Heath (New York: St. Martin's Press, 1980), p. 56. The inner ear can be described as a perceptual labyrinth, a pure architecture of sounds. It is a metaphor for learning. See Doob, The Idea of the Labyrinth, pp. 83–84.

25. From "I cannibali: Un Cri d'alarme." "Who are 'The Cannibals'? They are not men of power, paternally ferocious. This would be too easy. On the contrary, they are the young people and all those who do not side with power, with a particular system of power that shapes a particular society and rules with cruelty." From Cavani's film treatment of I cannibali (Archival Collection).

26. On this point, see Gilles Deleuze and Félix Guattari's study of savages, barbarians, and civilized men within the context of capitalism, in Anti-Oedipus: Capitalism and Schizophrenia, pref. M. Foucault, trans. Robert Hurley, Mark Seem, and Helen R. Lane

(Minneapolis: University of Minnesota Press, 1983), pp. 139–140. For a cultural discussion of the cannibalist trope in film, see Stam, *Subversive Pleasures*, chap. 4, "Of Cannibals and Carnivals."

27. "He must only see," says Cavani, "because the citizens have become blind. He must not speak, because in a revolution a word is already the beginning of a compromise toward defeat. . . . Clementi is at the same time the new and the old man." Faldini and Fofi, *L'avventurosa storia del cinema italiano raccontata dai suoi protagonisti*, p. 459. The director's approach to *I cannibali* is considerably different from that evidenced in *Galileo*. A popular actor such as Clementi, whose film image was shaped by the important roles he played in Buñuel's *Belle de jour* and Bertolucci's *Partner*, is instructed to perform entirely through corporeal visuality. Gianni Amelio, one of the assistant directors on the film, with Paola Tallarigo, comments on Clementi-Tiresias: "We filmed him wearing the same clothes he had when he first arrived in Rome. We did not give him any dialogue. He seemed unaware of interpreting a character; he was just there as an extraordinary presence, and he did the whole film in a very quiet way." Ibid. In an article Cavani wrote in 1972 in defense of Clementi (in prison for drug possession), she highlights the actor's figurative charisma: "Long black hair, ecstatic, big dark eyes, an elegant disposition, and sweet. The government official, the businessman, in short, the petit bourgeois, is physically the opposite of Pierre. . . . They see in Pierre someone 'different,' even if they don't know *why* and *in what* he is different: he is simply a *free man*. In my film he represents a free, innocent man; therefore he is also wise." "Pierre Clementi et la violence fasciste," in *I cannibali: Un film de Liliana Cavani*, French press kit, 1972. Cavani also explains her choice for Antigone: "I looked for a fashionable type, physically elegant, highly sophisticated, with a fragile grace disguising a strong character. She had to be 'physically' bourgeois. Britt is all of this." From "*I cannibali* secondo l'autore." Originally Cavani intended to cast the Redgraves and Franco Nero.

28. Like the seashell, the fish can also be identified with knowledge. The director rejects the association of the fish with Christ and calls for an anthropological interpretation. See Gérard Langlois, "Liliana Cavani: 'I cannibali,'" *Lettres Françaises*, 12 April 1972, p. 18. On the ambivalence of the fish symbol, see C. G. Jung, *Aion: Researches into the Phenomenology of the Self*, trans. R.F.C. Hull, Bollingen Series XX (New York: Pantheon, 1959), pp. 118 ff.; Gilbert Durand, *Les Structures anthropologiques de l'imaginaire: Introduction à l'archétypologie générale* (Paris: Bordas, 1984), pp. 243–247.

29. "'Cattolico di sinistra': Un'etichetta che respingiamo," *Cineforum* 10 (May–August 1970): 126. It was with this film that Moscati began a long collaboration with Liliana Cavani. He also coauthored the scripts of *Milarepa*, *Il portiere di notte*, *Al di là del bene e del male*, and *Dove siete? Io sono qui*. Cavani has consistently rejected the label of "cattolica del dissenso" (dissenting Catholic). On this subject, see her articles: "Un cinema libero," *Studium* 61 (September 1965): 598–602; "Realizzare il socialismo non significa riconoscere il fallimento del Vangelo," *Il nostro tempo*, 30 October 1966; "'Cattolici progressisti' una definizione pericolosa" (letter to the editor), *Il nostro tempo*, 31 December 1967; "Perché i giovani cattolici non dovrebbero protestare?" *Il nostro tempo*, 14 April 1968. And her interviews: Leone, "Contesto ma credo," p. 3; Maraini, *Ma tu chi eri?*, pp. 80–81; Clemente Ciattaglia, "Colloqui sul Vangelo: Incontro con Liliana Cavani," *Il popolo*, 16 May 1971, p. 9, reprinted in *Voci d'oggi sul vangelo* (Rome: Edizioni Cinque Lune, 1974), pp. 63–69; Barbara Giacomelli and Tonino Nieddu, "Liliana Cavani: Una religione senza complessi," *Vita pastorale* 62 (December 1974): 48–53. Cf.

also Cavani's review of Bergman's *Persona*, where she discusses the role of God in contemporary society: "Bergman affronta nel suo ultimo film il dramma della responsabilità umana," *Il nostro tempo*, 12 February 1967. For the polemical reception of *I cannibali*, see particularly Raniero La Valle, "Le due strade dei contestatori," *La stampa*, 1 May 1970, p. 2; G. Gr. "I cannibali," *Corriere della sera*, 3 May 1970, reprinted in G. Grazzini, *Gli anni settanta in cento film* (Bari: Laterza, 1978), pp. 38–40; M. Argentieri, "Un'Antigone del dissenso cattolico," *Rinascita*, 15 May 1970, p. 23, and "Il 'cattolicesimo' di Liliana Cavani," in Tallarigo and Gasparini, *Lo sguardo libero*, pp. 130–134; Elena De Sanctis, "I films scomodi di Liliana Cavani," *Vita francescana*, December 1970, p. 313.

30. *Tragedy and Philosophy* (Princeton, NJ: Princeton University Press, 1992), p. 216. For a discussion of the classical treatment of the Antigone story, see also pp. 217–225. Frye has defined the archetype of Prometheus as the central figure of tragedy, half-human and yet of a heroic size. See *Anatomy of Criticism*, p. 42.

31. *The Acoustic Mirror*, p. 223.

32. See Søren Kierkegaard, *Either/Or: Part I*, ed. and trans. with introd. and notes by Howard V. Hong and Edna H. Hong (Princeton, NJ: Princeton University Press, 1987), p. 158. In an interview with Gérard Langlois, Cavani states: "Words have no power. That is why the heroine refuses to speak at the end. To accept a dialogue means to sabotage the revolt." "Liliana Cavani: 'I cannibali,' " p. 18. On the importance of silence and speech in Sophocles' play, see particularly Josiah Ober and Barry Strauss, "Drama, Political Rhetoric, and the Discourse of Athenian Democracy," in *Nothing to Do with Dionysos? Athenian Drama in Its Social Context*, ed. John J. Winkler and Froma I. Zeitlin (Princeton, NJ: Princeton University Press, 1990), pp. 259–269.

33. *Anatomy of Criticism*, p. 238.

34. See Foucault, *Surveiller et punir*, pp. 173–174. Particularly relevant to my analysis of discourse is the chapter on the means of correct training, pp. 170–194.

35. The foot possesses a magical, generative power, often associated with seers. See C. G. Jung, *Symbols of Transformation: An Analysis of the Prelude to a Case of Schizophrenia*, trans. R.F.C. Hull, Bollingen Series XX (New York: Pantheon, 1956), pp. 126, 239. When Antigone is captured by the military police, she is wounded in one foot, a symbolic prefiguration of impending danger.

36. The ballad, entitled "Vorrei trovare un mondo" (I'd like to find a world), is by songwriter Gino Paoli. On pop music as cultural expression, Umberto Eco observes that even a song can become part of a controlling power structure. See *Apocalittici e integrati*, pp. 288–289.

37. *Language, Counter-Memory, Practice*, p. 210.

38. On this point, I refer to Stam's discussion of Roberto da Matta's analysis of carnival, *Subversive Pleasures*, pp. 129–130.

39. Cavani and Moscati, "I cannibali," p. 49.

40. See Bettina L. Knapp, *A Jungian Approach to Literature* (Carbondale and Edwardsville: Southern Illinois University Press, 1984), p. 24; Durand, *Les Structures anthropologiques de l'imaginaire*, pp. 363–369.

41. Cavani and Moscati, "I cannibali," p. 48.

42. Ibid. For Foucault, resistance is both a part of the functioning of power and a source of its perpetual disruption. See Hubert L. Dreyfus and Paul Rabinow, *Michel*

Foucault: Beyond Structuralism and Hermeneutics, 2d ed., afterword by and interview with M. Foucault (Chicago: University of Chicago Press, 1983), p. 147. Antigone's burial of Polynices defines a field of power and resistance.

43. See the stage directions to scenes 46 and 49, in Cavani and Moscati, "I cannibali," p. 49. Cf. the director's script notes to *I cannibali* (Archival Collection): "In the ancient tragedy the chorus is made of citizens who are accomplices in the misadventures fallen upon the city. The citizens of my city are impossible. Oh the gods! The anthropomorphic gods are questionable because of their human appearances. . . . The chorus of my city is impious. There is no catharsis."

44. "I cannibali," p. 49. At this point in the script, the director interjects herself as a speaking subject: "The crowd (the spectators) have had (wanted) a tragic ending. Will they applaud?" Ibid. On the role of the people in ceremonial executions, see Foucault, *Surveillir et punir*, pp. 61–62.

45. Ibid., p. 45. Few critics have commented on the role of the TV medium in *I cannibali*, among them Mira Liehm, who claims that Cavani's "television realism" undermines the film's metaphoric substance. *Passion and Defiance: Film in Italy from 1942 to the Present* (Berkeley and Los Angeles: University of California Press, 1984), p. 201. Cf. Deleuze and Guattari on TV as an apparatus of capture, a system of machinic enslavement and capitalist social subjection: "Modern power is not at all reducible to the classical alternative 'repression or ideology' but implies processes of normalization, modulation, modeling, and information that bear on language, perception, desire, movement, etc., and which proceed by way of microassemblages. This aggregate includes both subjection and enslavement taken to extremes." *A Thousand Plateaus: Capitalism and Schizophrenia*, trans. and foreword by Brian Massumi (Minneapolis: University of Minnesota Press, 1987), p. 458.

46. For an epistemological reading of the body as the ground of vision, I refer to Bruno, *Streetwalking on a Ruined Map*, pp. 68–69. Cf. Sontag on the function of the image-world created by the camera: "A capitalist society requires a culture based on images. It needs to furnish vast amounts of entertainment in order to stimulate buying and anesthetize the injuries of class, race, and sex. . . . The camera's twin capacities, to subjectivize reality and to objectify it, ideally serve these needs and strengthen them." *On Photography*, p. 178.

47. From the film treatment.

48. For the relationship of color to music, see Angela Dalle Vacche's discussion of the Tavianis' *Allosonfan*, a film also scored by Ennio Morricone. *The Body in the Mirror: Shapes of History in Italian Cinema* (Princeton, NJ: Princeton University Press, 1992), p. 169. Red signifies love, energy, and brotherhood. When Tiresias awakes on the beach, he is wrapped up in a black cloak, and he is associated with water. The sea, from which this *xenos* (foreigner) comes, is a favorite emblem of the unconscious. Red and white are alchemical colors, red representing the sun and white the moon. This cosmic association is potentially present in the scene of Tiresias holding Antigone in his arms "as a mother would her son." It provides the basis of an intersubjective mode of desire, later developed as cross-dressing. These shots are two-dimensional; they evoke a modern pietà. See Cavani's stage directions to scene 22, in "I cannibali," p. 44. For the alchemical significance of colors, see C. G. Jung, *Alchemical Studies*, trans. R.F.C. Hull, Bollingen Series XX (Princeton, NJ: Princeton University Press, 1967), p. 339.

49. See Cavani and Moscati, "I cannibali," p. 44.

50. *Il tamburo di carne*, pp. 44–45.

51. Ibid., pp. 46–47.

52. Cavani declares to an anonymous interviewer: "The cinema of ideas is not loved by power. Also the cinema that speaks of sex, if it is cinema of ideas, is hated by institutional power because one of its pillars is conformism . . . Pasolini says that when power becomes abnormal it expresses itself abnormally. And he exemplifies it through a tragic allegory. What can the audience possibly learn from this? That horror is not a part of a free nature but of a coerced nature." "Censura al cinema," *Nuova generazione*, 7 March 1976. For Gian Piero Brunetta, *I cannibali* finds its models in Pasolini's *Edipo re* and *Porcile*. See *Storia del cinema italiano dal 1945 agli anni ottanta*, p. 706.

53. Marcus's remarks apply to Pasolini's *Decameron*, a film she analyzes in terms of "writing with bodies." See *Filmmaking by the Book: Italian Cinema and Literary Adaptation* (Baltimore and London: Johns Hopkins University Press, 1993), p. 137.

54. *The Acoustic Mirror*, p. 224. In this sequence, the association of the bisexual consciousness of Dionysos and the feminine finds a poetic visualization in Antigone's madness, her irrational act of defiance translated into her many costumed disguises.

55. *Le nozze di Cadmo e Armonia* (Milan: Adelphi, 1989), p. 114. These words (vv. 613–614) are spoken by the chorus in Sophocles' *Antigone*.

56. "I cannibali," p. 49.

57. See Whitmont, *The Symbolic Quest*, p. 171; Gaston Bachelard, *La Terre et les rêveries du repos* (Paris: Corti, 1948), chap. 6. The cave dominates Antigone and Tiresias's action from the very beginning. Here they deposit the body of Polynices, enacting an initiatory rite of eating and drinking: a ceremony of incorporation into a new world. Antigone herself urges an analogy with a feminine principle during the interrogation scene. When asked where the rebels' bodies are hidden, she simply replies, "Nella madre" (in the mother). Cavani and Moscati, "I cannibali," p. 45.

58. "*I cannibali* secondo l'autore."

59. The association of desire with a space that bears on experiences of the feminine finds a compelling example in a crucial scene: when Anna is forced by her sister-in-law to wear a dull, formal dress instead of the bright, youthful one she has chosen. Anna becomes an exemplary case of female malady, a motif Cavani investigates by entering the interior, containing space of a mental institution filled with madwomen and supervising (male) doctors and nurses. The film was originally entitled *Facce nude* (Naked Faces). For an excellent reading of female madness in the cinematic context, see Bruno, *Streetwalking on a Ruined Map*, chap. 15, "Medical Figures: Hysteria and the Anatomy Lesson."

On the relationship of the Antigone complex and the Italian feminist critique, see especially Rossana Rossanda, who argues that Oedipus's daughter represents unlimited desire as opposed to male rationality, thus serving as a constant reminder of the boundaries of patriarchal government. See the introduction to Sofocle, *Antigone*, trans. Luisa Biondetti (Milan: Feltrinelli, 1987), pp. 7 ff. One of the most outspoken members within the Italian Communist Party's ranks in the sixties, Rossanda became a leader of the *Manifesto* group, publishers of a paper that attracted left-wing dissidents. She was expelled from the PCI in 1969.

Chapter 4
Toward a Negative Mythopoeia: Spectacle, Memory, and Representation
in *The Night Porter*

1. See Theodor W. Adorno's discussion of *passio* in *Kierkegaard: Construction of the Aesthetic*, trans., ed., and with foreword by Robert Hullot-Kentor (Minneapolis: University of Minnesota Press, 1989), pp. 119–122. For Kierkegaard, *passio* is a subjective category, a natural urge of the spirit that aims at the sacrifice of the self.

2. "Liliana Cavani: Le Mythe, le sexe et la révolte," p. 42.

3. L. Cavani, *Il portiere di notte* (Turin: Einaudi, 1974), p. 5.

4. Personal interview, 12 May 1990.

5. On this point, see Allan Casebier, *Film and Phenomenology: Toward a Realist Theory of Cinematic Representation* (Cambridge: Cambridge University Press, 1991), pp. 9–11.

6. Interview, 12 May 1990.

7. Introduction to *Il portiere di notte*, p. viii. The programs in the series were entitled "Hitler in Power," "The Splendors of the Third Reich," "Hitler überall," "The Third Reich Burns." Cavani also draws from films found at the Library of Congress, in Paris, and in the Federal Republic of Germany, from propaganda manifestos and George Grosz's 1930s cartoons. She constructs a topography of National Socialism by intercutting documentary footage with photographic materials. For a bibliography on Cavani's documentary period, see n. 9 to the introduction; also her inverview with Paolo Gobetti et al., "Liliana Cavani," in Amaducci et al., *Memoria, mito, storia*, pp. 45–53.

8. *Reflections of Nazism: An Essay on Kitsch and Death*, trans. Thomas Weyr (New York: Harper and Row, 1984), pp. 14–15. Friedländer argues that the fascination with Nazism in such films as *The Night Porter*, *Lacombe Lucien*, or *The Damned* derives from an aesthetization of the erotic plane and its hold on the masses (kitsch and the central motif of death). See also Sontag on Leni Riefenstahl's *Triumph of the Will*: "The document (the image) not only is the record of reality but is one reason for which the reality has been constructed, and must eventually supersede it." "Fascinating Fascism," in *Under the Sign of Saturn* (New York: Anchor Books, 1991), p. 83.

9. See Silverman, *The Acoustic Mirror*, p. 219.

10. *Visions of Excess*, p. 238.

11. Interview, 12 May 1990. Mann's use of quasi-stream-of-consciousness techniques is mirrored, for example, in Cavani's original script of *Il portiere di notte*, which contained various monologues to explain certain events. Only one short monologue made it into the film. After visiting Lucia's bedroom, Max, visibly shaken, reflects on his reaction, as he pours himself a beer in the hotel lobby: "All seemed lost. Instead something unexpected happened. The phantoms of memory have become physical . . . her voice, her body . . . is part of myself." Cavani, *Il portiere di notte*, p. 63.

12. As the director admitted, during the making of *Il portiere di notte*, she had an enormous faith in the capacity of cinema to express everything: "I was terrified to shoot too many compositions, and I cannot explain it rationally, but I felt from the beginning that I needed sequences. I deliberately wanted sequences with brief intercuts, as if the hotel were pulsating with this life, and you could feel the breathing and the heartbeat. I sensed the hotel lobby in this way. The symbol was Europe." Interview, 12 May 1990.

13. Ibid.

14. See *Kierkegaard: Construction of the Aesthetic*, pp. 40–46.

15. Cited by Walter Siti, "L'inconscio," in Asor Rosa, *Letteratura italiana*, 5:717. Cf. Cavani: "Cinema is for me a form of psychoanalysis that I apply to myself. That is why I shoot only what I like." Clouzot, "Liliana Cavani: Le Mythe, le sexe et la révolte," p. 42.

16. *Prophets of Extremity: Nietzsche, Heidegger, Foucault, Derrida* (Berkeley and Los Angeles: University of California Press, 1985), p. 34.

17. Introduction to *Il portiere di notte*, p. xiv. "The beauty of the figures of Klimt is dream, illusion, and it is tragic" (p. xiii).

18. "Liliana Cavani e Félix Guattari: Una conversazione," p. 175.

19. P. B. and S. T., "Anti-rétro: Entretien avec Michel Foucault," p. 12. For Canby, see " 'The Night Porter' Is Romantic Pornography," *New York Times*, 13 October 1974, D1, 19.

20. "Abelardo e Eloisa una storia d'amore e di anarchia," *Tuttolibri*, 8 December 1979, p. 20.

21. For a comprehensive selection of major reviews documenting the film's release and polemics, see *Il portiere di notte (critiche, fatti e polemiche): Dossier della critica*, ed. Ufficio Stampa dell'Italnoleggio Cinematografico (Rome), December 1974. Cavani wrote the screenplay in 1970; however, it was not until the end of 1972 that she found Robert Gordon Edwards, an American producer living in Rome, willing to finance the film. The decisive factor was Dirk Bogarde, who at first rejected the role but after seeing *Galileo* on French television committed himself to it. Essential to Bogarde's decision was also Visconti's backing of Cavani. Edwards also produced *La caduta degli dei* and *Morte a Venezia* (Death in Venice, 1971), in which the British actor had leading roles. For production details, see Bogarde's autobiography, *An Orderly Man* (London: Triad Grafton, 1984), pp. 168–178, 203–209, 231–238; and Edwards's interview with Alexander Stuart, "Collaboration," *Films and Filming* 20 (August 1974): 56–59. Cavani has acknowledged that one of her most valued collaborators was the producer, because of his distribution strategies, which determined the enormous success of the film. Edwards chose to premiere the film in Paris and not in Italy (where it was later censored and legally blocked for months). The American market went to Joseph Levin (Fellini's distributor in the United States), who skillfully arranged the X-rating and the negative reviews (particularly those of Pauline Kael and the *New York Times*) to the advertising advantage of the film. In Europe, the film's promotion was carefully staged through the backup of critics, intellectuals, and artists (among them Michel Foucault, Luchino Visconti, and Eduardo De Filippo).

Il portiere di notte was shot in 1973 for seven weeks in Rome and three in Vienna. The director's cut was 123 minutes long. On the making of the film, Cavani recounts: "*Il portiere di notte* is the conclusion to *Storia del Terzo Reich*. That documentary was my investigation into what happened to the generations that had preceded us. I wrote the treatment (just a short page) in one afternoon. Then I spent a year on the script. I inserted a lot more during the shooting. For example, I had not written the scene of the bathroom and the one when Max hits Lucia. Many explicatory scenes were cut either during the shooting or in the editing." Interview, 12 May 1990. Among the scenes that were cut, there is one in a restaurant near the end of the film where Max, dressed in his old SS uniform, spoon-feeds Lucia like a *bambina*.

22. Introduction to *Il portiere di notte*, p. ix.

23. Ibid., pp. ix–x. The film's working title was *Illecite relazioni* (Forbidden Affairs). One is reminded of Siegfried Kracauer's claim about *Das Cabinet des Dr. Caligari*, that once a strong sadism was unleashed, its reappearance on the screen testifies to its prominence in the German collective soul. See *From Caligari to Hitler: A Psychological History of the German Film* (Princeton, NJ: Princeton University Press, 1947), p. 74.

24. Cf. Cavani: "Dirk Bogarde's character is literally the porter—or gate-keeper—of the night." Alexander Stuart, "Consciousness and Conscience," *Films and Filming* 21 (February 1975): 11.

25. "Il portiere di notte," *Il tempo*, 14 April 1974, p. 12.

26. Introduction to *Il portiere di notte*, pp. vii–viii. On this subject (neglected by the official historiography), see Cavani's article in *Orizzonti* ("Le donne della resistenza," 4 April 1965, pp. 6–7), in which she reports that 4,563 women were arrested and tortured and over 3,000 were deported to Germany: very few came back. Among her readings for *Il portiere di notte* were the memoirs of Hitler's architect, Albert Speer's *Erinnerungen* (Inside the Third Reich, 1969) and Simon Wiesenthal's *The Murderers among Us* (1967).

27. On this issue, see Eric Santner's study of post-Holocaust discourses of mourning in German cinema, *Stranded Objects: Mourning, Memory, and Film in Postwar Germany* (Ithaca, NY, and London: Cornell University Press, 1990), pp. 7–8.

28. " 'Portiere di notte' di Liliana Cavani," *Letture* 73 (April 1974): 342. In an interview with François Courtet, Cavani describes the film as "the overture of the underground of a city—Vienna—where there was the highest percentage of Nazi criminals." "Les Rayons X du nazisme," *Nouvel Observateur*, 22 April 1974, p. 58.

29. See "Alfio Contini: Il cannocchiale rovesciato," in Consiglio and Ferzetti, *La bottega della luce*, p. 18.

30. Introduction to *Il portiere di notte*, p. ix.

31. Pasquale De Filippo, "Primo Levi, il testimone di quelli che non tornarono," *Gazzetta del mezzogiorno* (Bari), 10 December 1977.

32. Ibid. Levi returns to this subject in *I sommersi e i salvati* (The Drowned and the Saved) (Turin: Einaudi, 1986), pp. 34 ff. Ironically, he endorses *Salon Kitty* (1976) by Tinto Brass, a film Cavani was asked to direct but turned down after reading the script. Cf. Annette Insdorf: "One can see this merely as perversion and exploitation of the Holocaust for the sake of sensationalism. Or one can take seriously Max's confession. . . . His repressed guilt is perhaps as great as his initially repressed lust, and Max's ultimate action is to turn himself into a physically degraded and emotionally shattered prisoner." *Indelible Shadows: Film and the Holocaust* (Cambridge: Cambridge University Press, 1989), p. 138. Marguerite Waller offers an intelligent reading of the Holocaust as a feminist issue, departing from Primo Levi's remarks about *The Night Porter* and Bruno Bettelheim's critical review of Lina Wertmüller's *Seven Beauties* in the *New Yorker* ("Surviving," 2 August 1976, pp. 31–52). See "Signifying the Holocaust: Liliana Cavani's *Portiere di notte*," in *Feminisms in the Cinema*, ed. Laura Pietropaolo and Ada Testaferri (Bloomington: Indiana University Press, 1995), pp. 206–219.

33. Here I am paraphrasing Bataille's description of the ecstatic vision as catastrophe in *Visions of Excess*, p. 134. Maurice Blanchot has pointed out that the relation between Sade and the language of *excès* is construed as the representation of "le secret, l'obscurité de l'abîme, la solitude inviolable d'un cellule" (the mystery, the darkness of the abyss,

the inviolable solitude of a cell). *Lautréamont et Sade* (Paris: Editions de Minuit, 1963), pp. 17–18.

34. *Il portiere di notte*, p. 67.

35. From *"Il portiere di notte" di Liliana Cavani*, Italnoleggio Cinematografico press kit, 1974 (Archival Collection). In the flashback (played against *The Magic Flute*) in the infirmary, which Cavani calls "una zona tutta verde" (a green zone), Max tends to Lucia's wounds. The scene raises questions of female spectatorship, since it is directed to include various deployments of the gaze: at one edge of the frame, "recluse verdastre" (female prisoners bathed in green light) become visible witnesses. In exploring the spatial tension of female desire, Cavani's erotic mapping is located in a space (the infirmary) intended for (medical) examination of and experimentation on bodies. While the grayness of the dormitory is experientially male (in its association with sodomy) and the frozen stare of the deportees emphasizes their role as passive voyeurs, here voyeurism suggests involvement: Lucia "è coinvolta" (is a participant). Thus the act of seeing reclaims the spectatorial pleasures of the female gaze within the erotic boundaries. See Cavani's stage directions in *Il portiere di notte*, pp. 44–45. In this scene, the spectacular tonalities of soft lighting are transmuted into a spectrum of greenish hues, which is essentially atmospheric (coldness, disembodiment); it evokes sensations of distance and boundlessness. The color green conveys a kind of ethereal perspective, in contrast to the dark, unlit background of the dormitory scene. Initially, Lucia's reaction is a mixture of "ribrezzo e paura" (disgust and fear). Cf. Bataille: "I must say that repugnance, or horror, is the principle of desire." *L'Erotisme* (Paris: Editions de Minuit, 1957), p. 66.

36. Interview, 12 May 1990. Cf. R. M. Friedman: "The fact that nearly all the critics made the mistake of identifying Lucia as a Jewess, together with the form of the director's refutation, only underline the vitality of the stereotypes and, even, in Cavani's case, of antisemitic prejudices. There is clearly in her mind a Jewish type, incompatible with the fair elegance of the fragile Rampling." "Exorcising the Past: Jewish Figures in Contemporary Films," *Journal of Contemporary History* 19, no. 3 (1984): 518. Even such Italian critics as Moravia and Argentieri identified Lucia as an Austrian Jew (see respectively "C'è un nazista a pianterreno," *L'espresso*, 21 April 1974, p. 87, and "Liliana Cavani tra magia e storia," *Rinascita*, 26 April 1974, p. 23). Cavani is not antisemitic. A member of Amnesty International, she has viewed the film's themes as broadly inclusive from the very beginning. For the role of Lucia, she initially wanted Mia Farrow.

37. From *"Il portiere di notte" di Liliana Cavani*.

38. *Il portiere di notte*, p. 59. Cf. Cavani: "Max gazes at the woman, seeing not the 'woman' but the little girl he once knew." From "Trama del film: *Il portiere di notte*" (Archival Collection). The theme of the merry-go-round is fully developed in the initial treatment of the film (which is fourteen pages long). When Lucia encounters Max in 1957, she buys a curious gift for him: an antique carousel toy. Upon receiving it, Max decides to follow her to the opera, and their old affair is resumed. For an analysis of the film within the parameters of an Oedipal nostalgia, see K. Silverman, "Masochism and Subjectivity," *Framework* (University of East Anglia), no. 12 (1980): 6–7. Silverman approaches *Il portiere di notte* as an exemplary case of Freudian masochism/voyeurism, and in relation to Laura Mulvey's essay "Visual Pleasure and Narrative Cinema" (1975). Max's camera exemplifies a dynamic rapport between seeing and victimizing.

39. R. Caillois, *I giochi e gli uomini*, pref. Pier Aldo Rovatti, notes by Giampaolo Dossena (Milan: Bompiani, 1995), p. 155. Originally published as *Les Jeux et les hommes: Le Masque et le vertige* (Paris: Gallimard, 1967).

40. From "Incontro e lavoro con Kim Arcalli," 1977 (Archival Collection). Also: "Arcalli signified editing. He was the maximum form of Italian expression in editing. He rethought the film for you. Nobody does that anymore." Interview, 10 May 1990. Franco Arcalli ("Kim" to his friends) was the creative hand behind Bernardo Bertolucci's *Il conformista* (The Conformist, 1970). For Cavani, he also worked on *Milarepa* and *Al di là del bene e del male*. He died in 1977.

41. The motif of the fair plays a prominent role in Kracauer's analysis of *Caligari*. He views its diversity of thrilling amusements as the antithesis of tyranny and traces literary sources for its biblical images (Babel and Babylon alike). The fair becomes an enclave of anarchy and chaos in the sphere of entertainment: "For adults it is a regression into childhood days, in which games and serious affairs are identical, real and imagined things mingle, and anarchical desires aimlessly test infinite possibilities. By means of this regression the adult escapes a civilization which tends to overgrow and starve out the chaos of instincts. He escapes it to restore that chaos upon which civilization rests. Thus the fair is not freedom, but anarchy entailing chaos." *From Caligari to Hitler*, p. 73.

42. Cf. Cavani on eroticism: "A creative ritual that is not an empty gesture but purpose, an expression of life." Interview, 27 June 1989. On this issue, see also "La presa di posizione del Vaticano sul sesso," *Belfagor* 31 (March 1976): 233–234; "Eros non è il diavolo," *Tuttolibri*, 19 March 1977, p. 10; and the published text of a talk the director gave at the Teatro Eliseo in Rome on 4 February 1975, "Cinema ed erotismo," *Belfagor* 30 (March 1975): 157–168, reprinted as "Cinema e censura," in *Quaderni del centro culturale "Merolla" (1972–1975)*, ed. Salvatore Mignanò, no. 2 (1975): 221–240. Here she defines our culture as supported by two pillars: the horror of sex and the acceptance of violence in defense of property. She draws her conclusions from Bataille, Marcuse, Fritz Leist, and Guido Almansi's *L'estetica dell'osceno*. Of special interest is an unpublished letter written by Cavani to Pasolini at the time of the national debates on the abortion issue, where she discusses Sandor Ferenczi's biological subconscious as a thalassic regression. For Ferenczi, an individual regresses during coitus to the maternal amniotic fluids, thus recapturing his prebirth existence as an embryo. Cavani comments: "When Ferenczi speaks of an 'individual' during coitus, he speaks only of the male, and he confines the female to the [role of] marine symbol of man. Ferenczi never considers the woman as an individual, or an active partner, but rather as a passive object-symbol. She is seen as a part of nature, like the sky and the earth; of that nature within which man operates." After a three-page exposition, she concludes: "To accept the hypothesis of a thalassic regression means to accept the idea that a woman is 'an object' of nature (even if a beautiful one), an 'object' that seems to belong to everyone. It is unacceptable that a woman might be limited and emphasized solely as uterus in her social role. . . . Even those who are against abortion must deal with women as individuals" (Archival Collection). Cavani refers to a letter by Pasolini entitled "Thalassa," which was published in *Paese sera* on 25 January 1975. Pasolini, who supported all the referenda called by the Radicals, publicly declares his discomfort with the abortion law: "I am traumatized by the legalization of abortion, because, like many, I consider it a legalization of homocide. In dreams, and in everyday behavior—something

common to all men—I live my prenatal life, my happy immersion in the maternal fluids: and I know that there I existed." "Il coito, l'aborto, la falsa tolleranza del potere, il conformismo dei progressisti," in *Scritti corsari* (Milan: Garzanti, 1975), pp. 123–131, reprinted from "Sono contro l'aborto," *Corriere della sera*, 19 January 1975. The battle to reform the laws on abortion lasted until the mid-seventies. The signatures for a referendum were collected by the MLD (Movimento della Liberazione delle Donne Italiane) and the Radical Party in 1975. The bill legalizing abortion was ratified on 22 May 1978.

43. Cavani, *Il portiere di notte*, p. 73. For Cavani, the bathroom signifies the space of a ritual: "It is the locus where people look at themselves—there is always a mirror. It is a moment in which you are most exposed." Interview, 12 May 1990. Max's libidinal economy (symbolically enacted as desire for an absolute possession) finds another explicit application during the couple's erotic seige: the shattered jar of marmalade that they fiercely and playfully devour becomes the meal which sets up their final role reversal. Gian-Paolo Biasin has reminded us that at the foundation of the (Hegelian) master/slave dialectic one finds the ingestion of food as possession and transformation of the world. See *The Flavors of Modernity: Food and the Novel* (Princeton, NJ: Princeton University Press, 1993), pp. 17–18.

44. *Visions of Excess*, p. 222.

45. *Liliana Cavani*, pp. 104–105. At the climatic moment of death, in a preternatural silence, the couple transcends a world empowered by ceremonial language. "In Italy and Germany," says Cavani, "post-Fascism is primarily responsible for the ignorance of today's youth and for all its consequences. We must thank the fathers if the sons are criminals. They wanted to cover everything up with a stone. This cannot be done. As the Greek theater teaches us, he who has sinned through *hybris* must pay; otherwise the children pay. The Nazi crimes were possible owing to the complicity of the entire nation. Afterward, nobody knew anything. Those who lived near the extermination camps seem not to have had the nose to smell the burning of human flesh." Tassone, *Parla il cinema italiano*, 2:137.

46. I am referring respectively to Alexander Walker, "Two for the Pipshow," *Evening Standard*, 17 January 1974, p. 29; and to the title of Felix Barker's article in *Evening News*, 17 January 1974, p. 2C. *Last Tango in Paris* is a complex play of self-projection, in which Bertolucci explores the ambiguities of the cinematic and erotic experience. It became the point of reference among reviewers of Cavani's film. R. T. Witcombe writes: "Essentially, *The Night Porter* reveals the penchant of Italian directors for stories which put a man and a woman alone in a room together in order to see what passions and lusts emerge. Cavani's film, at its heart, is *Last Tango* transposed in time and place, but sharing the same sexual delineation." *The New Italian Cinema: Studies in Dance and Despair* (New York: Oxford University Press, 1982), p. 68. See also Vittorio Ricciuti, "Non ha dimenticato Bertolucci," *Il mattino*, 1 June 1974, and Federica Di Castro, "L'ultimo tango della Cavani," *Notiziario Arte Contemporanea*, July 1974, both reprinted in *Il portiere di notte (critiche, fatti e polemiche)*, pp. 32–33, 18–19; and Anna Paschetto, "Ultimo tango a Parigi e a Vienna," *Culture* (Milan), 1989, pp. 115–125.

47. " 'The Night Porter' Is Romantic Pornography," p. 1. Canby's position was echoed by several American critics: Nora Sayre claims that "the movie's visual virtues are negated by infinite absurdities—particularly by the sentimentality with which the director views this luckless couple" (" 'The Night Porter,' Portrait of Abuse, Stars Bogarde," *New York Times*, 2 October 1974, L58); Stanley Kauffmann writes about Cavani:

"She is apparently humorless and, in a basic sense, stupid. Only a humorless person could so often cross over into the ridiculous; only a stupid one could believe that all this sexual-homicidal blatancy was symbolically illuminating" ("Stanley Kauffmann on Films," *New Republic*, 5 October 1974, p. 33); Judith Crist describes the film as "a pretentious bit of pseudo-perversion that seems to be a nightmare mélange of *Last Tango* and *The Damned*" ("Winning Big," *New York*, 7 October 1974, p. 94); and Pauline Kael speaks of a "humanly and aesthetically offensive" porno gothic ("The Current Cinema: Stuck in the Fun," *New Yorker*, 7 October 1974, p. 151). On the other hand, Andrew Sarris writes that no one could possibly think that the film "is intended as a realistic reconstruction of the Nazi era," and that Cavani's style is "so seductive and so obsessive that one has to be willfully blind to ignore it." "The Nasty Nazis: History or Mythology?" *Village Voice*, 17 October 1974, p. 77. Canby's attack—which relies on the premise that Lucia is "the little Jewish girl"—is openly debated by Teresa De Lauretis in "Cavani's 'Night Porter': A Woman's Film," *Film Quarterly* 30 (Winter 1976–1977): 35–38. Also Molly Haskell defended the film in "Are Women Directors Different?" *Village Voice*, 3 February 1975, p. 73, reprinted in *Women and the Cinema*, ed. Karyn Kay and Gerald Peary (New York: Dutton, 1977), pp. 429–435. In a letter to the *New York Times*, Cavani comments on Canby's caustic remarks (which she believes to be commercially motivated) and compares his acritical stance with the European debates about her film (involving Moravia, Bory, the Freudian Institute in Paris, the Jungian Society in Rome). She concludes: "It should be clear that I am not protesting against negative criticism but rather the pertinence of its language. I have made films for eight years and I am used to being attacked; it becomes a part of my work. From many attacks I have learned something. In this case, I simply wanted to express my opinion on the controversy posed by the *New York Times*, for which no one asked my opinion—after all it is my film, and it is my skin. This is the reason why I am writing, because I truly believe in what I have learned to appreciate during my brief American visits, and that is the zest for the debate which is one of the most civilized, democratic traditions" (Archival Collection).

48. *Italian Cinema from Neorealism to the Present*, p. 349.

49. "The Challenge of Neo-Fascist Culture," *Cinéaste* 6, no. 4 (1975): 31. In the same issue of *Cinéaste*, there is an equally bitter review by Ruth McCormick, "Fascism à la Mode or Radical Chic?" (pp. 31, 33–34).

50. *Cahiers du Cinéma* devoted two issues to the subject of the *rétro* phenomenon, inviting Michel Foucault to debate on its "false archaeology of history." Foucault's discourse began with Marcel Ophüls's documentary *Le Chagrin et la pitié* (The Sorrow and the Pity, 1970) about French collaboration and resistance during World War II, and went on to include *Lacombe Lucien* and *Il portiere di notte*. He focused particularly on Louis Malle and Cavani to elucidate the interaction between the historical and the erotic. Specifically, *Lacombe Lucien*'s love theme has the simple function of rehabilitating the antihero; while in *Il portiere di notte* the crucial issue is *l'amour pour le pouvoir*: "In *Il portiere di notte*, it is interesting to see how, in Nazism, the power of one person was followed and enacted by many. The sort of false tribunal that has been constituted is very captivating. For there is the allure of a psychotherapy group, which indeed has the power structure of a secret society. Basically, it is a reconstituted SS cell, with a different judicial system, which opposes the central power." P. B. and S. T., "Anti-rétro: Entretien avec Michel Foucault," p. 12. See the articles by Bernard Sichère, "La Bête et le militant"

(*Cahiers du Cinéma*, nos. 251–252 [July–August 1974]: 19–29), and Pascale Bonitzer, "Le Secret derrière la porte" (*Cahiers du Cinéma*, nos. 251–252 [July–August 1974]: 31–36) for an analysis of the film within the context of a political petit-bourgeois unconscious and for its critical reception. See also Serge Daney's discussion of spectatorial embodiment in the scene of Max's last meeting with his ex-comrades on the rooftop of the Hotel zur Oper, in "Anti-rétro (suite) et fonction critique (fin)," *Cahiers du Cinéma*, no. 253 (October–November 1974): 30–31. It was *Le Monde* that opened the discussion on the *rétro* phenomenon with an article by Martin Even, "Les Ambiguités de la mode 'Rétro,' " 18 April 1974, pp. 18–19, and a follow-up debate published on 25 April, pp. 20–21 (which also includes a letter from Cavani); and Jacques Siclier, "Les Créateurs font marche arrière: Depuis trente-cinq ans, le cinéma raconte le nazisme," 18 April 1974, p. 18. In Italy, see particularly C. Quarantotto, "Achtung, nostalgia!" *Il borghese*, 28 April 1974, pp. 1067–1068; C. Cosulich, "Romeo e Giulietta nel lager," *Paese sera*, 16 June 1974, p. 9; L. Tornabuoni, "Il nazismo nel cinema," *Linus*, June 1974, pp. 60–66; and M. Argentieri, *Il film biografico* (Rome: Bulzoni, 1984), pp. 13–16. For the film's reception in Germany, see Renate Rasp, "Goldene Zeiten in KZ," *Der Spiegel*, 17 February 1975, pp. 121–126.

51. "Fascinating Fascism," in *Under the Sign of Saturn*, p. 105. Cf. Sichère: "Whips, chains, transvestism, Marlene, leather boots, hollow throbbing, march or die, jouissance, inviting mouths, Sade, Deleuze, subversive homosexuality, pulsating discharge, horrifying delight: the filthy beast and its coils. Fascism inhabits us: this is not an alarmed denunciation; it is a choking, shameful, elegant, exulting cry. Barbarity is at our doors. Better yet: it is within us, all of us." "La Bête et le militant," p. 19. On the theme of Fascist nostalgia, see also the debate organized by the weekly magazine *Panorama*, whose participants comprised Cavani, Pasolini, film critic Tullio Kezich, novelist Goffredo Parise, a psychiatrist, and a psychosexual analyst. The *rétro* phenomenon was identified within the terms of regression, patriarchy, fetishism, theatricality, and play. Cavani primarily views Nazism as a kind of occult religion. Emilia Granzotto and Giuliano Gallo, "Sedotti dal nero?" 9 October 1975, pp. 116–124. For the relationship of the film to history, see Pintus, *Storia e film*, pp. 99–100; Vito Attolini, *Sotto il segno del film (Cinema italiano 1968/76)* (Bari: Mario Adda Editore, 1983), pp. 244–248.

52. *Subversive Pleasures*, p. 170. Gilles Deleuze has coined a term (pornology) embracing Sade's and Masoch's works. Drawing from Bataille, he concludes that "the language of Sade is paradoxical *because it is essentially that of a victim.* Only the victim can describe torture; the torturer necessarily uses the hypocritical language of established order and power." *Sacher-Masoch: An Interpretation*, trans. Jean McNeil (London: Faber and Faber, 1971), pp. 16–17. Masoch is equally paradoxical in the matter of role reversals, because he exemplifies the language of the torturer. Like Deleuze, Cavani rejects the application of the term "pornography" to either author. See her article "There Are Degrees and Degrees of Sadomasochism," *Viva*, February 1975, pp. 113–114. On the issue of cinema and pornography, see particularly Roberto Nepoti, who includes *Il portiere di notte* as one of the "noble" examples among a number of films that exploit Nazism, Fascism, and sexuality. "Cinema pornoerotico: Le pratiche del dis-piacere," *Bianco e nero* 39, no. 5 (1978): 50–60. Nancy Huston sees Cavani's film and Pasolini's *Salò* as "an unfortunate attempt to reinject eroticism into genocide." *Mosaïque de la pornographie: Marie-Thérèse et les autres* (Paris: Denoel-Gonthier, 1982), p. 165. In discussing the films of *la mode rétro*, Naomi Greene criticizes Huston's position by claiming

that Pasolini rejects audience complicity, while trying to remove Eros from the tradition of romance and pornography. She calls *Il portiere di notte* and *Pasqualino settebellezze* (Seven Beauties, 1976) realistic melodramas that render sadomasochism erotic. *Pier Paolo Pasolini: Cinema as Heresy* (Princeton, NJ: Princeton University Press, 1990), p. 202.

53. Introduction to Maria Teresa Colonna, *Lilith la luna nera e l'eros rifiutato* (Florence: Edizioni del Riccio, 1980), p. 18. The Great Mother, Demeter, and the priest of the Sun are the antagonists of Tamino and Pamina, their love story being an initiation to the abolition of the masculine/feminine duality. This remarkable sequence has received little critical attention. The homologies of sadomasochism / death instinct and *The Magic Flute* / life instinct were suggested by Moravia, who saw in this scene a desacralization of the European tradition represented by the music of Mozart. "C'è un nazista a pianterreno," pp. 88. For a reading of Max and Lucia as compared to Pamina and Papageno, see Waller, "Signifying the Holocaust," pp. 214–216. Originally, the opera was *Don Giovanni*. The director comments on Mozart's treatment of the Don Juan myth in her article "Don Giovanni pensa e sconvolge il gioco," *Tuttolibri*, 8 March 1980, p. 15. Cavani has always wanted to make a film on Mozart. She has now completed a script (with Italo Moscati) entitled *I piccoli Mozart* (Mozart and Mozart, 1995). In 1979, Cavani made her operatic directorial debut at the Maggio Musicale Fiorentino with *Wozzeck*. Since then, she has worked on a regular basis at the Opéra de Paris and La Scala, among others, to great critical acclaim. For this aspect of Cavani's career, see Elena Doni, "Lirica Liliana," *Il messaggero*, 19 April 1979, p. 12; Mario Pasi, "La Cavani trema per la sua prima regia nella lirica," *Corriere della sera*, 17 April 1979, p. 20; Marcello De Angelis, "Wozzeck, 'omino' che si ribella solo a se stesso," *L'unità*, 27 April 1979, p. 12; Enrico Cavallotti, "La Cavani regista di 'Wozzeck' ha in cuore la musica di Mozart," *Il tempo*, 30 April 1979, p. 6; Giorgio Prosperi, "All'ombra del palazzo," *Il tempo*, 4 May 1979, p. 14; Enrico Cavallotti, "Aperto il Maggio: 'Wozzeck' di Berg ultima spiaggia del teatro in musica," *Il tempo*, 4 May 1979, p. 14; E. T. Glasow, "Gluck: 'Iphigenie en Tauride,' " *Opera News* 49, no. 3 (1984): 52–53; C. Pitt, "Cherubini: 'Medée,' " *Opera* 37, no. 6 (1986): 686–688; Armando Caruso, "Cavani e la Medea all'Opéra," *La stampa*, 2 March 1986, p. 21; Lorenzo Arruga, "Cavani, regista d'opera," in Tallarigo and Gasparini, *Lo sguardo libero*, pp. 150–152; Alfredo Mandelli, "Alla Scala tris d'assi nel nome della Callas," *Oggi*, 13 December 1993, p. 136; Luigi Chiavarone, "Il segreto della regia d'opera per Liliana Cavani," *Rivista illustrata del museo teatrale alla Scala* 8 (April 1995): 84–86; Roberta Emiliani, "Sì, questa Cavalleria una grande anima," *Corriere di Ravenna*, 19 July 1996, p. 33; Matthew Gurewitsch, "An Opera Director with a Cinematic Eye," *Wall Street Journal* (Europe), 12 June 1998, p. 13.

54. Cavani, *Il portiere di notte*, pp. 39, 40.

55. Ibid., p. 52.

56. On this point, cf. Bruno, *Streetwalking on a Ruined Map*, pp. 44. Elaborating on the notion of apparatus advanced by Jean-Louis Baudry, Bruno suggests that filmic desire itself is rooted in orality. Teresa De Lauretis has interpreted this scene as a metaphor of the female condition: "The way in which Lucia is victimized, the truth she discovers in herself and lives out, the imagery of her bondage to the Father (this is obviously the meaning of her being chained and hiding under the table), are a true metaphor, however magnified, of the female condition." "Cavani's 'Night Porter': A Woman's Film?" p. 37.

57. See Bataille, *Visions of Excess*, p. xiv.

58. Tiso, *Liliana Cavani*, p. 9. Within the context of cinematic reflections of Fascism, Visconti's *The Damned* is considered the Grand Opera approach to this historical period. At Visconti's death in 1976, Cavani remembered him as "a man of the spectacle like few others, a man of the Left, learned, cultivated, born to imagine scenes and create characters, but without rhetoric and demagogy. He hated ideological terrorism, almost as much as I do." "Un Homme contre le terrorisme," *Nouvelles Litteraires*, 25 March 1976, p. 3.

59. This is the full text of Visconti's letter: "The film 'Portiere di notte' by Liliana Cavani is a definite proof of the great maturity and wisdom of its author, whom I have already admired for such works as 'I cannibali' and 'Milarepa.' 'Portiere di notte' is an atrocious, cruel, and terrible film that leaves you breathless. It is acted to perfection by everyone, and especially by the magnificent protagonists Dirk Bogarde and Charlotte Rampling and also by Isa Miranda and Philippe Leroy. It is a film construed with rare wisdom and equilibrium, and it is a film that will remain as another dreadful witness to Nazism. I hope that Liliana Cavani's work will be soon released without cuts or absurd interferences. I am sure it will be successful with audiences all over the world" (Archival Collection). When the film failed to receive approval for distribution, Cavani issued a press release: "At the end of a private screening of *Il portiere di notte*, the director Liliana Cavani announced that the president of the third censorship commission asked her to completely cut out a scene that he called 'filthy and prostitution-like.' In addition to the journalists, at the screening there were Pier Paolo Pasolini, Laura Betti, Bernardo Bertolucci, Michelangelo Antonioni, Dacia Maraini, Mauro Bolognini, Alberto Moravia, and Marco Bellocchio. 'I reacted not just as a director but also as a woman: I do not see why a sexual act with the man on the top can pass censorship; however, if the woman is on the top it is considered prostitution. In order not to cut that scene—which I consider essential to the structure of my film—I asked the censors to rate the film for adults, but they refused and confiscated the film.' " Ansa, Rome, 28 April 1974 (Archival Collection). On censorship, see particularly G. B., "Il caso 'Portiere di notte': Come sempre censura d'idee. Assurde accuse al film di Liliana Cavani," *Il messaggero*, 29 March 1974, p. 12; C. Cosulich, "Il portiere di notte proibito," *Paese sera*, 31 March 1974, p. 3; C. C., "Il mondo del cinema contro la censura," *Il messaggero*, 19 April 1974, p. 11; "Reazioni del mondo del cinema al sequestro di 'Portiere di notte,' " *Il tempo*, 19 April 1971, p. 8; C. Costantini, "La censurata," *Il messaggero*, 27 April 1974, p. 3; A. Moravia, "Non placet," *L'espresso*, 28 April 1974, pp. 64–65; Remo Urbini, "L'obiettivo senza pudore," *Epoca*, 28 April 1974, pp. 128–129; and Cavani's letter to Gian Luigi Rondi published as "Cavani: E' democratico avere paura della realtà?" *Il tempo*, 25 April 1974, p. 13. At an assembly meeting of the ANICA (National Association of Cinema Authors), chaired by Edwards, Moravia, and Cavani, the film received the support of Rosi, Petri, Bellocchio, Bertolucci, Pasolini, the Tavianis, and Wertmüller, among others. Also Fellini wrote to Cavani, "How can we modify a somnolent, backward, childish psychology, that identifies with collective schemata and does not take individual stands, like us Italians?" This letter was published with three other Fellini letters in "Fellini: Caro Kubrick ti scrivo," *La stampa*, 17 January 1995, p. 17. On the role of censorship in Italian cinema, see M. Argentieri, *La censura nel cinema italiano* (Rome: Editori Riuniti, 1974).

60. Introduction to *Il portiere di notte*, p. x.

61. See Tiso, *Liliana Cavani*, p. 104. Tiso has defined the inherent ambiguity of the Cavanian character as "mythorealistic self-destruction." "L'ambiguità filmica e il suo equivoco," *Filmcritica*, no. 248 (October 1974): 331.

62. From a TV special on Cavani on the weekly program *Settimo Giorno*, aired on 18 July 1974 (RAI Film Archives). See also Bory's review, "Le Carnaval des spectres," *Nouvel Observateur*, 8 April 1974, p. 63, reprinted as "Il portiere di notte," *Settegiorni*, 28 April 1974, pp. 3–4.

63. *The Body in the Mirror*, p. 40.

64. "Visual Pleasure and Narrative Cinema," in *Film Theory and Criticism: Introductory Readings*, ed. Gerald Mast and Marshall Cohen (New York and Oxford: Oxford University Press, 1985), p. 810.

65. Antonin Artaud, *The Theater and Its Double*, trans. Mary Caroline Richards (New York: Grove Press, 1979), p. 104.

66. Stuart, "Consciousness and Conscience," p. 13. "The SS was a body endowed with a high potential for narcissism. Hitler's charisma is based on ambiguity: he is the 'virgin' while Mussolini was the 'male.'" Cavani's Introduction to *Il portiere di notte*, p. xiii.

67. From *"Portiere di notte" di Liliana Cavani*. Dietrich's song is interpreted by Charlotte Rampling. It was composed by Friedrich Hollander in 1930 at the Berlin cabaret Tingeltangel specifically for Dietrich. The role of Countess Stein is played by Isa Miranda, the diva of the thirties, a femme fatale icon of the Italian cinema of *telefoni bianchi* (white telephone films). She is primarily remembered for her role in *La signora di tutti* (Everybody's Lady, 1934) by Max Ophüls.

68. Cavani, *Il portiere di notte*, p. 70. In this scene, Lucia is a victim in a degenerate milieu.

69. What is implied here is a complete disavowal of the castration complex by the substituting of a fetish object, which is reassuring. On this point, see Mulvey, "Visual Pleasure and Narrative Cinema," p. 811; and Silverman, "Masochism and Subjectivity," pp. 5–6. Tullio Kezich attests to the difficulty of placing the Lucia/Salomè scene within the narrative logic of the story. See "Il portiere di notte," *Sipario*, no. 336 (May 1974): 42–43.

70. Renzo Fegatelli, "Il carnefice rivuole la bambina," *Fiera letteraria*, 12 May 1974, p. 27. For an exhaustive analysis of this topos, see Linda Mizejewski, *Divine Decadence: Fascism, Female Spectacle, and the Makings of Sally Bowles* (Princeton, NJ: Princeton University Press, 1992), esp. pp. 19–22, 78. For a reading of Lucia's performance as an exploration of bisexuality, see Beverle Houston and Marsha Kinder, "The Night Porter as Daydream," *Film/Literature Quarterly* 3 (Fall 1975): 367.

71. As René Girard has argued, we must forget the notion of Salomè as a professional seducer, because she is a child and she changes "from innocence to the convulsions of mimetic violence." *The Scapegoat*, trans. Yvonne Freccero (Baltimore: Johns Hopkins University Press, 1986), p. 131.

72. For an introduction to the literary and pictorial representations of Salomè, see Françoise Meltzer, *Salome and the Dance of Writing: Portraits of Mimesis in Literature* (Chicago and London: University of Chicago Press, 1987), esp. chap. 1. Two primary biblical sources tell us the story of Salomè: the Gospels of Mark and Matthew.

73. Cavani defines *Oltre la porta* as "un giallo psicologico" (a psychological thriller) that unfolds in a family conspiracy. Set in Marrakesh, the story is about a passionate

love affair between Nina (Eleonora Giorgi) and her stepfather Enrico (Marcello Mastroianni). Nina keeps Enrico in prison (where he serves time for the presumed murder of his wife) so that she can exert control over him. The couple's intense life is upset by the arrival of an American oil engineer (Tom Berenger), who relentlessly pursues Nina. The film then focuses on the defiance of traditional sexual boundaries: the negation of difference is made real by Enrico's willingness to submit to the power of a female voice. Cavani explains: "Going 'Beyond the door' is often a revelation that disturbs the cards. You may discover the truth or the appearance of truth. I love to observe and read about free human relationships or parental ones, because I think that the human being is the mammal we understand the least." From the press kit released by Cineriz in 1982 (Archival Collection).

Chapter 5
Staging the Gaze: *Beyond Good and Evil*

1. *Al di là del bene e del male* was first announced in 1974, at which time the director thought of casting Dirk Bogarde and Charlotte Rampling for the main roles. The film entered production in 1976–1977, and the Swedish actor Erland Josephson, who had worked with Bergman, was chosen to play Nietzsche. Dominique Sanda, a favorite of Bresson and Bertolucci, was cast as Lou, and Robert Powell, who had just completed *Gesù di Nazareth* (Jesus of Nazareth, 1977) with Franco Zeffirelli, played the role of Paul Rée. The shooting began in January 1977 and took eleven weeks. Exteriors were primarily shot in Rome, Venice, Munich, Lübeck, and Hamburg; the interior scenes were filmed at Cinecittà Studios. The film premiered in Paris the week of 4 October 1977 and was simultaneously released in Italy. Owing to various censorship battles, *Al di là del bene e del male* was eventually pulled out of distribution and, as a result, was blocked for one year. For production details and Cavani's approach to the film, see William Tuohy, "The Thinking Man's Triangle," *Los Angeles Times* 6 January 1977, p. 14; Pierre Montaigne, "Liliana Cavani, celle par qui le scandale arrive," *Le Figaro*, 4 October 1977, p. 29; Tassone, *Parla il cinema italiano*, 2:138. On the issue of censorship, see particularly Italo Moscati (the film's cowriter with Franco Arcalli), "Libertà d'opinione e libertà di film," *L'europeo*, 25 November 1977, p. 66; "Incredibile sequestro del film 'Al di là del bene e del male,' " *L'unità*, 9 November 1977, p. 9; Paolo D'Agostini, "Sequestrato, assolto, sequestrato: Era un film 'sorvegliato a vista,' " *La repubblica*, 10 November 1977, p. 14; "Italia: Le reazioni al sequestro del film di Liliana Cavani," *Il messaggero*, 10 November 1977, p. 12; C. Costantini, " 'Al di là del bene e del male': Quattro sequestri in un anno," *Il messaggero*, 22 October 1978, p. 12 (including "La risposta di Liliana Cavani"). The director addresses the legal controversies about her film in an article sent to *Il giorno* ("Liliana Cavani replica ai critici," 18 November 1977). In discussing this film, I refer to the original director's cut, which was 127 minutes long and included a ballet scene that was omitted from the American prints.

2. "Liliana Cavani and Félix Guattari: Una conversazione," pp. 173–174. The interview also appeared as "Liliana Cavani ou l'effet de trou noir amoureux," *Le Monde*, 10 November 1977, pp. 20–21.

3. *Male Subjectivity at the Margins* (New York and London: Routledge, 1992), p. 9. Feminist criticism has stressed the urgency of theorizing what Teresa De Lauretis has called the construction of gender as "the product and the process of both representa-

tion and self-representation" in relation to the female authorial voice. *Technologies of Gender*, p. 9.

4. Cavani, Arcalli, and Moscati, *Al di là del bene e del male*, p. 14. For Cavani, Lou is "a woman who lives her life as a total experience." Tassone, *Parla il cinema italiano*, 2:138.

5. *The Acoustic Mirror*, p. 216. These scenes were disturbing for many reviewers, who claimed that *Al di là del bene e del male* advanced erotic play beyond acceptable limits—primarily because a philosopher was involved. Paolo Valmarana calls them "heavy-handed, violent, and programmatically provocative" ("Il piacere dell'ambiguità," *Il popolo*, 29 October 1977, p. 5); Callisto Cosulich considers them disappointing ("La storia scende dal piedistallo e si fa scandalo," *Paese sera*, 29 October 1977, p. 15). For an account of the controversial reception of the film, see Cavani's reply to her critics in her interviews with Giorgio Calcagno, "La Cavani, regista dello scandalo," *La stampa*, 12 October 1977, p. 7; Enrico Rondoni, " 'A ciascuno il suo,' " *L'umanità*, 29 October 1977, p. 5; C. Costantini, "Al di là del vero e del falso," *Il messaggero*, 2 November 1977, p. 3; Lina Coletti, "Scandalo a tre," *L'europeo*, 11 November 1977, pp. 86–87. See also C. Costantini, "Ecce Omo," *Il messaggero*, 16 October 1977, p. 3; T. Kezich, "Una lezione d'amore accidentale e stravolta," *La repubblica*, 29 October 1977, p. 14. For an analysis of the critical attitude toward the film, see Gian Luigi Rondi, who expresses some reservations on the treatment of "Eros and the unconscious sold as culture when they are actually on the border of pornography" ("Al di là del bene e del male," *Il tempo*, 29 October 1977, p. 12); Vittorio Saltini, who compares Cavani's point of view to that of Nietzsche's hysterical sister Elizabeth ("Non ci sono genî per le cameriere," *L'espresso*, 30 October 1977, pp. 77–81; P. V. [P. Valmarana], "Chi ha paura di Liliana Cavani?" *Il popolo*, 5 November 1977, p. 5; Ruggero Guarini, "Donna è bello, il film invece no," *L'espresso*, 6 November 1977, p. 25. On the other hand, Claire Clouzot speaks of "a Faustian tale" ("Le Sexe de Nietzsche," *Le Matin*, 5 October 1977, p. 25); Guy Braucourt praises the film's "superbly Nietzschean beauty, force, lyricism" ("Audéla du bien e du mal," *Nouvelles Litteraires*, 6 October 1977, p. 27); Jacques Siclier singles out the director's modern approach ("La Nouvelle Morale de Liliana Cavani," *Le monde*, 8 October 1977, p. 31). For a reading of the film within the context of the gaze, see Giorgio Sassanelli and Giuseppe Vetrone, "Liliana Cavani o la capacità di guardare," *Belfagor* 33, no. 1 (1978): 101–104.

6. Simon Mizrahi and Martine Marignac, "Entretien avec Liliana Cavani, *Au-delà du bien et du mal*, French press kit, 1977 (Archival Collection). In Hayden White's words, Nietzsche's purpose as a philosopher was to transcend irony and to return consciousness to the enjoyment of its metaphorical powers or "its capacity to 'frolic in images,' to entertain the world as pure phenomena, and to liberate, thereby, man's poetic consciousness." *Metahistory*, p. 334. This requires the eradication of the killing illusions of the modern individual (the most dangerous being good and evil) and the liberation of consciousness from its capacity of illusion making.

7. Cavani, Arcalli, and Moscati, *Al di là del bene e del male*, p. 17.

8. Ibid., p. 23. In a letter from Leipzig in the autumn of 1882, Nietzsche defines Lou as the very embodiment of his notion of egoism: "You have within you this propensity for a sacred egoism that is also the tendency to submit oneself to what is the most elevated. But I do not understand how you could possibly confuse it with its opposite: the egoism and the desire to exploit, as with a cat that only wants to live." *La Vie de*

Frédéric Nietzsche d'après sa correspondance, ed. and trans. Georges Walz (Paris: Editions Rieder, 1932), pp. 359–360.

9. Cavani, who credits costume designer Piero Tosi for his fine eye in creating an ambience, recalls how he succeeded in dressing Lou as a character "for the future." Personal interview, 12 May 1990. For Tosi's artistic career, see Caterina D'Amico de Carvalho, *Piero Tosi: Costumi e scenografie* (Milan: Leonardo, 1997).

10. *Foucault*, trans. and ed. Seán Hand, foreword by Paul Bové (Minneapolis: University of Minnesota Press, 1988), p. 130.

11. "Liliana Cavani and Félix Guattari: Una conversazione," p. 176. For Cavani's approach to Lou, see especially her interviews with Hector Bianciotti, "Liliana Cavani: 'La Plus Belle Création de Lou Andréas Salomé, c'est sa vie,' " *Nouvel Observateur*, 10 October 1977, p. 76–77; A. M. Mori, "E Zarathustra è una femmina," *La repubblica*, 29 October 1977, p. 15.

12. "Liliana Cavani and Félix Guattari: Una conversazione," p. 174. Cavani inscribes the following Nietzschean dictum in the French press kit: "When man invented hell, in actuality he produced his paradise."

13. " 'Perché il mio cinema è sempre crudele,' " *Corriere della sera*, 4 November 1977, p. 3.

14. Mizrahi and Marignac, "Entretien avec Liliana Cavani." Cavani sees the relationship of the masculine and the feminine as a conflict embedded in culture and subjectivity (a position held by Salomé herself). For Lou's heterosexual life experiences, see Biddy Martin, *Woman and Modernity: The (Life)Styles of Lou Andreas-Salomé* (Ithaca, NY, and London: Cornell University Press, 1991), pp. 10–11. Cavani's Lou transcends the role of the mere passive muse of traditional iconography. She asserts her own independent thoughts. Nietzsche specifically complains about this matter in a letter to Paul Rée dated 1882: "The Lou that we met at Orta *was* a different being from the one I found later: a being without ideals, goals, duties. . . . She herself told me that she had no morality— and I thought that, like me, she had a *more severe* one! and that every day, every hour, she offered to her god some of her in sacrifice." *La Vie de Frédéric Nietzsche d'après sa correspondance*, p. 361. As Jacques Derrida points out, Nietzsche's writings portray woman either as concealed truth or as the affirmative (Dionysian) being, who survives castration. See *Spurs: Eperons* (Chicago: University of Chicago Press, 1979), p. 101.

15. From a letter dated 18 August 1882, cited in Lou Andreas-Salomé, *Mon Expérience de l'amitié avec Nietzsche et Rée* (Paris: Societé Française d'Etudes Nietzschéennes, 1954), p. 11.

16. From aphorism 125, in *The Portable Nietzsche*, selected and translated, with an introduction, prefaces, and notes by Walter Kaufmann (New York: Viking Press, 1954), p. 96.

17. See Costantini, "Ecce Omo," p. 3. Cavani explains: "Nietzsche was a true lyrical character, whose life was original and unique. If I had made a historical film of his life, it would have been an absurdity, since he was so much against historians and 'historicism.' " C. Clouzot, "Liliana Cavani, Nietzsche et l'éros," *Le Matin*, 6 October 1977, p. 26; reprinted as "Entretien avec Liliana Cavani," *Ecran*, 15 November 1977, pp. 55–56. For the characterization of Salomé, Cavani relies primarily on the biography by H. F. Peters, *My Sister, My Spouse*, and Lou's letters to Freud. Several reviewers lamented Cavani's lack of historical fidelity in her interpretation of Nietzsche. See, for example, Guglielmo Biraghi, "Al di là del bene e del male," *Il messaggero*, 29 October

1977, p. 12; Roberto Escobar, "Lo scrittore tedesco non c'entra con il film," *L'avanti*, 29 October 1977, p. 14; A. Savioli, "Un terzetto scombinato," *L'unità*, 29 October 1977, p. 11; Alberto Arbasino, "La Bile Nera, le maschere, il sesso, tre mezze calze e tanti orrori. . .," *La repubblica*, 30 November 1977, p. 14. In a letter to *Le Monde* (which dedicated an entire page to the film), the director responds to the attack against her by philosopher Jean-Marie Benoist ("Une Voyure du pauvre," 10 November 1977, pp. 20–21): "The art of the Renaissance is characterized by three common factors: the patrons were cardinals, popes, and princes; the theme and title were generally sacred; art was profane. The Italian art of the Renaissance expresses a freedom that for the bigots of the time must have appeared lascivious. So much flesh and nature for a religion that recognized mainly the soul and heaven! Prior to the Counter-Reformation, the Church was enlightened, 'reborn.' Through the artists of the trecento and quattrocento, the Church was recapturing its faith in the body and in life. People like Benoist also existed during that time. They are like erudite, fanatical monks who condemn and mock art, hoping to build bonfires for pagan pictures and books. Enlightened popes and princes held them at bay. . . . Nobody expects a Benoist to make a sound analysis of a film, a book, or a picture: they usually despise, insult, and destroy. I know all this, but often I am so naive as to believe that the Benoist times are over: this is an unforgivable naïveté" (Archival Collection).

18. *The Portable Nietzsche*, p. 184. Foucault has called Zarathustra the Nietzschean "sign of rupture." *Language, Counter-Memory, Practice*, p. 195.

19. The influence of Thomas Mann can be seen in the flashback of Nietzsche's contamination with syphilis in a brothel in Cologne, and his encounter with the beautiful Sicilian girl (his decision to spurn the warning is reminiscent of Adrian Leverkühn's own experience), and also in Nietzsche's representation during Lou's last visit to Naumburg (a "shrunken face, an *Ecce homo* countenance," "a mouth opened in pain and unseeing eyes"). See *Doctor Faustus*, trans. John E. Woods (New York: Knopf, 1997), pp. 165, 533. In both scenes, Nietzsche seems exhaustedly passive. For Paul, the act of watching the prostitute in Berlin, or the young boys at the Palatine, implies a gradual freeing of repressed sexuality; for Fritz, the encounter with the Sicilian prostitute (and later in Venice with the mysterious Dulcamara) causes him to confront the last masks: death and madness. Nietzsche's loss of virginity follows the legend of the transient philology student diverted to a brothel, where he becomes infected with syphilis. This scene evokes a sense of liberation for the visitor, as he walks up a dark stairway leading to the house of sensual pleasures. The brothel seems subterranean, with low ceilings and closed doors. It encompasses a bourgeois, decadent vision (Biedermeyer furniture, smoky shafts of light from windows, a dreamy opiated atmosphere), which is defied in the philosopher's transgression of the warning (from another visitor) and in his acceptance of the syphilitic southern girl: "I have never been able to think of that encounter without a religious shudder—for in that embrace, one party forfeited his salvation, the other found hers. The traveler from afar refused to reject her no matter what the risk—and to the wretched girl that must have come as a purifying, justifying, elevating blessing; and it appears that she offered him all the sweetness of her womanhood in repayment for what he was risking for her." Ibid., p. 165. For Bataille, "in prostitution, the prostitute is consecrated to transgression. The sacred and prohibited aspects of the sexual act do not disappear: her entire life is devoted to the violation of the interdict." *L'Erotisme*, p. 147. The Sicilian prostitute plays a major role as expression of a universal

human value: she frees Nietzsche from the cultural bounds of his family. In Visconti's *Morte a Venezia*, Tadzio plays "Für Elise" on the piano, the theme associated with the young syphilitic girl.

20. For the evolution of *passio* in the direction of spiritual dynamic and strong will, see Spengler, *The Decline of the West*, 1:320 n. 2.

21. See Tornabuoni, " 'Perché il mio cinema è sempre crudele,' " p. 3. In relation to the prominent male figures with whom she was associated, Lou has been construed either as a phallic mother or, more positively, as an inspirational muse. Cavani's Salomé is not grounded in patriarchy. For a traditional account of the relationship of the "holy trinity," see H. F. Peters, *My Sister, My Spouse: A Biography of Lou Andreas-Salomé* (New York: Norton, 1962), pp. 81–148; Angela Livingston, *Salomé: Her Life and Work* (Mt. Kisco, NY: Moyer Bell, 1984), pp. 32–58; and for Lou in the context of feminism, see Martin, *Woman and Modernity*, pp. 61–91.

22. Cf. Cavani: "For Nietzsche, 'all that is profound tries to mask itself.' If the revolution is truly a profound project—as we believe—then she loves to wear masks. Fritz, Lou, and Paul have attempted to transform themselves: I recount their experiences moving from one mask to the other until I reach another end . . . or perhaps until I reach their reality." From *Au-delà du bien et du mal*, French press kit, 1977. From the Greek *persona*, mask indicates the public role of a man, which in classical antiquity meant his essence.

23. This scene was initially censored along with the scenes at the Palatine and at the Berlin train station. Jung associates the arrow symbolism (which has a masculine connotation) with repressed desires, and pain with erotic libido. That is, the wounding and painful shafts of the arrows come not from outside but from our unconscious. See *Symbols of Transformation*, pp. 287–288. Cf. Nietzsche on the Dionysian as "temporary identification with the principle of life (including the voluptuousness of the martyr)." *The Will to Power*, ed. with commentary by Walter Kaufmann, new trans. by W. Kaufmann and R. J. Hollingdale (New York: Random House, 1967), bk. 2, no. 417 (1883–1888), p. 224. For the convergence of mystical and erotic idealizations, see Lou Salomé's essay on love, *Die Erotik*, published in 1910.

24. *The Portable Nietzsche*, p. 364. Cavani locates the essence of Paul's homosexuality in an affirmation of desire. In this scene, as well as the one at the Berlin station, he is in a theatrical rapport with his own nascent identity as other.

25. See Jung, *Symbols of Transformation*, p. 292.

26. "Laughter only assumes its fullest impact on being at the moment when, in the fall that it unleashes, a representation of death is cynically recognized. It is not only the composition of elements that constitutes the incandescence of being, but its decomposition in its mortal form. The difference in levels that provokes common laughter—which opposes the lack of an absurd life to the plenitude of successful being—can be replaced by that which opposes the summit of imperative elevation to the dark abyss that obliterates all existence. Laughter is thus assumed by the totality of being." *Visions of Excess*, p. 177.

27. *Subversive Pleasures*, p. 89.

28. Mizrahi and Marignac, "Entretien avec Liliana Cavani." Guattari has interpreted this scene as a reversal of Eurydice's myth: a journey to the underworld to look for Paul/Orpheus in death. See "Liliana Cavani e Félix Guattari: Una conversazione," p.

180. The Spiritualistic movement and the séance (which is generated by the magnetic temperament of the medium and visualized through physical and kinetic manifestations) form an important cultural topos of the second half of the nineteenth century. As in the case of Paul, apparitions demanded the direct involvement of the medium, since they could become visible only through the hypnotic state of the mediumistic body.

29. *Foucault*, p. 59. Visibilities function as points of conflict in relation to which social practices are transgressed. On this point, see particularly Foucault's reading of Velásquez's painting *Las Meninas* in *The Order of Things: An Archaeology of the Human Sciences* (New York: Vintage Books, 1970), pp. 3–16, a translation of *Les Mots et les choses* (Paris: Gallimard, 1966).

30. Cf. Cavani: "*Al di là del bene e del male* is a Nietzschean film in the sense that it translates the chiaroscuro of the contradiction that is typical of Nietzsche's thought. Nietzsche has the reputation of being an extremely 'serious' philosopher. However, he used to say that if he ever had a disciple, it was indispensable that he would learn to laugh." Mizrahi and Marignac, "Entretien avec Liliana Cavani."

31. See *Language, Counter-Memory, Practice*, p. 50.

32. On the genealogical configuration of fire as a source of light, see Bruno De Marchi, *Umbra dei e palpebra del cinema, luce* (Milan: Euresis Edizioni, 1996), pp. 95–113. Fires "are indexes of everlasting life. They are indexes of perpetuity, similar to, but less irenic than, permanent foliage of evergreen trees. Therefore, fire remains an excellent cue for cinema, *animated photography*" (p. 113). For the sexualization of fire, see G. Bachelard, *La Psychanalyse du feu* (Paris: Gallimard, 1949), pp. 75–97; and Durand, *Les Structures anthropologiques de l'imaginaire*, pp. 380–385, 390. Particularly Durand establishes a connection between the archetypal meaning of fire and its messianic significance in creating the symbol of the Cross. One is reminded of the image of Francis of Assisi holding a torch in front of the crucifix of San Damiano.

33. *Streetwalking on a Ruined Map*, p. 59. Bruno reads *curiositas* in the Augustinian mode of "the lust of the eyes," which I am applying here.

34. Cavani, Arcalli, and Moscati, *Al di là del bene e del male*, pp. 19–20.

35. See Omar Calabrese, *Neo-Baroque: A Sign of the Times*, trans. Charles Lambert, with foreword by U. Eco (Princeton, NJ: Princeton University Press, 1992), p. 59; originally published as *L'età neobarocca* (Rome and Bari: Laterza, 1987).

36. Tornabuoni, " 'Perché il mio cinema è sempre crudele,' " p. 3.

37. From Cavani's stage directions in Cavani, Arcalli, and Moscati, *Al di là del bene e del male*, p. 20.

38. "Liliana Cavani e Félix Guattari: Una conversazione," p. 175.

39. Tornabuoni, " 'Perché il mio cinema è sempre crudele,' " p. 3.

40. Mizrahi and Marignac, "Entretien avec Liliana Cavani." Cavani sees Lou's "androgynous mentality" as the will to take charge of her life instead of being a follower. See D. H., "Cavani chez Nietzsche," *L'Express magazine*, 3 August 1977, p. 59. In discussing the figure of the androgyne (which had been idealized by the Romantics), George L. Mosse stresses the fact that, by the end of the nineteenth century, it "was perceived as a monster of sexual and moral ambiguity, often identified with other 'outsiders' such as masochists, sadists, homosexuals, and lesbians." *Nationalism and Sex-*

uality: Respectability and Abnormal Sexuality in Modern Europe (New York: Fertig, 1985), p. 104.

41. "The world of (Dionysian) eroticism is on the opposite pole of the servile world of utilitarianism and production; it has in itself an aim, a meaning, and a justification. If this is the world of the Feminine, the episteme of the Feminine is anarchy." Introduction to Colonna, *Lilith la luna nera e l'eros rifiutato*, p. 17. At the time of the release of *Al di là del bene e del male*, Cavani announced that her next film would be based on Wedekind's play *Lulu*, with Romy Schneider in the role of the femme fatale who meets her fate at the hands of Jack the Ripper. The screenplay was written in collaboration with Enrico Medioli and Franco Arcalli. The filming was scheduled to begin in London during the winter of 1977–1978. The project did not materialize owing to contractual complications with Schneider. In an interview with Mary Blume, Cavani emphasizes that *Lulu* was "an analysis of femininity, not women but femininity, and the people who are its enemies." "Liliana Cavani's Aim: 'I Sow Disquiet,' " *International Herald Tribune*, 22–23 October 1977, p. 12. Among Cavani's unfilmed scripts that involve prominent female roles are *Il giorno del successo* (the story of an orchestra conductor and her beginnings in the classical music world) and one on Simone Weil (1909–1943). This last script was published as L. Cavani and I. Moscati, *Lettere dall'interno: Racconto per un film su Simone Weil* (Turin: Einaudi, 1974). For the title role, Cavani approached Helena Bonham Carter during the shooting of *Francesco*, and she accepted. RAI, however, never committed to the project. See the transcript of the Incontro a Carpi (1990) organized by Luca Goldoni, pp. 66–67 (Archival Collection). Selected papers from this retrospective were published in Tallarigo and Gasparini, *Lo sguardo libero*.

42. From the stage directions in Cavani, Arcalli, and Moscati, *Al di là del bene e del male*, p. 48.

43. Elizabeth's biography of her brother (*Das Leben Friedrich Nietzsche*, 1897–1904) played a major role in shaping the views of the Nietzsche-Salomé friendship. As a Russian Jew, Lou represented political subversion and danger.

44. Clouzot, "Liliana Cavani, Nietzsche et l'éros," p. 26. Also: "The good sentiments of the bourgeois society of the nineteenth century are betrayed so Evil becomes Good, in the sense that it crumbles the walls of hypocrisy. By being killed by Evil, Good renews its vitality. 'They have separated us,' says Ducamara (Evil). This is fundamentally a Nietzschean concept. The Devil, Evil, and Dionysos were a part of Christ. Later, priests and intellectuals separated them. In several instances during my film, Good is killed by its opponent. These scenes are Nietzschean in the sense that one cannot be a Christian unless one participates in the assassination of God, as God himself desired. The true covenant is in death." Mizrahi and Marignac, "Entretian avec Liliana Cavani." Alberto Moravia sees "a Luciferian type of sinner" in Cavani's Nietzsche and suggests that the ballet scene is reminiscent of the Devil's apparition to Ivan Karamazov. "Diavolo di un Nietzsche," *L'espresso*, 13 November 1977, p. 150. Cf. also Gabriel Matzneff, "Au-delà du bien et du mal," *Le Monde*, 15 October 1977, p. 2. As I have already noted, the ballet was censored (and completetly eliminated) for the American audience. For the (negative) reception of the film in the United States, see John Coleman, "Saddle Soap," *New Statesman*, 26 October 1979, p. 653; Janet Maslin, "The Screen: 'Beyond Good and Evil,' " *New York Times*, 18 May 1984, C14; Marcia Pally, "The Perils of Libideology," *Village Voice*, 29 May 1984, p. 60.

45. From the stage directions in Cavani, Arcalli, and Moscati, *Al di là del bene e del male*, pp. 101–102.

46. "Il superuomo, la superdonna e il terzo incomodo," *Corriere della sera*, 29 October 1977, p. 16.

47. From aphorism 215, *Beyond Good and Evil*, in F. W. Nietzsche, *The Philosophy of Nietzsche* (New York: The Modern Library, [1947]), p. 520.

Chapter 6
Theatricality and Reflexivity in *The Berlin Affair*

1. From Cavani's production notes in *The Berlin Affair*, Cannon press kit, 1985 (Archival Collection). Cavani also declared that she was drawn to Tanizaki (1886–1965) because of his dramatic "intensity and extreme economy, his capacity to bring us, as nearly breathless spectators, inside the meaning of seemingly insignificant details." Ibid. *Manji* was published as a serial novel in a literary magazine between 1928 and 1930. Sonoko, the first-person narrator, recounts her own story to a prominent writer as a long monologue that constitutes the novel itself. It is the story of a passionate love affair with Mitsuko that eventually involves her husband and Watanuki, an impotent, effeminate dandy. For his psychological insight, Tanizaki has been compared to the eighteenth-century libertine novelists and to D. H. Lawrence. Mitsuko is actually the name of Tanizaki's third wife. She inspired several of his novels, including *Kagi* (The Key, 1956), on which Tinto Brass based his film with Stefania Sandrelli (*La chiave*, 1983). Also there is an earlier version by Yukio Mishima, *Kagi* (Odd Obsession, 1959). For a further discussion of Cavani's adaptation, see her interview with Antonella Barone, "Cavani interior," *Prima visione cinematografica*, December 1985, pp. 36–37; and my "Narratività e storia in *Interno berlinese* di Liliana Cavani," in *Romance Languages Annual 1989*, ed. Ben Lawton and Anthony Julian Tamburri (West Lafayette, IN: Purdue Research Foundation, 1990), 1:52–55.

2. The Japanese story within a German setting was widely criticized, especially at the Berlin Film Festival in February of 1986. For example, Giovanni Grazzini views the filmmaker's choice of the historical context as "inessential" ("A porte chiuse in un inferno," *Corriere della sera*, 15 November 1985, p. 23), while Angelo Solmi endorses Cavani's opposition between "the Nazi rigid conformism and the 'scandalous' eroticism of the affair" ("A qualcuna piace femmina," *Oggi*, 4 December 1985, p. 118). See also G. L. Rondi, "Interno berlinese," *Il tempo*, 31 October 1985, p. 12; S. Borelli, "Sesso e alta diplomazia," *L'unità*, 31 October 1985, p. 13; T. Kezich, "Passioni e Germania nazista," *La repubblica*, 2 November 1985, p. 28, and "Più avvincente che convincente," *Panorama*, 24 November 1985, p. 13; Ernesto G. Laura, "Una storia giapponese in versione occidentale," *Il popolo*, 13 November 1985, p. 11; M. Morandini, "Cavani: Una erotica elegante Germania," *Il giorno*, 15 November 1985, p. 16; Giusto Orsera, "Poco corpo niente anima," *Il borghese*, 24 November 1985, pp. 754–755; Iannis Katsahanias, "La Croix et la bannière," *Cahiers du Cinéma* 383–384 (May 1986): 87. On this subject, Cavani replied with an article ("E' cinema europeo") published in *La repubblica*, 5 November 1985, p. 6.

3. Barone, "Cavani interior," p. 38.

4. From "Liliana Cavani gira 'Interno berlinese,'" Ansa press release dated 8 May 1985 (Archival Collection). *Interno berlinese* was the first film produced by Menahem

Golan and Yoram Globus in Italy for Cannon (which had just bought out Gaumont). It was shot in Rome (De Paolis Studios) and Vienna from April to July 1985 for a budget of approximately four million dollars. It premiered in Milan on 23 October 1985. Gudrun Landgrebe, one of the discoveries of the new German cinema, had appeared in Robert van Ackeren's *Die Flambierte Frau* (The Woman in Flames, 1982–1983), Edgar Reitz's *Heimat* (1984), and István Szabó's *Colonel Redl* (1985). Casting the role of Mitsuko proved to be more challenging. Cavani went to Tokyo looking for a model of beauty that could balance seductiveness with an iron will. She found it in the twenty-four-year-old actress and pop singer Mio Takaki. For Cavani's approach to the film, see particularly A. M. Mori, "Passione a quattro con idolo in kimono," *La repubblica*, 18 April 1985, p. 17; Mariangiola Castrovilli, "Cavani, ancora uno scandalo," *Il giornale*, 30 June 1985, p. 17; S. Robiony, "Liliana Cavani: 'Berlin Interior non è un film, è la mia libertà,'" *La stampa*, 30 June 1985, p. 18; G. Gs., "Per Liliana Cavani una passione in svastica e kimono," *Corriere della sera*, 30 June 1985, p. 21; F. Fer., "Mistica seduzione," *Il messaggero*, 30 June 1985, p. 12; L. Saitta, "Tra Vienna e Berlino per raccontare tre vite private che diventano 'caso,'" *Il tempo*, 1 July 1985, p. 8; Rino Alessi, "Tanizaki nel Terzo Reich," *La repubblica*, 2 July 1985, p. 20; Renata Pisu, "Vi svelo i segreti del mio amico Tanizaki," *Tuttolibri*, 3 August 1985, p. 3.

5. From the Greek *eidolon* (simulacrum), "idol" denotes the image of deity. Its archaic meaning includes "shadow" and "phantasm." Cf. Cavani: "There exist passions for ideas as well as for people, which after all is the same thing, because we endow the person we love with our own ideas and fantasies. Francesco's passion for Christ was an idea he personified, and that kind of passion triggers great energy which liberates our fantasy." Barone, "Cavani interior," p. 38.

6. As Louise recounts in the opening sequence: "I was leading a hygienic life, in line with the directives of the party. I followed the ideal program that women's magazines called the art and culture for the German woman." Taken from the film's dialogue.

7. The swastika is among the most ancient of symbols. It is found in Asia, India, Central America, and northern Europe. "Its graphic design indicates a rotation around a center and symbolizes action, a regenerative cycle. It is often associated with the (true or false) saviors of humanity: Christ, Buddha, Charlemagne, Hitler. . . . Rotation represents the cosmic and the transcendental. However, when rotation follows the direction of a clock (the swastika of Charlemagne), it represents the temporal and the profane (it is the 'evil' of the Hitlerian swastika). This equally armed cruciform figure symbolizes the square root of four, or the number sixteen: it indicates absolute dynamism, total power, and the realization of material power. Jakob Böehme saw in it an exaltation of pride, an unruly will to power, and, finally, the symbol of the abyss, the opposite of nirvana. In the positive sense, the swastika indicates the cyclical return of human endeavors toward spiritual redemption." From "Le Symbolism du svastika," L. Cavani, *The Berlin Affair*, Cannon French press kit, 1986 (Archival Collection). As Carl Jung suggests, a counterclockwise movement of the cross indicates movement toward the unconscious, while a clockwise movement goes toward consciousness (spinning out of the unconscious chaos). The one is sinister, the other rightful. See *The Archetypes and the Collective Unconscious*, trans. R.F.C. Hull, 2d ed., Bollingen Series XX (Princeton, NJ: Princeton University Press, 1969), p. 320.

8. R. Pisu, "Una passione privata e scandalosa nel Giappone tedesco della Cavani," *La stampa*, 22 February 1985, p. 23.

9. Mori, "Passione a quattro con idolo in kimono," p. 17. Cavani's remarks echo a Schopenhauerian vision of history. For, according to the German philosopher, men have the capacity to withdraw from action (the fortunate ones). Those who choose to act are defeated. However, they can experience the pleasure of contemplating pure form.

10. For the etymological derivation of "represent" from *repraesentatio* ("to show," "to bring back"), see Devoto, *Avviamento alla etimologia italiana*, p. 348.

11. See A. L., "Un interno berlinese per fare karakiri," *L'avanti*, 6 November 1985, p. 6.

12. *Metahistory*, p. 238.

13. The film contains two musical tracks: one (Wagnerian) represents the Western characters; the other belongs to the "religious" presence of Mitsuko. Sound can also function as a realistic detail. In the title sequence, the tapping of the professor's typewriter and the sound of the doorbell strictly govern the rhythm-bound tension that announces Louise's arrival.

14. *Foucault*, p. 107.

15. On this point, see Bruce F. Kawin, *Mindscreen: Bergman, Godard and First-Person Film* (Princeton, NJ: Princeton University Press, 1978), pp. 7–8. Kawin refers to what a character sees in contrast with what he thinks, or the eye of the mind. Thus the meaning of "idea" (from the Greek *idein* "to see"), which etymologically connotes "form," "appearance," is not strictly the Platonic eternal models, apprehensible only to the eye of the mind.

16. Cf. Susan Sontag on the Nazi aesthetic of the 1930s: "The fascist style at its best is Art Deco, with its sharp lines and blunt massing of material, its petrified eroticism." "Fascinating Fascism," in *Under the Sign of Saturn*, p. 94. Cavani chose to shoot in Vienna (instead of Berlin) owing to its prewar atmosphere and architecture. For the sophisticated interior sets, she hired art director Luciano Ricceri, who had worked with Visconti and on several of Ettore Scola's films, including *Una giornata particolare* (A Special Day, 1977), set in 1938 Fascist Rome.

17. See "Inferno berlinese," *L'espresso*, 1 December 1985, p. 198.

18. Nostalgia comes from the Greek *nóstos* ("return") and *-alg\a* ("suffering" for the desire to return). In Tanizaki, this word opens and closes the novel. It represents Sonoko's hysterical longing for an unworthy man; this is the reason why she begins to attend the art lessons. At the end, it is applied to Mitsuko: "After all," says the narrator, "it is useless to hate those who are already dead; even now, whenever I think of Mitsuko, rather than feel resentment or anger, I feel a deep sense of nostalgia. . . ." *La croce buddista*, trans. Lydia Origlia, 3d ed. (1982; Parma: Guanda, 1987), p. 149. These same words close *Interno berlinese*.

19. *Luchino Visconti: Un profilo critico* (Venice: Marsilio, 1996), p. 65.

20. Saul Friedländer has offered a similar characterization of the motif of death for the Nazis. See *Reflections of Nazism*, p. 42. Cf. Sonoko: "In the end we had become like empty shells: she wanted us not to have any other desire or interest in the world but to live exclusively of the light from a sun called Mitsuko." Tanizaki, *La croce buddista*, p. 144.

21. For gender roles in *Interno berlinese*, see Chantal Nadeau, "Girls on a Wired Screen: Cavani's Cinema and Lesbian S/M," in *Sexy Bodies: The Strange Carnalities of*

Feminism, ed. Elizabeth Grozs and Elspeth Probyn (London and New York: Routledge, 1995), pp. 211–230.

22. See Stam, *Subversive Pleasures*, p. 175. On the issue of transgressive *écriture*, I find Robert Stam's discussion of eroticism in Buñuel and Bataille extremely useful and illuminating.

23. In accordance with alchemical ritual, drinking engenders emotion and conflict, but it can also alter movement into inertia, stupor, and dissolution. Heinz and Louise's lethargy is due to Mitsuko's large doses of narcotics, which she forces upon them. Eric Neumann locates the primordial mysteries of the Feminine at the beginning of human culture. The preparation of food and drink, the fashioning of garments, the house, all express a spiritual character transcending the merely real. Poisons are numinous substances that have been acquired in mysterious wise. Those who convey and administer them (almost always women) are sacral figures, or priestesses. In the mysteries of stupor, consciousness is regressively dissolved, poisoned by negative orgiastic sexuality. Intoxicants and poisons belong to the sphere of seduction by the young witch. See *The Great Mother*, pp. 59–60, 74.

24. Personal interview, 13 June 1989. At the same time, suicide can be viewed as the physical toll paid for trespassing, an act that entails a resistance to the oppression of the exterior.

25. "Essentially, the domain of eroticism is the domain of violence, the domain of violation." *L'Erotisme*, p. 23. Cavani's images suggest this desire for an extreme state: female desire becomes the desire to live intensely to the boundaries of the possible.

26. From Cavani's production notes in *The Berlin Affair* (1985).

27. *To the Distant Observer: Form and Meaning in the Japanese Cinema*, rev. and ed. Annette Michelson (Berkeley and Los Angeles: University of California Press, 1979), p. 173. Burch defines Japanese arts, particularly the Kabuki and the doll theater, as essentially presentational versus the representational approach adopted by any Western theatrical practice (see pp. 69–72). Ozu typically sets up his camera so as to create unleveled eyeline matches. *Interno berlinese* achieves a kind of transcendental stasis. Some critics have called it "la sacralizzazione delle forme" (the sacredness of forms) in Cavani's cult of the ambiguous. See Grazzini, "A porte chiuse in un inferno," p. 23.

28. "In the aesthetic mode of contemplation we have found *two inseparable constituent parts*—the knowledge of the object, not as individual thing but as Platonic Idea, that is, as the enduring form of this whole species of things; and the self-consciousness of the knowing person, not as individual, but as *pure will-less subject of knowledge*." *The World as Will and Idea* (London: Routledge & Kegan Paul, 1957), 1:253. For Schopenhauer, in art, the individuation process is refracted onto the contemplation of the pure idea (he rejects the Kantian distinction between beautiful and sublime).

29. For Cavani, "the political category that is most important is beauty. Beauty is the fundamental value of one's existence." Interview, 13 June 1989.

30. See C. G. Jung, *The Structure and Dynamics of the Psyche*, trans. R.F.C. Hull, 2d ed., Bollingen Series XX (Princeton, NJ: Princeton University Press, 1981), p. 211. Cavani's discourse, inspired by a metaphysics of beauty, is bound to a fetishism of the signified, to a seduction with objects as sexuality and power, objects that are mere simulacra.

31. "Inferno berlinese," p. 198.

32. Interview, 12 May 1990. On this point, see also Robiony, "Liliana Cavani: 'Berlin Interior non è un film, è la mia libertà,' " p. 18.

33. From Cavani's production notes in *The Berlin Affair* (1985). Some American reviewers totally misrepresented this aspect of the film by calling it fetishistic and exploitive. See Laurie Stone, "Faking it," *Village Voice*, 27 January 1987, p. 62; Caryn James, "Wartime Obsessions," *New York Times*, 15 July 1988, C12.

34. *From Caligari to Hitler*, p. 280. Kracauer's observations refer to the Nazi propaganda war film.

35. For the costuming of Mitsuko, Cavani relied on a noted Japanese artist, Jusaburo Tsujimura. For the elaborate psychological use of the kimono in the film, see Paolo Cervone, "Liliana Cavani: 'Eros in kimono,' " *Corriere della sera*, 17 April 1985, p. 23; Fabrizio Corallo, "Il piacere è tutto mio," *Panorama*, 6 October 1985, p. 8.

36. "Quando la luce diventa racconto," *Videoregistratore* (Milan), November 1985, p. 70. Cavani credits her cinematographer for the successful look of the film: "He was able to create in a very special way the idea, the anguish, and the inner spaces that are the key to the film." Giacomo Puma, "Il cinema dietro le quinte: Interno berlinese," Ibid., p. 69. Spinotti was primarily known for his association with Fabio Carpi's *Quartetto Basileus* (Basileus Quartet, 1982). In 1998, he was nominated for an Oscar for *LA Confidential* by Curtis Hanson. Ernesto Novelli at Technicolor Labs in Rome developed the E.N.R. process in order to achieve purer blacks on print film (without altering the purity of the other colors). This technique was first used for Vittorio Storaro, who photographed *Reds* for Warren Beatty.

37. Hata Kohei, a scholar and a personal friend of Tanizaki, explains the aesthetic resonance of darkness in Japanese culture: "The Japanese day begins at sunset and ends at sunset; this means that the most essential things happen in darkness, in the uncertain nocturnal light. Our calendar proceeds from night to day, but in order to see in the dark, you need the contrast with white. . . . The Janapese admire light, the whiteness of the skin; however, they never forget the role of shadow, that darkness which you call morbosity." Pisu, "Vi svelo i segreti del mio amico Tanizaki," p. 3.

38. Interview, 10 May 1990.

39. See *Streetwalking on a Ruined Map*, p. 6. Bruno refers to Jessica Benjamin's notion of intersubjectivity as theorized in "A Desire of One's Own: Psychoanalytic Feminism and Intersubjective Space," in *Feminist Studies/Critical Studies*, ed. T. De Lauretis (Bloomington: Indiana University Press, 1986).

Chapter 7
The Architectonics of Form: *Francesco* and *Milarepa*

1. Giovanna Grassi, "E venne un uomo chiamato Francesco," *Settegiorni illustrati dal Corriere della sera*, 9 April 1988, p. 60. On the controversial casting of Rourke, see, among others, Irene Bignardi, "Uno, nessuno centomila Mickey Rourke," *Venerdì di repubblica*, 22 January 1988, pp. 101–103; S. Robiony, "Cavani: 'Solo con Rourke posso rifare la storia di Francesco,' " *La stampa*, 13 February 1988, p. 16; L. Saitta, " 'Il mio Francesco avrà il volto di Mickey Rourke,' " *Il tempo*, 14 February 1988, p. 18. On her choice of actors, Cavani confesses: "In a film, the selection of the protagonist is fundamental. I need actors who are very creative, who transfer their energy onto the character. If their persona does not correspond with my interpretation of the film, then

everything falls apart." Personal interview, 12 May 1990. As Silverman has pointed out, Cavani's authorial subjectivity relies heavily on her imaginary rapport with her male characters; thus the actor provides a vehicle leading to imaginary mastery. See *The Acoustic Mirror*, p. 215. On this issue, cf. Tiso, *Liliana Cavani*, pp. 66–67. See also Cavani's article "Note sull'attore cinematografico," *Studium* 57 (July–August 1961): 549–554, which is a revised version of an essay she wrote at the Centro Sperimentale di Cinematografia during the academic year 1960–1961.

2. Renato Gaita, "Tredici settimane e mezzo, ma stavolta come un santo," *Il messaggero*, 13 February 1988, p. 25. The film Cavani refers to is *Il giorno del successo*, which originally had an orchestra conductor as the main character (see chap. 5, n. 41).

Francesco was produced by Scanni with the collaboration of Raiuno and Royal Film of Monaco. It was shot on location in Umbria and Abruzzo, beginning in February of 1988, for fourteen weeks. It premiered in Rome on 21 March 1989. For production details, see Cavani's interviews with Grassi, "E venne un uomo chiamato Francesco," pp. 60–70; Paolo Cervone, "S. Francesco ha il volto di Rourke," *Corriere della sera*, 13 February 1988, p. 27; Vittorio Spiga, "Mickey, un santo per la Cavani," *La nazione*, 14 February 1988, p. 11; Italo Carmignani, "Francesco non torna ad Assisi," *La stampa*, 18 February 1988, p. 10; Simone Fortuna, "Ma Francesco gira lontano da Assisi," *La nazione*, 19 February 1988, p. 9; A. M. Mori, "Cavani: Francesco un uomo completo," *La repubblica*, 18 November 1988, p. 29. *Francesco* represented Italy at the Cannes Film Festival, along with *Splendor* by Ettore Scola and *Nuovo cinema paradiso* by Giuseppe Tornatore. At Cannes, the film's screening was applauded by the audience and was highly praised. The French press had mixed reviews. On the other hand, the British press capitalized on Rourke's connections with the IRA and caused a controversy that unfairly hurt the outcome for the film. Mickey Rourke—who was supposed to have had a press conference in order to clear up this issue—was advised not to answer any further questions.

3. Grassi, "E venne un uomo chiamato Francesco," p. 70. See also Gloria Satta, "Un altissimo contatto," *Il messaggero*, 4 October 1988, p. 14.

4. Francesco recites these words for Chiara's initiation ceremony. For a plot outline of the Franciscan itinerary, see chapter 1. On the characterization of Chiara of Assisi, Cavani says: "Chiara was not a passive object but a subject who collaborated with the spiritual project of Francesco. If at that time there existed such a thing as a copyright for the project, both of them would have had to sign it. When Francesco was in doubt, especially during crucial moments, he asked Chiara for her opinion." From Cavani's lecture "Donna e libertà di espressione" at the Convegno-Centenario Josefa Segovia, "La donna nelle grandi trasformazioni del nostro tempo," Rome, 15–16 May 1992, Centre d'Etudes Saint-Louis de France (Archival Collection). The text was revised and published in *Donna e modernità*, ed. Elena Cavalcanti (Rome: Edizioni Dehoniane, 1993), pp. 121–134. For Cavani's approach to the character of Chiara of Assisi, see my article "Ideologia, creatività e iconografia nella Chiara di Liliana Cavani," in *Italian Women Mystics*, ed. Dino Cervigni, *Annali d'italianistica* 13 (1995): 387–400.

5. Interview, 27 June 1989. Cf. Cavani: "I may be anticlerical; in fact I am. But I am not antireligious. Any form of knowledge interests me." Cavani, *Milarepa*, p. 42.

6. See "Gabriella Cristiani: La magia del montaggio," in AA. VV., *Gabriella Cristiani: Omaggio a Kim Arcalli* (Bari: Assessorato alla Cultura, 1988), pp. 24–25. Cristiani acknowledges the influence of comic strips. At Arcalli's death in 1978, Cristiani completed

the editing of *Luna* for Bernardo Bertolucci. In 1988, she won an Oscar for *The Last Emperor*. For a cultural history of Italian editors, see S. Masi, *Nel buio della moviola: Introduzione alla storia del montaggio* (L'Aquila: La Lanterna Magica, 1985); Marco Giusti and Enrico Ghezzi, eds., *Kim Arcalli, montare il cinema* (Venice: Marsilio, 1980).

7. See Gennep, *The Rites of Passage*, p. 20.

8. "In making the film, I was thinking of the difference between charisma and structure, that is, between those people who have this charisma, or *charis* (grace), and the ones who want to possess it but do not have it. It is a little like the rapport between Mozart and Salieri; between the head of the structure and Francesco with his *charis*." "Il Vangelo alla lettera: Una conversazione tra Liliana Cavani e Pierre Riches," in L. Cavani and Roberta Mazzoni, *Francesco* (Milan: Leonardo, 1989), p. 126. In the early Catholic Church, we witness the institutional desacralization of charisma, the replacement of grace with structure. Francesco's charisma is his ability to transcend the conformity of a hierarchical culture. His concrete approach to experiencing his new life is due, in part, to his practical education in the house of a wealthy merchant.

9. In the published script, the word "vision" is substituted for "image." Ibid., p. 8.

10. "Un grande 'Francesco,' " *Il tempo*, 22 March 1989, p. 15; reprinted as " 'Francesco' di Liliana Cavani," *Rivista del cinematografo* 59 (May 1989): 12. For the critical response to the film, see S. Borelli, "Francesco-Rourke: il sangue e l'estasi," *L'unità*, 23 March 1989, p. 25; Massimo Monteleone, "Francesco uomo vero e Santo," *Il popolo*, 23 March 1989, p. 9; F. Bolzoni, "Quel Francesco per amico," *L'avvenire*, 23 March 1989, p. 15; T. Kezich, "Rourke, 9 settimane e mezzo da santo," *Corriere della sera*, 23 March 1989, p. 21; S. Frosali, "Mickey a tu per tu con Dio," *La nazione*, 24 March 1989, p. 10; M. Morandini, "Santo Francesco senza uccellini," *Il giorno*, 24 March 1989, p. 24; L. Tornabuoni, "Povero e nudo," *Panorama*, 9 April 1989, p. 16; Virgilio Fantuzzi, " 'Francesco' di Liliana Cavani," *Civiltà cattolica*, 17 June 1989, pp. 568–581.

11. Originally Cavani was going to open the film with a series of close-ups juxtaposing Francesco's feet, eyes, and hands in the present and in the past. See script description for the opening scene, *Francesco*, p. 7.

12. "Santo con stile," *L'espresso*, 30 April 1989, p. 144.

13. Film critic Alberto Farassino expresses some reservations on Cavani's use of corporeality, particularly her scenes of nudity. He supports his argument by singling out this specific episode. See "Francesco va per il mondo," *La repubblica*, 24 March 1989, p. 25. On this issue, there was an insert signed by Brutus ("Ci dispiace") following Gian Luigi Rondi's review of the film in *Rivista del cinematografo*. It reads: "We regret that a film of such value as *Francesco* is contaminated by an abundance of male nudity and by one perverse scene of eroticism. Are these included for commercialism? Is it an obsession, or even an increasing rudeness? Surely, they are stylistic choices out of place that add nothing to the film. They just load it with ambiguity; they purposely upset the linear narrative rhythm; they distract the attention of the spectator where he really needed concentration. We regret it, because the film is valuable, engaging, and important. It did not deserve to slip on a banana peel."

14. From "*Francesco*: Le tappe salienti e i luoghi delle riprese," Istituto Luce press kit, 1989 (Archival Collection).

15. Interview, 12 May 1990. *Blade Runner* is a hybrid science fiction film set in Los Angeles in the year 2019. Cinematographer Jordan Cronenwerth created a haunting look for a dreadful city destroyed by its own technology.

16. Frye, *Anatomy of Criticism*, p. 48.

17. Cf. Cavani: "The first film represented an initial encounter with Francesco, a beautiful impression, however, incomplete; the second film intensified the search for a contact with God, which the first time around was not as developed. Nothing says that I could not make another one. This encounter may continue, because I think that anybody can undertake a 'revolutionary' itinerary: the only viable revolution is the one that involves ourselves." Massimo Giraldi, "La 'folle libertà' di Francesco d'Assisi," *Popoli e missione* 5, no. 12 (December 1991): 44. In *Francesco*'s press kit, Cavani writes: "In trying to understand this man, I experience the expansion of consciousness" (Archival Collection).

18. Incorruptibility, permanence, and divinity are the attributes of the stone. For its symbolism and also for its lapis-Christ parallelism, see Jung, *Alchemical Studies*, p. 95; Eliade, *Images and Symbols*, pp. 41–56.

19. Cervone, "S. Francesco ha il volto di Rourke," p. 27. Cavani explains that Donati carefully selected materials which existed during that time and applied them to the sets. He also researched medieval color dyes for the costumes. For Francesco and his friars, he chose a coarse smock (used for prayer and work), instead of the Franciscan habit. Interview, 12 May 1990. The director's approach was to avoid the classical costume film. See Titta Fiore, "Un santo del futuro," *Il mattino*, 18 March 1989, p. 14. For his costumes, Donati was awarded the Davide di Donatello in 1989. Donati is best known for his collaboration with Visconti (especially his theatrical productions), Fellini, and Pasolini. He won two Oscars: for *Romeo and Juliet* (1968) by Franco Zeffirelli and for Fellini's *Casanova* (1976).

20. "Il Vangelo alla lettera," in *Francesco*, pp. 133–134. In reviewing the film, Giovanni Grazzini emphasizes a similar point: "Dressed in rags, Francesco drags himself along stone walls, woods, and fields, from the Middle Ages to the present, and from the present he projects himself, eternal utopia, toward tomorrow. He is the protagonist captured in a new technological rendition of the Bardi altarpiece that in the duecento illustrated the life of the saint." "L'uomo nuovo del Duecento," *Il messaggero*, 23 March 1989, p. 18.

21. See Mori, "Passione a quattro con idolo in kimono," p. 17.

22. Interview, 12 May 1990. Several critics recognized a direct analogy between Francesco/Rourke and the character of Milarepa. See, for example, M. Argentieri, "L'amaro poverello," *Rinascita*, 8 April 1989, p. 20.

23. "Per seminare inquietitudine," in Cavani, *Milarepa*, p. 42. The idea of the film was presented by Cavani to Ludovico Alessandrini, who had it produced by RAI. In the spring of 1970, at the Spoleto Festival, while screening *I cannibali*, the director announced the production of her new film. She had just returned from location scouting in Nepal, where initially *Milarepa* was to be shot. However, owing to production restrictions as well as some aesthetic considerations, it was filmed during the autumn of 1972 in Abruzzo, with the working title of "L'avventura di Milarepa" (The Adventure of Milarepa). It premiered on 28 December 1973 in Pistoia and was released in January 1974. The film was aired on television that June. *Milarepa* was selected for the Cannes Film Festival in the special category on cultural studies. Owing to its artistic merit, it was entered into competition and became eligible for the Palm d'or—which went to Francis F. Coppola's *The Conversation*. That year at Cannes, Italy was represented by Fellini's *Amarcord* (out of competition), by Pasolini's *Il fiore delle mille e una notte* (The Arabian

Nights), which won the jury's special prize, and by *Delitto d'amore* by Luigi Comencini. For production details, see "L'avventura di Milarepa: Nuovo film TV di Liliana Cavani," *L'avanti*, 22 August 1973, p. 5; Valerio Riva, "Lui, Milarepa," *L'espresso*, 29 October 1973, pp. 16–17.

At the time Cavani was producing *Milarepa*, she also announced the making of a new film adapted from a Polish novel, *Addio all'autunno* (Farewell to Autumn, 1926), by Stanislaw I. Witkiewicz. Set in a corrupt society, the story recounts the adventures of Attanasius Bazakbal, an individual molded on Musil's characters. "Young Attanasius is essentially a superfluous man who escapes from contemporary reality through eroticism, an exotic taste, and drugs. He is defeated by reality when he chooses to confront it. Totally controlled by his passion for the 'demonic' Hela Bertz, and after undergoing many misadventures, in the end Attanasius manifests his true nature: he is the product of a society destined for extinction; he is unable to understand the society of the future." From "Sullo schermo 'Addio all'autunno' con la regia di Liliana Cavani," Ansa press release, April 1970 (Archival Collection). The film script was cowritten with Italo Moscati and was scheduled to begin production in January of 1971. *Addio all'autunno* was never realized owing to budgetary concerns.

24. "La pazzesca razionalità della geometria religiosa," *Cinema nuovo* 23, no. 229 (May–June 1974): 184–185. Also Gian Piero Brunetta singles out the film's "figurative abstraction" and "stylistic ascetism," in *Storia del cinema italiano dal 1945 agli anni ottanta*, p. 706.

25. Loretta Guerrini, "Un cinema alla ricerca dell'ingaggio migliore," in AA. VV., *Il signore ti dia pace*, Celebrazioni centenarie dell'ordine francescano secolare, Dalla regola di Niccolò IV ad oggi 1289–1989 (Bologna: Edizioni Francescane, [1991]), p. 169.

26. "Il 'viaggio' del protagonista," in Cavani, *Milarepa*, p. 54. The Hungarian actor Lajos Balàzsovitz was particularly known for his work with Miklós Jancsó and Marta Mészáros. His name was recommended by Luchino Visconti, who was planning to have him in *Proust*, a project he never realized. On the actors who had worked with her up to that point (Castel, Clementi, Peter Gonzales, Balàzsovitz), Cavani states: "They are not only good actors, they are truly for me the corporeal image of my four films: *Francesco, The Cannibals, The Guest, Milarepa*. Four poets, four madmen, four disturbing and sweet faces in which I identified myself and in which I see my time identified. They have not acted 'the part of. . . .' They are physically those four 'characters' (and they knew it instantly). Thus the term 'characters' has to be redefined because the soul of the film is in them." Ibid.

27. "Una notizia sulla liberazione," Ibid., p. 25.

28. J. Bacot, ed., *Vita di Milarepa: I suoi delitti, le sue prove, la sua liberazione* (Milan: Adelphi, 1989), p. vii. For a reconstruction of Milarepa's popularity in the West, see V. R. [Valerio Riva], "Ci sono cento modi per diventare guru," *L'espresso*, 28 October 1973, p. 17.

29. Interview, 12 May 1990.

30. " 'Sogno di fare un film sulla Resurrezione,' " *La discussione* (Rome), 1 June 1991, p. 17. Cavani also refers to Pasolini's "Lettera su un giovane poliziotto" (Letter about a Young Policeman), in which he claims that today's proletarians are indeed the young policemen who are assigned to contain the students' upheavals, and not the revolutionaries themselves, who come from wealthy bourgeois families.

31. Luisella Re, "La guerra dei sexy," *Stampa sera*, 31 January 1974, p. 9.

32. *Orientalism* (New York: Vintage Books, 1979), p. 3.

33. On Milarepa's itineraries, see Cavani, "Per seminare inquietudine," in *Milarepa*, pp. 43–44. As for the critics' attitude toward the film, most of them considered it to be Cavani's best. Alberto Moravia speaks of "structurally original forms" ("Budda è salito in cima all'Appennino," *L'espresso*, 16 December 1973, p. 23); and Lino Miccichè emphasizes the film's "enchanted lyricism" ("Mito e realtà in 'Milarepa,' " *L'avanti*, 23 March 1974, p. 3, reprinted in *Cinema italiano degli anni '70: Cronache 1969–1978* [Venice: Marsilio, 1980], pp. 195–197). See also: G. B. Cavallaro, "Il primo giorno dopo il diluvio," *Settegiorni*, 30 December 1973, pp. 24–25; L. Pestelli, "La speranza è nel Tibet?" *La stampa*, 1 February 1974, p. 7; S. Frosali, " 'Milarepa': La Cavani migliore," *La nazione*, 23 February 1974, p. 9; Bir., "Milarepa," *Il messaggero*, 23 March 1974, p. 12; G. L. Rondi, "Milarepa," *Il tempo*, 24 March 1974, p. 14; P. Valmarana, " 'Milarepa' di Liliana Cavani: Un invito a vivere secondo la verità," *Il popolo*, 26 March 1974, p. 7; Robert Chazal, " 'Milarepa': Le Voyage au bout de la connaissance," *France-Soir*, 21 February, 1975, p. 21. On the other hand, some reservations were expressed by Francesco Savio, who calls *Milarepa* a purely decorative film, therefore "inutile" (of no use) ("Senza mistero," *Il mondo*, 18 April 1974, p. 22); and Mino Argentieri, who laments the lack of historical materialism in the interpretation of Milarepa's story ("Liliana Cavani tra magia e storia," p. 23).

34. "Il 'viaggio' del protagonista," in *Milarepa*, p. 50.

35. *Bar* means in between, and *do* means island or mark; a kind of landmark that stands between two things. On this subject, see W. Y. Evans-Wentz, ed., *The Tibetan Book of the Dead* (London and Oxford: Oxford University Press, 1960), pp. 2–10; Claes Corlin, "The Journey through the Bardo: Notes on the Symbolism of Tibetan Mortuary Rites and the Tibetan Book of the Dead," in *On the Meaning of Death: Essays on Mortuary Rituals and Eschatological Beliefs*, ed. S. Cederroth, C. Corlin, and J. Lindström, introd. Maurice Bloch (Stockholm: Almqvist & Wiksell International, 1988), pp. 63–75.

36. Cavani, *Milarepa*, p. 70.

37. Ibid., p. 80.

38. *Anatomy of Criticism*, p. 150. It also suggests the bardo retreat, a dangerous form of practice that consists of seven days of meditation in darkness.

39. For the *mandala* symbolism and its use in Lamaistic literature, see Jung, *The Archetypes and the Collective Unconscious*, pp. 357–358. The Sanskrit word *mandala* means "circle." It is the Hindu term for the magic circles drawn in religious rituals. In pictorial representations, red is one of the principal colors associated with the Earth Mother. Ibid., p. 185. For Milarepa's consecration, Marpa also draws an elaborate mandala. The most significant mandalas are found in the realm of Tibetan Buddhism.

40. Silverman, *The Acoustic Mirror*, pp. 228–229. I am much intrigued by Kaja Silverman's excellent reading of the intersubjective exchanges between Milarepa and his mother. She claims that the marginal existence of the mother within the village is emblematic of female subjectivity as such. For the feminist critic, the discourse of yoga becomes a metaphor "for the collapse of all binary oppositions that support the present symbolic order, and that keep power and privilege in place—particularly those bearing upon sexual difference, with its 'impure' or culturally coercive vision of biological distinction" (p. 230).

41. See Stam, *Subversive Pleasures*, p. 126.

42. *The Acoustic Mirror*, p. 231.

43. On this point, see Gennep, *The Rites of Passage*, pp. 15–25.

44. Cavani, *Milarepa*, p. 90. On the regenerative symbology of the fish, see Knapp, *A Jungian Approach to Literature*, pp. 248–249; Jung, *The Archetypes and the Collective Unconscious*, p. 141.

45. Guerrini, "Un cinema alla ricerca dell'ingaggio migliore," p. 169.

46. *Cosmos and History*, p. 36.

47. Silverman suggests that, in this process, Milarepa is stripped of the phallic attributes of male subjectivity. This sequence contains the utopian vision of a subjective space beyond sexual difference. See *The Acoustic Mirror*, pp. 229–231. On the other hand, Tiso speaks of an essential, ironic cruelty that aims at the total disintegration of one's own alienation. In *Milarepa*, sadism becomes the method for search and renewal. See *Liliana Cavani*, pp. 94–95.

48. *L'Epreuve du labyrinthe: Entretiens avec Claude-Henri Rocquet* (Paris: Pierre Belfond, 1978), p. 211.

49. "Mito e realtà in 'Milarepa,' " p. 3.

Chapter 8
The Essential Solitude: A Conclusion

1. Gs., "Per Liliana Cavani una passione in svastica e kimono," p. 21. *La pelle* (The Skin, 1980), adapted from Curzio Malaparte's 1949 novel, charts the avenues of resistance to the oppression of the Allied forces in 1943 Naples. The overtly political dimensions of the scenes involving General Mark Cork (Burt Lancaster) and Malaparte (Marcello Mastroianni) are infused with the theme of the Tower of Babel and its apocalyptic imagery. Cavani defies the propagandistic image of the American soldier by exhibiting what is left of the horrors of history: the artifacts of war (food, clothing); the powerful accumulation of tanks, weapons, explosions, and scenes of destruction. What we have is a confusion of tongues that translate into a vast body of metaphorical identifications. In the original version of the film, the actors speak many languages (from English to the Neapolitan dialect).

2. Mori, "Passione a quattro con idolo in kimono," p. 17. See also L. Tornabuoni, "Cavani nella tragedia di Moro," *La stampa*, 2 October 1984, p. 19. The film on Moro, with Gian Maria Volonté in the title role, was never made by Cavani. Eventually, it was Giuseppe Ferrara, a director known for his documentarian approach, who executed *Il caso Moro* in 1986.

3. *Histoire de la Sexualité*, vol. 2, *L'Usage des plaisirs* (Paris: Gallimard, 1984), p. 16.

4. The idea of the film originated when Cavani visited a Catholic mission in Carpi, where a group of deaf children was giving a Christmas recital. She recounts: "While everybody around me became happy, I couldn't help becoming sad. I was thinking: they don't hear each other. I noticed in the audience some other deaf children who were communicating in lively gestures. Somehow the body finds its own equilibrium as a form of compensation." Costa, "Sogno di fare un film sulla Resurrezione," p. 16. The film was produced by Giuseppe Bertolucci for San Francisco Film in collaboration with RAI UNO. It was entered in competition at the 1993 Venice Film Festival. Anna Bonaiuto (Fausto's mother) won the Coppa Volpi as best supporting actress. Cavani and her cowriter Italo Moscati thoroughly researched the subject by personally visiting several institutions and communities for the deaf ("non udenti"), and also consulted

several books, including *Seeing Voices: A Journey into the World of the Deaf* (1989) by neurologist Oliver W. Sacks. For production details, see Cristiana Paternò, " 'Sordità, la mia nuova eresia,' " *L'unità*, 15 August 1991, p. 22; Giuseppina Manin, "Cavani: Storia d'amore senza parole," *Corriere della sera*, 1 December 1991, p. 35; Andrea Piersanti, "Al di là del rumore," *Rivista del cinematografo*, n.s., 62 (April 1992): 7–10; L. Tornabuoni, "Cavani: Una guerra d'amore nel mondo del silenzio," *La stampa*, 17 January 1993, p. 23; Emma Neri, "Sordo e son desto," *Il sabato*, 21 August 1993, pp. 58–59; N. Aspesi, "Tra il silenzio e la famiglia due donne narrano il dolore: Le difficili scelte di Cavani e Issermann," *La repubblica*, 2 September 1993, p. 27.

5. G. Grassi, " 'Un amore oltre i rumori della vita,' " *Corriere della sera*, 24 August 1993, p. 20. Also: "At first this was a working title, and then we became attached to it. . . . For us it meant the search for a human contact and the desire to communicate. It is somehow like the disorienting birth of a chick pushing its way out of an eggshell, and while looking around frightened, it asks itself: 'Where are you? I'm here.' " From L. Cavani and I. Moscati's film treatment of *Dove siete? Io sono qui* (Archival Collection). In her introduction to the published script, the director also recalls that the title was inspired by a book by Austrian biologist Konrad Lorenz, *The Year of the Greylag Goose* (1978). One of the founders of a new science, ethology, Lorenz studies animal behavioral patterns in which our perceptual mechanisms play a vital role. See L. Cavani and I. Moscati, "Viaggio in un''etnia' e oltre," in L. Cavani and I. Moscati, *Dove siete? Io sono qui* (Venice: Marsilio, 1993), pp. 1–2. The film received the FEDIC prize (Federazione Italiana dei Cineclub) at the Fiftieth Venice Film Festival. The jury, presided over by Giovanni Grazzini, stated: "Liliana Cavani explores a relevant social theme, with a highly controlled language that favors an indispensable civil consciousness." From an Ansa press release dated 10 September 1993 (Archival Collection). For the critical reception of the film, see, among others, I. Bignardi, "Se il telefono non squilla . . . Cavani racconta la vita con l'handicap," *La repubblica*, 2 September 1993, p. 26; F. Bolzoni, "Giulietta e Romeo vincono il silenzio," *L'avvenire*, 2 September 1993, p. 19; M. Morandini, "Nel film della Cavani, la forza del silenzio," *Il giorno*, 2 September 1993, p. 15; Anton Giulio Mancino, "Dalla parte dei più disagiati," *Paese sera*, 2 September 1993, p. 21; T. Kezich, "E dalla Cavani tutte le emozioni del silenzio," *Corriere della sera*, 2 September 1993, p. 23; G. L. Rondi, "Cavani, l'importanza del silenzio," *Il tempo*, 27 September 1993, p. 18.

6. From the film treatment.

7. Butoh, a humanistic form of theater dance that developed in post–World War II Japan, expresses the darkness and the desperation felt by the Japanese people after the bombing of Hiroshima and Nagasaki. It is influenced by German expressionism and has some stylistic affinities with No and Kabuki traditions. On the subject, see *Butō: La "nuova danza" giapponese*, introd. Maria Pia D'Orazi (Rome: Editori Associati, 1997); Mark Holborn et al., *Butoh: Dance of the Dark Soul* (New York: Aperture, 1987).

8. From the director's written interview with Lorella Silvagni, which later appeared as "Liliana Cavani," in *Non capovolgere* (Mantua), no. 4 (September 1993): 35–43 (Archival Collection). The published script describes the impact of Akira's dance on Fausto as spellbinding and subjugating. He witnesses the "resurrection of a perfect body." See Cavani and Moscati, *Dove siete? Io sono qui*, p. 54.

9. On the difference between the *nikutai* and the social mask in the Japanese conception of the body, see D'Orazi, "L'ingenuità della carne: La ricerca di autenticità nella danza giapponese Buto," in *Butō*, pp. 7–8.

10. From "Ai Amour," in *Butō*, p. 204.

11. According to the original film treatment, written with Italo Moscati in 1991, Elena dies following a violent attack by a group of young boys who mock and persecute her difference. She becomes a *pharmakos*, an innocent victim of social prejudices and contradictions.

12. From the film treatment of *Galileo* (Archival Collection).

13. Cavani and Moscati, *Lettere dall'interno*, p. 123. The lines ("Il gioco è divino perché non c'è nessuna promessa / o speranza di guadagno") are from Elsa Morante's "Canzone degli F. P. e degli I. M." in *Il mondo salvato dai ragazzini e altri poemi* (1968).

Filmography

Shorts

1961 **INCONTRO DI NOTTE** (Night Encounter)
Producer: Centro Sperimentale di Cinematografia (Rome). *Story*: Liliana Cavani. *Screenplay*: Liliana Cavani. *Photography*: Giulio Spadini. *Sound*: Domenico Curia. *Set design*: Marco Morelli. *Assistant director*: Roberto Triana Arenas. *Production organizer*: Titano Cervone. *Cast*: Romano Ghini, Annabella Incontrera, Samba Ababacan. *Director*: Liliana Cavani. Released by Centro Sperimentale di Cinematografia. Italy: 35mm, black and white. 10 minutes.

1962 **LA BATTAGLIA** (The Battle)
Producer: Centro Sperimentale di Cinematografia (Rome). *Story*: Liliana Cavani. *Screenplay*: Liliana Cavani. *Photography*: Antonio Piazza. *Costumes*: Rosalba Menichelli. *Assistant director*: Sergio Tau. *Music*: Béla Bartók. *Production organizer*: Titano Cervone. *Cast*: Antonio Menna, Daniela Igliozzi, Samba Ababacan, Rosanna Santoro, Ireneo Petruzzi, Nili Arutay, Pal Bang-Hansen. *Director*: Liliana Cavani. Released by Centro Sperimentale di Cinematografia. Italy: 35mm, black and white. 30 minutes. Selected for the 1962 San Sebastian Film Festival. *Awards*: "Ciak d'oro" for best biennial short, Centro Sperimentale di Cinematografia, 1962.

Documentaries

1961 **LA VITA MILITARE** (The Military Life)
Producer: RAI Radiotelevisione Italiana. *Editing*: Franco Attenni. *Animation*: Recta Film. *Director*: Liliana Cavani. Aired on RAI-2 in the series *Racconti dell'Italia di ieri*. Italy: 16mm, black and white. 11 minutes.

1961 **GENTE DI TEATRO** (Theater People)
Producer: RAI Radiotelevisione Italiana. *Photography*: Franco De Cristofaro. *Editing*: Franco Attenni. *Director*: Liliana Cavani. Aired on RAI-2 in the series *Racconti dell'Italia di ieri*. Italy: 16mm, black and white. 12 minutes.

1961–62 **STORIA DEL TERZO REICH** (History of the Third Reich)
Producer: RAI Radiotelevisione Italiana. *Consultant*: Mario Bendiscioli. *Narration*: Giacomo Cesaro, Italo A. Chiusano, Boris Ulianich. *Editing*: Franco Attenni, Ettore Salvi. *Music*: Daniele Paris. *Director*: Liliana Cavani. A four-part documentary aired on RAI-1 and -2, in the series *Anni d'Europa*. Italy: 35mm and 16mm, black and white. 203 minutes.

1962 **ETÀ DI STALIN** (The Age of Stalin)
Producer: RAI Radiotelevisione Italiana. *Consultant*: Giorgio Galli. *Narration*: Giorgio Galli. *Editing*: Ettore Salvi. *Music*: Daniele Paris. *Director*: Liliana Cavani. A three-part documentary aired on RAI-2, in the series *Anni d'Europa*. Italy: 16mm, black and white. 184 minutes.

1963 **L'UOMO DELLA BUROCRAZIA** (The Bureaucrat)
Producer: RAI Radiotelevisione Italiana. *Collaboration*: Livio Zanetti, Luigi Villa. *Sketches*: Pino Zac. *Photography*: Colombo Pieraccioli. *Editing*: Gianbattista Mussetto.

Director: Liliana Cavani. Aired on RAI-2, in the series *Osservatorio*. Italy: 16mm, black and white. 16 minutes.

1963 **ASSALTO AL CONSUMATORE** (Assault on the Consumer)
Producer: RAI Radiotelevisione Italiana. *Collaboration*: Nello Ajello. *Sketches*: Pino Zac. *Photography*: Ettore Carnevali. *Editing*: Franca Di Lorenzo. *Director*: Liliana Cavani. Aired on RAI-2, in the series *Osservatorio*. Italy: 16mm, black and white. 18 minutes.

1964 **LA CASA IN ITALIA** (Housing in Italy)
Producer: RAI Radiotelevisione Italiana. *Consultants*: Alberto Ronchey, Filippo Ponti. *Narration*: Fabrizio Dentice. *Collaboration*: Rina Macrelli, Salvatore Conoscente. *Photography*: Franco Solito. *Editing*: Franco Attenni. *Music*: Peppino De Luca. *Narrators*: Arnoldo Foà, Alberto Lupo. *Production organizers*: Gianmaria Messeri, Aldo Scimonelli. *Director*: Liliana Cavani. A four-part series aired on RAI-1. Italy: 16mm, black and white. 165 minutes.

1964 **GESÙ MIO FRATELLO** (My Brother Jesus)
Producer: RAI Radiotelevisione Italiana. *Collaboration*: Rina Macrelli. *Photography*: Sandro Messina. *Editing*: Domenico Gorgolini. *Music*: Peppino De Luca. *Narrator*: Giancarlo Sbragia. *Production organizer*: Amedeo Puthod. *Director*: Liliana Cavani. Aired on RAI-2. Italy: 16mm, black and white. 46 minutes. *Awards*: "Premio Italia," UNDA, 1964.

1965 **IL GIORNO DELLA PACE** (Day of Peace)
Producer: RAI Radiotelevisione Italiana. *Narration*: Alfonso Gatto. *Collaboration*: Rina Macrelli. *Photography*: Sandro Messina, Klaus Philipp. *Editing*: Franco Attenni. *Music*: Peppino De Luca. *Narrator*: Arnoldo Foà. *Production organizer*: Remo Odevaine. *Director*: Liliana Cavani. Aired on RAI-2. Italy: 16mm, black and white. 49 minutes.

1965 **LA DONNA NELLA RESISTENZA** (The Women of the Resistance)
Producer: RAI Radiotelevisione Italiana. *Narration*: Paolo Glorioso. *Collaboration*: Rina Macrelli. *Photography*: Mario Dolci. *Sound*: Enzo D'Alfonso. *Editing*: Jenner Menghi. *Music*: Antonio Tealdo. *Narrator*: Riccardo Cucciolla. *Director*: Liliana Cavani. Aired on RAI-2, in the series *Prima pagina*. Italy: 16mm, black and white. 48 minutes. *Awards*: "Medusa d'argento," Premio dei Colli, Este, 1965.

1965 **PHILIPPE PÉTAIN: PROCESSO A VICHY** (Trial at Vichy)
Producer: RAI Radiotelevisione Italiana. *Research*: Franca Caprino. *Photography*: Misha Tzigoyan, Sandro Messina. *Editing*: Domenico Gorgolini. *Music*: Peppino De Luca. *Narrator*: Giancarlo Sbragia. *Production organizers*: Eva De Muschietti Chiesa, Amedeo Puthod. *Director*: Liliana Cavani. Aired on RAI-2, in the series *Prima pagina*. Italy: 16mm, black and white. 47 minutes. *Awards*: "Leone d'oro," Venice Film Festival (documentary section), 1965; "Targa Este," Premio dei Colli, 1966.

Feature Films

1966 **FRANCESCO DI ASSISI** (Francis of Assisi)
Producer: RAI Radiotelevisione Italiana. *Screenplay*: Tullio Pinelli, Liliana Cavani. *Historical consultant*: Boris Ulianich. *Assistant director*: Lina Macrelli. *Sets and costumes*: Ezio Frigerio. *Editing*: Luciano Gigante. *Photography*: Giuseppe Ruzzolini. *Sound*: Nino Renda. *Music*: Peppino De Luca. *Cast*: Lou Castel (Francesco), Giancarlo Sbragia (Pietro Bernardone), Grazia Marescalchi (Pica), Riccardo Cucciolla (Leone), Ludmilla

Lvova (Chiara), Ken Belton (Innocent III), Marco Bellocchio (Pietro di Stacia), Giuseppe Campodifiori (Giovanni), Teodoro Cicogna (Egidio), Roberto Di Massimo (Guido), Gerig Domain (Cardinal Colonna), Marcello Formica (Gentiluccio), Giampiero Frondini (Pietro Cattani), Gerard Herter (Elia da Cortona), Franco Marchesi (Corrado), Oscar Mercurelli (Angelo), Maurizio Tocchi (Masseo), Gianni Turillazzi (Rufino). *Production organizer*: Sergio Iacobis. *Director*: Liliana Cavani. Released by RAI Radiotelevisione Italiana. Italy: 16mm (blown up to 35mm), black and white. 119 minutes. Selected for: XXVII Venice Film Festival ("Sezione informativa"), 1966; IX Gran Premio Bergamo, 1966; "Premio Italia," Palermo, 1966; Les Rencontres Internationales du film pour la jeunesse, 1967. *Awards*: "Noci d'oro," 1966; "Labaro d'oro," Valladolid Film Festival (ex-aequo with *Akahige* by Akira Kurosawa), 1967; "Prix Unda," Montecarlo TV Festival, 1967.

1968 GALILEO

Producer: Leo Pescarolo for Fenice Cinematografica (Venice), Rizzoli Film (Rome), and Kinozenter (Sofia). *Screenplay*: Tullio Pinelli, Liliana Cavani. *Script collaborator*: Fabrizio Onofri. *Historical consultant*: Boris Ulianich. *Assistant director*: Lina Macrelli. *Photography*: Alfio Contini. *Editing*: Nino Baragli. *Sets and costumes*: Ezio Frigerio. *Music*: Ennio Morricone. *Cast*: Cyril Cusack (Galileo), Giulio Broggi (Sagredo), Paolo Graziosi (Bernini), Gigi Ballista (Dominican Inquisitor), Gheorghi Cerkelov (Bellarmine), Nicolai Doicev (Inchofer), Gheorghi Kaloiancev (Giordano Bruno), Nevena Kokanova (Marina), Marcello Turilli (Acquapendente), Pietro Vida (Urban VIII), and special appearance by Lou Castel (Father Charles). *Production organizer*: Sergio Iacobis. *Director*: Liliana Cavani. Released by Cineriz. Italy-Bulgaria: 35mm, Eastmancolor. 92 minutes (original version 105'). Selected for the 1968 Film Festivals of Venice and Montecarlo. *Awards*: "Premio Cineforum" (ex-aequo with *Faces* by John Cassavetes), 1968.

1969 I CANNIBALI (The Cannibals)

Producers: Enzo Doria, Bino Cicogna for Doria–San Marco Film. *Assistant directors*: Gianni Amelio, Ugo Novello, Paola Tallarigo. *Music*: Ennio Morricone. *Editing*: Nino Baragli. *Sets and costumes*: Ezio Frigerio. *Photography*: Giulio Albonico. *Production director*: Federico Tofi. *Production organizer*: Giuseppe Francone. *Story*: Liliana Cavani. *Screenplay*: Italo Moscati, Liliana Cavani. *Cast*: Pierre Clementi (Tiresias), Britt Ekland (Antigone), Francesco Leonetti (Haemon's father), Delia Boccardo (Ismene), Marino Masè (Ismene's fiancé), Cora Mazzoni (Antigone's mother), Francesco Arminio (Antigone's father), the actors of the "Comunità teatrale Emilia Romagna," and special appearance by Tomas Milian (Haemon). *Director*: Liliana Cavani. Released by Euro International Films. Italy: 35mm, color, Techniscope. 88 minutes. Selected for the 1970 Film Festivals of Spoleto, Cannes ("Quinzaine des réalisateurs"), New York, San Francisco, London. *Awards*: "Targa AIACE," 1970.

1971 L'OSPITE (The Guest)

Producer: Lotar Film for RAI Radiotelevisione Italiana. *Screenplay*: Liliana Cavani. *Photography*: Giulio Albonico. *Editing*: Andreina Casini. *Sets and costumes*: Fiorella Mariani. *Assistant Director*: Paola Tallarigo. *Production organizer*: Sergio Iacobis. *Music*: Gioacchino Rossini. *Cast*: Lucia Bosè (Anna), Glauco Mauri (Piero), Peter Gonzales (Luciano), Alvaro Piccardi (Anna's brother), Giancarlo Caio (Doctor), Gian Piero Frondini, Alfio Galardi, Maddalena Gillia, Maria Luisa Salmaso, Lorenzo Piani. *Direc-*

tor: Liliana Cavani. Released by Sacis. Italy: 16mm (blown up to 35mm), Eastmancolor. 93 minutes. Selected for the 1971 Film Festivals of Venice and Cannes ("Quinzaine des réalisateurs"). *Awards*: "Targa AIACE," 1972; "Timone d'oro," 1972.

1973   **MILAREPA**

Producer: Lotar Film for RAI Radiotelevisione Italiana. *Story*: Liliana Cavani. *Screenplay*: Liliana Cavani, Italo Moscati, adapted from *Tibet's Great Yogi Milarepa* (Oxford University Press). *Historical consultant*: Boris Ulianich. *Assistant director*: Paola Tallarigo. *Editing*: Franco Arcalli. *Photography*: Armando Nannuzzi. *Sets and costumes*: Jean Marie Simon. *Music*: Daniele Paris. *Production organizer*: Sergio Iacobis. *Cast*: Lajos Balàzsovits (Lumley/Milarepa), Paolo Bonacelli (Professor Bennett/Marpa), Marisa Fabbri (Lumley/ Milarepa's mother), Marcella Michelangeli (Karin/Damema). *Director*: Liliana Cavani. Released by RAI Radiotelevisione Italiana. Italy: 35mm, color. 113 minutes. Selected for the 1974 Cannes Film Festival. *Awards*: "Carpine d'oro," 1973.

1974   **IL PORTIERE DI NOTTE** (The Night Porter)

Producers: Robert Gordon Edwards, Esa De Simone for Lotar Film. *Editing*: Franco Arcalli. *Photography*: Alfio Contini. *Music*: Daniele Paris. *Set design*: Jean Marie Simon, Nedo Azzini. *Costumes*: Piero Tosi. *Screenplay*: Liliana Cavani, Italo Moscati. *Assistant directors*: Franco Cirino, Paola Tallarigo. *Cast*: Dirk Bogarde (Max), Charlotte Rampling (Lucia), Philippe Leroy (Klaus), Gabriele Ferzetti (Hans), Giuseppe Addobbati (Stumm), Isa Miranda (Countess Stein), Nino Bignamini (Adolf), Marino Masè (Atherton), Amedeo Amodio (Bert), Geoffrey Coplestone (Kurt), Manfred Freiberger (Dobson), Ugo Cardea (Mario), Hilde Gunther (Greta), Nora Ricci (Fräulein Holler). *Director*: Liliana Cavani. Released by Italnoleggio Cinematografico. Italy: 35mm, color. 113 minutes (original version 123′). Selected for the 1975 Film Festivals of Belgrade and Teheran. *Awards*: "Consorzio Stampa Cinematografica," 1974; "Premio Riccione" for best director, 1974; "Premio Eur," 1974; Grand Prix Cinéma de 'Elle,' " Paris, 1974.

1977   **AL DI LÀ DEL BENE E DEL MALE** (Beyond Good and Evil)

Producer: Robert Gordon Edwards for Clesi Cinematografica, Lotar Film, Les Productions Artistes Associés (Paris), Artemis Gmbh (Berlin). *Story*: Liliana Cavani. *Screenplay*: Liliana Cavani, Franco Arcalli, Italo Moscati. *Set Design*: Lorenzo Mongiardino. *Art director*: Nedo Azzini. *Costumes*: Piero Tosi. *Music*: Daniele Paris. *Photography*: Armando Nannuzzi. *Associate producer*: Esa De Simone. *Editing*: Franco Arcalli. *Assistant directors*: Paola Tallarigo, Albino Cocco. *Cast*: Dominique Sanda (Lou), Erland Josephson (Fritz), Robert Powell (Paul), Virna Lisi (Elisabeth), Philippe Leroy (Peter Gast), Carmen Scarpitta (Malvida), Amedeo Amodio (Ducamara), Michael Degen (Karl Andreas), Nicoletta Machiavelli (Amanda), and special appearance by Elisa Cegani (Franziska Nietzsche) and Umberto Orsini (Bernard). *Director*: Liliana Cavani. Released by Italnoleggio Cinematografico. Italy-France-Germany (BDR): 35mm, color. 127 minutes. Selected for the Film Festivals of Teheran, 1977; Belgrade, 1978; Brussels, 1978. *Awards*: "Palladio d'oro," 1977; "Nastro d'argento" to Virna Lisi for best supporting actress, Venice Film Festival, 1977.

1980   **LA PELLE** (The Skin)

Producer: Renzo Rossellini for Opera Film Produzione (Rome), Gaumont SA (Rome). *Set Design*: Dante Ferretti. *Costumes*: Piero Tosi. *Music*: Lalo Schifrin. *Assistant director*: Paola Tallarigo. *Photography*: Armando Nannuzzi. *Editing*: Ruggero Mastroianni. *Exec-*

utive producer: Manolo Bolognini. *Screenplay*: Robert Katz, Liliana Cavani, adapted from *La pelle* by Curzio Malaparte. *Cast*: Marcello Mastroianni (Malaparte), Burt Lancaster (General Mark Cork), Claudia Cardinale (Princess Caracciolo), Ken Marshall (Jimmy Wren), Alexandra King (Deborah Wyatt), Carlo Giuffré (Eduardo Mazzullo), Yann Babilée, Jacques Sernas, Jeanne Valerie, Liliana Tari, Giuseppe Barra, Cristina Donadio, Maria Rosaria Della Femmina. *Director*: Liliana Cavani. Released by Gaumont. Italy-France: 35mm, color. 131 minutes. Selected for the Film Festivals of Cannes, 1981; Montreal, 1981; Manila, 1981; Chicago, 1982. *Awards*: "Biglietto d'oro Anec/Agis," 1982.

1982   **OLTRE LA PORTA** (Beyond Obsession)
Producer: Francesco Giorgi for Futur Film '80, RAI Radiotelevisione Italiana, Cineriz Distributori Associati. *Screenplay*: Liliana Cavani, Enrico Medioli. *Photography*: Luciano Tovoli. *Set design*: Dante Ferretti. *Set dresser*: Verde Visconti. *Costumes*: Piero Tosi. *Music*: Pino Donaggio. *Production manager*: Roberto Giussani. *Editing*: Ruggero Mastroianni. *Assistant director*: Paola Tallarigo. *Sound*: Jean Pierre Ruh. *Cast*: Marcello Mastroianni (Enrico), Eleonora Giorgi (Nina), Tom Berenger (Matthieu), Michel Piccoli (Mutti), Cecily Brown (Mrs. Moretti), Paolo Bonetti (Assam), Maria Sofia Amendola, Enrico Bergier, Marcia Briscoe. *Director*: Liliana Cavani. Released by Cineriz, Sacis. Italy: 35mm, color. 108 minutes. Selected for the 1982 Film Festivals of Venice ("Sezione Vittorio De Sica"), and San Sebastian. *Awards*: "Segno d'argento," 1983.

1985   **INTERNO BERLINESE** (The Berlin Affair)
Producers: Menahem Golan, Yoram Globus for Cannon Productions (Rome), Italian International Film (Rome), KF-Kinofilm Produktions Gmbh (Munich). *Music*: Pino Donaggio. *Set design*: Luciano Ricceri. *Set dresser*: Verde Visconti. *Assistant director*: Paola Tallarigo. *Costumes*: Alberto Verso; Mio Takaki's costumes by Jusaburo Tsujimura. *Editing*: Ruggero Mastroianni. *Production organizer*: Mario Cotone. *Story*: Liliana Cavani. *Screenplay*: Liliana Cavani, Roberta Mazzoni, adapted from *The Buddhist Cross* by Junichirō Tanizaki. *Executive producer*: John Thompson. *Cast*: Gudrun Landgrebe (Louise), Kevin McNally (Heinz), Mio Takaki (Mitsuko), Massimo Girotti (Werner), Philippe Leroy (Herbert), William Berger (The Professor), Andrea Prodan (Joseph Benno), John Steiner, Enrico Maria Scrivano, Claudio Lorimer, Tomoko Tanaka. *Director*: Liliana Cavani. Released by Italian International Film. Italy-Germany (BDR): 35mm, color. 122 minutes. Selected for the XXVI Berlin Film Festival, 1986.

1989   **FRANCESCO**
Producer: Giulio Scanni for Karol Film, RAI Radio Televisione Italiana RAI UNO, Istituto Luce, Royal Film (Münich). *Story*: Liliana Cavani. *Screenplay*: Liliana Cavani, Roberta Mazzoni. *Assistant director*: Paola Tallarigo. *Sets and costumes*: Danilo Donati. *Photography*: Giuseppe Lanci; for the three weeks in Perugia, Ennio Guarnieri. *Editing*: Gabriella Cristiani. *Music*: Vangelis. *Cast*: Mickey Rourke (Francesco), Helena Bonham Carter (Chiara), Andrea Ferreol (Pica), Mario Adorf (Cardinal Ugolino), Paolo Bonacelli (Pietro Bernardone), Fabio Bussotti (Leone), Riccardo de Torrebruna (Pietro Cattani), Alexander Dubin (Angelo), Stanko Molnar (Elia), Paco Reconti (Rufino), Diego Ribon (Bernardo), Maurizio Schmidt (Masseo), Paolo Proietti (Pacifico), Peter Berling (Bishop of Assisi), Nikolaus Dutsch (Cardinal Colonna), Hanns Zischler (Innocent III). *Director*: Liliana Cavani. Released by Istituto Luce Italnoleggio Cinematografico, Sacis. Italy: 35mm, color. 155 minutes. Selected for the Cannes Film Festival,

1989. *Awards*: "David di Donatello" to Danilo Donati for best costumes, 1989; "Nastro d'argento" to Fabio Bussotti for best supporting actor, 1989; "Premio Internazionale Ascoli Piceno," 1991.

1993   **DOVE SIETE? IO SONO QUI** (Where Are You? I'm Here)
Producer: Giovanni Bertolucci for San Francisco Film, RAI Radio Televisione Italiana RAI UNO and Sacis. *Story and Screenplay*: Liliana Cavani, Italo Moscati. *Assistant director*: Paola Tallarigo. *Costumes*: Alberto Verso. *Set design*: Luciano Ricceri. *Set dresser*: Egidio Spugnini. *Photography*: Armando Nannuzzi. *Editing*: Angelo Nicolini. *Music*: Pino Donaggio. *Production manager*: Tullio Lullo. *Sound*: Candido Raini. *Cast*: Chiara Caselli (Elena), Gaetano Carotenuto (Fausto), Anna Bonaiuto (Fausto's mother), Valeria D'Obici (Fausto's aunt), Giuseppe Perruccio (Fausto's father), Doriana Chierici (Elena's mother), Ines Nobili (Maria), Ko Morobushi (Butoh dancer). *Director*: Liliana Cavani. Released by I.I.F. Italian International Film and Sacis. Italy: 35mm, color. 108 minutes. Selected for the Venice Film Festival, 1993. *Awards*: "Coppa Volpi" to Anna Buonaiuto for best supporting actress, Venice Film Festival.

Operas

1979   **WOZZECK**, by Alban Berg.
Conductor: Bruno Bartoletti. Opening night, Forty-second Maggio Musicale Fiorentino. Teatro Comunale.

1984   **IFIGENIA IN TAURIDE**, by Christopher W. Gluck.
Conductor: Gerd Albrecht. Opéra de Paris.

1986   **MEDEA**, by Luigi Cherubini.
Conductor: Pinchas Steinberg. Opéra de Paris.

1986   **MEDEA**, by Luigi Cherubini.
Conductor: Bruno Bartoletti. Opening night, "Firenze capitale della cultura europea," sponsored by CEE. Teatro Comunale, Florence. *Awards*: "Franco Abbiati Prize" for best opera of 1985–1986.

1990   **LA TRAVIATA**, by Giuseppe Verdi.
Conductor: Riccardo Muti. Teatro alla Scala, Milan. *Awards*: "Amici del loggione," 1990; First Prize at the International Opera Screen IMZ Festival for best program recorded in high-definition television.

1991   **CARDILLAC**, by Paul Hindemith.
Conductor: Bruno Bartoletti. Opening night, Fifty-fourth Maggio Musicale Fiorentino. Teatro Verdi, Florence.

1993   **JENUFA**, by Leos Janàcek.
Conductor: Semyon Bychkov. Opening night, Fifty-sixth Maggio Musicale Fiorentino. Teatro Comunale, Florence. *Awards*: "Franco Abbiati Prize" for best opera of 1992–1993.

1993   **LA VESTALE**, by Gaspare Spontini.
Conductor: Riccardo Muti. Opening night 1993–1994 Season, Teatro alla Scala, Milan.

1995   **LA CENA DELLE BEFFE**, by Umberto Giordano.
Conductor: Bruno Bartoletti. Zürich Opera.

1996   **CAVALLERIA RUSTICANA**, by Pietro Mascagni.
   Conductor: Riccardo Muti. Ravenna Festival.
1998   **MANON LESCAUT**, by Giacomo Puccini.
   Conductor: Riccardo Muti. Teatro alla Scala, Milan.

Screenwriter

1969   **IL CASO LIUZZO**.
   Directed by Giuseppe Fina for the RAI Television series *Teatro-inchiesta*.

Bibliography

ADDITIONAL bibliographical references are cited in the discussion of individual films.

Writings by Cavani

Screenplays

"Francesco di Assisi." Part 1. *Rivista del cinematografo* 41 (August 1968): 503–512.

"Francesco d'Assisi." Part 2. *Rivista del cinematografo* 41 (September–October 1968): 577–587.

"I dialoghi del film Galileo." *Cineforum* 8 (October 1968): 598–624.

Francesco e Galileo: Due film. Introduction by Leo Pestelli. Turin: Gribaudi, 1970.

"I cannibali." In collaboration with Italo Moscati. *Sipario* 25 (February 1970): 40–49.

Milarepa. Edited by Italo Moscati. Bologna: Cappelli, 1974.

Il portiere di notte. Turin: Einaudi, 1974.

El portero de noche. Barcelona: Icaria, 1976.

Al di là del bene e del male. In collaboration with Franco Arcalli and Italo Moscati. Turin: Einaudi, 1977.

Oltre la porta. In collaboration with Enrico Medioli. Turin: Einaudi, 1982.

Francesco. In collaboration with Roberta Mazzoni. Milan: Leonardo, 1989.

Dove siete? Io sono qui. In collaboration with Italo Moscati. Venice: Marsilio, 1993.

Unfilmed Screenplays

"Uno 'Spiritual cinematografico': Black Jesus." In collaboration with Ludovico Alessandrini. *Fiera letteraria*, 12 December 1965, pp. 6–7.

Lettere dall'interno: Racconto per un film su Simone Weil. In collaboration with Italo Moscati. Turin: Einaudi, 1974.

Essays, Reviews, and Other Writings

"Profilo all'opera di Ingmar Bergman." *Studium* 56 (November 1960): 786–789.

Note sull'attore cinematografico. Rome: Centro Sperimentale di Cinematografia, Anno Accademico 1960–1961. Reprinted as "Note sull'attore cinematografico." *Studium* 57 (July–August 1961): 549–554.

"L'avventura, la notte e la critica." *Studium* 57 (March 1961): 195–198.

"La discesa all'inferno della regista S. Clarke." *Rivista del cinematografo* 34 (July 1961): 239–240.

"Il cinema francese e il 'nuovo' romanzo." *Studium* 58 (January 1962): 32–35.

"Cesare, l'idraulico, pensa che anche lui ha 'I giorni contati.' " *Il nostro tempo*, 26 April 1962.

"Per Antonioni solo nell'Eclisse l'uomo moderno trova la verità. *Il nostro tempo*, 3 May 1962, p. 8.

"All'armi, siam fascisti!" *Il nostro tempo*, 7 June 1962.

"L'eclisse." *Studium* 58 (September 1962): 631–635.

"Quante storie di giovani borghesi che non sanno né vogliono vivere." *Il nostro tempo*, 6 September 1962, p. 8.

"John Ford è ancora il migliore con il suo sano film western." *Il nostro tempo*, 11 October 1962, p. 8.

"Un coraggioso film americano sui retroscena dell'alta politica." *Il nostro tempo*, 1 November 1962.

"Banditi a Orgosolo." *Il nostro tempo*, 30 November 1962.

"Cinema 1962." *Studium* 59 (April 1963): 284–286.

"Quattro films ed una osservazione." *Studium* 59 (July–August 1963): 524–531.

"Cinema-Moravia." *Studium* 60 (February 1964): 115–118.

"Il teleschermo avvelenato." *Corriere della sera*, 10 May 1964, p. 5.

"Fantapolitica e verità." *Studium* 60 (July–August 1964): 523–526.

"Una regista alla ricerca dei piccoli fratelli di Gesù." *Rivista del cinematografo*, no. 1 (January 1965): 46–47.

"I fratelli di Gesù nella bidonville." *Orizzonti*, 17 January 1965, pp. 24–26.

"Le donne della resistenza." *Orizzonti*, 4 April 1965, pp. 6–7.

"Un cinema libero." *Studium* 61 (September 1965): 598–602.

"Realizzare il socialismo non significa riconoscere il fallimento del Vangelo." *Il nostro tempo*, 30 October 1966.

"Il ribelle in perfetta letizia." *Cinecircoli* 5 (January–February 1967): 3.

"Bergman affronta nel suo ultimo film il dramma della responsabilità umana." *Il nostro tempo*, 12 February 1967.

" 'Cattolici progressisti' una definizione pericolosa" (letter to the editor). *Il nostro tempo*, 31 December 1967.

"Liliana Cavani scrive a Cineforum." *Cineforum* 2, nos. 76–80 (1968): 592–593.

"Perché i giovani cattolici non dovrebbero protestare?" *Il nostro tempo*, 14 April 1968.

"Un cinema antirazzista non è ancora nato." *Rivista del cinematografo*, nos. 6–7 (June–July 1968): 374–375.

"Il vizio di appellarsi alle 'persone autorevoli.' " *Il nostro tempo*, 8 December 1968, p. 2.

"Andare a Venezia." *Settegiorni*, 17 October 1971, p. 33.

"Quando un regista recita un copione." *Presente imperfetto* (1972), pp. 113–116.

"Le leggi dell'improbabilità." In *Maestri del cinema in TV: Buster Keaton*, pp. 62–63. Rome: RAI, Appunti del servizio stampa no. 45 (1972).

"I cannibali: Un Cri d'alarme." In *I cannibali: Un film de Liliana Cavani*, pp. 6–8. French press kit, 1972.

"Pierre Clementi et la violence fasciste." In *I cannibali: Un film de Liliana Cavani*, pp. 19–21. French press kit, 1972.

"Perché ho fatto il film." *Paese sera*, 31 March 1974, p. 3.

"Cavani: E' democratico avere paura della realtà?" *Il tempo*, 25 April 1974, p. 13.

"Hanno offeso il pubblico." *Settegiorni*, 28 April 1974, p. 3.

"There Are Degrees and Degrees of Sadomasochism." *Viva*, February 1975, pp. 113–114.

"Cinema ed erotismo." *Belfagor* 30 (March 1975): 157–168. Reprinted as "Cinema e censura," in *Quaderni del Centro Culturale "Merolla" (1972–1975)*, edited by Salvatore Mignanò, no. 2 (1975): 221–240.

"Herren der Gaskammern unter uns." *Der Spiegel*, 3 March 1975, p. 10.

"Pasolini." *"La Biennale"-Annuario* (1976), p. 1039.

"La presa di posizione del Vaticano sul sesso." *Belfagor* 31 (March 1976): 233–234.

"Un Homme contre le terrorisme." *Nouvelles Litteraires*, 25 March 1976, p. 3.

"Eros non è il diavolo." *Tuttolibri*, 19 March 1977, p. 10.

"Grida dal manicomio." *Tuttolibri*, 9 July 1977, p. 4.

"La risposta di Liliana Cavani." *Il messaggero*, 22 October 1978, p. 12.

"Lo scandalo di Sibilla." *Tuttolibri*, 9 December 1978, p. 10.

"Abelardo e Eloisa una storia d'amore e di anarchia." *Tuttolibri*, 8 December 1979, p. 20.

"Gli spettri al festino." *Tuttolibri*, 22 December 1979, p. 148.

Introduction to Maria Teresa Colonna, *Lilith la luna nera e l'eros rifiutato*, pp. 5–20. Florence: Edizioni del Riccio, 1980.

"Il paziente non è un suddito." *Tuttolibri*, 9 February 1980, p. 16.

"Don Giovanni pensa e sconvolge il gioco." *Tuttolibri*, 8 March 1980, p. 15.

"Il disco capsula." In *Sul disco*, pp. 18–19. Rome: Associazione Fonici Italiani, 1981.

"La pelle." *L'araldo*, 22–23 May 1981, pp. 8–9.

"Da Malaparte alla Cavani: 'La pelle' fa ancora scandalo." *Tuttolibri*, 26 September 1981, p. 1.

"Senza pace né guerra." *Il mattino*, 2 October 1981, p. 5.

"C'è ancora quella battaglia da vincere (la censura)." *L'altro cinema* (Aiace) (1982), p. 29.

"Con i miei attori nel turbine di Marrakech tra stupori, amori e misteri." *Corriere della sera*, 24 April 1982, p. 15.

"A quindici anni dal mio film." In *Francesco un 'pazzo' da slegare*, pp. 336–339. Assisi: Cittadella Editrice, 1983.

"Sulla pelle filmica d'Europa." *Belfagor* 39, no. 3 (1984): 354–358.

"Cinema e TV fra due ideologie." *Il popolo*, 24 January 1984, p. 9.

"Perché mi ha ispirato un film." *Tuttolibri*, 3 August 1985, p. 3.

"E' cinema europeo." *La repubblica*, 5 November 1985, p. 6.

"Annunciazione a Roma di Elio Fiore." *Belfagor* 41, no. 4 (1986): 466–467.

"La donna partorì il mito e l'uomo lo adottò." *Tuttolibri*, 17 May 1986, pp. 4–5.

"Nel Sud un esilio misterioso." *Tuttolibri*, 5 September 1987, p. 2.

"Poi rispunta un moralista intelligente e fa baccano." *Gulliver* 6 (December 1987): 4.

"Così abbiamo dato l'Oscar europeo." *Corriere della sera*, 27 November 1988, p. 24.

"Pensare e ascoltare." *Annuario AIC* (1989), p. 15.

"Francesco." *Première*, May 1989, pp. 148–151.

"Ricordo Moravia." *La repubblica*, 2 October 1990, p. 12.

"Ho visto il mio Francesco 'convertire' anche Stalin." *Corriere della sera*, 29 July 1991, p. 20.

"Mondanità e amicizia." *Amadeus*, January 1992, p. 36.

"Esiste discriminazione?" *Emigrazione* 24, no. 3 (1992): 47–48.

"Donna e libertà d'espressione." In *Donna e modernità*, edited by Elena Cavalcanti, pp. 121–134. Rome: Edizioni Dehoniane, 1993.

"Il cinema per capire." In *Il cinema di Liliana Cavani*, edited by Primo Goldoni, pp. 23–29. Bologna: Grafis Edizioni, 1993.

"L'Europa rischia il sottosviluppo." *La stampa*, 13 October 1993, p. 23.

"Savater sbaglia: Il cinema europeo si difende cosi." *L'unità*, 6 February 1994, p. 1.

"Ci vuole una 'carta delle regole.' " *Letture* 50, no. 522 (1995): 6–8.

"La democrazia, la cultura e il potere della comunicazione." *Il popolo*, 7 October 1995, p. 6.
"Il cinema e l'arcobaleno." In *Parlare il cinema*, edited by Elio Girlanda et al., pp. 2–3. Rome: Editrice A.V.E., 1996.
"Fuori della mischia." *Rivista del cinematografo* 66 (January 1996): 19.
"Un ministero per la cultura." *La repubblica*, 2 February 1996, p. 10.

Interviews

The following is a selection of Cavani's discussions of her art, including comments on specific films, and of her contributions to debates on cultural affairs. The interviewer's name is listed if it is acknowledged in a byline. The order is chronological.

Benedetti, Mario. "Baracche e ville con piscina: Queste le case degli italiani." *Incom*, 3 May 1964, pp. 10–14.
Bolzoni, Francesco. "Una regista televisiva tra i 'piccoli fratelli di Gesù.'" *Osservatore romano*, 2–3 January 1965, p. 3.
Saviano, Leonardo. "La provinciale coraggiosa." *Tutto Carpi*, July 1965, pp. 30–32.
Trasatti, Sergio. "L'inquietante Francesco." *Cinecircoli* 4 (March 1966): 28–29.
Foglietti, Mario. "San Francesco come noi." *Il popolo*, 26 April 1966, p. 3.
Bolzoni, Francesco. "Lo scandalo di Francesco." *Orizzonti*, 5 June 1966, pp. 27–33.
Lucchini, Mario, and Alessandro Zaina. "Intervista a Liliana Cavani." *Il cammino* (Annali francescani), November 1966, pp. 281–283.
Sermonti, Bianca. "Quando il regista è donna: Liliana Cavani." *Rivista del cinematografo*, nos. 4–5 (1967): 259–262.
"Quattro domande a Liliana Cavani regista." *Se vuoi*, no. 5 (1967): 13.
Michetti Ricci, Luciano. "Il vero pericolo è l'autocensura." *Settegiorni*, 2 July 1967, p. 37.
"Quattro domande agli uomini di cinema." *Rinascita*, 25 August 1967, p. 26.
Foglietti, Mario. "Tra un Brecht e un antibrecht c'è il posto per un altro Galileo." *Il popolo*, 25 November 1967, p. 11.
Gh., G. "Ho realizzato il mio film per combattere l'intolleranza." *La stampa*, 3 September 1968, p. 7.
Calcagno, Giorgio. "La regista del 'Galileo' spiega perché fa dei film anticlericali." *La stampa*, 21 August 1969, p. 7.
Stampa, Carla. "La regista dei film che scottano." *Epoca*, 17 May 1970, pp. 134–139.
Sorteni, Marco. "Una cinepresa sull'anima dei giovani." *Domenica del corriere*, 26 May 1970, p. 36.
"Crisi e avvenire del cinema nel giudizio dei giovani autori." *Voce repubblicana*, 14–15 July 1970, p. 5.
Calcagno, Giorgio. "Siamo tutti cannibali." *Gioventù*, 19 July 1970, pp. 23–27.
Foglietti, Mario. "Cinema politico in Italia." *Rivista del cinematografo*, no. 11 (November 1970): 517–524.
De Sanctis, Elena. "I films scomodi di Liliana Cavani." *Vita francescana*, December 1970, pp. 312–315.
Ciattaglia, Clemente. "Colloqui sul Vangelo: Incontro con Liliana Cavani." *Il popolo*, 16 May 1971, p. 9.

"Il questionario: Per chi si scrive un romanzo? Perché si gira un film?" *Bianco e nero* 33, nos. 5–6 (1972): 68–116.

Langlois, Gérard. "Liliana Cavani: 'I cannibali.' " *Lettres Françaises*, 12 April 1972, p. 18.

Cervoni, Albert. "Autour de 'I cannibali.' " *L'Humanité*, 19 April 1972, p. 10.

Verdi, E. "Entretien avec Liliana Cavani." *Cinéma* (Paris) 167 (June 1972): 144–147.

"Il parere di." *Skema* 4 (July 1972): 47–48.

Maraini, Dacia. "Liliana Cavani." In *Ma tu chi eri? Interviste sull'infanzia*, pp. 75–87. Milan: Bompiani, 1973.

Santuari, Aurora. "Gli assassini fanno mea culpa." *Paese sera*, 27 February 1973, p. 3.

Surchi, Sergio. "I nazisti si confessano." *La nazione*, 6 March 1973, p. 9.

Zambonini, Franca. "Le battaglie di Liliana Cavani." *Famiglia cristiana*, 24 June 1973, pp. 27–31.

Saitta, Luigi. "Una vicenda di criminali di guerra." *Osservatore romano*, 18 July 1973, p. 5.

Leone, Anna Maria. "Contesto ma credo." *Il messaggero*, 16 December 1973, p. 3.

Ciattaglia, Clemente. "Incontro con Liliana Cavani, regista." In *Voci d'oggi sul vangelo*, pp. 63–69. Rome: Edizioni Cinque Lune, 1974.

Zanelli, Dario. "Cinema italiano ultima leva." *Skema* 6 (January 1974): 7–10.

Rondi, Gian Luigi. "Liliana Cavani: 'Milarepa è un viaggio nel contrario.' " *Il tempo*, 27 January 1974, p. 12.

Re, Luisella. "La guerra dei sexy." *Stampa sera*, 31 January 1974, p. 9.

C., G. [Calcagno, Giorgio]. "Dal Tibet alle SS." *La stampa*, 6 February 1974, p. 6.

Fegatelli, Renzo. "Milarepa il San Francesco del Tibet." *Fiera letteraria*, 10 March 1974, pp. 3–6.

Grant, Jacques. "Liliana Cavani: La Révolution démocratique." *Combat*, 5 April 1974, p. 13.

Tremois, Claude-Marie. "Nous avons tous en nous un 'piccolo' de nazisme." *Télérama*, 6 April 1974, pp. 64–66.

Lane, John Francis. "Italy's Liliana Cavani—Appreciated More Abroad." *Daily American*, 14–15 April 1974, p. 5.

Courtet, François. "Les Rayons X du nazisme." *Nouvel Observateur*, 22 April 1974, pp. 58–59.

Costantini, Costanzo. "La censurata." *Il messaggero*, 27 April 1974, p. 3.

Nobécourt, Jacques. "Liliana Cavani: 'Ho cercato di spiegare cosa c'è dietro il crimine nazista.' " *Il globo* (Rome), 28 April 1974, p. 7.

Beria, Chiara. "Sei donna? Sotto." *Panorama*, 2 May 1974, pp. 98–100.

"Liliana Cavani: Perché ho fatto questo film sulla peste 1920–45." *L'umanità*, 6 May 1974, p. 26.

Clouzot, Claire. "Liliana Cavani: Le Mythe, le sexe et la révolte." *Ecran*, no. 26 (June 1974): 36–46.

Maillet, Dominique. "Entretien avec Liliana Cavani." *Cinématographe*, no. 8 (June–July 1974): 37–39.

Giacomelli, Barbara, and Tonino Nieddu. "Liliana Cavani: Una religione senza complessi." *Vita pastorale* 62 (December 1974): 48–53.

Stuart, Alexander. "Consciousness and Conscience." *Films and Filming* 21 (February 1975): 10–15.

Arias, Juan. "Democrazia è rivoluzione." *Critica meridionale*, 20 March 1975, pp. 5–6.

"Liliana Cavani." *Playboy* (Italian ed.), May 1975, pp. 21–26.

Granzotto, Emilia, and Giuliano Gallo. "Sedotti dal nero?" *Panorama*, 9 October 1975, pp. 116–124.

Mori, Anna Maria. "Insieme ai critici, anche gli spettatori hanno votato contro gli angeli custodi." *La repubblica*, 11 May 1976, p. 12.

"Liliana Cavani e Félix Guattari: Una conversazione." In L. Cavani, Franco Arcalli, and Italo Moscati, *Al di là del bene e del male*, pp. 171–180. Turin: Einaudi, 1977.

Brancourt, G. "Breve rencontre . . . avec Liliana Cavani." *Ecran*, 15 March 1977, pp. 10–11.

"Liliana Cavani . . . al di là del bene e del male." *Vogue* (Italian ed.), April 1977, pp. 114–117, 137–138.

Gasperi, Anne de. "Liliana Cavani au 'Quotidien': Nous vivons sur le crépuscule des idéologies des autres siècles." *Quotidien de Paris*, 5 October 1977, p. 15.

Clouzot, Claire. "Liliana Cavani, Nietzsche et l'éros." *Le Matin*, 6 October 1977, p. 26.

Bianciotti, Hector. "Liliana Cavani: 'La Plus Belle Création de Lou Andréas Salomé, c'est sa vie.' " *Nouvel Observateur*, 10 October 1977, pp. 76–77.

Calcagno, Giorgio. "La Cavani, regista dello scandalo." *La stampa*, 12 October 1977, p. 7.

Fanali, Rossella. "E il 'superuomo' si arrese alla . . . superdonna." *Giorni*, 12 October 1977, pp. 51–54.

Rondoni, Enrico. " 'A ciascuno il suo.' " *L'umanità*, 29 October 1977, p. 5.

Costantini, Costanzo. "Al di là del vero e del falso." *Il messaggero*, 2 November 1977, p. 3.

Tornabuoni, Lietta. " 'Perché il mio cinema è sempre crudele.' " *Corriere della sera*, 4 November 1977, p. 3.

Coletti, Lina. "Scandalo a tre." *L'europeo*, 11 November 1977, pp. 86–87.

Clouzot, Claire. "Entretien avec Liliana Cavani." *Ecran*, 15 November 1977, pp. 55–56.

Arias, Juan. "Cavani: Un enforque erótico de la vida de Nietzsche." *El País*, 7 January 1978, p. 33.

———. "Asi es Cavani." *El País*, 2 April 1978, pp. 26–31.

Galimberti, Carlo. "Sfumata 'Lulu' la Cavani si dà al teatro." *Corriere della sera*, 14 September 1978, p. 19.

Giglio, Rolando. "E Stipo mormorò: Che passi lo straniero." *Il messaggero*, 15 February 1979, p. 3.

"Tre miliardi di spettatori." *La repubblica*, 18 March 1979, p. 8.

Moscati, Italo. "Liliana mi ha tolto la pelle." *Amica*, 3 October 1979, pp. 61–62.

Mori, Anna Maria. "Il Galileo arriva in TV? Liliana Cavani (forse) ha vinto la sua battaglia." *La repubblica*, 24 November 1979, p. 14.

Garcia del Vall, Arnoldo. *Liliana Cavani*. Madrid: Editorial Fundamentos, 1980.

Pisano, Isabel. "Liliana Cavani." In *Alla ricerca di un sogno: Appuntamento con il cinema italiano*, pp. 117–127. Rome: Edizioni dell'Ateneo, 1980.

Tassone, Aldo. "Liliana Cavani." In *Parla il cinema italiano*, 2:107–142. Milan: Il Formichiere, 1980.

Santuari, Aurora. "Liliana Cavani: Positiva ambiguità." *Paese sera*, 29 May 1980, p. 19.

Rienzi, Maria Teresa. "Napoli, una Babilonia al centro del mondo." *L'unità*, 29 January 1981, p. 11.

Rondi, Gian Luigi. "Liliana Cavani: 'La pelle' ricordando anche Malaparte." *Il tempo*, 22 March 1981, p. 12.

Tornabuoni, Lietta. " 'La pelle è una nostra bandiera.' " *La stampa*, 23 May 1981, p. 3.

Porro, Maurizio. "Malaparte? Non mi interessa: Io non ho voluto raccontare tutta quella storia." *Corriere della sera*, 23 May 1981, p. 26.

Zampa, Fabrizio. "Ho un solo messaggio: Raccontare." *Il messaggero*, 7 June 1981, p. 10.

Mita, Alina. "Cavani: Non invento crudeltà." *Giornale di Sicilia*, 6 October 1981, p. 3.

Arias, Juan. "Liliana Cavani: 'La piel somo todos.' " *El Paìs*, 28 November 1981, pp. 4–5.

Cassano, Dolores. "Ahi, Carpi, Carpi mia!" *Bologna incontri*, December 1981, pp. 40–41.

Spartà, Santino. "Il servo spietato." In *Vuole scegliere una parabola?*, pp. 123–128. Milan: Edizioni Paoline, 1982.

Rondi, Gian Luigi. "Liliana Cavani: Oltre la porta un segreto di famiglia." *Il tempo*, 10 January 1982, p. 12.

———. "Liliana Cavani: Ho fatto un film come mi piaceva farlo." *Il tempo*, 4 September 1982, p. 13.

"Al cinema con Liliana Cavani." *La repubblica*, 7 January 1983, p. 7.

"L'Italia? Io la vedo in questo quadro." *Tuttolibri*, 24 September 1983, pp. 4–5.

Paolozzi, Letizia. "Ora voglio fare quello scomodo film sulla Weil." *L'unità*, 23 November 1983, p. 9.

Spaak, Catherine. "Liliana Cavani." In *Ventisei donne*, pp. 113–119. Milan: Mondadori, 1984.

Tornabuoni, Lietta. "Cavani nella tragedia di Moro." *La stampa*, 2 October 1984, p. 19.

Pisu, Renata. "Una passione privata e scandalosa nel Giappone tedesco della Cavani." *La stampa*, 22 February 1985, p. 23.

Cervone, Paolo. "Liliana Cavani: 'Eros in kimono.' " *Corriere della sera*, 17 April 1985, p. 23.

Mori, Anna Maria. "Passione a quattro con idolo in kimono." *La repubblica*, 18 April 1985, p. 17.

Pisu, Renata. "Vi svelo i segreti del mio amico Tanizaki." *Tuttolibri*, 3 August 1985, p. 3.

Pavoni, Anna. "Liliana Cavani: Amo l'amore." *Ciak* 1 (October 1985): 82–84.

Corallo, Fabrizio. "Il piacere è tutto mio." *Panorama*, 6 October 1985, p. 8.

Monteverdi, Germana. "Ho scoperto i sentimenti." *Oggi*, 30 October 1985, pp. 57–58.

Bellentani, Luciana. "I peccati di Berlino." *Amica*, 28 November 1985, pp. 70, 74–75.

Mölter, Margit. "Eine Italienerin Schreibt Filmgeschichte." *Harper's Bazaar* (German ed.), November–December 1985, pp. 110–114.

Barone, Antonella. "Cavani interior." *Prima visione cinematografica*, December 1985, pp. 36–38.

Caruso, Armando. "Cavani e la Medea all'Opéra." *La stampa*, 2 March 1986, p. 21.

Montaigne, Pierre. "Liliana Cavani: Amours interdites." *Le Figaro*, 23 April 1986, p. 37.

Joecker, Jean-Pierre. "Liliana Cavani." *Masques*, no. 5 (May 1986): 52–57.

Paloscia, Alberto. "Medea fa la rivoluzione." *L'unità*, 26 September 1986, p. 13.

Palazzeschi, Massimo. "Liliana Cavani: 'Io ed il cinema.' " *Piazza Grande* (Arezzo) 3, no. 23 (February 1987): 44–45.

Vaccari, Luigi. "Quel numero parla." *Il messaggero*, 2 February 1987, p. 5.

Clavarino, Ferdinando. "Creatività e successo del manager . . . ovvero la moltiplicazione del proprio prodotto." *Kybernetes*, no. 10 (December 1987): 18–20.

Spiga, Vittorio. "Mickey, un santo per la Cavani." *La nazione*, 14 February 1988, p. 11.

Cambria, Adele. "Liliana Cavani: Dal Galileo al S. Francesco." *Minerva dossier*, no. 10 (October 1988): 25–26.

Satta, Gloria. "Un altissimo contatto." *Il messaggero*, 4 October 1988, p. 14.

Mori, Anna Maria. "Cavani: Francesco un uomo completo." *La repubblica*, 18 November 1988, p. 29.

Riches, Pierre. "Il Vangelo alla lettera." In L. Cavani and R. Mazzoni, *Francesco*, pp. 125–143. Milan: Leonardo, 1989.

"A colloquio con Liliana Cavani." *Immagine e pensiero* 6 (January–March 1989): 26–28.

B., P. "Non è Francesco." *Epoca*, 5 March 1989, p. 65.

Fiore, Titta. "Un santo del futuro." *Il mattino*, 18 March 1989, p. 14.

Crespi, Alberto. "Francesco parte seconda: Il contatto con Dio." *L'unità*, 21 March 1989, p. 20.

Saitta Luigi, "Liliana Cavani: 'Ho filmato il sogno di San Francesco.' " *Il tempo*, 21 March 1989, p. 16.

Satta, Gloria. "Ecco l'uomo Francesco." *Il messaggero*, 21 March 1989, p. 18.

Spiga, Vittorio. "Laudato sii, San Francesco." *La nazione*, 21 March 1989, p. 9.

"La sua esperienza ci costringe a ridare bellezza ad ogni uomo." *L'avvenire*, 23 March 1989, p. 15.

Cavallo, Rita. "San Francesco: Un modello di vita possibile (per tutti)." *Prospettive nel mondo*, 14 (April 1989), 145–147.

Di Palma, Guido, and Anne Grillet-Aubert. "Liliana Cavani." *Orologi* (Rome), April 1989, pp. 78–82.

Parodi, Enrico. "Ecco il cantico per fratello Gol: 'Oggi il mio San Francesco predica tra i tifosi.' " *Gazzetta sportiva*, 2 April 1989, p. 11.

Poltronieri, Federica. "Di questo fraticello sono quasi innamorata." *Oggi*, 12 April 1989, p. 110.

Balsamo, Beatrice. "Il mio Francesco e la sua nudità." *Avvenimenti* (Rome), 19 April 1989, pp. 68–69.

Moretti, Paola. "Intervista con Liliana Cavani, regista di 'Francesco.' " *Video-star* (Milan), May 1989, pp. 20–25.

Ferenczi, Aurélien. "Le Miracle de Saint Rourke." *Quotidien de Paris*, 19 May 1989, p. 31.

Tranchant, Marie-Noëlle. "Une Auréole pour 'la Cavani.' " *Le Figaro*, 19 May 1989, p. 41.

"Mickey, Francesco, Dieu, l'IRA at les autres." *Le Figaro*, 22 May 1989, p. 35.

Neri, Emma. "Non è Francesco." *Il sabato*, 27 May 1989, pp. 66–67.

Magno, Vito. "Liliana Cavani: Cambia la vita chi si avvicina a Dio." *Rogate Ergo* (Rome) 2, nos. 6–7 (1989): 23–26.

"Liliana parla di Chiara." *Laurentianum* 31, nos. 1–2 (1990): 405–412.

Marrone, Gaetana. "L'attualità di *Francesco*: Incontro con Liliana Cavani." *L'Anello che non tiene* 2 (Fall 1990): 43–55.

Paternò, Cristiana. "Registi in coro: La guerra è solo stupida." *L'unità*, 16 January 1991, p. 12.

Guerrini, Loretta. "La soglia della filmabilità del sacro." *Il cantico* 58, nos. 1–2 (1991): 8–9.

———. "Un cinema alla ricerca dell'ingaggio migliore." In AA. VV., *Il Signore ti dia pace*, pp. 165–172. Celebrazioni centenarie dell'ordine francescano secolare. Dalla regola di Niccolò IV ad oggi 1289–1989. Bologna: Edizioni Francescane, [1991].

Gianeri, Donata. "Cavani: 'Un film per dare voce al silenzio.' " *Stampa sera*, 25 March 1991, p. 21.

Costa, Silvia. " 'Sogno di fare un film sulla Resurrezione.' " *La discussione* (Rome), 1 June 1991, pp. 16–17. Reprinted in *Tra l'anima e il mondo*, edited by Mauro Calcagno and Piero Martino, pp. 47–55. Rome: Edizioni Cinque Lune, 1991.

Paternò, Cristiana. " 'Sordità, la mia nuova eresia.' " *L'unità*, 15 August 1991, p. 22.

Madeo, Liliana. "Liliana Cavani: Comunione e provocazione." *La stampa*, 9 November 1991, p. 15.

Neri Emma. "Diversi, ma normali." *Il sabato*, 30 November 1991, pp. 83–84.

Manin, Giuseppina. "Cavani: Storia d'amore senza parole." *Corriere della sera*, 2 December 1991, p. 35.

Zordan Amalia. "Liliana Cavani: I luoghi della memoria." In *Carpi*, edited by Cristina Brigidini and Pier Paride Tedeschini, pp. 26–28. Milan: Edizioni Condé Nast, 1992.

Neri, Emma. "Figli di un dio minore sulla via di damasco." *Film cronache* (ANCCI) 6, no. 29 (1992): 32–36.

"Esiste discriminazione?" *Emigrazione* 24 (March 1992): 47–48.

Manin, Giuseppe. "La Cavani 'tuona': Disobbedite alla TV." *Corriere della sera*, 14 March 1992, p. 39.

Giannelli, Luca. "Quali valori per la società di domani." *Il popolo*, 14 March 1992, p. 15.

Piersanti, Andrea. "Al di là del rumore." *Rivista del cinematografo*, n.s., 62 (April 1992): 7–10.

Pullmann, Richard. "Mickey Rourke: Dal Ring a 'WhiteSands.' " *Harper's Bazaar* (Italian ed.), July–August 1992, pp. 118–121.

Tornabuoni, Lietta. "Cavani: Una guerra d'amore nel mondo del silenzio." *La stampa*, 17 January 1993, p. 23.

Sossi, Tiziano. "L'ambizione dell'autenticità." *Film cronache*, no. 35 (January–February 1993): pp. 47–51.

Guerrini, Loretta. "Dove siete? Io sono qui: Conversazione con Liliana Cavani." *Cineclub* (Rome), no. 7 (January–March 1993): 43–45.

———. "La dignità dell'esistenza." *Il cantico* (Rome) 60, no. 5 (1993): 26–27.

Paniccia, Valeria. "Il coraggio e l'amore." *Elite*, no. 6 (June 1993): 118–121.

Porcari, Giulia. "Dove siete? Io sono qui." *V.S.P.* (Voci Silenzi Pensieri), no. 33 (June–July 1993): 31–33.

Bolzoni, Francesco. "Cavani: Difendo i sordomuti." *L'avvenire*, 18 August 1993, p. 19.

Neri, Emma. "Sordo e son desto." *Il sabato*, 21 August 1993, pp. 58–60.

Grassi, Giovanna. " 'Un amore oltre i rumori della vita.' " *Corriere della sera*, 24 August 1993, p. 20.

Cervone, Paolo. "Le voci del silenzio." *Corriere della sera* (Supplemento), 26 August 1993, pp. 68–71.

Bagnoli, Marco. "Liliana Cavani: 'Dove siete? io sono . . . a Carpi.' " *Resto del Carlino*, 27 August 1993, p. 9.

"Liliana Cavani." *Non capovolgere* (Mantua), no. 4 (September 1993): 35–43.

Detassis, Piera. "Dove Siete? Io sono qui." *Ciak*, no. 9 (September 1993): p. 17.

Aspesi, Natalia. "Tra il silenzio e la famiglia due donne narrano il dolore: Le difficili scelte di Cavani e Isserman." *La repubblica*, 2 September 1993, p. 27.

Corradi, Corrado. "Al confronto, miseri dialoghi i nostri." *Il giorno*, 2 September 1993, p. 15.

V., S. [Spiga, Vittorio]. "Cavani: Dalla parte del pudore." *Resto del Carlino*, 2 September 1993, p. 17.

Mancino, Anton Giulio. "Dalla parte dei pù disagiati." *Paese sera*, 2 September 1993, p. 21.

Vaccari, Luigi. "Alla fine arriva la parola." *Il messaggero*, 2 September 1993, p. 19.

"Libertà e coercizione nella esperienza culturale della donna di oggi: Intervista a Liliana Cavani." *Psicologia, Psicopatologia e Psicosomatica della donna* 2, no. 1 (1994): 33–34.

"Liliana Cavani." In *Memoria, mito, storia*, edited by Alessandro Amaducci et al., pp. 45–54. Turin: Archivio Nazionale Cinematografico della Resistenza, 1994.

"Liliana Cavani." *Rassegna di storia contemporanea* (Modena) 1, no. 2 (1994): 166–169.

Guerrini, Loretta. "Conversazione con Liliana Cavani." *Cineclub*, no. 21 (January–March 1994): 13–15.

"Liliana Cavani." *Non capovolgere* (Mantua), no. 5 (February 1994): 32–33.

"I giovani registi sono costretti a pensare in piccolo." *Momento sera* (Rome), 22 April 1994, p. 27.

Mérigeau, Pascal. "Les Mots qu'il faut." *Le Monde*, 28 April 1994, p. 7.

Nayeri, Farah. "The Serenity of Speech Cloaked in Silence." *European Élan*, 29 April 1994, p. 7.

Di Fortunato, Eleonora, and Mario Paolinelli. "Il doppiaggio e gli autori." *Produzione e cultura* (Rivista bimestrale del sindacato nazionale scrittori) 8 (May–August 1994): 42–46.

Tornabuoni, Lietta. "Cavani: Solo la Storia ci salverà." *La stampa*, 2 July 1994, p. 13.

———. "Riscopriamo la Storia." *Rivista del cinematografo e delle comunicazioni sociali* 64 (August–September 1994): 36–37.

Durante, Francesco. "Quella volta che la RAI mi censurò." *Il mattino*, 3 August 1994, p. 13.

Moscati, Italo. "Liliana Cavani: 'Ignoranza, madre di tutti i nazismi.'" *Il messaggero*, 14 September 1994, p. 19.

Grassi, Giovanna. "Così spezzate il cuore al mio Francesco." *Corriere della sera*, 2 October 1994, p. 31.

T., L. [Tornabuoni, Lietta]. "Cavani: La Rai? Un manicomio." *La stampa*, 2 October 1994, p. 24.

"A proposito delle biblioteche." In *La biblioteca desiderata*, edited by Massimo Cecconi, pp. 114–115. Milan: Provincia di Milano, 1995.

Almansi, Guido. *Tra cinema e teatro*. Venice: Marsilio, 1995.

"Liliana Cavani." In *Parigi-Roma: 50 anni di coproduzioni italo-francesi (1945–1995)*, edited by Jean A. Gili and Aldo Tassone, pp. 66–68. Florence: Editrice Il Castoro, 1995.

Amicone, Luigi. "Bastian contrario." *Tracce* (Rivista di comunicazione e liberazione) 22 (May 1995): 42–43.

Camisasca, Massimo. "Liliana Cavani." In *Volti e incontri*, pp. 29–30. Milan: Jaca Book, 1996.

Man., S. "La regista di 'Francesco': Un doppio premio." *La stampa*, 24 February 1996, p. 14.

"La regista riflette." *Dante* (Utrecht), June 1996, pp. 12–14.

Calcagno, Giorgio. "Liliana Cavani: Un padre trovato alla RAI." *La stampa*, 7 August 1996, p. 21.

Works about Cavani

A., L. "Britt Ekland a Milano." *Corriere della sera*, 3 April 1969, p. 15.

A., M. "Si è conclusa la storia di un santo senza retorica." *Stampa sera*, 9 May 1966, p. 8.

A., R. "Milarepa." *L'unità*, 23 March 1974, p. 9.

Accolti Gil, Mario. "Al di qua del bene e del male." *Mondo operaio* (Rome), November 1977, pp. 135–136.

Acconciamessa, Mirella. "Una storia d'amore sul filo della follia." *L'unità*, 11 June 1971, p. 7.

Adler, S. "Liliana Cavani." *Cinema Papers* (Melbourne) 41 (December 1982): 524–527, 579.

Alessandrini, Ludovico. "Momenti delle telecamere." *Osservatore romano*, 10 May 1964, p. 5.

———. "Momenti delle telecamere." *Osservatore romano*, 1 January 1965, p. 3.

Alessi, Rino. "Tanizaki nel Terzo Reich." *La repubblica*, 2 July 1985, p. 20.

Alichino. "La pericolosa Cavani." *Settegiorni*, 15 September 1968, p. 32

Allezaud, Robert. "Un Nouveau Visage du fascisme." *Télécinè*, no. 189 (June 1974): 16–18.

———. "Au-delà. . . ." *Télécinè*, no. 223 (December 1977): 39–40.

Amaducci, Alessandro, et al., eds. "Liliana Cavani." In *Memoria, mito, storia*, pp. 45–54. Turin: Archivio Nazionale Cinematografico della Resistenza, 1994.

Appiotti, Mirella. "Liliana Cavani spara a zero sui cannibali." *Stampa sera*, 23 April 1970, p. 6.

Arbasino, Alberto. "La Bile Nera, le maschere, il sesso, tre mezze calze e tanti orrori. . . ." *La repubblica*, 30 November 1977, p. 14.

Argentieri, Mino. "A Venezia è morta la vecchia mostra." *Rinascita*, 13 September 1968, p. 26.

———. "Il tarlo del censore." *Rinascita*, 20 September 1968, pp. 23–24.

———. "Un'Antigone del dissenso cattolico." *Rinascita*, 15 May 1970, p. 23.

———. "Portiere di notte." *Quadrangolo* (1974), pp. 68–70.

———. "Liliana Cavani tra magia e storia." *Rinascita*, 26 April 1974, p. 23.

———. "Storia di una celebre trinità." *Rinascita*, 18 November 1977, p. 38.

———. " 'La pelle': Una Napoli da presepe." *Rinascita*, 23 October 1981, p. 32.

———. "Natale al buio della sala." *Rinascita*, 28 December 1985, p. 20.

———. "L'amaro poverello." *Rinascita*, 8 April 1989, p. 20.

Aspesi, Natalia. "Scusi, qual è il colore della disperazione?" *La repubblica*, 23 May 1981, p. 17.

Assayas, Olivier. "L'Académie du cinéma." *Cahiers du Cinéma* 326 (1981): 16–21.

Augias, C. "Sotto la frusta di Lou Salomè." *La repubblica*, 28 July, 1977, pp. 12–13.

Auty, Martyn. "Oltre la porta." *Monthly Film Bulletin* 51 (March 1984): 81.

"L'avventura di Milarepa: Nuovo film TV di Liliana Cavani." *L'avanti*, 22 August 1973, p. 5.

B., A. "Tra San Francesco e Lawrence D'Arabia." *Il borghese*, 21 May 1989, pp. 180–181.

B., C. [Bechtold]. "Portier de nuit." *Cinématographe* (Paris), no. 8 (June–July 1974): 36–37.

B., C. "Nietzsche persegue un'idea fissa e non è certamente la filosofia." *L'avanti*, 29 October 1977, p. 14.

B., G. "Il caso 'Portiere di notte': Come sempre censura d'idee. Assurde accuse al film di Liliana Cavani." *Il messaggero*, 29 March 1974, p. 12.

———. "Sequestrati 'Simona' e 'Il portiere di notte.' " *Il messaggero*, 18 April 1974, p. 15.

B., J. "En competition gangsters (Altman) et sages (Cavani)." *Le Monde*, 17 May 1974, p. 23.

———. "Milarepa." *Le Monde*, 26 February 1975, p. 23.

B., P. "Cannibali riscattati da giovani in rivolta." *Il giorno*, 22 April 1970, p. 19.

———. "Antigone a Milano." *Il giorno*, 3 May 1970, p. 17.

B., P. [Bonitzer, Pascal], and S. T. "Anti-rétro: Entretien avec Michel Foucault." *Cahiers du Cinéma*, nos. 251–252 (July–August 1974): 5–15.

———. "Au delà du bien et du mal." *Cahiers du Cinéma*, no. 284 (January 1978): 55.

B., S. G. "Il guitto di Waterloo e l'inchiesta nascosta." *Giornale d'Italia*, 12 May 1964, p. 13.

———. "Un 'Francesco' tendenzioso e Marilyn agli esordi." *Giornale d'Italia*, 10 May 1966, p. 13.

B., V. "TV: 'Anni d'Europa' e il paroliere di turno." *Corriere della sera*, 20 October 1962, p. 8.

———. "Le donne sapienti." *Corriere della sera*, 22 December 1962, p. 8.

Babert, Caroline. "Liliana Cavani: Au-delà de la morale." *Le Matin*, 25 November 1981, p. 31.

Bachmann, Gideon. "La pelle senza Malaparte." *Gioia*, 27 April 1981, pp. 32–37.

Baignères, Claude. "La Fête de l'horreur." *Le Figaro*, 23–24 May 1981, p. 28.

———. "Les Horreurs d'une guerre." *Le Figaro*, 26 November 1981, p. 27.

———. "Fatalité de l'inceste." *Le Figaro*, 4 May 1983, p. 28.

———. "Galipettes." *Le Figaro*, 26–27 April 1986, p. 35.

———. "Odeurs . . . de sainteté." *Le Figaro*, 20–21 May 1989, p. 34.

Banti, Anna. "Un maestro e un'esordiente." *Approdo letterario*, October–December 1968, pp. 151–154.

Baracco, Adriano. "Cannibalismo retorico." *Lo specchio*, 10 May 1970, p. 34.

Barbato, Andrea. "Non confondere sacro e profano." *L'espresso*, 21 August 1988, p. 21.

Barbry, F.-R. "Portier de nuit, Liliana Cavani sur fond de barbarie." *Cinéma* (Paris), no. 444 (June 1988): 29.

Bardelli, Luigi. "Finalmente dalla negazione una risposta positiva." *Cineforum* 10 (May–August 1970): 126–129.

Barker, Felix. "The Classic You May Never See." *Evening News*, 17 January 1974, p. 2C.

Baroncelli, Jean de. " 'Sunday, Bloody Sunday' de John Schlesinger, présenté à Venise." *Le Monde*, 7 September 1971, p. 18.

———. " 'I cannibali,' de Liliana Cavani." *Le Monde*, 14 April 1972, p. 27.

————. " 'Portier de nuit,' de Liliana Cavani." *Le Monde*, 5 April 1974, p. 25.

Baudin, Brigitte. "Liliana Cavani dans le monde du silence." *Le Figaro*, 29 April 1994, p. 31.

Béhar, Henri. "Mickey Rourke ne parle pas aux oiseaux." *Le Monde*, 11 May 1989, p. 6. Reprinted as "Rourke: 'La Cavani? Mi ha tolto tutte le inibizioni.' " *La stampa*, 19 May 1989, p. 25.

Bellocchio, Piergiorgio. "Era meglio Malaparte." *Panorama*, 16 November 1981, p. 161.

Beltramo Ceppi, Claudia. "Nietzsche-Cavani nel bene e nel male: La vera storia della 'trinità.' " *La repubblica*, 29 October 1977, p. 15.

Benoist, Jean-Marie. "Une Voyure du pauvre." *Le Monde*, 10 November 1977, pp. 20–21.

Ber. "Senza smalto." *Il piccolo*, 24 May 1964, p. 6.

————. "Vita di San Francesco." *Il piccolo*, 7 May 1966, p. 7.

Berenice. "Quando incontrai il Nietzsche della Cavani." *Paese sera*, 30 October 1977, p. 16.

Berets, Ralph. "Recent Cinematic Images of Nazism: 'The Night Porter' and 'Seven Beauties.' " *Film and History* 9 (December 1979): 73–81.

Bernari, Carlo. "Quei giorni terribili, quel terribile Curzio: L'incubo che spaccò Napoli." *Il mattino*, 13 November 1980, p. 5.

Bianchi, Riccardo. "Ma per la Cavani resta un mistero." *L'europeo*, 18 November 1977, p. 9.

Bignardi, Irene. "Uno, nessuno centomila Mickey Rourke." *Venerdì di repubblica*, 22 January 1988, pp. 101–103.

————. "Se il telefono non squilla . . . Cavani racconta la vita con l'handicap." *La repubblica*, 2 September 1993, p. 26.

Binet, Violaine. "L'Art d'être femme." *L'Epress* (Paris), 10 March 1989, p. 77.

Bir. [Biraghi]. "L'ospite." *Il messaggero*, 11 March 1972, p. 12.

————. "Milarepa." *Il messaggero*, 23 March 1974, p. 12.

————. "Il portiere di notte." *Il messaggero*, 14 April 1974, p. 14.

Biraghi, Guglielmo. "Un Galileo moderno." *Il messaggero*, 3 September 1968, p. 10.

————. "Carné contro il sistema giudiziario." *Il messaggero*, 5 September 1971, p. 12.

————. "Al di là del bene e del male." *Il messaggero*, 29 October 1977, p. 12.

————. "Morbosità e incomprensioni fra vincitori e vinti." *Il messaggero*, 2 October 1981, p. 9.

————. "I sequestrati di Marrakesh." *Il messaggero*, 29 October 1982, p. 10.

————. "Se il sesso è potere." *Il messaggero*, 31 October 1985, p. 15.

Blasi, Bruno. "E io dissi: O Mickey o niente." *Panorama*, 26 March 1989, p. 145.

Blume, Mary. "Liliana Cavani and the Young." *International Herald Tribune*, 15–16 April 1972, p. 14.

————. "Liliana Cavani's Aim: 'I Sow Disquiet.' " *International Herald Tribune*, 22–23 October 1977, p. 12.

Bo, Fabio. "Evviva Francesco." *Il messaggero*, 15 March 1989, p. 33.

Bo, L. "La Cavani: 'Il nazismo non è morto del tutto.' " *Corriere della sera*, 2 April 1974, p. 13.

Bocchi, Lorenzo. "La Cavani nell'inferno del sesso." *Corriere della sera*, 6 October 1977, p. 16.

Bodard, Lucien. "Derrière la guerre: Le Cortège des horreurs." *Le Figaro*, 25 November 1981, p. 30.

Bogani, Giovanni. "Giotto e gli altri." *La nazione*, 24 March 1989, p. 11.

Bogarde, Dirk. *An Orderly Man*. London: Triad Grafton, 1986.

Bolzoni, Francesco. " 'Cannibali' destinati a polemiche." *L'avvenire*, 26 April 1970, p. 12.

———. "Quel Francesco per amico." *L'avvenire*, 23 March 1989, p. 15.

———. "Terapia di gruppo." *Rivista del cinematografo* 59 (May 1989): 13.

———. "Giulietta e Romeo vincono il silenzio." *L'avvenire*, 2 September 1993, p. 19.

———. "La creatività degli handicappati." *Film cronache*, no. 39 (September–October 1993): 14–15.

Bondanella, Peter. *Italian Cinema from Neorealism to the Present*. New expanded ed. New York: Continuum, 1993.

Bongiovanni, Marco. "Temi e prospettive dei film di Venezia." *Rivista del cinematografo* 40 (November 1966): 688–691.

Bonitzer, Pascal. "Le Secret derrière la porte." *Cahiers du Cinéma*, nos. 251–252 (July–August 1974): 31–36.

Bonne-Ville, L. "La Peau." *Séquences*, no. 105 (July 1981): 12.

Bonuomo, Michele. "Un libro maledetto che affascinò la Cavani." *Mattino illustrato*, 15 November 1980, pp. 21–23.

Borelli, Sauro. "Le genti di Babele sono arrivate tra i dolori di Napoli." *L'unità*, 2 October 1981, p. 9.

———. "Sesso e alta diplomazia." *L'unità*, 31 October 1985, p. 13.

———. "Francesco-Rourke: il sangue e l'estasi." *L'unità*, 23 March 1989, p. 25.

———. "Cannes '89, il festival non fa la rivoluzione." *L'unità*, 7 May 1989, p. 20.

Bory, Jean-Louis. "Le Carnaval des spectres." *Nouvel Observateur*, 8 April 1974, p. 63. Reprinted as "Il portiere di notte." *Settegiorni*, 28 April 1974, pp. 3–4.

Bosisio, Paolo. "Liliana Cavani." *Belfagor* 33, no. 2 (1978): 173–190, 158.

Boujut, Michel. "Naples au baiser de fiel." *Nouvelles Littéraires*, 26 November 1981, p. 30.

Branca, Vittore. "Quando vedere è credere." *Il messaggero*, 7 June 1989, p. 18.

Braucourt, Guy. "Zakouski et premier choix." *Nouvelles Littéraires*, 13 May 1974, p. 23.

———. "Le Petit Juge, l'industriel et le mystique." *Nouvelles Littéraires*, 17 February 1975, p. 15.

———. "Au-delà du bien et du mal." *Nouvelles Littéraires*, 6 October 1977, p. 27.

Braudeau, Michel. "La Foi de Mickey." *Le Monde*, 21–22 May 1989, p. 9.

Brown, Geoff. "I cannibali." *BFI-Monthly Film Bulletin* 42 (December 1975): 258–259.

Brunetta, Gian Piero. *Forma e parola nel cinema*. Introduced by Gianfranco Folena. Padua: Liviana, 1970.

———. *Storia del cinema italiano dal 1945 agli anni ottanta*. Rome: Editori Riuniti, 1982.

———. *Cent'anni di cinema italiano*. Rome-Bari: Laterza, 1991.

Bursi, Giovanna. "A proposito di 'Francesco.' " *Frate Francesco* (Reggio Emilia), no. 5 (May 1989): 19–20.

Burvenich, Jos. "Tre autori a Venezia: Pasolini, Bene, Cavani." *Cineforum* 8 (October 1968): 565–566.

———. "Lo sguardo del cinema sul cristianesimo." *Cineforum* 10 (September 1970): 211–214.

Buscemi, Francesco. *Invito al cinema di Liliana Cavani*. Milan: Mursia, 1996.

Bz., U. "Il flagello della svastica." *La stampa*, 20 October 1962, p. 4.

―――. "Berlino in fiamme." *La stampa*, 27 October 1962, p. 4.

―――. "Donne intellettuali di trecento anni fa." *La stampa*, 22 December 1962, p. 4.

―――. "Una serata politica." *La stampa*, 29 December 1962, p. 4.

―――. "Burocrazia sotto accusa." *La stampa*, 24 May 1963, p. 4.

―――. "Mina recita 'Otello' accanto a Renzo Ricci." *La stampa*, 3 May 1964, p. 5.

―――. "Deludente il 'Cantatutto' con Milva, Villa e Arigliano: Vigorosa e coraggiosa puntata dell'inchiesta 'La casa in Italia.' " *La stampa*, 17 May 1964, p. 5.

―――. "I dispiaceri del sabato sera." *La stampa*, 24 May 1964, p. 5.

―――. "La donna e la Resistenza in un'inchiesta televisiva." *La stampa*, 6 August 1964, p. 4.

―――. "L'imputato Pétain." *La stampa*, 5 June 1965, p. 4.

―――. "Stasera il film 'Francesco di Assisi.' " *La stampa*, 6 May 1966, p. 4.

―――. "Francesco spaccato a metà." *La stampa*, 7 May 1966, p. 5.

C. "La parabola della Cavani." *La nazione*, 25 May 1973, p. 11.

C., A. "Cavani: Dove siete? Io sono qui." *Il giornale* (Milan), 28 September 1993, p. 21.

C., C. "La Cavani nell'inferno del manicomio." *Il messaggero*, 12 June 1971, p. 12.

―――. "Un film della Cavani sul tema della colpa." *Il messaggero*, 25 February 1973, p. 14.

―――. "Il mondo del cinema contro la censura." *Il messaggero*, 19 April 1974, p. 11.

―――. "Piano di lotta contro la censura delle forze del cinema italiano." *Il messaggero*, 20 April 1974, p. 15.

C., E. [Carrère]. "Au-delà du bien et du mal." *Positif* (Paris), no. 203 (February 1978): 73–74.

C., E. [Comuzio]. "La pelle." *Cineforum* 21 (November 1981): 78–80.

C., F. [Chalais, François]. "Le Scandale n'est plus ce qu'il était." *Le Figaro*, 6 September 1993, p. 29.

C., G. [Cremonini]. "Litanie storiche." *L'unità*, 20 October 1962, p. 7.

―――. "Germania demoniaca." *L'unità*, 27 October 1962, p. 7.

―――. "Controcanale: 'Stalin dal '34 al '40.'" *L'unità*, 22 December 1962, p. 7.

―――. "Controcanale: Conclusione infantile." *L'unità*, 29 December 1962, p. 7.

―――. "Controcanale: 'Ribalta' senza luci." Review of *La casa in Italia*. *L'unità*, 3 May 1964, p. 4.

―――. "Indagine sulla pace." *L'unità* (Milan), 8 May 1965, p. 9.

―――. "La donna nella Resistenza." *L'unità* (Milan), 10 May 1965, p. 6.

―――. "L''eroe' traditore." *L'unità* (Milan), 5 June 1965, p. 9.

―――. "Milarepa." *Cinema nuovo* 23 (May–June 1974): 216–217.

―――. "L'erotismo del nuovo cinema contro un sesso 'degradato.' " *La stampa*, 1 February 1975, p. 7.

―――. "Oltre la porta." *Cinema nuovo* 32 (February 1983): 55.

C., I. [Cipriani, Ivano]. "Galileo nelle mani di una donna." *Paese sera*, 19 October 1966, p. 1 (Radio-TV).

―――. "Cavani risponde ai suoi critici." *Paese sera*, 5 September 1968, p. 14.

C., J. L. [Cros]. "Au-delà du bien et du mal." *Revue du Cinéma*, no. 332 (October 1978): 25–26.

C., L. [Cordelli]. "Oltre la porta." *Positif*, no. 261 (November 1982): 41.

C., M. [Chion]. "Portier de nuit." *Positif*, no. 159 (May 1974): 74–75.

———. "La pelle." *Positif*, nos. 244–245 (July–August 1981): 101–102.

———. "Derrière la porte." *Cahiers du Cinéma* 347 (1983): 73–74.

C., U. "I cannibali." *L'unità*, 1 May 1970, p. 13.

Calabrese, Pietro. "Strehler e la Cavani protagonisti a Parigi." *Il messaggero*, 7 October 1977, p. 10.

Canby, Vincent. " 'The Night Porter' Is Romantic Pornography." *New York Times*, 13 October 1974, D1, 19.

———. "The Art of Turning Bad Reviews into Good Quotes." *New York Times*, 27 October 1974, D17.

———. "Ici Se Habla Euro-English." *New York Times*, 4 June 1989, sec. 2, pp. 1, 19. Translated as "Le lingue tagliate dei registi." *La stampa*, 10 June 1989, p. 13.

I cannibali: Guida alla lettura del film. Scheda Filmografica SPF no. 5. Rome: Centro Studi Sampaolofilm, 1982.

Cantelli, Alfio. "Napoli aspra della Cavani sulle tracce di Malaparte." *Giornale nuovo*, 25 September 1981, p. 11.

———. "Una giapponese amante-carnefice." *Giornale nuovo* (Milan), 15 November 1985, p. 19.

———. "Giallo a Venezia, Woody sogghigna: E il cinema italiano entra in gara con gli amori silenziosi di 'Dove siete? Io sono qui.' " *Il giornale* (Milan), 2 September 1993, p. 19.

Capdenac, Michel. "Cannes: Un Festival différent." *Lettres Françaises*, 27 May 1970, pp. 18–19.

Cappabianca, Alessandro. "Prodigi e incidenti sulle vie del cinema italiano." *Filmcritica* 25 (April 1974): 123–128.

Cappelletti, Vincenzo. "Le false certezze dell'accusato e degli inquisitori." *Retrospettive libri*, October 1981, pp. 18–20.

Cappelli, Valerio. "Io, enigmatica Santa Chiara." *Corriere della sera*, 5 April 1988, p. 27.

Caprara, Valerio. "Quei giorni crudeli delle signorine: La Cavani gira 'La pelle.' " *Mattino illustrato*, 15 November 1980, pp. 10–16.

———. "C'è un dandy che passeggia nell'inferno." *Il mattino*, 2 October 1981, p. 5.

———. "Francesco, il vagabondo di Dio." *Il mattino*, 25 March 1989, p. 13.

Carabba, Claudio, "Sui sentieri della banalità universale." *L'europeo*, 12 October 1981, p. 66.

———. "Storia di eros e di furore." *L'europeo*, 21 December 1985, p. 52.

———. "Il giullare di Io." *L'europeo*, 14 April 1989, p. 105.

Carancini, Gaetano. "Il 'Galileo' di Liliana Cavani dramma attuale dell'uomo di scienza." *Voce repubblicana*, 3–4 September 1968, p. 4.

———. "Galileo: Un occhiale contro l'inquisizione." *Voce repubblicana*, 24–25 February 1969, p. 5.

———. " 'I cannibali': Un film che affronta il problema del potere e della repressione." *Voce repubblicana*, 4–5 May 1970, p. 5.

Carbone, Giorgio. "Cavani commuove con l'amore tra 'i figli di un Dio minore.' " *La notte*, 2 September 1993, p. 15.

Cardini, Franco. "Fede e povertà." *Storia illustrata*, no. 376 (March 1989): 12–21.

Carmignani, Italo. "Francesco non torna ad Assisi." *La stampa*, 18 February 1988, p. 10.

Carotenuto, Aldo. "Quella minaccia che viene dall'alto." *Il mattino*, 3 September 1993, p. 15.

Caruso, S. Lucio. "Francesco, uomo normale." *Rivista del cinematografo* 40 (February 1966): 108–112. Reprinted in *Il mattino*, 6 May 1966, p. 9.

Casazza, Sandro. "Scandalosa trinità della Cavani." *La stampa*, 30 November 1977, p. 7.

Casolaro, Mario. "Galileo." *Film mese* 2 (August–September 1968): 99.

Castellano, Gianni. "I matti siamo noi." *Resto del Carlino*, 5 September 1971, p. 9.

Castello, Giulio Cesare. "Proibito scendere nel sottosuolo con la regista di notte." *Umanità*, 6 May 1974, p. 27.

Castrovilli, Mariangiola. "Cavani, ancora uno scandalo." *Il giornale*, 30 June 1985, p. 17.

Cavallaro, G. B. "Galileo." *Rivista del cinematografo* 41 (September–October 1968): 525–526.

———. "Il primo giorno dopo il diluvio." *Settegiorni*, 30 December 1973, pp. 24–25.

Cavallo, Angelo. "Un S. Francesco televisivo in formato ridottissimo." *Il mattino*, 9 May 1966, p. 17.

"Cavani: 'Ogni tre anni la stessa cosa.' " *La repubblica*, 10 November 1977, p. 14.

Cavicchioli, Luigi. "Cristo fra le automobili." *Domenica del corriere*, 12 May 1970, p. 100.

———. "Il nazi-portiere che ha dato scandalo." *Domenica del corriere*, 19 May 1974, pp. 68, 70.

Celani, Filippo. "Lo spettacolo della settimana: 'Francesco d'Assisi.' " *Osservatore romano*, 9–10 May 1966, p. 3.

Cervone, Paolo. "S. Francesco ha il volto di Rourke." *Corriere della sera*, 13 February 1988, p. 27.

———. " 'Mickey Rourke? Un santo perfetto.' " *Corriere della sera*, 21 March 1989, p. 25.

Cervoni, Albert. "En quête d'une 'morale.' " *L'Humanité*, 19 October 1977, p. 10.

Cesareo, Giovanni. " 'Francesco d'Assisi' storia di un ribelle." *L'unità* (Milan ed.), 7 May 1966, p. 11.

———. "Francesco non si piega alle regole." *L'unità*, 9 May 1966, p. 7.

Chalais, François. "Nietzsche dans la cloaque," *Le Figaro*, 8–9 October 1977, p. 29.

Champlin, Charles. "Love at First Rite in 'Night Porter.' " *Los Angeles Times*, 30 October 1974, sec. 4, p. 13.

Chapier, Henry. " 'François d'Assise' de Liliana Cavani compte parmi les véritables 'découvertes' de Venise." *Combat*, 20 September 1966, p. 8.

———. "La Grande Fête des cinéastes anarchistes." *Combat*, 6 September 1971, p. 13.

———. "*Au-delà* . . . de Liliana Cavani: Une nouvelle polémique autour de Nietzsche." *Quotidien de Paris*, 5 October 1977, p. 15.

Charesol, Georges. "Le Dernière Valse à Vienne." *Nouvelles Littéraires*, 15 April 1974, p. 21.

Chauvet, Louis. "Portier de nuit." *Le Figaro*, 6–7 April 1974, p. 24.

———. "Stavisky vu par Renais." *Le Figaro*, 15 May 1974, p. 26.

———. "Films au féminin." *Le Figaro*, 11 October 1977, p. 29.

Chazal, Robert. " 'Les Cannibales' contre tous les fascismes." *France-Soir*, 14 April 1972, p. 13.

Chauvet, Louis. " 'Portier de nuit' . . . L'amour monstre." *France-Soir*, 4 April 1974, p. 17.

——. " 'Milarepa': L'Aventure de l'esprit." *France-Soir*, 16 May 1974, p. 19.

——. " 'Milarepa': Le Voyage au bout de la conaissance." *France-Soir*, 21 February 1975, p. 21.

Ciment, M. "A Synopsis of the 1981 Cannes Film Festival." *Positif*, no. 144 (1981): 81–84.

Cincotti, Guido. "Francesco di Assisi." *Bianco e nero* 27 (July–August 1966): 186–188.

"Cinema italiano mobilitato contro censura e sequestri." *Corriere della sera*, 27 April 1974, p. 13.

"Il cinema reagisce contro i sequestri." *Il tempo*, 27 April 1974, p. 8.

Cini, Letizia. "E finalmente Mickey parlò." *La nazione*, 16 March 1988, p. 9.

Cip. [Cipriani, Ivano]. "Obiettivo su Hitler scatenato." *Paese sera*, 20 October 1962, p. 9.

——. "Si cerca il seme della follia nazi." *Paese sera*, 27 October 1962, p. 9.

——. "Il terzo Reich brucia." *Paese sera*, 27 October 1962, p. 9.

——. "Un telerapporto sul culto della personalità di Stalin." *Paese sera*, 22 December 1962, p. 9.

——. "Donne e Resistenza." *Paese sera*, 10 May 1965, p. 13.

——. "Il vecchio traditore." *Paese sera*, 5 June 1965, p. 15.

——. "Germania '36–37 tra riti pagani e primi lager." *Paese sera*, 13 September 1977, p. 13.

——. "Il mito della razza negli anni di Hitler." *Paese sera*, 20 September 1977, p. 15.

——. "Comincia la rotta di Hitler." *Paese sera*, 27 September 1977, p. 13.

Cipriani, Ivano. "Stalin alla TV." *Rinascita*, 29 December 1962, p. 26.

——. "Una rissa alle soglie della TV." *Paese sera*, 8 May 1964, p. 3.

——. "La casa in Italia, oggi." *Rinascita*, 9 May 1964, p. 27.

——. "La TV ha sospeso la 'Casa in Italia.' " *Paese sera*, 10 May 1964, p. 19.

——. "La giungla." *Paese sera*, 17 May 1964, p. 19.

——. "Diciotto minuti di tagli per la 'Casa in Italia.' " *Paese sera*, 19 May 1964, p. 11.

——. "Il giorno della pace." *Paese sera*, 8 May 1965, p. 13.

——. "Francesco d'Assisi un ribelle del '200." *Paese sera*, 7 May 1966, p. 13.

——. "La ribellione non è finita." *Paese sera*, 9 May 1966, p. 13.

——. "Francesco sul video." *Rinascita*, 14 May 1966, pp. 22–23.

——. "Un irlandese ribelle nei panni di Galileo." *Paese sera*, 23 September 1967, p. 3.

Cixous, Hélène. "Est-ce que le nazisme c'était ça?" *Combat*, 11 April 1974, p. 13.

Clouzot, Claire. "Le Sexe de Nietzsche." *Le Matin*, 5 October 1977, p. 25.

Cohen, Larry. "Italy's 'Cannibals' Needs, Deserves U.S. Distributor." *Hollywood Reporter*, 22 September 1970, pp. 3–4.

Coleman, John. "Room Service." *New Statesman* (London), 25 October 1974, p. 592.

——. "Saddle Soap." *New Statesman*, 26 October 1979, p. 653.

Coletti, Lina. "Come Liliana Cavani rischia 'La pelle.' " *L'europeo*, 24 May 1979, pp. 170–173.

Colpart, Gilles. "La Peau." *Revue du Cinéma*, f.s., 26 (1982): 256–257.

——. "Derrière la porte." *Revue du Cinéma*, 383 (May 1983): 33.

Compagnone, Luigi. "Napoli, sotto la pelle." *L'unità*, 4 October 1981, p. 3.

Consiglio, Stefano, and Fabio Ferzetti, eds. *La bottega della luce: I direttori della fotografia.* Preface by Emilio Tadini. Milan: Ubulibri, 1983.

Cornand, André. "Les Cannibales." *Revue du Cinéma*, no. 262 (June–July 1972): 86–88.

———. "Portier de nuit." *Revue du Cinéma*, nos. 288–289 (October 1974): 282–284.

Cos., E. "La televisione ci svela i misteri dell'atmosfera." *Gazzetta del popolo*, 7 May 1966, p. 6.

Costantini, Costantino. "La ragazza di notte." *Il messaggero*, 2 June 1974, p. 3.

Costantini, Costanzo. "Antibrechtiano il primo film su Galileo Galilei." *Il messaggero*, 21 June 1967, p. 10.

———. "Ecce Omo." *Il messaggero*, 16 October 1977, p. 3.

———. " 'Al di là del bene e del male': Quattro sequestri in un anno." *Il messaggero*, 22 October 1978, p. 12.

Costantini, Luigi. "Un Galileo precursore del Concilio." *Panorama*, 15 February 1968, pp. 51–52.

Cosulich, Callisto. "Cadaveri a Milano." *A.B.C.* (Milan), 27 March 1970, pp. 25–28.

———. "Credere, disobbedire e combattere." *A.B.C.*, 7 July 1972, p. 62.

———. "Milarepa di L. Cavani: Francesco del Tibet nostro santo liberatore." *Paese sera*, 23 March 1974, p. 14.

———. "Il portiere di notte proibito." *Paese sera*, 31 March 1974, p. 3.

———. "Il portiere di notte assassino in congedo." *Paese sera*, 14 April 1974, p. 19.

———. "Romeo e Giulietta nel lager." *Paese sera*, 16 June 1974, p. 9.

———. "L'anno di Liliana Cavani." *Paese sera*, 3 August 1974, p. 6.

———. "La storia scende dal piedistallo e si fa scandalo." *Paese sera*, 29 October 1977, p. 15.

———. " 'La pelle' della Cavani irrita ma interessa." *Paese sera*, 23 May 1981, p. 16.

———. "Losey, Odorisio e Cavani due delusioni e un tonfo." *Paese sera*, 6 September 1982, p. 13.

———. "Melodramma a Marrakech." *Paese sera*, 29 October 1982, p. 15.

———. "Cavani, la voce di chi non sente." *Paese sera*, 2 September 1993, p. 20.

Cowie, Peter. "I cannibali." *International Film Guide* (1973), pp. 180–181.

Cri., R. "La chiesa assegna i suoi Oscar." *La stampa*, 24 February 1996, p. 14.

Crist, Judith. "Winning Big." *New York*, 7 October 1974, pp. 93–96.

Curtiss, Thomas Quinn. "Tying Nietzsche's Romantic Knot." *International Herald Tribune*, 5 October 1977, p. 5.

———. "Liliana Cavani's Garish 'The Skin.' " *International Herald Tribune*, 16 December 1981, p. 5.

D'Agostini, Paolo. "Sequestrato, assolto, sequestrato: Era un film 'sorvegliato a vista.' " *La repubblica*, 10 November 1977, p. 14.

Dalle Vacche, Angela. *The Body in the Mirror: Shapes of History in Italian Cinema.* Princeton, NJ: Princeton University Press, 1992.

Daney, Serge. "Anti-rétro (suite) et fonction critique (fin)." *Cahiers du Cinéma*, no. 253 (October–November 1974): 30–36.

Debenedetti, Antonio. "Come la Cavani rifà la 'pelle.' " *Corriere della sera illustrato*, 13 September 1980, pp. 25–27, 62.

De Giorgis, Ettore. "L'impegno umano e artistico di Liliana Cavani." *Vita sociale*, 29 (July–October 1972): 371–377.

De Lauretis, Teresa. "Cavani's 'Night Porter': A Woman's Film?" *Film Quarterly* 30 (Winter 1976–1977): 35–38.

————. *Technologies of Gender: Essays on Theory, Film and Fiction*. Bloomington: Indiana University Press, 1987.

Del Buono, Oreste. "Il portiere apre la porta al nazismo." *L'europeo*, 9 May 1974, p. 143.

Delclos, Tomas. "Liliana Cavani reivindica en Barcelona la vigencia del Renacimiento y de Galileo." *El Pais*, 5 February 1983, p. 25.

Del Re, Giancarlo. "Un fascino dal breve sorriso." *Il messaggero*, 3 September 1968, p. 10.

Del Rio, Domenico. "Il poverello è un eroe popolare." *La repubblica*, 24 March 1989, p. 25.

De Sanctis, Gino. "Dopo Dante la TV 'attualizzerà' San Francesco." *Il messaggero*, 18 April 1966, p. 3.

Di Giacomo, Filippo. "Pacifica rivoluzione." *Il messaggero*, 4 October 1988, p. 14.

Di Giammatteo, Fernaldo. "La seconda volta del 'Portiere di notte.' " *Rivista del cinematografo* 66 (January 1966): 18–19.

————. *Lo sguardo inquieto: Storia del cinema italiano (1940–1990)*. Florence: La Nuova Italia, 1994.

Di Janni, Gisa. "L'ospite." *Politica*, 3 June 1973, pp. 25–26.

Di Rienzo, Maurizio. "Il rumore del silenzio." *Giornale di Napoli*, 2 September 1993, p. 20.

Dol., M. [Doletti, Mino]. "Hitler überall." *Il tempo*, 20 October 1962, p. 10.

————. "L'età di Stalin." *Il tempo*, 22 December 1962, p. 12.

————. "Le donne nella Resistenza." *Il tempo*, 10 May 1965, p. 11.

————. "Primo piano: Pétain." *Il tempo*, 5 June 1965, p. 8.

————. "Francesco d'Assisi." *Il tempo*, 7 May 1966, p. 8.

————. "Francesco d'Assisi." *Il tempo*, 9 May 1966, p. 12.

Doletti, Mino. "La casa in Italia." *Il tempo*, 3 May 1964, p. 6.

————. "Il messaggio di 'Milarepa.' " *Il tempo*, 14 June 1974, p. 9.

Doni, Rodolfo. "Portiere di notte." *La nazione*, 18 May 1974, p. 3.

Dorigo, Francesco. "Cinema e istituzioni: Concorso alla riforma delle strutture ospedaliere," *Rivista del cinematografo*, no. 6 (June 1972): 262–265.

Dorr, John H. "The Night Porter." *Hollywood Reporter*, 1 October 1974, p. 4.

Dossena, Giampaolo. "Scoperta la vera 'eresia' di Galileo." *Tuttolibri*, 24 September 1983, p. 1.

Durgnat, Raymond. "Skin Games." *Film Comment* 17, no. 6 (1981): 28–32.

Duvignaud, Jean. "Les Amours de Friedrich et de Lou." *Nouvelles Littéraires*, 6 October 1977, p. 13.

Dzieduszycki, Michele. "Al di là dell'amore." *Epoca*, 16 November 1977, pp. 112–119.

Earle, Anita. " 'The Cannibals' at S.F. Film Festival." *San Francisco Chronicle*, 26 October 1970, p. 43.

Ellero, Roberto. "Stavolta la Cavani ha deluso." *L'avanti*, 7 September 1982, p. 16.

Enrile, Andrea. "Un simbolico viaggio immaginario: 'Milarepa' di Liliana Cavani." *Cinema 60*, no. 96 (March–April 1974): 46–48.

Escobar, Roberto. "Lo scrittore tedesco non c'entra con il film." *L'avanti*, 29 October 1977, p. 14.

————. " 'Al di là del bene e del male': Cavani contro Nietzsche." *Cineforum* 18, nos. 1–2 (1978): 21–26.

Estève, M. "Au delà du bien et du mal." *Lumière du Cinéma*, 9 November 1977, pp. 18–33.

Even, Martin. "Les Ambiguités de la mode 'Rétro.' " *Le Monde*, 18 April 1974, pp. 18–19.

F., A. "Uccidete il vitello grasso e arrostitelo—I cannibali." *Cinema nuovo* 19 (July–August 1970): 297–299.

F., L. "Il San Francesco della TV non è un film comunista." *La stampa*, 10 May 1966, p. 4.

F., U. "Magia tra vita e morte." *L'avanti*, 22 May 1974, p. 5.

Fabbretti, Nazareno. "Chi sono i santi." *Domenica del corriere*, 5 June 1966, p. 20.

————. "Difendere 'Galileo' dal clericalismo laico." *Gazzetta del popolo*, 21 September 1968, p. 3.

Faldini, Franca, and Goffredo Fofi, eds. *L'avventurosa storia del cinema italiano raccontata dai suoi protagonisti 1960–1969*. Milan: Feltrinelli, 1981.

Fallica, Alfredo. "Perché difendo il film della Cavani." *Giornale di Sicilia*, 4 December 1977, p. 8.

Fantuzzi, Virgilio. " 'Francesco' di Liliana Cavani." *Civiltà cattolica*, 17 June 1989, pp. 568–581.

Farassino, Alberto. "Francesco va per il mondo." *La repubblica*, 24 March 1989, p. 25.

Fava, Claudio G. "Il cinema e il santo di Assisi: Che simpatico poverello!" *Storia illustrata*, no. 376 (March 1989): 16.

Fegatelli, Renzo. "Il carnefice rivuole la bambina." *Fiera letteraria*, 12 May 1974, p. 27.

"Fellini: Caro Kubrick ti scrivo," *La stampa*, 17 January 1995, p. 17.

Fer., F. "Mistica seduzione." *Il messaggero*, 30 June 1985, p. 12.

Fernandez Santos, J. "Una mujer excepcional." *El País*, 27 May 1978, p. 28.

"Un ferragosto con San Francesco." *L'espresso*, 29 August 1965, p. 21.

Ferrari, Franco. "Liliana Cavani regista controcorrente." *Tutto Carpi*, June 1966, pp. 39–40.

"Un festival belle époque: Una lettera di Bellocchio in polemica con la Cavani." *Paese sera*, 26 August, 1971, p. 9.

"Film 'I cannibali' per Britt Ekland." *Corriere della sera*, 25 March 1969, p. 13.

"Film: Was ist am Faschismus so sexy?" *Der Spiegel*, 17 February 1975, pp. 121–126.

Fini, Massimo. "Né bene né male, solo volgare." *L'europeo*, 18 November 1977, p. 101.

Fiore, Antonio. "La pelle di Napoli non era quella." *Il mattino*, 2 October 1981, p. 1.

Fiore, Titta. "Cinema Babilonia." *Il mattino*, 14 February 1988, p. 17.

Fiorucci, Alvaro. "Andate a vederlo è uno dei migliori." *La repubblica*, 24 March 1989, p. 25.

Fofi, Goffredo. *Il cinema italiano: Servi e padroni*. Milan: Feltrinelli, 1971.

————. "Il vangelo secondo Hulk." *L'unità*, 1 May 1989, p. 5.

————. "Giovani ma belli." *Panorama*, 8 August 1993, pp. 98–100.

Fortuna, Simone. "Ma Francesco gira lontano da Assisi." *La nazione*, 19 February 1988, p. 9.

Fotia, Maria. "L'ospite." *Rivista del cinematografo*, no. 5 (May 1972): 237–238.

"Francesco." *Famiglia cristiana*, 26 April 1989, p. 29.

Frezzato, Achille. "I film d'autore in concorso." *Rivista di Bergamo* 17, nos. 8–9 (1966): 25–44.

———. "Le strutture della mostra di Venezia rispecchiano gli intenti di una società che non esiste più." *Cineforum* 8 (October 1968): 583–586.

Friedman, R. M. "Exorcising the Past: Jewish Figures in Contemporary Films." *Journal of Contemporary History* 19, no. 3 (1984): 511–527.

Frosali, Sergio. "Galileo e l'Inquisizione." *La nazione*, 3 September 1968, p. 8.

———. "Visconti e Fellini premiati a Spoleto." *La nazione*, 26 April 1970, p. 7.

———. "Milarepa." *Sipario*, no. 333 (February 1974): 53–54.

———. 'Milarepa': La Cavani migliore." *La nazione*, 23 February 1974, p. 9.

———. "Vecchi fantasmi a Vienna." *La nazione*, 14 April 1974, p. 11.

———. "Il massacro di Nietzsche." *La nazione*, 18 November 1977, p. 3.

———. " 'La pelle' di Malaparte-Cavani: L'umanesimo della sopravvivenza." *La nazione*, 23 May 1981, p. 17.

———. "Nel ventre di Napoli con Malaparte." *La nazione*, 25 September 1981, p. 15.

———. "Interno berlinese." *La nazione*, 30 November 1985, p. 6.

———. "Mickey a tu per tu con Dio." *La nazione*, 24 March 1989, p. 10.

Fusco, Maria Pia. "Il bisogno di raccontare Francesco in cerca di Dio." *La repubblica*, 21 March 1989, p. 28.

G. [Gramigna, Giuliano]. "Alla TV: Pirandello." *Corriere della sera*, 25 November 1961, p. 6.

———. "TV: 'Sesto piano.' " *Corriere della sera*, 27 October 1962, p. 8.

———. "TV: Debutto felice del 'San Francesco.' " *Corriere della sera*, 7 May 1966, p. 13.

G., A. "Sui teleschermi: Primo canale." Review of *La casa in Italia*. *Il messaggero*, 24 May 1964, p. 10.

———. "Primo canale: Abbiamo visto." Review of *Francesco di Assisi: Part I*. *Il messaggero*, 7 May 1966, p. 10.

———. "Primo canale: Vedremo oggi." Review of *Francesco di Assisi: Part II*. *Il messaggero*, 8 May 1966, p. 12.

———. "Primo canale: Abbiamo visto." Review of *Francesco di Assisi: Part II*. *Il messaggero*, 9 May 1966, p. 12.

G., D. "Portier de nuit." *Image et Son* (Paris) 284 (May 1974): 125.

G., G. "Il tormento di Galileo Galilei." *Bollettino italiano*, September 1967, p. 10.

Gaita, Renato. "Tredici settimane e mezzo, ma stavolta come un santo." *Il messaggero*, 13 February 1988, p. 25.

Galileo: Guida alla lettura del film. Scheda Filmografica SPF no. 9. Rome: Centro Studi Sampaolofilm, 1986.

Galimberti, Carlo. "Diventa film dopo 24 anni 'La pelle' di Malaparte." *Corriere della sera*, 12 December 1973, p. 13.

Gambetti, Giacomo. "Il sesto 'Premio dei Colli' rilancia l'inchiesta filmata." *Osservatore romano*, 18 October 1965, p. 3.

Gaudio, Silvana. "Torna al lavoro in patria la 'diva' esiliata a Londra." *Il mattino*, 14 February 1973, p. 11.

Gearing, Nigel. "Galileo." *Monthly Film Bulletin* 42 (April 1975): 81–82.

Gerus, Patrizio. "Tre illustri letterati che fanno solo l'amore." *La repubblica*, 7 October 1977, p. 13.

Ghiotto, Renato. "Al di là del bene e del male." *Bianco e nero* 39 (January–February 1978): 111–114.

Ghirelli, Antonio. " 'La pelle' di Napoli, una città vinta: Il fascino inquietante dell'atrocità." *Il mattino*, 2 October 1981, p. 5.

Gi., Massimo. " 'Milarepa' è un viaggio nei 'perché' di un mago Tibetano." *Il globo*, 7 April 1974, p. 9.

———. "Risultati troppo inferiori alle intenzioni." *Il globo*, 28 April 1974, p. 7.

Giacci, Vittorio. "Lucia e Lucien, due volti del fascismo che da ambigui diventano equivoci." *Cineforum* 15 (May 1975): 305–314.

Giacomelli, Barbara. " 'Galileo' un uomo interroga il potere." *Vita pastorale*, January 1972, pp. 54–56.

Gilles, Jacob. "Portier de nuit." *L'Express* (Paris), 1 April 1974, p. 6.

Ginzburg, Natalia. "La Cavani racconta l'orrore di Hitler." *Corriere della sera*, 21 September 1977, p. 15.

Giraldi, Massimo. "La 'folle libertà' di Francesco d'Assisi." *Popoli e missione* 5 (December 1991): 43–44.

Giroux, Henry. "The Challenge of Neo-Fascist Culture." *Cinéaste* 6, no. 4 (1975): 30–32.

Giuliani, Gianna. *Le strisce interiori: Cinema italiano e psicanalisi.* Preface by Piero Bellanova. Rome: Bulzoni, 1980.

Godard, Colette. "Le Théâtre de la dictature, de la mort et du travesti." *Le Monde*, 18 April 1974, p. 19.

Gold. "I cannibali." *Variety*, 30 September 1970, p. 24.

Goldoni, Primo, ed. *Il cinema di Liliana Cavani.* Atti del Convegno: Carpi, 25 February– 3 March 1990. Casalecchio di Reno, Bologna: Grafis Edizioni, 1993.

Golo Stone, Mirto. "The Feminist Critic and Salomé: On Cavani's *The Night Porter.*" In *Romance Languages Annual 1989*, edited by Ben Lawton and Anthony Julian Tamburri, 1:41–44. West Lafayette, IN: Purdue Research Foundation, 1990.

Gonano, Gian Luigi. "Frate Francesco e l'istanza sociale." *La notte* (Milan), 9 May 1966, p. 13.

Gov., G. "E' colpa della carriera." *L'avanti*, 10 May 1966, p. 5.

Gr., G. [Grossini, Giancarlo]. "Al di là del bene e del male." *Cinema nuovo* 27 (January–February 1978): 55–56.

———. "La pelle." *Cinema nuovo* 31 (April 1982): 53–54.

Grassi, Giovanna. "E venne un uomo chiamato Francesco." *Settegiorni illustrati del Corriere della sera*, 9 April 1988, pp. 58–75.

———. "La Cavani, entusiasmo a Mosca, filmoteca a Carpi." *Corriere della sera*, 25 July 1991, p. 23.

———. "Già 'scomparso' il film della Cavani." *Corriere della sera*, 12 October 1993, p. 30.

Grazzini, Giovanni. " 'La camorra' vince ad Este." *Corriere della sera*, 10 October 1965, p. 13.

———. "Settimo 'Premio dei Colli': Il cinema fruga la realtà." *Corriere della sera*, 4 October 1966, p. 13.

———. "Galileo: Ieri come oggi." *Corriere della sera*, 3 September 1968, p. 13.

———. "I cannibali." *Corriere della sera*, 3 May 1970, p. 15. Reprinted in *Gli anni Settanta in cento film*, pp. 38–40. Bari: Laterza, 1978.

Gr., G. [Grossini, Giancarlo]. "Venezia: Carné fra due italiani." *Corriere della sera*, 5 September 1971, p. 15.

———. "Viaggio con la Cavani nell'orrore del nazismo." *Corriere della sera*, 1 June 1974, p. 13.

———. "Il superuomo, la superdonna e il terzo incomodo." *Corriere della sera*, 29 October 1977, p. 16.

———. *Eva dopo Eva: La donna nel cinema italiano dagli anni Settanta a oggi*. Bari: Laterza, 1980.

———. "Cannes divisa sulla 'Pelle' della Cavani." *Corriere della sera*, 23 May 1981, p. 26.

———. "Oggi 'La pelle' non fa polemica." *Corriere della sera*, 25 September 1981, p. 3. Reprinted in *Cinema '81*, pp. 130–133. Bari: Laterza, 1982.

———. "Dietro la porta della Cavani l'enigma delle grandi passioni." *Corriere della sera*, 8 October 1982, p. 25. Reprinted in *Cinema '82*, pp. 130–132. Bari: Laterza, 1983.

———. "A porte chiuse in un inferno." *Corriere della sera*, 15 November 1985, p. 23. Reprinted in *Cinema '85*, pp. 155–157. Bari: Laterza, 1986.

———. "L'uomo nuovo del Duecento." *Il messaggero*, 23 March 1989, p. 18. Reprinted in *Cinema '89*, pp. 55–57. Bari: Laterza, 1990.

———. "Dove siete? Io sono qui." In *Cinema '93*, pp. 72–73. Bari: Laterza, 1994.

Greene, Naomi. "Fascism in Recent Italian Films." *Film Criticism* 6, no. 1 (1981): 31–42.

Greenspun, Roger. " 'Cannibals,' Modern Version of 'Antigone.' " *New York Times*, 21 September 1970, p. 55.

Grelier, Robert. "La Peau." *Revue du Cinéma* 366 (November 1981): 42–44.

Grieco, Gianfranco. "Quale Francesco?" *Rivista del cinematografo* 59 (May 1989): 14.

Grossini, Giancarlo. *Cinema e follia: Stati di psicopatologia sullo schermo (1948–1982)*. Bari: Edizioni Dedalo, 1984.

Gs., G. "Per Liliana Cavani una passione in svastica e kimono." *Corriere della sera*, 30 June 1985, p. 21.

Guarda, Guido. "L'autore come personaggio." *Osservatore romano*, 5–6 September 1966, pp. 3, 5.

———. "Dal 'Francesco' a 'La Prise du pouvoir.' " *Osservatore romano*, 19–20 September 1966, p. 5.

Guardincerri, Attilio. "Una storia d'amore in mezzo alla contestazione." *Cineforum* 10 (May–August 1970): 122–124.

Guarini, Ruggero. "Al di là del male e del peggio." *L'espresso*, 30 October 1977, pp. 70–75.

———. "Donna è bello, il film invece no." *L'espresso*, 6 November 1977, p. 25.

Guarrini, Ruggero. "Sotto tiro." *L'espresso*, 25 October 1981, p. 126.

Guattari, Félix. "Meglio lo scandalo del matrimonio." *L'espresso*, 30 October 1977, pp. 81–83.

———. "Liliana Cavani au l'effet de trou noir amoureux." *Le Monde*, 10 November 1977, pp. 20–21.

Guerri, Giordano Bruno. "Quell'addormentato di Mastroianni non assomiglia a mio fratello." *Domenica del corriere*, 13 June 1980, pp. 58–65.

———. "Ma forse questa volta ha esagerato." *Panorama*, 24 November 1981, p. 181.

Guerrini, Loretta M. "Cenerentola del film: Per un'analisi della sceneggiatura." In L. Cavani and I. Moscati, *Dove siete? Io sono qui*, pp. 105–119. Venice: Marsilio, 1993.

Guglielmino, Gian Maria. "Galileo 'omino ingenuo' schiacciato tra scienza e potere." *Gazzetta del popolo* (Turin), 3 September 1968, p. 7.

———. "Milarepa." *Gazzetta del popolo*, 1 February 1974, p. 6.

Guidi, Gabriella. "Liliana Cavani prepara un'inchiesta sulla casa." *Rivista del cinematografo*, nos. 3–4 (March–April 1964): 164–166.

Gurewitsch, Matthew. "An Opera Director with a Cinematic Eye." *Wall Street Journal* (Europe), 12 June 1998, p. 13.

H., D. "Cavani chez Nietzsche." *L'Express*, 3 August 1977, pp. 56, 59.

Haskell, Molly. "After the Revolution (2)." *Village Voice*, 1 October 1970, p. 57.

———. "Are Women Directors Different?" *Village Voice*, 3 February 1975, p. 73.

Heymann, Danièle. "Bonheur de rire, doleur de rire." *Le Monde*, 4 September 1993, p. 19.

Hinxman, Margaret, and Susan D'Arcy. *The Films of Dirk Bogarde*. Introduction by Joseph Losey. London: Literary Services and Production, 1974.

Houston, Beverle, and Marsha Kinder. "*The Night Porter* as Daydream." *Film Quarterly/Literature* 3 (Autumn 1975): 363–370.

Houston, Penelope. "Cannes 70." *Sight and Sound* 39 (Summer 1970): 121–123.

Huston, Nancy. *Mosaïque de la pornographie: Marie-Thérèse et les autres*. Paris: Denoël-Gonthier, 1982.

Ialli. "Hitler al potere." *L'unità*, 25 November 1961, p. 8.

Iarussi, Oscar. "E la Cavani esplora il mondo della sofferenza." *La gazzetta del mezzogiorno* (Bari), 2 September 1993, p. 17.

"Incredibile sequestro del film 'Al di là del bene e del male.' " *L'unità*, 9 November 1977, p. 9.

Infusino, Gianni. "Maledetto fu il libro, e chi lo scrisse. . . ." *Il mattino*, 13 November 1980, p. 5.

Insdorf, Annette. *Indelible Shadows: Film and the Holocaust*. Cambridge: Cambridge University Press, 1989.

"Italia: Le reazioni al sequestro del film di Liliana Cavani." *Il messaggero*, 10 November 1977, p. 12.

Jaccard, Roland. "Le Roman du film 'Svastika.' " *Le Monde*, 29 April 1986, p. 17.

James, Caryn. "Wartime Obsessions." *New York Times*, 15 July 1988, C12.

Jatt., E. [Jattarelli, Emidio]. "Tra cronaca e melodramma 'L'ospite' della Cavani." *Il tempo*, 5 September 1971, p. 12.

Jattarelli, Emidio. "L'ospite." *Il tempo*, 11 March 1972, p. 7.

Jenny, Urs. "Falscher Riecher." *Der Spiegel*, 7 September 1981, p. 218.

Kael, Pauline. "The Current Cinema: Stuck in the Fun." *New Yorker*, 7 October 1974, pp. 151–156.

Katsahnias, Iannis. "La Croix et la bannière." *Cahiers du Cinéma* 383–384 (May 1986): 87.

Kauffmann, Stanley. "Stanley Kauffmann on Films.' " *New Republic*, 5 October 1974, pp. 18, 33.

Kay, Karyn, and Gerard Peary, eds. *Women and the Cinema*. New York: Dutton, 1977.

Keyser, L. J. "Three Faces of Evil: Fascism in Recent Movies." *Journal of Popular Film* 4, no. 1 (1975): 21–31.

Kezich, Tullio. "Galileo." *Bianco e nero*, nos. 5–6 (1969): 146–147.

———. "I cannibali." *Panorama*, 7 May 1970, p. 15.

———. "Milarepa." *Panorama*, 28 February 1974, p. 15.

———. "Il portiere di notte." *Sipario*, no. 336 (May 1974): 42–43.

———. "Il portiere di notte." *Panorama*, 2 May 1974, p. 31.

———. "Una lezione d'amore accidentale e stravolta." *La repubblica*, 29 October 1977, p. 14.

———. "Al di là del bene e del male." *Panorama*, 15 November 1977, p. 33.

———. "La vita per un pugno di lire." *La repubblica*, 23 May 1981, p. 17.

———. "Ecco a voi uno scrittore all'inferno." *La repubblica*, 25 September 1981, p. 15.

———. "La pelle." *Panorama*, 12 October 1981, p. 33.

———. "Oltre la porta." *Panorama*, 8 November 1982, p. 18.

———. "Passioni e Germania nazista." *La repubblica*, 2 November 1985, p. 28.

———. "Più avvincente che convincente." *Panorama*, 24 November 1985, p. 13.

———. "Rourke, 9 settimane e mezzo da santo." *Corriere della sera*, 23 March 1989, p. 21.

———. "Le parole sono pietre." *Corriere della sera*, 2 August 1993, p. 19.

———. "E dalla Cavani tutte le emozioni del silenzio." *Corriere della sera*, 2 September 1993, p. 23.

———. "Quando la voce dell'amore vince la sordità." *Corriere della sera*, 27 September 1993, p. 26.

Kroll, Jack. "Cannes: The Dream Bazaar." *Newsweek*, 8 June 1981, p. 61.

L., A. "Un interno berlinese per fare karakiri." *L'avanti*, 6 November 1985, p. 6.

L., J. "Milarepa." *Image et Son* 285 (June 1974): 29–30.

L., R. [Rosario Lizzio]. "Silenziosamente Liliana." *La Sicilia*, 2 September 1973, p. 29.

Lane, John Francis. "Who Are the Real Cannibals?" *Daily American* (Rome), 28 April 1970, p. 5.

———. "Cannon's Carte Blanche for Director Cavani's 'Berlin.' " *Screen International*, 24 August 1985, p. 68.

Lattes, Wanda. "Intimità sì, ma intellettuale." *La nazione*, 25 November 1977, p. 3.

Laura, Ernesto G. "Una storia giapponese in versione occidentale." *Il popolo*, 13 November 1985, p. 11.

———. "La chiamata di Dio, la risposta di Francesco." *La discussione* (Rome), 25 March 1989, p. 23.

Laurenzi, Carlo. "Una stella spenta nel medioevo." *Giornale nuovo*, 23 March 1989, p. 3.

La Valle, Raniero. "Un Francesco inquietante." *Avvenire d'Italia*, 15 May 1966, p. 1.

———. "Le due strade dei contestatori." *La stampa*, 1 May 1970, p. 2.

Le Fanu, Mark. "Beyond the Door." *Films and Filming*, no. 355 (April 1984): 32–33.

Lefèvre, Raymond. "Portier de nuit." *Cinéma* (Paris) 187 (May 1974): 105–106.

———. "Au-delà du bien et du mal." *Revue du Cinéma*, no. 322 (November 1977): 89–90.

Levantesi, Alessandra. "La Cavani presenta il suo San Francesco." *L'avanti*, 21 March 1989, p. 18.

———. "Rimane sospeso il conto con Dio." *L'avanti*, 24 March 1989, p. 19.

Levi, Primo. *I sommersi e i salvati*. Turin: Einaudi, 1986.

Lichtenstein, Grace. "In Liliana Cavani's Love Story, Love Means Always Having to Say Ouch." *New York Times*, 13 October 1974, D19.

Liehm, Mira. *Passion and Defiance: Film in Italy from 1942 to the Present.* Berkeley and Los Angeles: University of California Press, 1984.

Liliana Cavani. Schede Registi SPF no. 8. Rome: Centro Studi Sampaolofilm, 1975.

"Liliana Cavani lleva al cine 'La piel,' de Malaparte." *El Pais*, 23 July 1980, p. 40.

Lilli, Laura. "Ritorno alla Casa Rossa." *La repubblica*, 21 September 1979, pp. 12–13.

Liverani, Maurizio. "Un Galileo come Dubcek nel film della Cavani." *Momento sera* (Rome), 3–4 September 1968, p. 13.

Lizzani, Carlo. *Il cinema italiano dalle origini agli anni ottanta.* Filmography by Roberto Chiti. 2d ed. Rome: Editori Riuniti, 1982.

Locchi, Giorgio. "Ambiguo per i francesi 'il portiere' della Cavani." *Il tempo*, 10 April 1974, p. 10.

Lucchini, Gabriele. "Varata la sezione del film d'autore." *Rivista del cinematografo* 40 (November 1966): 682–684.

Lucidi, Marcantonio. "Il saio? Meglio il pigiama." *Il messaggero*, 13 March 1988, p. 15.

M., A. [Angelo Merisi]. "Tristi amori in Marocco e in Calabria." *Giornale di Sicilia*, 6 September 1982, p. 15.

M., A. M. "Cavani: 'E' straordinario.' " *La repubblica*, 14 January 1989, p. 8.

M., G. "Ancora sul poverello." *Resto del Carlino*, 8 May 1966, p. 6.

M., G. M. "Consegnati i 'Premi Spoleto per il cinema.' " *Resto del Carlino* (Bologna), 26 April 1970, p. 9.

M., I. [Moscati, Italo]. "Ancora su Francesco." *Avvenire d'Italia*, 8 May 1966, p. 5.

———. "Ed ora non dimentichiamo." *Avvenire d'Italia*, 10 May 1966, p. 5.

———. "Il 'Galileo' della Cavani." *L'avanti*, 22 February 1969, p. 3.

M., L. "La regista Cavani a fior di pelle ma con bravura." *L'avanti*, 7 October 1981, p. 15.

M., P. "Milarepa." *Fiches du Cinéma*, March 1975, p. 17.

———. "Les Gestes qui sauvent." *Le Monde*, 28 April 1994, p. 7.

M., S. " 'L'ospite' della Cavani." *Giornale d'Italia*, 25–26 May 1973, p. 14.

McArthur, Colin. "Moralist Iconography of Nazism." *Tribune* (London), 8 November 1974, p. 7.

Maccario, Angelo. "Un film a colori su Galileo per la regia di Liliana Cavani." *Il messaggero*, 27 February 1967, p. 12.

———. "Tutti severi meno uno." *Corriere della sera*, 23 May 1981, p. 26.

McCormick, Ruth. "Fascism à la Mode or Radical Chic?" *Cinéaste* 6, no. 4 (1975): 31, 33–34.

Magny, J. "Le Cas Cavani." *Téléciné*, no. 223 (December 1977): 40.

Malcolm, Derek. "Anyone for Venice." *Guardian*, 8 September 1971, p. 8.

———. "Lonesome Wow Boy." *Guardian*, 24 October 1974, p. 12.

———. "Bloch and Tackle." *Guardian*, 30 October 1975, p. 8.

———. "Assegais and Dolls." *Guardian*, 25 October 1979, p. 9.

Mancini, Michele. "Galileo." *Filmcritica* 20 (May 1969): 180.

Manet, Eduardo. "L'Affaire 'Portier de nuit.' " *Combat*, 1 April 1974, p. 13.

Mangiacapre, Lina. *Cinema al femminile.* Padua: Mastrogiacomo, 1980.

Manin, Giuseppina. "Serenamente a Cannes il santo della Cavani." *Corriere della sera*, 20 May 1989, p. 27.

Manin, Giuseppina. "Due o tre cose che so di San Paolo." *Corriere della sera*, 9 November 1991, p. 29.

―――. "Vi racconterò due piccoli Mozart." *Corriere della sera*, 25 March 1994, p. 37.

Maraldi, Antonio, ed. *Fotografi di scena del cinema italiano: Mario Tursi*. Cesena: Editrice Il Ponte Vecchio, 1996.

Mardore, Michel. "La Cavani récidive." *Nouvel Observateur*, 25 April 1986, p. 64.

Marino, Ruggero. "Lucia Bosé per una vita 'ospite' di un manicomio." *Il tempo*, 10 June 1971, p. 12.

Marmori, Giancarlo. "Un dubbio: Non avrò sbagliato film?" *L'espresso*, 30 October 1977, p. 73.

Marrone, Gaetana. "Narratività e storia in *Interno berlinese* di Liliana Cavani." In *Romance Languages Annual 1989*, edited by Ben Lawton and Anthony Julian Tamburri, 1:52–55. West Lafayette, IN: Purdue Research Foundation, 1990.

―――. "Liliana Cavani negli USA." In *Lo sguardo libero*, edited by Paola Tallarigo and Luca Gasparini, pp. 145–147. Florence: La Casa Usher, 1990.

―――. "The Staging of Cavani's *Galileo*: The Historiographer's Art." In *Etica cristiana e scrittori del Novecento*, edited by Floridan M. Iannace. *Forum Italicum*, Filibrary no. 5 (1993): 139–146.

―――. "Ideologia, creatività e iconografia nella Chiara di Liliana Cavani." In *Italian Women Mystics*, edited by Dino Cervigni. *Annali d'italianistica* 13 (1995): 387–400.

Martin, Marcel. "Au-Delà du bien et du mal." *Ecran*, 15 November 1977, pp. 54–55.

Martineau, R. "La Peau." *Séquences* (Montreal) 111 (January 1983): 88–90.

Maslin, Janet. "The Screen: 'Beyond Good and Evil.' " *New York Times*, 18 May 1984, C14.

Matzneff, Gabriel. "Au-delà du bien et du mal." *Le Monde*, 15 October 1977, p. 2.

Maurin, François. "Journée déconcertante au Festival de Cannes: 'Stavinsky' d'Alain Resnais, 'Milarepa' de Liliana Cavani." *L'Humanité*, 15 May 1974, p. 12.

Mayor, Francis. "Un Film fasciné par le nazisme." *Télérama*, 6 April 1974, pp. 63–64.

Mazzi, Libero. " 'Galileo' impegnato ufficialmente e (in privato) la satira di Caprioli." *Il piccolo*, 3 September 1968, p. 7.

Me., L. " 'Il portiere di notte' di Liliana Cavani." *Il manifesto*, 13 June 1974, p. 6.

Meccoli, Domenico. "Milarepa." *Epoca*, 7 April 1974, pp. 120–121.

―――. "Nell'albergo di Dirk Bogarde è passato Dostoievski." *Epoca*, 28 April 1974, p. 139.

―――. "Al di là del bene e del male." *Epoca*, 16 November 1977, p. 130.

Meccoli, Sandro. "Ecco il 'cartellone' delle ultime giornate." *Corriere della sera*, 3 September 1968, p. 13.

Mei, Francesco. "I connotati dello sterminio." *Il popolo*, 9 October 1977, p. 7.

Meneghini, Anna Luisa. "Francesco d'Assisi: Testimone dei suoi tempi." *Così*, 8 May 1966, pp. 15–19.

Miccichè, Lino. "Un salto nella verità." *L'avanti*, 29 September 1968, p. 8.

―――. "L'ospite." *L'avanti*, 12 March 1972, p. 13.

―――. "Mito e realtà in 'Milarepa.' " *L'avanti*, 23 March 1974, p. 3.

―――. *Cinema italiano degli anni '70: Cronache 1969–1975*. Venice: Marsilio, 1980.

"Milarepa." *Cinéma* (Paris) 188 (June 1974): 72.

Milne, Tom. "Postscript on Venice." *Observer*, 12 September 1971, p. 27.

Mizejewski, Linda. *Divine Decadence: Fascism, Female Spectacle, and the Makings of Sally Bowles*. Princeton, NJ: Princeton University Press, 1992.

Mohort, Michel. " 'Milarepa' de Liliana Cavani." *Le Figaro*, 19 February 1975, p. 21.

Monitor, "Il tamburo dei tedeschi." *Il paese*, 25 November 1961, p. 3.

Montaigne, Pierre. "Liliana Cavani, celle par qui le scandale arrive." *Le Figaro*, 4 October 1977, p. 29.

———. "Mastroianni et Lancaster mobilisés." *Le Figaro*, 16 November 1981, p. 23.

———. "Liliana Cavani sur un terrain miné." *Le Figaro*, 4 May 1983, p. 28.

Montanelli, Indro. "Il teleschermo avvelenato." *Corriere della sera*, 6 May 1964, p. 3.

Monteleone, Massimo. "Francesco uomo vero e Santo." *Il popolo*, 23 March 1989, p. 9.

Montesi, Antonella. "Ho filmato il sogno di San Francesco." *Tutto spettacolo*, 1–15 April 1989, pp. 5–6.

Morandini, Morando. "Biografie obiettive." *Il giorno*, 24 November 1967, p. 3.

———. "Napoli '43 arriva la peste." *Il giorno* (Milan), 25 September 1981, p. 12.

———. "Cavani: Una erotica elegante Germania." *Il giorno*, 15 November 1985, p. 16.

———. "Santo Francesco senza uccellini." *Il giorno*, 24 March 1989, p. 24.

———. "Nel film della Cavani, la forza del silenzio." *Il giorno*, 2 September 1993, p. 15.

Moravia, Alberto. " 'Galileo' di Liliana Cavani: In ginocchio davanti ai censori." *L'espresso*, 22 September 1968, p. 23.

———. "Antigone si arrende ai tecnocrati." *L'espresso*, 10 May 1970, p. 23.

———. " 'L'ospite' di Liliana Cavani: In purgatorio sarò tua." *L'espresso*, 19 March 1972, p. 23.

———. "Faccia feroce fa carriera." *L'espresso*, 25 June 1972, p. 23.

———. "Budda è salito in cima all'Appennino." *L'espresso*, 16 December 1973, p. 23.

———. "C'è un nazista a pianterreno." *L'espresso*, 21 April 1974, pp. 87–88.

———. "Non placet." *L'espresso*, 28 April 1974, pp. 64–65.

———. "Diavolo di un Nietzsche." *L'espresso*, 13 November 1977, pp. 150–151.

———. "Inferno berlinese." *L'espresso*, 1 December 1985, p. 198.

———. "Santo con stile." *L'espresso*, 30 April 1989, pp. 143–144.

Mori, Anna Maria. "E Zarathustra è una femmina." *La repubblica*, 29 October 1977, p. 15.

———. "Perché amiamo Francesco." *La repubblica*, 18 March 1989, p. 6.

Moscati, Italo. "Francesco uomo d'oggi." *Avvenire d'Italia*, 6 May 1966, p. 5.

———. "Il fuoco fatuo dei critici TV." *Civiltà dell' immagine*, July 1966, pp. 9–12.

———. "Un Francesco 'nuovo.' " *Rivista del cinematografo* 40 (July 1966): 482–485.

———. "La TV come mezzo di espressione: Si apre un dibattito sulle sabbie mobili." *Civiltà dell'immagine*, October 1966, pp. 91–99.

———. "Un Galileo 'anti-Brecht.' " *Osservatore romano*, 18–19 September 1967, p. 5.

———. " 'Francesco di Assisi' di Liliana Cavani: Metodologia evangelica." *Rivista del cinematografo* 41 (August 1968): 503.

———. "Il Galileo di Liliana Cavani." *Cineforum* 8 (October 1968): 594–597.

———. " 'Cattolico di sinistra': Un'etichetta che respingiamo." *Cineforum* 10 (May–August 1970): 124–126.

———. " 'Portiere di notte' di Liliana Cavani." *Letture* 73 (April 1974): 340–343.

———. "Accanto alla Cavani c'è un Mozart che dorme." *Paese sera*, 24 March 1976, p. 11.

Moscati, Italo. "Libertà d'opinione e libertà di film." *L'europeo*, 25 November 1977, p. 66.

Mosk. "The Night Porter." *Variety*, 3 April 1974, p. 14.

——. "Oltre il bene e il male." *Variety*, 12 October 1977, p. 17.

Mughini, Giampiero. "La sfida di Nietzsche e Savinio." *Paese sera*, 5 November 1977, p. 3.

N., E. [Natta]. "La pelle." *Rivista del cinematografo* 54 (December 1981): 683.

N., G. [Napoli, Gregorio]. "Milarepa della Cavani." *Giornale di Sicilia*, 19 April 1974, p. 8.

——. "L'ambiguo gioco della vittima e del boia." *Giornale di Sicilia*, 3 October 1982, p. 9.

——. "Interno berlinese." *Giornale di Sicilia*, 24 November 1985, p. 21.

Nacache, J. "La Peau." *Cinéma*, nos. 271–272 (July–August 1981): 130–131.

Nadeau, Chantal. "Girls on a Wired Screen: Cavani's Cinema and Lesbian S/M." In *Sexy Bodies: The Strange Carnalities of Feminism*, edited by Elizabeth Grosz and Elspeth Probyn, pp. 211–230. London and New York: Routledge, 1995.

Napoli, Carlo. "Il vero volto di San Francesco." *Orizzonti*, 10 April 1966, pp. 21–24.

Napoli, Gregorio. "Drammatico dibattito fra la scienza e la fede." *Giornale di Sicilia*, 3 September 1968, p. 8.

——. "Una malinconica fiaba sull'agonia dell'uomo." *Giornale di Sicilia*, 3 May 1970, p. 8.

——. "Elogio dei maniaci." *Giornale di Sicilia*, 5 September 1971, p. 8.

——. "Napoli '44 in un girone infernale." *Giornale di Sicilia*, 2 October 1981, p. 9.

——. "La passione macabra di Assisi." *Giornale di Sicilia*, 25 March 1989, p. 20.

Natta, Enzo. "Galileo a braccetto con Marcuse." *Dimensioni* 6 (November 1968): 50–58.

——. "Due cannibali tra i ribelli insepolti." *Dimensioni* 7 (June 1969): 70–74.

——. "Liliana e Francesco." *Famiglia cristiana*, 5 April 1989, pp. 40–41.

Nediani, Antonio. "La Cavani alle prese con la vita di Galileo." *L'avanti*, 18 October 1967, p. 5.

Nepoti, Roberto. "Cinema pornoerotico: Le pratiche del dis-piacere." *Bianco e nero* 39, no. 5 (1978): 3–65.

——. "Un cinema senza parole." *La repubblica*, 23 September 1993, p. 9.

"Nietzsche in mutande." *Stampa sera*, 29 November 1977, p. 23.

Nobécourt, Jacques. "*Portiere di notte* tra Freud e Hitler: Bisogna saper affrontare le cose inquietanti." *Il globo*, 28 April 1974, p. 7.

Nourissier, François. "Antigone chez les gauchistes." *L'Express* (Paris), 17 April 1972, p. 47.

Orsera, Giusto. "Poco corpo niente anima." *Il borghese*, 24 November 1985, pp. 754–755.

Orsini, Onorato. "L'eretico globale." *La notte*, 3 September 1968, p. 12.

" 'L'ospite' della Cavani." *Il popolo*, 24 May 1973, p. 9.

O'Toole, Lawrence. "Allusions to Grandeur." *MacLeans*, 20 August 1979, p. 41.

P., G. [Peruzzi, Giuseppe]. "Il portiere di notte." *Cinema nuovo* 23 (July–August 1974): 285–287.

Pacifici, Alberto. "Nove signore in cabina di regia." *Settimana Incom*, 5 April 1964, pp. 24–28.

Pally, Marcia. "The Perils of Libideology." *Village Voice*, 29 May 1984, p. 60.

Papa, Antonio. "Napoli americana." *Belfagor* 37, no. 3 (1982): 249–264.

Paschetto, Anna. "Ultimo tango a Parigi e a Vienna." *Culture* (Milan) (1989), pp. 115–125.

Pasolini, Pier Paolo. "La pazzesca razionalità della geometria religiosa." *Cinema nuovo* 23, no. 229 (May–June 1974): 184–187.

———. *Scritti corsari*. Milan: Garzanti, 1975.

———. "L'ambiguità." *Recensione* (Monza) 1 (April–May 1975): 9–13.

Passek, Jean Loup. "Liliana Cavani ou l'itinéraire." *Combat*, 16 May 1974, p. 13.

Pasti, Daniela. "Sotto la 'pelle' della Cavani." *La repubblica*, 21 September 1979, p. 13.

———. "Bello, asciutto, estatico: E' il santo che fa scena." *La repubblica*, 26 September 1981, p. 4.

Pat., P. "Sanda e Nietzsche: Amore e scandalo." *La stampa*, 6 October 1977, p. 7.

Patania, Sonia. "Ha fatto il pugile come Rourke l'ultima scoperta della Cavani." *Giornale di Sicilia*, 2 June 1993, p. 22.

Pecora, Elio. "Al di là del bene e del male c'è solo lo scandalo." *Voce repubblicana*, 29 October 1977, p. 3.

Per., P. "La regista Cavani a Torino con il suo Galileo." *Stampa sera*, 5–6 March 1969, p. 6.

———. "Con l'anima nel Tibet." *Stampa sera*, 1 February 1974, p. 7.

Pérez, Michel. "La Peau de Liliana Cavani." *Le Matin*, 23 May 1981, p. 24.

Perona, Piero. "La Cavani metà bene e metà male." *Stampa sera*, 30 November 1977, p. 25.

———. "Non sta nella 'Pelle' la Napoli 1943?" *Stampa sera*, 25 September 1981, p. 21.

———. "Sesso difficile." *Stampa sera*, 30 November 1985, p. 32.

Perrone, Paolo. "Oggi Lucia Bosé sarà l''Ospite' che la società non sa aiutare." *Corriere di Napoli*, 4–5 September 1971, p. 3.

Perrotti, Paolo. "Portiere di notte." *Quadrangolo* (1974), pp. 71–73.

"Un persiano naif e i 'mostri sacri.' " *Paese sera*, 27 August 1971, p. 13.

Pesce, Alberto. "I due 'Francesco' di Liliana Cavani." *Madre*, no. 3 (March 1989): 56–59.

Pestelli, Leo. "La lotta fra verità e potere nel 'Galileo' di Liliana Cavani." *La stampa*, 3 September 1968, p. 7.

———. "Il 'Galileo' della Cavani." *La stampa*, 6 March 1969, p. 7.

———. "Antigone fra i grattacieli." *La stampa*, 1 May 1970, p. 7.

———. "Pietà per i pazzi al Festival." *La stampa*, 5 September 1971, p. 7.

———. "La speranza è nel Tibet?" *La stampa*, 1 February 1974, p. 7.

———. "Gli 'incubi' del nazismo." *La stampa*, 1 June 1974, p. 9.

Petley, Julian. "Interno berlinese." *Monthly Film Bulletin* 54 (January 1987): 22–23.

Petrucci, Antonio. "Quasi un diario." *Osservatore romano*, 11 May 1966, p. 3.

———. "Dietro i capelli lunghi dei 'provos' l'homo ludens reagisce all'homo faber." *Fiera letteraria*, 1 September 1966, p. 24.

Philippon, Alain. "Le Défi d'une cinéaste." *Cahiers du Cinéma* 330 (December 1981): 55–57.

Pillitteri, Paolo. "I rapporti fra l'uomo e il potere nell'ottimo 'Galileo' della Cavani." *L'avanti*, 3 September 1968, p. 5.

Pintus, Pietro. *Storia e film: Trent'anni di cinema italiano (1945–1975)*. Rome: Bulzoni, 1980.

Piscitelli, Salvatore. "La vittima e il carnefice: 'Il portiere di notte' di Liliana Cavani." *Cinema 60*, no. 96 (March–April 1974): 54–55.

Plazy, Gilles. "Liliana Cavani, cinéaste italienne." *Le Monde*, 13 April 1972, p. 29.

Poggialini, Mirella. "Iniziò coi documentari RAI." *L'avvenire*, 23 March 1989, p. 15.

———. "Cavani fra sentimento e ragione: 'Siamo tutti incapaci di comunicare ma vivere significa incontrare.' " *L'avvenire*, 2 September 1993, p. 19.

Polacco, Giorgio. "Galileo visto dall'unica donna regista presente alla rassegna." *Stampa sera*, 3–4 September 1968, p. 6.

———. "Volerò via subito sul mio cavallo azzurro." *Momento sera*, 28 April 1970, p. 11.

———. "Lucia Bosè: Una vita in manicomio." *Momento sera*, 11–12 June 1971, p. 15.

Polese, Ranieri. "Il mio schermo, le mie battaglie." *La nazione*, 30 November 1985, p. 6.

Porro, Gabriele. "Cavani: Un film sul clan Mozart." *La repubblica*, 25 April 1994, p. 33.

Porro, Maurizio. "L'Eros è diffamato da una cultura con i tabù." *Corriere della sera*, 4 February 1975, p. 13.

———. "Tre sorrisi di donna e un regista pensieroso." *Corriere della sera*, 6 September 1982, p. 18.

"Portier de nuit: Film de Liliana Cavani." *Avant-Scène* 147 (May 1974): 53–58.

Il portiere di notte (critiche, fatti e polemiche): Dossier della critica. Edited by Ufficio Stampa dell'Italnoleggio Cinematografico (Rome), December 1974.

Porzio, Domenico. "Liliana Cavani." In *Primi piani*, preface by Enzo Biagi, pp. 48–51. Milan: Mondadori, 1976.

Powell, Dilys. "Prisoners of Passion." *Sunday Times* (London), 20 January 1974, p. 27.

———. "Passion Laid Bare." *Sunday Times*, 27 October 1974, p. 33.

———. "Braving the New World." *Sunday Times*, 2 November 1975, The Arts, p. 37.

Preci, Walter. "TV: Un Francesco ravvicinato." *Gioventù*, June 1966, pp. 30–31.

Preda, Gianna, ed. "Domande e risposte: Santi televisivi." *Il borghese*, 19 May 1966, p. 155.

Prezioso, Sonia. "Un'esperienza del cinema italiano: Liliana Cavani." *Ragionamenti* (Rome) 3, nos. 30–31 (1976): 57–69.

Prisco, Michele. "Al di là del bene e del male." *Il mattino*, 19 November 1977, p. 11.

"Protesta alla TV per 'Francesco d'Assisi.' " *Il messaggero*, 15 May 1966, p. 12.

Puma, Giacomo. "Il cinema dietro le quinte: Interno berlinese." *Videoregistratore* (Milan), November 1985, pp. 68–69.

Putti, Laura. "Vangelis e le macchine." *La repubblica*, 28 March 1989, p. 36.

Q., L. "Francesco d'Assisi." In *Tradizione e innovazione nel cinema degli autori emiliano-romagnoli*, edited by Adelio Ferrero, pp. 43–45. Modena: Ufficio Cinema del Comune di Modena, 1976.

Qu., C. "Milarepa." *Giornale d'Italia*, 23–24 March 1974, p. 14.

Quaglietti, Lorenzo. "La pelle di Liliana Cavani." *Cinema sessanta*, no. 142 (November–December 1981): 58–59.

Quarantotto, Claudio. "Una lezione di storia che non convince." *Giornale d'Italia*, 3–4 September 1968, p. 3.

————. "Cronache di una Mostra salvata dai borghesi." *Il borghese*, 12 September 1968, pp. 92–93.

————. "Un Galileo 'contestatore.' " *Giornale d'Italia* (Rome), 22 February 1969, p. 13.

————. "Oscar e 'cannibali' una sera, a Spoleto." *Giornale d'Italia*, 27–28 April 1970, p. 15.

————. "I russi chiudono la porta." *Giornale d'Italia*, 6 September 1971, p. 12.

————. "Il portiere di notte." *Giornale d'Italia*, 16 April 1974, p. 14.

————. "Achtung, nostalgia!" *Il borghese*, 28 April 1974, pp. 1067–1068.

Quilici, Lia. "Madame direttore." *L'espresso*, 20 April 1969, pp. 13–17.

Quinzio, Sergio. "Né sacerdote né monaco." *Il messaggero*, 4 October 1981, p. 3.

R., C. "Manifestazioni cinematografiche." In *Biennale-Annuario 1978*, p. 343. Venice: La Biennale, 1979.

R., G. L. [Rondi, Gian Luigi]. "I cannibali." *Il tempo*, 26 April 1970, p. 10.

————. "Oltre la porta." *Il tempo*, 29 October 1982, p. 12.

R., S. "Napoli, l'inferno della Cavani." *La stampa*, 25 September 1981, p. 17.

R., V. "Ci sono cento modi per diventare guru." *L'espresso*, 28 October 1973, p. 17.

Raban, Jonathan. "Venetian Mixed Fish." *New Statesman*, 10 September 1971, p. 341.

Rabaurdin, D. "Berlin Affair." *Cinéma* (Paris), no. 351 (April 1989): p. 5.

Raboni, Giovanni. "Antigone ribelle anche a Milano." *L'avvenire*, 6 May 1970, p. 9.

"Racconto dei concetti." *Fiera letteraria*, 28 March 1968, p. 29.

Raffaelli, Sergio. " 'I cannibali' di Liliana Cavani." *Lettere*, nos. 8–9 (August–September 1970): 593–597.

Rasp, Renate. "Goldene Zeiten im KZ." *Der Spiegel*, 17 February 1975, p. 122.

Rayns, Tony. "Al di là del bene e del male." *Monthly Film Bulletin* 46 (December 1979): 247.

Rea, Domenico. "La teoria dello scoop." *Il mattino*, 2 October 1981, p. 5.

"Reazioni del mondo del cinema al sequestro di 'Portiere di notte.' " *Il tempo*, 19 April 1974, p. 8.

Reggiani, Stefano. "Tanto sangue, poca passione." *La stampa*, 23 May 1981, p. 3.

————. "Cavani, le passioni congelate." *La stampa*, 29 November 1985, p. 23.

————. "Rourke, la follia del santo." *La stampa*, 24 March 1989, p. 25.

Renaud, Tristan. "Le Temps des assassins: 'I cannibali' de Liliana Cavani." *Lettres Françaises*, 19 April 1972, pp. 13, 16.

————. "I cannibali: Morts sans sépultures." *Cinéma* (Paris), no. 167 (June 1972): 151.

Rensi, Emilia. "Eppur si muove. . . ." *Umanità nuova* (Rome), 1 March 1969, pp. 2, 4.

Ricciuti, Vittorio. " 'Galileo' un film decoroso ma di troppo rigore storico." *Il mattino*, 3 September 1968, p. 9.

————. "Un cinema del tutto inedito nel film di Augusto Tretti." *Il mattino*, 5 September 1971, p. 11.

————. "Cinema e sesso." *Il mattino*, 30 April 1974, p. 3.

Richetti, Donata, "La Cavani fa la dura, Agosti l'agitatore." *Il giornale*, 2 September 1993, p. 19.

Rinaudo, Fabio. "Un Galileo non fa primavera." *Film mese* 2 (August–September 1968): 104.

Ripa, Ornella. "Solo i cannibali salveranno la città." *Gente*, 11 May 1970, pp. 107–108.

Riva, Sonja. "Alla scoperta di un paese straniero." *Galatea*, September 1993, pp. 85–87.

Riva, Valerio. "Lui Milarepa." *L'espresso*, 29 October 1973, pp. 16–17.

Rizzon, Gianpiero. "Dopo quella di Brass la matta della Cavani." *Il gazzettino*, 5 September 1971, p. 3.

Robiony, Simonetta. "Liliana Cavani: 'Berlin Interior non è un film, è la mia libertà.' " *La stampa*, 30 June 1985, p. 18.

——. "Cavani: 'Solo con Rourke posso rifare la storia di Francesco.' " *La stampa*, 13 February 1988, p. 16.

——. "Cavani: 'Senza Rourke non avrei mai girato Francesco.' " *La stampa*, 21 March 1989, p. 21.

——. "La forza degli infelici." *La stampa*, 2 September 1993, p. 19.

Rocher, Thérèse. "Berlin Affair." *Cinématographe* (Paris) 118 (April 1986): 61.

Rondi, Gian Luigi. "Un suggestivo 'Galileo' sullo schermo della Mostra." *Il tempo*, 3 September 1968, p. 7.

——. "Lunga notte delle stelle per gli 'Oscar italiani.' " *Il tempo*, 26 Appril 1970, p. 10.

——. "Milarepa." *Il tempo*, 24 March 1974, p. 14.

——. "Il portiere di notte." *Il tempo*, 14 April 1974, p. 12.

——. "A Cannes il dramma di due solitudini." *Il tempo*, 17 May 1974, p. 12.

——. "Al di là del bene e del male." *Il tempo*, 29 October 1977, p. 12.

——. "Ritorna il Malaparte che aveva sempre ragione." *Il tempo*, 23 May 1981, p. 10.

——. "La pelle." *Il tempo*, 2 October 1981, p. 10.

——. "Trote per Losey sequestri d'amore per Liliana Cavani." *Il tempo*, 6 September 1982, p. 19.

——. "Interno berlinese." *Il tempo*, 31 October 1985, p. 12.

——. "Un grande 'Francesco.' " *Il tempo*, 22 March 1989, p. 15.

——. " 'Francesco' di Liliana Cavani." *Rivista del cinematografo* 59 (May 1989): 12.

——. "Cavani, l'importanza del silenzio." *Il tempo*, 27 September 1993, p. 18.

Rondoni, Enrico. "Così parlò Nietzsche sul sentiero di Liliana Cavani." *L'umanità*, 29 October 1977, p. 5.

Rosenbaum, Jonathan. "Portiere di notte." *Monthly Film Bulletin* 41 (November 1974): 255–256.

Rouchy, Marie-Elisabeth. "Liliana Cavani: La Belle Indifférente." *Le Matin*, 4 May 1983, p. 32.

Roud, Richard. "Rebirth of Realism." *Guardian* (Manchester), 2 August 1966, p. 7.

——. "On the Road to Venice." *Guardian*, 14 August 1971, p. 6.

Ryweck, Charles. " 'Beyond Good and Evil': Intriguing, Controversial Work." *Hollywood Reporter*, 9 July 1984, p. 23.

S., G. "Un uomo come noi." *Azione sociale* (Rome), 22 May 1966, p. 15.

S., N. "Il respiro calmo della verità." *L'avanti*, 3 May 1964, p. 6.

——. "Un ordine e un metodo." *L'avanti*, 17 May 1964, p. 6.

——. "L'inchiesta sul tetto che scotta." *L'avanti*, 31 May 1964, p. 6.

S., R. "Divieto di sepoltura." *La notte*, 4 May 1970, p. 15.

Sa., Ag. [Savioli, Aggeo]. "Le prime: Galileo." *L'unità*, 21 February 1969, p. 7.

——. "L'ospite." *L'unità*, 11 March 1972, p. 9.

Sa., Au. [Santuari, Aurora]. " 'L'ospite' di Rondi rompe il silenzio." *Paese sera*, 24 August 1971, p. 11.

——. " 'Oltre la porta': Tanto sui miei film dopo ci ripensate." *Paese sera*, 7 September 1982, p. 13.

Sacchi, Filippo. "Misteri della censura: 'Galileo' vietato ai minori di 18 anni." *Epoca*, 22 September 1968, p. 130.

———. "Ritorna con Antigone il dramma del potere assoluto." *Epoca*, 3 May 1970, p. 135.

Saitta, Luigi. "Tra Vienna e Berlino per raccontare tre vite private che diventano 'caso.' " *Il tempo*, 1 July, 1985, p. 8.

———. " 'Il mio S. Francesco avrà il volto di Mickey Rourke.' " *Il tempo*, 14 February 1988, p. 18.

"Saltata l'inchiesta sulla casa." *L'avanti*, 10 May 1964, p. 6.

Saltini, Vittorio. "Non ci sono genî per le cameriere." *L'espresso*, 30 October 1977, p. 77–81.

———. "Al di là del bene e del vaso." *L'espresso*, 20 November 1977, pp. 95–97.

Salvatorelli, Luigi. "San Francesco alla TV." *La stampa*, 19 May 1966, p. 3.

Sanfilippo, Mario. "Scomodo e allineato." *Il messaggero*, 4 October 1981, p. 3.

Santuari, Aurora. "L'ospite' è sacro pure in manicomio." *Paese sera*, 10 June 1971, p. 21.

Sarris, Andrew. "The Nasty Nazis: History or Mythology?" *Village Voice*, 17 October 1974, pp. 77–78.

Sassanelli, Giorgio, and Giuseppe Vetrone. "Liliana Cavani o la capacità di guardare." *Belfagor* 33, no. 1 (1978): 101–104.

Saviane, Sergio. "I tranelli del teleobiettivo." *L'espresso*, 31 May 1964, p. 27.

———. "Il fratello della luna." *L'espresso*, 15 May 1966, p. 31.

Savio, Francesco. "Senza mistero." *Il mondo*, 18 April 1974, p. 22.

Savioli, Aggeo. "Il 'Galileo' ha trovato l'ambiente meno adatto." *L'unità*, 3 September 1968, p. 7.

———. " 'I cannibali': Antigone 1970." *L'unità*, 26 April 1970, p. 10.

———. "Il nazismo intimista." *L'unità*, 14 April 1974, p. 9.

———. "Un terzetto scombinato." *L'unità*, 29 October 1977, p. 11.

———. "Quel sequestro è una prova d'amore." *L'unità*, 6 September 1982, p. 8.

Sayre, Nora. " 'The Night Porter,' Portrait of Abuse, Stars Bogarde." *New York Times*, 2 October 1974, L58.

Sc., A. [Scagnetti, Aldo]. "L'ospite." *Paese sera*, 11 March 1972, p. 13.

Scagnetti, Aldo. " 'Galileo': Un film su potere e libertà." *Paese sera*, 21 February 1969, p. 11.

———. "Ex criminali nazisti in un film della Cavani." *Paese sera*, 7 February 1971, p. 19.

Scandolara, Sandro. "L'amore, i morti e altre cose." *Cineforum* 10 (May–August 1970): 130–135.

Scap. [Scaparro, Maurizio]. "La notte dei lunghi coltelli di Hitler." *L'avanti*, 25 November 1961, p. 5.

Schettino, Daniela. "La cinematografia di Liliana Cavani." Diss., Università degli Studi di Lecce: Facoltà di Lettere e Filosofia, 1976–1977.

Schickel, Richard. "Out of the Night." *Time*, 21 October 1974, pp. 12, K6.

Segneri, Ettore. "Dove siete? Io sono qui di Liliana Cavani." *Rivista del cinematografo* 11 (November 1993): 15.

Ser., G. "Dibattito alla Camera su un film 'immorale.' " *Il tempo*, 6 May 1978, p. 17.

Serceau, Daniel. "Berlin Affair." *Revue du Cinéma* 416 (May 1986): 64–65.

Sermonti, Giuseppe. "Non fu uno sperimentatore." *Retrospettive libri*, October 1981, pp. 13–18.

Serra, Silvestro, and Maria Simonetti. "Sulla pelle di Curzio." *Panorama*, 24 November 1980, pp. 178–182.

Shorter, Eric. "Travelling in Good Faith." *Daily Telegraph*, 26 October 1979, p. 15.

Sichère, Bernard. "La Bête et le militant." *Cahiers du Cinéma*, nos. 251–252 (July–August 1974): 19–29.

Siciliano, Enzo. "Metti un ciak sulle bugie di Malaparte." *Corriere della sera illustrato*, 13 September 1980, pp. 22–25.

Siclier, Jacques. "Les Créateurs font marche arrière: Depuis trente-cinq ans, le cinéma raconte le nazisme." *Le Monde*, 18 April 1974, p. 18.

———. "La Nouvelle Morale de Liliana Cavani." *Le Monde*, 8 October 1977, p. 31.

———. "Liliana Cavani, Malaparte et l'enfer de Naples." *Le Monde*, 26 May 1981, p. 19.

———. "L'Esthète et la Bostonienne dans l'enfer de Naples." *Le Monde*, 28 November 1981, p. 23.

———. "Les Mystères de Marrakech." *Le Monde*, 7 May 1983, p. 23.

———. "Berlin Affair." *Le Monde*, 29 April 1989, p. 17.

Silverman, Kaja. "Masochism and Subjectivity." *Framework* (University of East Anglia), no. 12 (1980): 2–9.

———. *The Acoustic Mirror: The Female Voice in Psychoanalysis and Cinema*. Bloomington and Indianapolis: Indiana University Press, 1988.

———. *Male Subjectivity at the Margins*. New York and London: Routledge, 1992.

Six, Jean-François. "On n'a jamais fini d'aimer." *Le Monde*, 5–6 May 1974, pp. 9–10.

———. "Milarepa, est-ce une drogue?" *Le Monde*, 23–24 March 1975, p. 11.

Solmi, Angelo. "Galileo raccontato da una donna." *Oggi*, 26 September 1968, pp. 87, 89.

———. "La gentile signora parla di cadaveri." *Oggi*, 26 May 1970, p. 135.

———. "Smettiamola di punire i coraggiosi." *Oggi*, 8 May 1974, p. 161.

———. "Nostalgia del 'Portiere.'" *Oggi*, 12 June 1974, p. 109.

———. "Non è Nietzsche, ma è un gran film." *Oggi*, 19 November 1977, p. 147.

———. "A qualcuna piace femmina." *Oggi*, 4 December 1985, pp. 118–119.

———. "Somiglia a un samurai." *Oggi*, 12 April 1989, p. 109.

Sorgi, Claudio. "Critica e anticritica." *Osservatore romano*, 20–21 November 1967, p. 3.

———. "Accolto il 'Galileo' con buona dose di consensi e polemiche." *Osservatore romano*, 4 September 1968, p. 5.

Spiga, Vittorio. "L'ambiguo potere del sesso." *Resto del Carlino*, 1 November 1985, p. vii.

———. "Atomica, mai più: E Liliana Cavani parla del suo 'Francesco.'" *La nazione*, 19 May 1989, p. 9.

———. "Benvenuta, sorella voce." *Resto del Carlino*, 2 September 1993, p. 17.

Spinotti, Dante. "Quando la luce diventa racconto." *Videoregistratore* (Milan), November 1985, p. 70.

Stein, Elliott. "Berlin Stories." *Village Voice*, 20 January 1987, p. 57.

Stone, Laurie. "Faking It." *Village Voice*, 27 January 1987, p. 62.

Stuart, Alexander. "Collaboration." *Films and Filming* 20 (August 1974): 56–59.

Su., S. [Surchi, Sergio]. "La tecnica della dittatura." *Il popolo*, 25 November 1961, p. 5.

———. "Videosera: Congedo di 'Osservatorio.' " *Il popolo*, 29 June 1963, p. 7.

———. "Videosera: I 'bassi' e le baracche." *Il popolo*, 3 May 1964, p. 5.

———. " 'L'ospite': Un mondo di esiliati senza ritorno." *Il popolo*, 25 May 1973, p. 7.

Sulik, Boleslaw. "London Film Festival." *Tribune* (London), 11 December 1970, p. 11.

Sultanik, Aaron. "World War II as Nightmare and as Human Folly." *Midstream* (New York) 21 (January 1975): 67–70.

Surchi, Sergio. "San Francesco alla TV soltanto umano." *Il popolo*, 17 May 1966, p. 3.

———. "Drammatizzare mai distorcere se si vuole insegnare qualcosa." *Il popolo*, 15 November 1967, p. 7.

———. "Visione obbiettiva con filtro moderno." *Il popolo*, 25 November 1967, p. 11.

———. "Occhi puntati sul manicomio." *La nazione*, 26 June 1971, p. 9.

T., G. "Sui teleschermi: Secondo canale." Review of *Storia del Terzo Reich*. *Il messaggero*, 20 October 1962, p. 8.

———. "Sui teleschermi: Secondo canale." Review of *Storia del Terzo Reich*. *Il messaggero*, 27 October 1962, p. 8.

———. "Sui teleschermi: Secondo canale." Review of *Età di Stalin*. *Il messaggero*, 22 December 1962, p. 8.

———. "Sui teleschermi: Secondo canale." Review of *L'uomo della burocrazia*. *Il messaggero*, 23 May 1963, p. 8.

———. "Sui teleschermi: Secondo canale." Review of *Il giorno della pace*. *Il messaggero*, 8 May 1965, p. 10.

———. "Sui teleschermi: Secondo canale." Review of *La donna nella resistenza*. *Il messaggero*, 10 May 1965, p. 12.

———. "Sui teleschermi: Secondo canale." Review of *Philippe Pétain: Processo a Vichy*. *Il messaggero*, 5 June 1965, p. 10.

———. "Sui teleschermi: Secondo canale." Review of *Francesco di Assisi*. *Il messaggero*, 24 March 1967, p. 10.

T., L. [Tornabuoni, Lietta]. "Occasione sprecata dalla Cavani." *La stampa*, 6 September 1982, p. 6.

———. "Liliana Cavani, il silenzio." *La stampa*, 2 September 1993, p. 19.

———. "Quando si ama nel silenzio." *La stampa*, 24 September 1993, p. 26.

T., P.-L. [Thirard]. "Les Cannibales." *Positif* 139 (June 1972): 63.

Tallarigo, Paola, and Luca Gasparini, eds. *Il cinema di Liliana Cavani: Lo sguardo libero*. Florence: La Casa Usher, 1990.

Taylor, John Russell. "Idiot Delights." *Times* (London), 7 September 1971, The Arts, p. 7.

"Terrore e miseria del III Reich." *La stampa*, 25 November 1961, p. 4.

Testaferri, Ada, ed. *Donna: Women in Italian Culture*. Ottawa: Dovehouse Editions, 1989.

Tiso, Ciriaco. "L'ambiguità filmica e il suo equivoco." *Filmcritica* 248 (October 1974): 239–335.

———. *Liliana Cavani*. Il Castoro cinema, no. 21. Florence: La Nuova Italia, 1975.

Tornabuoni, Lietta. "Come è bello farsi dirigere da una donna." *L'europeo*, 19 June 1969, p. 82.

———. "Il nazismo nel cinema." *Linus*, June 1974, pp. 60–66.

Tiso, Ciriaco. "Cavani, suspense con passione dopo le amarezze de 'La pelle.' " *La stampa*, 29 December 1981, p. 15.

———. "Povero e nudo." *Panorama*, 9 April 1989, p. 16.

———. "I guai della 'Berlitz Era.' " *La stampa*, 11 June 1989, p. 3.

———. "Chi vive nella Berlitz Era?" *La stampa*, 13 June 1989, p. 3.

Torresin, Brunella. "Un santo per amico." *La repubblica*, 5 May 1989, p. 9.

Tournès, A. "Liliana Cavani." *Jeune Cinéma* 63 (May–June 1972): 20–24.

Tr. [Trifiletti]. "TV: Francesco senza aureola." *Voce repubblicana*, 8 May 1966, p. 5.

———. "TV: Si comincia a 'pensare.' " *Voce repubblicana*, 10 May 1966, p. 5.

Trasatti, Sergio. "Alla TV un film su Francesco d'Assisi: Una proposta culturale dedicata ai giovani." *Osservatore romano*, 12–13 April 1966, p. 5.

———. "Amorale e insignificante il film di Schlesinger." *Osservatore romano*, 6–7 September 1971, p. 3.

———. "Quale Francesco nel cinema contemporaneo?" *Osservatore romano*, 3–4 April 1989, p. 3.

Tremois, Claude-Marie. "Cannes: Dévoré par 'Les cannibales.' " *Télérama*, 30 May 1970, pp. 61–62.

———. " 'Portier de nuit': Un film contre l'horreur nazie." *Télérama*, 6 April 1974, pp. 62–63.

Trifiletti, Aldo. "Nel film d'autore il cinema cerca il proprio rinnovamneto." *Voce repubblicana*, 15–16 September 1966, p. 5.

Trionfera, Claudio. "Il misterioso mondo dei sordi e quello di Manhattan." *Il tempo*, 2 September 1993, p. 23.

Trischitta, Domenico. *Francesco: Percorsi cinematografici*. Catania: Boemi Prampolini, 1996.

Tuohy, William. "The Thinking Man's Triangle." *Los Angeles Times*, 6 January 1977, p. 14.

"Gli uomini ambigui di Liliana Cavani." *Giornale d'Italia*, 8–9 March 1973, p. 15.

Urbano, Micaela. "Quasi quindici miliardi per un divo americano e tanti attori tutti giovani." *Il messaggero*, 21 March 1989, p. 18.

Urbini, Remo. "L'obiettivo senza pudore." *Epoca*, 28 April 1974, pp. 128–129.

V., L. "Il mondo del cinema unito nella lotta contro la repressione." *Il messaggero*, 27 April 1974, p. 8.

V., P. [Valmarana, Paolo]. "Chi ha paura di Liliana Cavani?" *Il popolo*, 5 November 1977, p. 5.

Valmarana, Paolo. "Esempio di chiarezza il film della Cavani." *Il popolo*, 3 September 1968, p. 5.

———. "Occhi di oggi rifanno Galileo." *Il popolo*, 21 February 1969, p. 7.

———. " 'Milarepa' di Liliana Cavani: Un invito a vivere secondo la verità." *Il popolo*, 26 March 1974, p. 7.

———. "L'inferno nazista." *Il popolo*, 14 April 1974, p. 7.

———. "Il piacere dell'ambiguità." *Il popolo*, 29 October 1977, p. 5.

———. "Lo scandalo è fuori dalle righe." *Il popolo*, 3 October 1981, p. 25.

"Il valore del dissenso." *L'avanti*, 26 April 1970, p. 9.

Venegoni, Marinella. "Sullo schermo la donna è ancora 'contorno' per i padri padroni." *La stampa*, 11 December 1977, p. 9.

Venezia, Alessandra. "Laudata sia Liliana." *Panorama*, 26 March 1989, pp. 142–145.

Verdone, Mario. "La XXIX Mostra di Venezia, contestazione a parte." *Bianco e nero*, nos. 9–10 (September–October 1968): 73–97.

Vergani, Leonardo. "La Cavani non taglia il film che scotta." *Corriere della sera*, 15 May 1974, p. 15.

Vice. "Televisione: Gli anni tragici dell'Europa." *L'avanti*, 2 December 1961, p. 5.

———. "Una trasmissione sul nazismo." *L'avanti*, 20 October 1962, p. 5.

———. "L'età di Stalin." *L'avanti*, 22 December 1962, p. 5.

———. "Sui teleschermi: Primo canale." Review of *La casa in Italia*. *Il messaggero*, 9 May 1964, p. 8.

———. "Da cantatutto ai pirati." *L'unità*, 17 May 1964, p. 11.

———. "Controcanale: Un'assurda riforma." *L'unità*, 24 May 1964, p. 9.

———. "Controcanale: C'è casa e casa." *L'unità*, 31 May 1964, p. 9.

———. "Antigone (oggi) muore a Milano." *Gazzetta del popolo*, 1 May 1970, p. 7.

———. "Le prime: Francesco d'Assisi." *L'unità*, 22 June 1972, p. 7.

Video. "Donne coraggiose." *Paese sera*, 3 May 1964, p. 12.

Vinciguerra, Claudia. "Liliana Cavani: 'L'*Interno berlinese* è la storia di una ragazza giapponese, che nel 1938 sconvolge la vita di una coppia borghese e nazista.'" *Il giorno*, 30 June 1985, p. 14.

Vitrano, Salvo. "Nella rete delle verità." *Il mattino*, 28 September 1982, p. 14.

———. "Perversioni esotiche all'ombra del III Reich." *Il mattino*, 4 November 1985, p. 23.

Vogel, Amos. "One Festival Plus One." *Village Voice*, 9 July 1970, pp. 51, 57–58.

Walker, Alexander. "Two for the Pipshow." *Evening Standard*, 17 January 1974, p. 29.

Waller, Marguerite. "Signifying the Holocaust: Liliana Cavani's *Portiere di notte*." In *Feminisms in the Cinema*, edited by Laura Pietropaolo and Ada Tagliaferri, pp. 206–219. Bloomington: Indiana University Press, 1995.

Walsh, Moira. "The Night Porter." *America*, 26 October 1974, p. 234.

Werb. "Galileo." *Variety*, 11 September 1968, p. 6.

———. "L'ospite." *Variety*, 22 September 1971, p. 14.

———. "Milarepa." *Variety*, 17 April 1974, p. 20.

———. "La pelle." *Variety*, 3 June 1981, p. 15.

Witcombe, R. T. *The New Italian Cinema: Studies in Dance and Despair*. New York: Oxford University Press, 1982.

Wlaschin, Ken. "Liberated Women: Venice '71." *Films and Filming* 18 (November 1971): 26–30.

"The Year of the Cannibals." *Filmfacts* 16, no. 1 (1973): 10–11.

Yung. "Oltre la porta." *Variety*, 15 September 1982, p. 16.

———. "Interno berlinese." *Variety*, 6 November 1985, p. 28.

———. "Francesco." *Variety*, 12 April 1989, p. 20.

———. "Francesco." *Variety*, 20 May 1989, p. 3.

Z., D. [Zanelli, D.]. "Un Tibet abruzzese." *Resto del Carlino*, 17 March, 1974, p. 9.

Z., P. D. [Zimmerman]. "Trampling on Rampling." *Newsweek*, 7 October 1974, p. 95.

Zanelli, Dario. "Un 'Galileo' che fa pensare a Dubcek." *Resto del Carlino*, 3 September 1968, p. 9.

———. "'Fritz' Nietzsche e la superdonna." *Resto del Carlino*, 20 November 1977, p. vi.

Other Works Cited

Abruzzese, Alberto, et al. *Spettacolo e metropoli*. Naples: Liguori, 1981.

Adorno, Theodor W. *Kierkegaard: Construction of the Aesthetic*. Translated, edited, and with foreword by Robert Hullot-Kentor. Minneapolis: University of Minnesota Press, 1989.

Andreas-Salomé, Lou. *Mon Expérience de l'amitié avec Nietzsche et Rée*. Paris: Societé Française d'Etudes Nietzschéennes, 1954.

Argentieri, Mino. *La censura nel cinema italiano*. Rome: Editori Riuniti, 1974.

———. *Il film biografico*. Rome: Bulzoni, 1984.

Artaud, Antonin. *The Theater and Its Double*. Translated by Mary Caroline Richards. New York: Dover, 1979.

Asor Rosa, Alberto, ed. *Letteratura italiana*. 6 vols. Turin: Einaudi, 1982.

Attolini, Vito. *Sotto il segno del film (Cinema italiano 1968/76)*. Bari: Mario Adda Editore, 1983.

Bachelard, Gaston. *La Terre et les rêveries du repos*. Paris: Corti, 1948.

———. *La Psychanalyse du feu*. Paris: Gallimard, 1949.

———. *La Poétique de l'espace*. Paris: Presses Universitaires de France, 1967.

Bacot, Jacques, ed. *Vita di Milarepa: I suoi delitti, le sue prove, la sua liberazione*. Milan: Adelphi, 1989.

Bataille, Georges. *L'Erotisme*. Paris: Editions de Minuit, 1957.

———. *Visions of Excess: Selected Writings 1927–1939*. Edited and introduced by Allan Stoekl, translated by A. Stoekl et al. Minneapolis: University of Minnesota Press, 1985.

Bazin, André. *What Is Cinema?* Edited and translated by Hugh Gray. 2 vols. Berkeley and Los Angeles: University of California Press, 1967.

Bendix, Reinhard. *Max Weber: An Intellectual Portrait*. Garden City, NY: Anchor Books, 1960.

Benjamin, Jessica. "A Desire of One's Own: Psychoanalytic Feminism and Intersubjective Space." In *Feminist Studies/Critical Studies*, edited by T. De Lauretis, pp. 78–101. Bloomington: Indiana University Press, 1986.

Benjamin, Walter. *Illuminations*. New York: Harcourt, Brace and World, 1968.

Biasin, Gian-Paolo. *The Flavors of Modernity: Food and the Novel*. Princeton, NJ: Princeton University Press, 1993.

Blanchot, Maurice. *Lautrémont et Sade*. Paris: Editions de Minuit, 1963.

Bordwell, David. *The Films of Carl-Theodor Dreyer*. Berkeley and Los Angeles: University of California Press, 1981.

Brunette, Peter. *Roberto Rossellini*. New York: Oxford University Press, 1987.

Bruno, Giuliana. *Streetwalking on a Ruined Map: Cultural Theory and the City Films of Elvira Notari*. Princeton, NJ: Princeton University Press, 1993.

Buci-Glucksmann, Christine. *La Folie du voir: De l'esthétique baroque*. Paris: Editions Galilée, 1986.

Burch, Noël. *To the Distant Observer: Form and Meaning in the Japanese Cinema*. Revised and edited by Annette Michelson. Berkeley and Los Angeles: University of California Press, 1979.

Butō: La "nuova danza" giapponese. Introduced by Maria Pia D'Orazi. Rome: Editori Associati, 1997.

Caillois, Roger. *I giochi e gli uomini.* Preface by Pier Aldo Rovatti, notes by Giampaolo Dossena. Milan: Bompiani, 1995.

Calabrese, Omar. *Neo-Baroque: A Sign of the Times.* Translated by Charles Lambert, with foreword by U. Eco. Princeton, NJ: Princeton University Press, 1992.

Calasso, Roberto. *Le nozze di Cadmo e Armonia.* Milan: Adelphi, 1989.

Campbell, Joseph. *The Hero with a Thousand Faces.* 2d ed. Bollingen Series XVII. Princeton, NJ: Princeton University Press, 1968.

Carroll, Noël. *Philosophical Problems of Classical Film Theory.* Princeton, NJ: Princeton University Press, 1988.

Casebier, Allan. *Film and Phenomenology: Toward a Realist Theory of Cinematic Representation.* Cambridge: Cambridge University Press, 1991.

Cassirer, Ernst. *Substance and Function and Einstein's Theory of Relativity.* Translated by William Curtis Swabey and Marie Collins Swabey. New York: Dover, 1953.

Cavell, Stanley. *The Claiming of Reason: Wittgenstein, Skepticism, Morality and Tragedy.* New York: Oxford University Press, 1979.

Cederroth, S., C. Corlin, and J. Lindström, eds. *On the Meaning of Death: Essays on Mortuary Rituals and Escatological Beliefs.* Introduced by Maurice Bloch. Stockholm: Almqvist & Wiksell International, 1988.

Corti, Maria. *Il viaggio testuale: Le ideologie e le strutture semiotiche.* Turin: Einaudi, 1978.

D'Amico de Carvalho, Caterina. *Piero Tosi: Costumi e scenografie.* Milan: Leonardo, 1997.

Deleuze, Gilles. *Sacher-Masoch: An Interpretation.* Translated by Jean McNeil. London: Faber and Faber, 1971.

———. *Nietzsche and Philosophy.* Translated by Hugh Tomlinson. New York: Columbia University Press, 1983.

———. *Foucault.* Translated and edited by Seán Hand, foreword by Paul Bové. Minneapolis: University of Minnesota Press, 1988.

Deleuze, G., and Félix Guattari. *Anti-Oedipus: Capitalism and Schizophrenia.* Preface by M. Foucault, translated by Robert Hurley, Mark Seem, and Helen R. Lane. Minneapolis: University of Minnesota Press, 1983.

———. *A Thousand Plateaus: Capitalism and Schizophrenia.* Translated and with foreword by Brian Massumi. Minneapolis: University of Minnesota Press, 1987.

De Marchi, Bruno. *Umbra dei e palpebra del cinema, luce.* Milan: Euresis Edizioni, 1996.

Derrida, Jacques. *Spurs: Eperons.* Chicago: University of Chicago Press, 1979.

Doane, Mary Ann. "Ideology and the Practice of Sound Editing and Mixing." In *The Cinematic Apparatus,* edited by T. De Lauretis and Stephen Heath, pp. 47–56. New York: St. Martin's Press, 1980.

Doob, Penelope Reed. *The Idea of the Labyrinth from Classical Antiquity through the Middle Ages.* Ithaca, NY, and London: Cornell University Press, 1990.

Dreyfus, Hubert L., and Paul Rabinow. *Michel Foucault: Beyond Structuralism and Hermeneutics.* 2d ed. Afterword by and interview with M. Foucault. Chicago: University of Chicago Press, 1983.

Durand, Gilbert. *Les Structures anthropologiques de l'imaginaire: Introduction à l'archétypologie générale.* Paris: Bordas, 1984.

Eco, Umberto. *La struttura assente: Introduzione alla ricerca semiologica.* Milan: Bompiani, 1968.

Eco, Umberto. *Apocalittici e integrati*. Milan: Bompiani, 1977.

Eliade, Mircea. *Cosmos and History: The Myth of the Eternal Return*. New York: Harper, 1959.

———. *Images and Symbols: Studies in Religious Symbolism*. Translated by Philip Mairet. New York: Sheed and Ward, 1961.

———. *L'Epreuve du labyrinthe: Entretiens avec Claude-Henri Rocquet*. Paris: Pierre Belfond, 1978.

Evans-Wentz, W. Y., ed. *The Tibetan Book of the Dead*. London and Oxford: Oxford University Press, 1960.

Fleming, John V. *From Bonaventure to Bellini: An Essay in Franciscan Exegesis*. Princeton, NJ: Princeton University Press, 1982.

Fortini, Arnaldo. *Francesco d'Assisi e l'Italia del suo tempo*. Rome: Biblioteca di Storia Patria, 1968.

Foucault, Michel. *The Order of Things: An Archaeology of the Human Sciences*. New York: Vintage Books, 1970.

———. *Histoire de la folie à l'âge classique*. Paris: Gallimard, 1972.

———. *Surveiller et punir: Naissance de la prison*. Paris: Gallimard, 1975.

———. *Histoire de la sexualité*. Vol. 1, *La Volonté de savoir*. Vol. 2, *L'Usage des plaisirs*. Paris: Gallimard, 1976, 1984.

———. *Language, Counter-Memory, Practice: Selected Essays and Interviews*. Edited and introduced by Donald F. Bouchard, translated by D. F. Bouchard and Sherry Simon. Ithaca, NY: Cornell University Press, 1977.

Fraser, J. T. *Of Time, Passion, and Knowledge: Reflections on the Strategy of Existence*. 2d ed. Princeton, NJ: Princeton University Press, 1990.

Friedländer, Saul. *Reflections of Nazism: An Essay on Kitsch and Death*. Translated by Thomas Weyr. New York: Harper and Row, 1984.

Frugoni, Chiara. *A Distant City: Images of Urban Experience in the Medieval World*. Translated by William McCuaig. Princeton, NJ: Princeton University Press, 1991.

———. *Francesco e l'invenzione delle stimmate: Una storia per parole e immagini fino a Bonaventura e Giotto*. Turin: Einaudi, 1992.

Frye, Northrop. *Anatomy of Criticism: Four Essays*. Princeton, NJ: Princeton University Press, 1957.

Galilei, Galileo. *Opere*. 13 vols. Milan: Società Tipografica De' Classici Italiani, 1808–1811.

Gennep, Arnold van. *The Rites of Passage*. Introd. S. T. Kimball, translated by M. B. Vizedon and G. L. Caffee. 1960. 3d ed. Chicago: University of Chicago Press, 1964.

Genovese, Nino, ed. *Barbaro e Chiarini: I teorici del cinema dietro la macchina da presa*. Messina: Edizioni De Spectaculis, 1988.

Girard, René. *The Scapegoat*. Translated by Yvonne Freccero. Baltimore: Johns Hopkins University Press, 1986.

Giusti, Marco and Ghezzi, Enrico, eds. *Kim Arcalli, montare il cinema*. Venice: Marsilio, 1980.

Green, Julien. *God's Fool: The Life and Times of Francis of Assisi*. Translated by Peter Heinegg. New York: Harper and Row, 1985.

Greene, Naomi. *Pier Paolo Pasolini: Cinema as Heresy*. Princeton, NJ: Princeton University Press, 1990.

Hauser, Arnold. *The Social History of Art*. 2 vols. New York: Knopf, 1952.

Holborn, Mark, et al. *Butoh: Dance of the Dark Soul*. New York: Aperture, 1987.

Jung, Carl G. *Symbols of Transformation: An Analysis of the Prelude to a Case of Schizophrenia*. Translated by R.F.C. Hull. Bollingen Series XX. New York: Pantheon, 1956.

————. *Aion: Researches into the Phenomenology of the Self*. Translated by R.F.C. Hull. Bollingen Series XX. New York: Pantheon, 1959.

————. *Alchemical Studies*. Translated by R.F.C. Hull. Bollingen Series XX. Princeton, NJ: Princeton University Press, 1967.

————. *The Archetypes and the Collective Unconscious*. Translated by R.F.C. Hull. Bollingen Series XX. 2d ed. Princeton, NJ: Princeton University Press, 1969.

————. *The Structure and Dynamics of the Psyche*. Translated by R.F.C. Hull. 2d ed. Bollingen Series XX. Princeton, NJ: Princeton University Press, 1981.

Kantorowicz, Ernst H. *The King's Two Bodies: A Study in Mediaeval Political Theology*. Princeton, NJ: Princeton University Press, 1957.

Kaufmann, Walter. *Tragedy and Philosophy*. Princeton, NJ: Princeton University Press, 1992.

Kawin, Bruce F. *Mindscreen: Bergman, Godard and First-Person Film*. Princeton, NJ: Princeton University Press, 1978.

Kierkegaard, Søren. *Either/Or: Part I*. Edited and translated with introduction and notes by Howard V. Hong and Edna H. Hong. Princeton, NJ: Princeton University Press, 1987.

Knapp, Bettina L. *A Jungian Approach to Literature*. Carbondale and Edwardsville: Southern Illinois University Press, 1984.

Kracauer, Siegfried. *From Caligari to Hitler: A Psychological History of the German Film*. Princeton, NJ: Princeton University Press, 1947.

Lemert, Charles C. and Garth Gillian. *Michel Foucault: Social Theory as Transgression*. New York: Columbia University Press, 1982.

Leprohon, Pierre. *The Italian Cinema*. Translated by R. Graves and O. Stallybrass. New York: Praeger, 1972.

Livingston, Angela. *Salomé: Her Life and Work*. Mt. Kisco, NY: Moyer Bell, 1984.

Lortz, Joseph. *Un santo unico*. Rome: Edizioni Paoline, 1958.

Lukács, Geörgy. *Estetica*. Translated by Fausto Codino. 2 vols. Turin: Einaudi, 1970.

Mann, Thomas. *Doctor Faustus*. Translated by John E. Woods. New York: Knopf, 1997.

Marcus, Millicent. *Filmmaking by the Book: Italian Cinema and Literary Adaptation*. Baltimore and London: Johns Hopkins University Press, 1993.

Martin, Biddy. *Woman and Modernity: The (Life)Styles of Lou Andreas-Salomé*. Ithaca, NY, and London: Cornell University Press, 1991.

Masi, Stefano. *Nel buio della moviola: Introduzione alla storia del montaggio*. L'Aquila: La Lanterna Magica, 1985.

————. "Gabriella Cristiani: La magia del montaggio." In AA. VV., *Gabriella Cristiani: Omaggio a Kim Arcalli*. Bari: Assessorato alla Cultura, 1988.

Megill, Allan. *Prophets of Extremity: Nietzsche, Heidegger, Foucault, Derrida*. Berkeley and Los Angeles: University of California Press, 1985.

Meltzer, Françoise. *Salome and the Dance of Writing: Portraits of Mimesis in Literature*. Chicago and London: University of Chicago Press, 1987.

Mereu, Italo. *Storia dell'intolleranza in Europa: Sospettare e punire. Il sospetto e l'Inquisizione romana nell'epoca di Galilei*. Milan: Mondadori, 1979.

Miccichè, Lino. *Luchino Visconti: Un profilo critico*. Venice: Marsilio, 1996.

Morpurgo-Tagliabue, Guido. *I processi di Galileo e l'epistemologia*. Rome: Armando, 1981.

Mosse, George L. *Nationalism and Sexuality: Respectability and Abnormal Sexuality in Modern Europe*. New York: Fertig, 1985.

Mulvey, Laura. "Visual Pleasure and Narrative Cinema." In *Film Theory and Criticism: Introductory Readings*, edited by Gerald Mast and Marshall Cohen, pp. 803–816. New York andOxford: Oxford University Press, 1985.

Neumann, Erich. *The Origins and History of Consciousness*. Foreword by C. G. Jung. Translated by R.F.C. Hull. Bollingen Series XLII. Princeton, NJ: Princeton University Press, 1973.

———. *The Great Mother: An Analysis of the Archetype*. Translated by Ralph Manheim. Bollingen Series XLVII. Princeton, NJ: Princeton University Press, 1974.

Nicholson, Alfred. *Cimabue: A Critical Study*. Princeton, NJ: Princeton University Press, 1932.

Nietzsche, Friedrich. *La Vie de Frédéric Nietzsche d'après sa correspondance*. Edited and translated by Georges Walz. Paris: Editions Rieder, 1932.

———. *The Philosophy of Nietzsche*. New York: The Modern Library, [1947].

———. *The Portable Nietzsche*. Selected and translated with introduction, prefaces, and notes by Walter Kaufmann. New York: Viking Press, 1954.

———. *Philosophy in the Tragic Age of the Greeks*. Translated and introduced by Marianne Cowan. Chicago: Gateway, 1962.

———. *The Will to Power*. Edited with commentary by Walter Kaufmann. New translation by W. Kaufmann and R. J. Hollingdale. New York: Random House, 1967.

Oudemans, C. W., and A.P.M. Lardinois. *Tragic Ambiguity: Anthropology, Philosophy and Sophocles' Antigone*. Leiden and New York: E. J. Brill, 1987.

Peters, H. F. *My Sister, My Spouse: A Biography of Lou Andreas-Salomé*. New York: Norton, 1962.

Redondi, Pietro. *Galileo Heretic*. Translated by Raymond Rosenthal. Princeton, NJ: Princeton University Press, 1987.

Rossanda, Rosanna. Introduction to Sofocle, *Antigone*, pp. 7–60.. Translated by Luisa Biondetti. Milan: Feltrinelli, 1987

Said, Edward W. *Orientalism*. New York: Vintage Books, 1979.

Salvatorelli, Luigi. *Vita di san Francesco d'Assisi*. 1926. Turin: Einaudi, 1982.

Sandberg Vavalà, Evelyn. *La croce dipinta italiana e l'iconografia della passione*. Verona: Casa Editrice Apollo, 1929.

Santner, Eric. *Stranded Objects: Mourning, Memory, and Film in Postwar Germany*. Ithaca, NY, and London: Cornell University Press, 1990.

Schopenhauer, Arthur. *The World as Will and Idea*. Vol. 1. London: Routledge and Kegan Paul, 1957.

Simson, Otto von. *The Gothic Cathedral: Origins of Gothic Architecture and the Medieval Concept of Order*. Bollingen Series XLVIII. Princeton, NJ: Princeton University Press, 1956.

Sitney, P. Adams. *Vital Crises in Italian Cinema: Iconography, Stylistics, Politics*. Austin: University of Texas Press, 1995.

Skoller, Donald, ed. *Dreyer in Double Reflection*. New York: Dutton, 1973.

Sontag, Susan. *On Photography*. New York: Delta Book, 1977.

———. *Under the Sign of Saturn*. New York: Anchor Books, 1991.

Sophocles. *The Three Theban Plays: Antigone, Oedipus the King, Oedipus at Colonus*. Translated by Robert Fagles, introduction and notes by Bernard Knox. Harmondsworth: Penguin, 1984.

Spampanato, Vincenzo. *Documenti della vita di Giordano Bruno*. Florence: Olschki, 1933.

Spengler, Oswald. *The Decline of the West*. 2 vols. in 1. New York: Knopf, 1932.

Stam, Robert. *Subversive Pleasures: Bakhtin, Cultural Criticism, and Film*. Baltimore and London: Johns Hopkins University Press, 1989.

Steiner, George. *Antigones*. New York and Oxford: Oxford University Press, 1984.

Tanizaki, Junichirō. *La croce buddista*. Translated by Lydia Origlia. 1982. 3d ed. Parma: Guanda, 1987.

Turner, Victor W. *The Forest of Symbols: Aspects of Ndembu Ritual*. Ithaca, NY: Cornell University Press, 1967.

————. *The Ritual Process: Structure and Anti-Structure*. London: Routledge & Kegan Paul, 1969.

Weber, Max. *Economy and Society: An Outline of Interpretative Sociology*. Edited by Guenther Roth and Claus Wittich. Berkeley and Los Angeles: University of California Press, 1978.

White, Hayden. *Metahistory: The Historical Imagination in Nineteenth-Century Europe*. Baltimore and London: Johns Hopkins University Press, 1973.

Whitmont, Edward C. *The Symbolic Quest: Basic Concepts of Analytical Psychology*. Princeton, NJ: Princeton University Press, 1978.

Winkler, John J., and Froma I. Zeitlin, eds. *Nothing to Do with Dionysos? Athenian Drama in Its Social Context*. Princeton, NJ: Princeton University Press, 1990.

Index

Adorno, Theodor W., 87
Albonico, Giulio, 62
Al di là del bene e del male, 5, 9, 10, 11, 82, 86, 116–139, 157, 188, 192
Alessandrini, Ludovico, 34
Andreas-Salomé, Lou, 116
Antamoro, Giulio, 17
Antonioni, Michelangelo, 161
Arcalli, Franco, 99–100, 124, 146, 163, 223n.40
Aristotelian, 6, 11, 54,
Aristotle, 40, 57; *Politics*, 57
Artaud, Antonin, 80, 95, 101, 147
Azzini, Nedo, 83

Bacot, Jacques: *Vita di Milarepa*, 174
Bakhtin, Mikhail, 19
Bakunin, Mikhail, 3
Balàzsovitz, Lajos, 174
Banti, Anna, 5
Barberini, Maffeo (Pope Urban VIII), 43
Barthes, Roland, 75
Bataille, Georges, 12, 80, 81, 101, 147, 149; and eroticism, 86, 89, 150; on laughter, 125
Bazin, André, 8, 43, 46, 105
Beardsley, Aubrey, 114
Belázs, Béla, 57
Bellarmine, Robert, 53
Bellissima (Visconti), 107
Bellocchio, Marco, 3, 17; *Pugni in tasca, I*, 17
Berlin Affair, The. See *Interno berlinese*
Bernini, Giovanni Lorenzo, 47, 56
Bertolucci, Bernardo, 3, 83, 100, 101; *Il conformista*, 83
Beyond Good and Evil. See *Al di là del bene e del male*
Beyond Obsession. See *Oltre la porta*
Blade Runner (Ridley Scott), 168, 243n.15
body: Cavani's concept of, 18, 27, 44, 47, 56, 66–68, 73, 161–163, 167–168, 170–171, 174, 176
Bogarde, Dirk, 86, 89, 90, 100, 104, 108, 220n.21

Bondanella, Peter, 103, 205n.1
Bonham Carter, Helena, 163
Bonnet, Jules, 131
Bory, Jean-Louis, 108
Brecht, Bertold, 209n.32
Bresson, Robert, 12
Brunetta, Gian Piero, 200n.1, 205n.37, 245n.24
Bruno, Giordano, 39, 53–54, 55
Bruno, Giuliana, 63, 129, 156–157, 207n.11
Buddha, 171
Buddhism, and Buddhist, 177, 183
Buñuel, Luis, 7, 147
Burch, Noël, 149
Butoh, 189–191, 192, 193, 248n.7

Caduta degli dei, La (Visconti), 107
Caillois, Roger, 99
Calasso, Roberto, 74
Campbell, Joseph, 16, 29
Canby, Vincent, 4, 89, 103
Cannibali, I, 6, 10, 11, 36, 37, 57–77, 90, 171, 189
Cannibals, The. See *I cannibali*
Carotenuto, Gaetano, 188
Caselli, Chiara, 188
Castel, Lou, 17, 27, 165
Catullus, 192
Cavallari, Giobatta, 17
Cavani, Liliana: on actors, 241–242n.1, 245n.26; biographical sources on, 3–4, 195n.3; and censorship, 54, 197n.10, 210n.40, 228n.59, 230n.1; and De Sica, 7, 207n.17; as documentarian, 5–6, 219n.7; —, *La casa in Italia*, 4, 5; —, *La donna nella Resistenza*, 91; —, *Età di Stalin*, 5; —, *Gesù mio fratello*, 201n.3; —, *Storia del Terzo Reich*, 5, 83–84, 91; and ideology, 4, 6–7, 62, 213n.16; as opera director, 227n.53; and Pier Paolo Pasolini, 4, 34–35, 204–205n.37; and RAI-TV, 5–6, 17, 196n.9; and realism, 6–8, 10, 30, 40, 81, 155; shorts: *La battaglia*, 202n.11; —, *Incontro di notte*, 201–202n.11; unfilmed scripts,

Cavani, Liliana (*cont.*)
  198n.13, 206n.4, 227n.53; — *Addio all'au-
  tunno*, 245n.23; —, *Il caso Liuzzo*, 6,
  198n.13; —, *Il giorno del successo*,
  236n.41; —, *Lettere dall'interno: Racconto
  per un film su Simone Weil*, 336n.41; —,
  Lulu, 236n.41; and Luchino Visconti, 7,
  228n.58
Cavell, Stanley, 54
Chomsky, Noam, 64
Christ, 18–19, 22, 23, 24, 27–29, 124, 136,
  138, 163, 168
Cimabue, Giovanni, 168
Clementi, Pierre, 64
Clouzot, Claire, 82
Cocteau, Jean, 11
Conformista, Il (Bertolucci), 83
Contini, Alfio, 46, 92
corporeality, 46, 73, 146, 157, 170–171,
  243n.13
Corti, Maria, 36
Costa, Silvia, 174
Cristiani, Gabriella, 163
Cusack, Cyril, 43

Dalle Vacche, Angela, 110
dance, 108–114, 136–138, 147, 167, 189–
  192, 193
De Lauretis, Teresa, 225n.47, 227n.56,
  230n.3
Deleuze, Gilles, 119, 125, 144
De Sica, Vittorio, 43, 193; *Ladri di biciclette*, 7;
  Umberto D, 7, 43
Devoto, Anna, 174
Dietrich, Marlene, 111
Dionysos, and Dionysian, 68, 88, 94, 108,
  122, 123, 125, 138, 139, 193
Doane, Mary Ann, 63
Dr. Strangelove (Kubrick), 60
Donaggio, Pino, 144
Donati, Danilo, 170, 244n.19
Doria, Enzo, 57
Dostoievsky, Feodor, 6, 12, 90, 91, 160, 168;
  The Idiot, 60
Dove siete? Io sono qui, 11, 188–193
Dreyer, Carl-Theodor, 7, 37, 48; *Vampyr*, 7

Eco, Umberto, 62
Ekland, Britt, 59
Eliade, Mircea, 183
Engels, Friedrich, 3
Eros, 89, 114, 142, 147, 150

eroticism, 95, 110–111, 147; Cavani on,
  223n.42
Euripides, 12

Fascism, and Fascist, 3, 4, 13, 73, 84, 92,
  103, 111, 114
Faust (Gounod), 119
Fellini, Federico, 193
Förster-Nietzsche, Elizabeth, 133–134
Foucault, Michel, 4, 9, 12, 18, 27, 29, 66–67,
  101, 127, 188; on confession, 209n.34; *Les
  Mots et les choses*, 77, 119; *Surveiller et
  punir*, 43, 208n.29
Francesco, 4, 11, 22, 29, 161–171, 193
Francesco di Assisi, 5, 8, 9, 10, 17–36, 37, 50,
  57, 82, 84, 163, 168, 170
Francis of Assisi. See *Francesco di Assisi*
Frazer, J. T., 46
Freud, Sigmund, 89, 119, 124
Friedländer, Saul, 84, 219n.8
Frigerio, Ezio, 46
Frugoni, Chiara, 32
Frye, Northrop, 65, 177

Galen, 44
Galilei, Galileo: *Dialogo sopra i due massimi sis-
  temi*, 48; *Il saggiatore*, 39
Galileo, 6, 10, 37–56, 57, 64, 82, 83, 84
game, 8, 23, 50, 71, 88, 99, 101, 107, 110,
  119, 121, 127–128, 130, 131, 136, 143,
  147–149, 153
Gaze, 9, 11, 27, 47, 65, 67, 68, 70, 80, 86,
  97, 105, 108, 111, 116, 124, 125, 127,
  128, 130, 131, 143, 149, 151, 157, 173
Gennep, Arnold van, 23
Ginzburg, Natalia, 198n.11
Giotto, 22, 168
Giroux, Henry, 103
Gramsci, Antonio, 4
Grazzini, Giovanni, 4, 138
Green, Julien, 19
Guarnieri, Ennio, 161
Guattari, Félix, 5, 89, 116, 119, 131
Guest, The. See *L'ospite*
Guglielmi, Angelo, 5

Hegel, Georg W. F., 57
Hijikata, Tatsumi, 192
Hitchcock, Alfred, 7
Hitler, Adolf, 84, 87, 113, 140, 142, 149,
  151, 153

Innocente, L' (Visconti), 107
intérieur, 87, 105, 157, 155–156, 175
interior, 9, 22, 32, 37, 80, 82, 90, 108, 114, 126, 140, 142, 143, 147–149, 153–154, 162, 167, 168, 175. See also *intérieur*
Interno berlinese, 9, 10, 82, 83, 86, 87, 88, 107, 108, 140–157, 188

Jesus, 23, 63. *See also* Christ
Joan of Arc, 7
Josephson, Erland, 116
Jung, C. G., 215n.28, 216n.35, 234n.23, 238n.7, 246n.39

Kabuki, 152, 154
Kafka, Franz, 89
Kandinsky, Wassily, 89
Kaufmann, Walter, 64
Kierkegaard, Søren, 87, 144
Kierkegaardian, 65, 80, 144
Kipling, Rudyard, 70
Klee, Paul, 89
Klimt, Gustav, 89
Kracauer, Siegfried, 154

labyrinth, 9–10, 39, 75, 82, 101, 103, 130, 168, 177–178, 183. *See also* maze
labyrinthine, 9–18, 27, 29, 43, 47, 60, 127, 129, 170, 177, 180
Ladri di biciclette (De Sica), 7
Lanci, Giuseppe, 161
Landgrebe, Gudrun, 140, 146
Lang, Fritz, 7
Levi, Primo, 92–94
Lisi, Virna, 134
Lukács, Geörgy, 40
Lumière, August and Louis, 3

Mahler, Gustav, 118–119
Mann, Thomas, 12, 86, 116; *Doktor Faustus*, 122
Mao Tse-Tung, 173
Marcus, Millicent, 73
Marx, Karl, 3
Masi, Stefano, 163
masochism, 86, 108, 116, 124
Mastroianni, Ruggero, 146
Matte Blanco, Ignacio, 88
maze, 18, 29, 47, 63, 71, 127, 129, 180
Mazzoni, Roberta, 161
McNally, Kevin, 140
Megill, Allan, 89

merry-go-round, 98–100, 222n.38, 223n.41
Micciché, Lino 146, 186
Milarepa, 8, 10, 37, 75, 84, 100, 163, 168, 170, 171–187
Montanelli, Indro, 4
Morante, Elsa, 174
Moravia, Alberto, 5, 37, 62, 146, 151, 167
Moreau, Gustave, 114
Moro, Aldo, 188
Morobushi, Ko, 189, 192
Morricone, Ennio, 47, 54, 60, 73
Morte a Venezia (Visconti), 146
Moscati, Italo, 18, 64, 92, 171, 174
Mozart, Wolfgang Amadeus: 104, 227n.53; *Die Zauberflöte*, 104
Mulvey, Laura, 110
Munch, Edward, 89
Murnau, F. W., 7
Musil, Robert, 12

Nazi, 91, 92, 97, 103, 111, 115, 147, 154, 155, 165
Nazism, 4, 5–6, 13, 84, 90, 105, 107–108, 110, 114, 140, 142, 144, 150, 151, 153–154, 155
Nexus (Miller), 63
Nietzsche, Friedrich, 6, 12, 89, 117–119, 122, 124, 125, 126, 127, 170; *Also Sprach Zarathustra*, 122, 124; *Ecce Homo*, 122; *The Gay Science*, 121; on Lou Andreas-Salomé, 231n.8, 232n.14
Nietzschean, 8, 87, 104, 117, 119, 121, 122, 124, 125, 126, 131, 138, 170, 193
Night Porter, The. See Il portiere di notte
Novelli, Ernesto, 155, 241n.36

Oltre la porta, 10, 94, 114, 229–230n.73
Ōno, Kazuo, 192
Ospite, L', 10, 11, 75–77, 189, 218n.59
Ossessione (Visconti), 7
Ozu, Yasujiro, 149, 154

Pabst, Georg Wilhelm, 7
Paris, Daniele, 90
Pasolini, Pier Paolo, 4, 7, 34, 73, 173, 186; *Salò*, 73
passio, 13, 81, 89, 107, 165, 170
passion, 86, 142, 143, 152. See also *passio*
Pelle, La, 10, 11, 188, 247n.1
Pelléas et Mélisande (Maeterlinck), 77
Pes, Aurelio, 16
Pisacane, Carlo, 7

Plato, 105
Platonic, 144, 150, 151, 155
play, 8, 11, 18, 81, 94, 95, 129, 130, 147, 193. *See also* game
Portiere di notte, Il, 4–5, 6, 9–10, 11, 46, 75, 81–115, 146, 157, 188, 192
Powell, Robert, 116
Prise de pouvoir par Louis XIV, La (Rossellini), 17
Prodan, Andrea, 140
Pugni in tasca, I (Bellocchio), 17

Rampling, Charlotte, 89, 100, 108
Redondi, Pietro, 47
Riches, Pierre, 171
Rilke, Rainer Maria, 119
Rondi, Gian Luigi, 90, 165
Rosenkavalier, Der (Strauss), 110
Rossellini, Roberto, 17, 37; *La prise de pouvoir par Louis XIV*, 17
Rossini, Gioacchino, 77
Rourke, Mickey, 161, 167, 168, 170

Sabatier, Paul, 168
Sade, marquis de, 6, 82, 90, 95, 103, 127, 147; Blanchot on, 221n.33; *La Philosophie dans le boudoir*, 147
sadism, 86, 88, 103, 108, 113
sadomasochism, and sadomasochistic, 82, 88, 90, 95, 100, 114–115, 188, 226n.52
Said, Edward W., 174
Salò (Pasolini), 73
Salomè, 114, 229n.71
Sanda, Dominique, 116
scandal, 38, 48, 68, 89, 119, 129
scandalous, 4, 8, 18, 21, 31, 37, 44, 81, 82, 89, 103, 123, 125, 142, 147
Scanni, Giulio, 161
Schiele, Egon, 89, 110
Schopenhauer, Arthur, 140, 143, 151
Servant, The (Losey), 100
Seven Days in May (Frankenheimer), 60
Seventh Circle, 193
Silverman, Kaja, 18, 19, 64–65, 73, 116, 117, 180
Simon, Leonard, 193
Sitney, P. Adams, 205n.37
Skin, The. See *La pelle*
Socrates, 188

Sontag, Susan, 61, 103, 219n.8, 239n.16
Sophocles, 10, 12, 57–59, 63; *Antigone*, 57, 58–59; *Oedipus Rex*, 63
Spengler, Oswald, 45
Spinotti, Dante, 155, 241n.36
Spongano, Raffaele, 3
Stam, Robert, 103, 125

Takaki, Mio, 83, 140, 146, 154
Tanizaki, Junichirō, 140, 147; *Manji*, 140, 237n.1
Tassone, Aldo, 53
Te Deum (Haydn), 47
Terra trema, La (Visconti), 7
theatricality, 40, 147, 153, 154, 157
Thomas Aquinas, St., 44
Thomas of Celano, 167
Tiso, Ciriaco, 3, 21, 101
Tornabuoni, Lietta, 120
Tosi, Piero, 83, 107
transgression, 11, 18, 23, 86, 89, 126–127, 130, 133, 144, 147, 151
transgressive, 36, 40, 129, 138, 140, 147, 161, 163, 170, 192, 193
Tsujimura, Jusaburo, 83

Umberto D (De Sica), 7, 43

Vampyr (Dreyer), 7
Vangelis, 168, 170
Visconti, Luchino, 7, 83, 105–107, 146, 193, 228n.59; *Bellissima*, 107; *La caduta degli dei*, 107; *L'innocente*, 107; *Morte a Venezia*, 146; *Ossessione*, 7; *La terra trema*, 7
voyeur, 122, 125, 126, 130, 143
voyeurism, and voyeuristic, 9, 70, 86, 97, 113, 127, 131, 157

Wagner, Otto, 82
Weber, Max, 23
Wedekind, Frank, 119; *Lulu*, 236n.41
Where Are You? I'm Here. See *Dove siete? Io sono qui*
White, Hayden, 21, 143
Wilde, Oscar, 114

Zarri, Adriana, 34
Zavattini, Cesare, 43